SUZUKA

8

Kouji Seo

TRANSLATED AND ADAPTED BY
David Ury

LETTERED BY
North Market Street Graphics

NORTH BAY
PUBLIC LIBRARY

NORTH BAY
DISCARDED
AUG 18 2009
PUBLIC LIBRARY

DEL
REY

BALLANTINE BOOKS · NEW YORK

Suzuka volume 8 is a work of fiction. Names, characters, places, and incidents are the products of the author's imagination or are used fictitiously. Any resemblance to actual events, locales, or persons, living or dead, is entirely coincidental.

A Del Rey Manga/Kodansha Trade Paperback Original

Suzuka volume 8 copyright © 2005 by Kouji Seo
English translation copyright © 2008 by Kouji Seo

All rights reserved.

Published in the United States by Del Rey Books, an imprint of The Random House Publishing Group, a division of Random House, Inc., New York.

DEL REY is a registered trademark and the Del Rey colophon is a trademark of Random House, Inc.

Publication rights arranged through Kodansha Ltd.

First published in Japan in 2005 by Kodansha Ltd., Tokyo

ISBN 978-0-345-50167-7

Printed in the United States of America

www.delreymanga.com

9 8 7 6 5 4 3 2

Translator/adapter: David Ury
Lettering: North Market Street Graphics

Contents

A Note from the Author

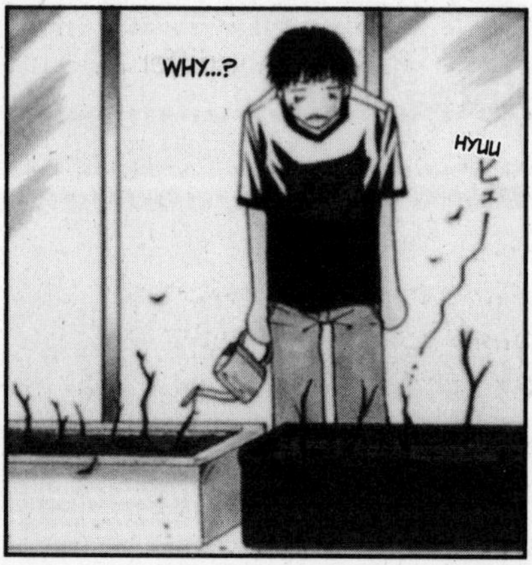
WHY...?
HYUU
ヒュ

ALL OF MY TOMATOES HAVE DIED.
I'LL HAVE TO POSTPONE MY BIG TOMATO PARTY UNTIL NEXT YEAR...

Honorifics Explained

Throughout the Del Rey Manga books, you will find Japanese honorifics left intact in the translations. For those not familiar with how the Japanese use honorifics and, more important, how they differ from American honorifics, we present this brief overview.

Politeness has always been a critical facet of Japanese culture. Ever since the feudal era, when Japan was a highly stratified society, use of honorifics—which can be defined as polite speech that indicates relationship or status—has played an essential role in the Japanese language. When addressing someone in Japanese, an honorific usually takes the form of a suffix attached to one's name (example: "Asuna-san"), is used as a title at the end of one's name, or appears in place of the name itself (example: "Negi-sensei," or simply "Sensei!").

Honorifics can be expressions of respect or endearment. In the context of manga and anime, honorifics give insight into the nature of the relationship between characters. Many English translations leave out these important honorifics and therefore distort the feel of the original Japanese. Because Japanese honorifics contain nuances that English honorifics lack, it is our policy at Del Rey not to translate them. Here, instead, is a guide to some of the honorifics you may encounter in Del Rey Manga.

-san: This is the most common honorific and is equivalent to Mr., Miss, Ms., or Mrs. It is the all-purpose honorific and can be used in any situation where politeness is required.

-sama: This is one level higher than "-san" and is used to confer great respect.

-dono: This comes from the word "tono," which means "lord." It is an even higher level than "-sama" and confers utmost respect.

-kun: This suffix is used at the end of boys' names to express familiarity or endearment. It is also sometimes used by men among friends, or when addressing someone younger or of a lower station.

-chan: This is used to express endearment, mostly toward girls. It is also used for little boys, pets, and even among lovers. It gives a sense of childish cuteness.

Bozu: This is an informal way to refer to a boy, similar to the English terms "kid" and "squirt."

**Sempai/
Senpai:** This title suggests that the addressee is one's senior in a group or organization. It is most often used in a school setting, where underclassmen refer to their upperclassmen as "sempai." It can also be used in the workplace, such as when a newer employee addresses an employee who has seniority in the company.

Kohai: This is the opposite of "sempai" and is used toward underclassmen in school or newcomers in the workplace. It connotes that the addressee is of a lower station

Sensei: Literally meaning "one who has come before," this title is used for teachers, doctors, or masters of any profession or art.

[blank]: This is usually forgotten in these lists, but it is perhaps the most significant difference between Japanese and English. The lack of honorific means that the speaker has permission to address the person in a very intimate way. Usually, only family, spouses, or very close friends have this kind of permission. Known as *yobisute*, it can be gratifying when someone who has earned the intimacy starts to call one by one's name without an honorific. But when that intimacy hasn't been earned, it can be very insulting.

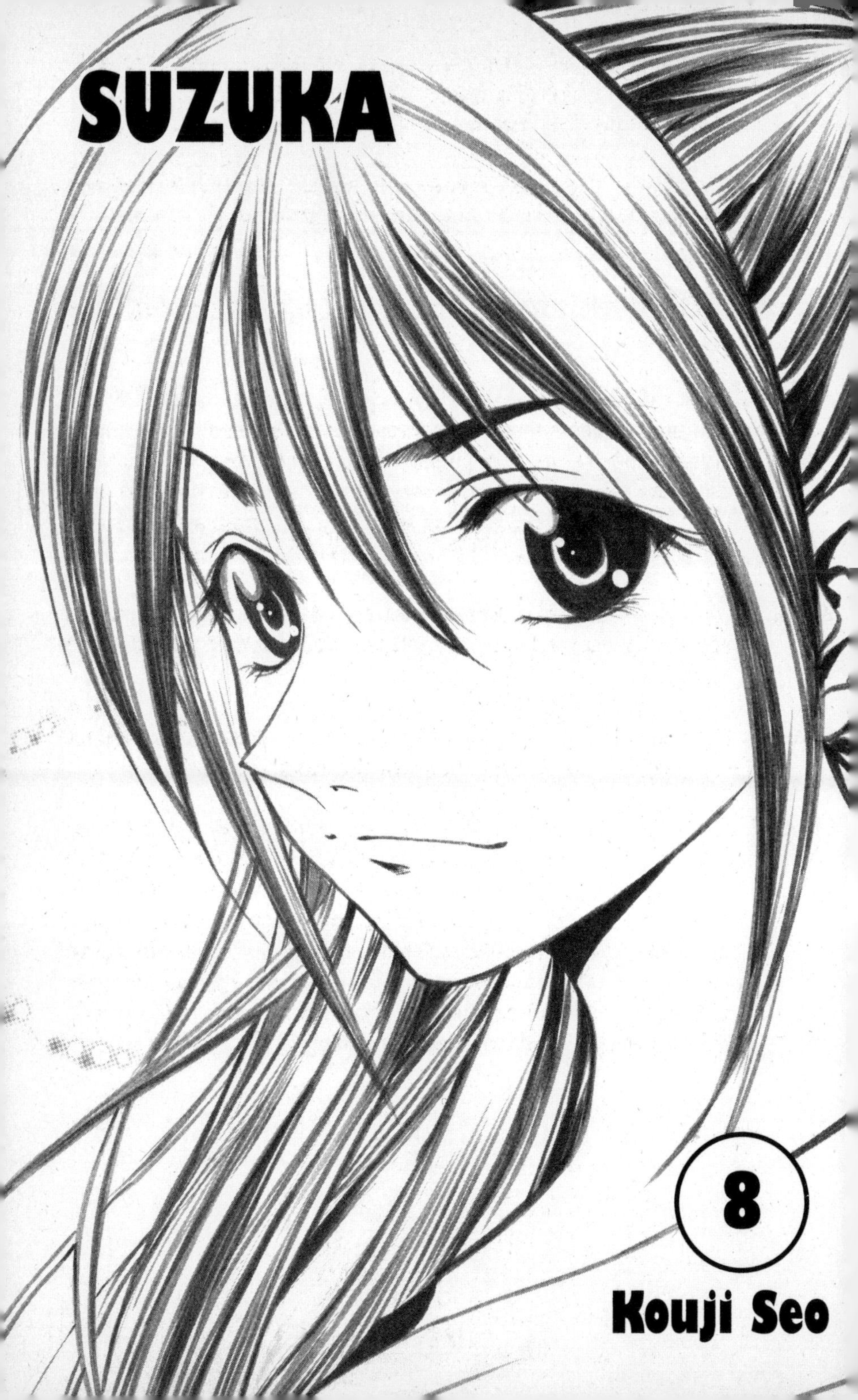
SUZUKA
8
Kouji Seo

CONTENTS

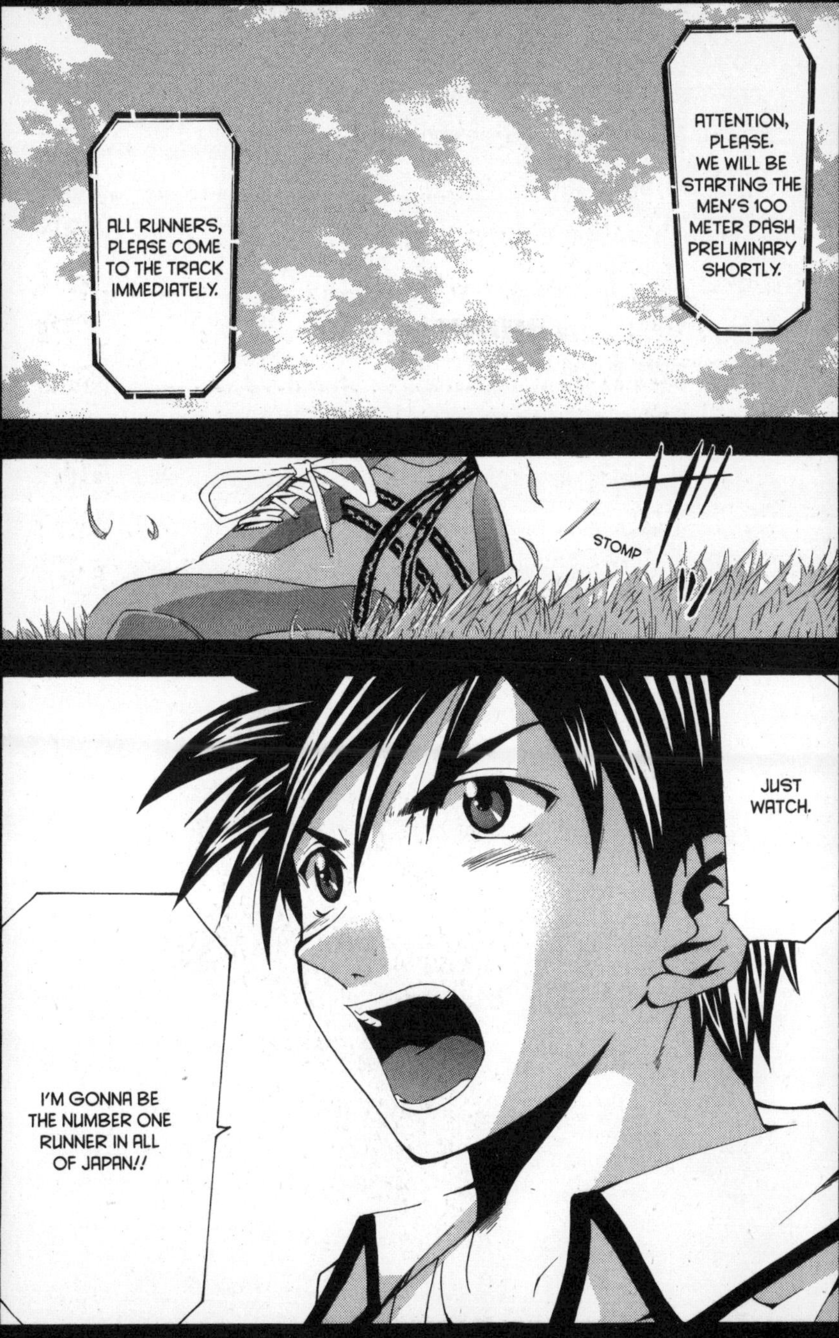
ATTENTION, PLEASE. WE WILL BE STARTING THE MEN'S 100 METER DASH PRELIMINARY SHORTLY.
ALL RUNNERS, PLEASE COME TO THE TRACK IMMEDIATELY.
STOMP
JUST WATCH.
I'M GONNA BE THE NUMBER ONE RUNNER IN ALL OF JAPAN!!

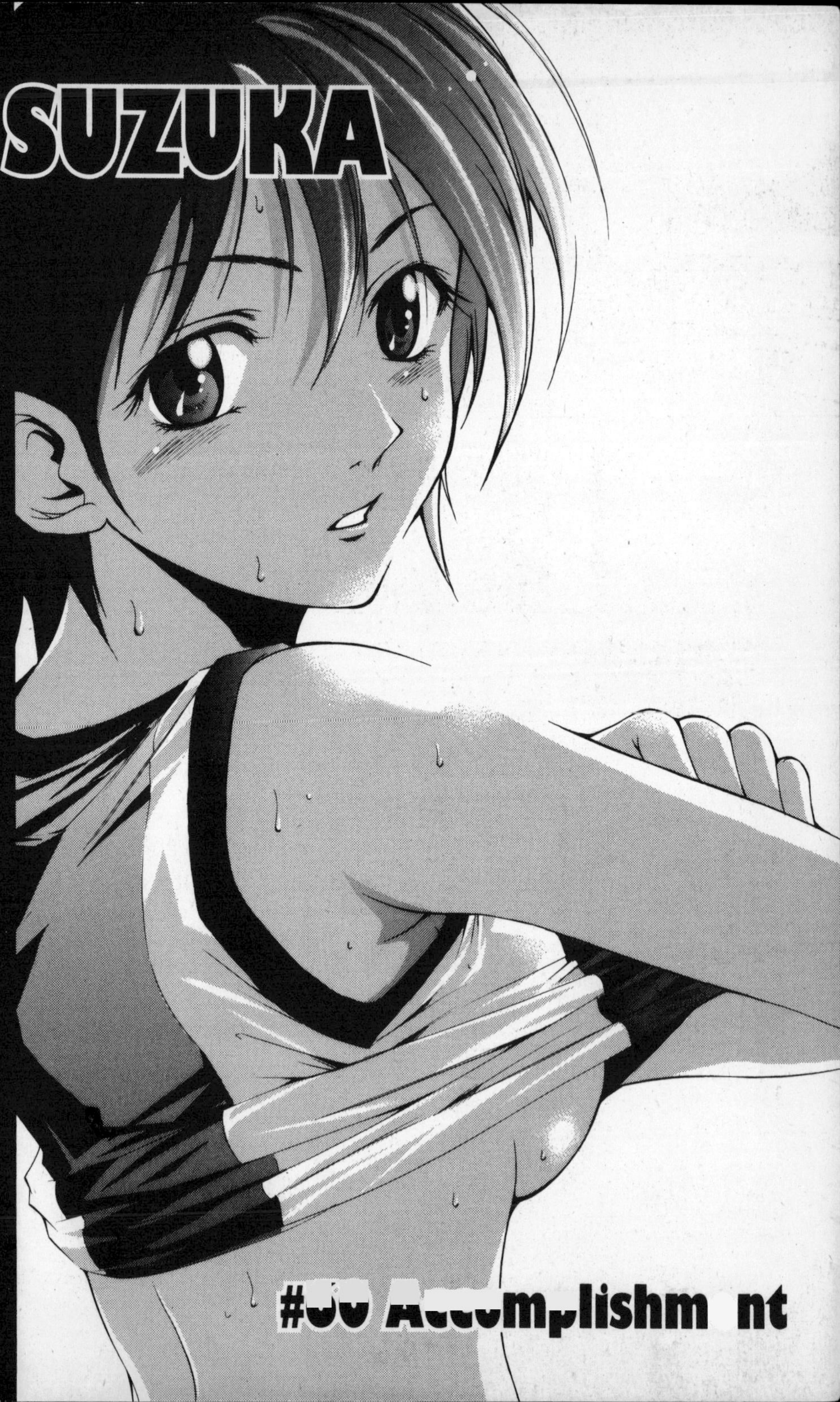
SUZUKA
Accomplishment

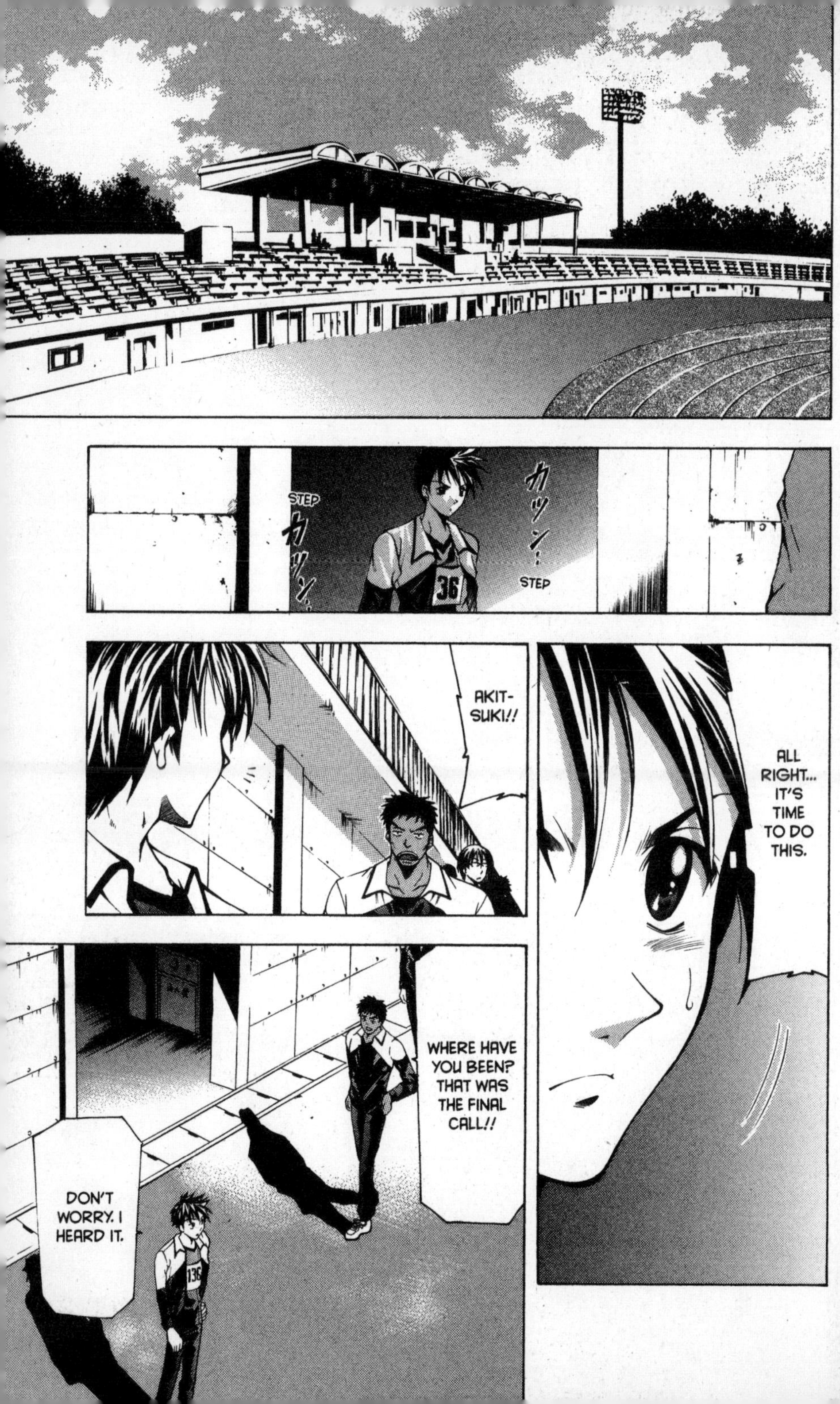
カツン…
STEP
STEP
カツン…
ALL RIGHT... IT'S TIME TO DO THIS.
AKIT-SUKI!!
WHERE HAVE YOU BEEN? THAT WAS THE FINAL CALL!!
DON'T WORRY. I HEARD IT.

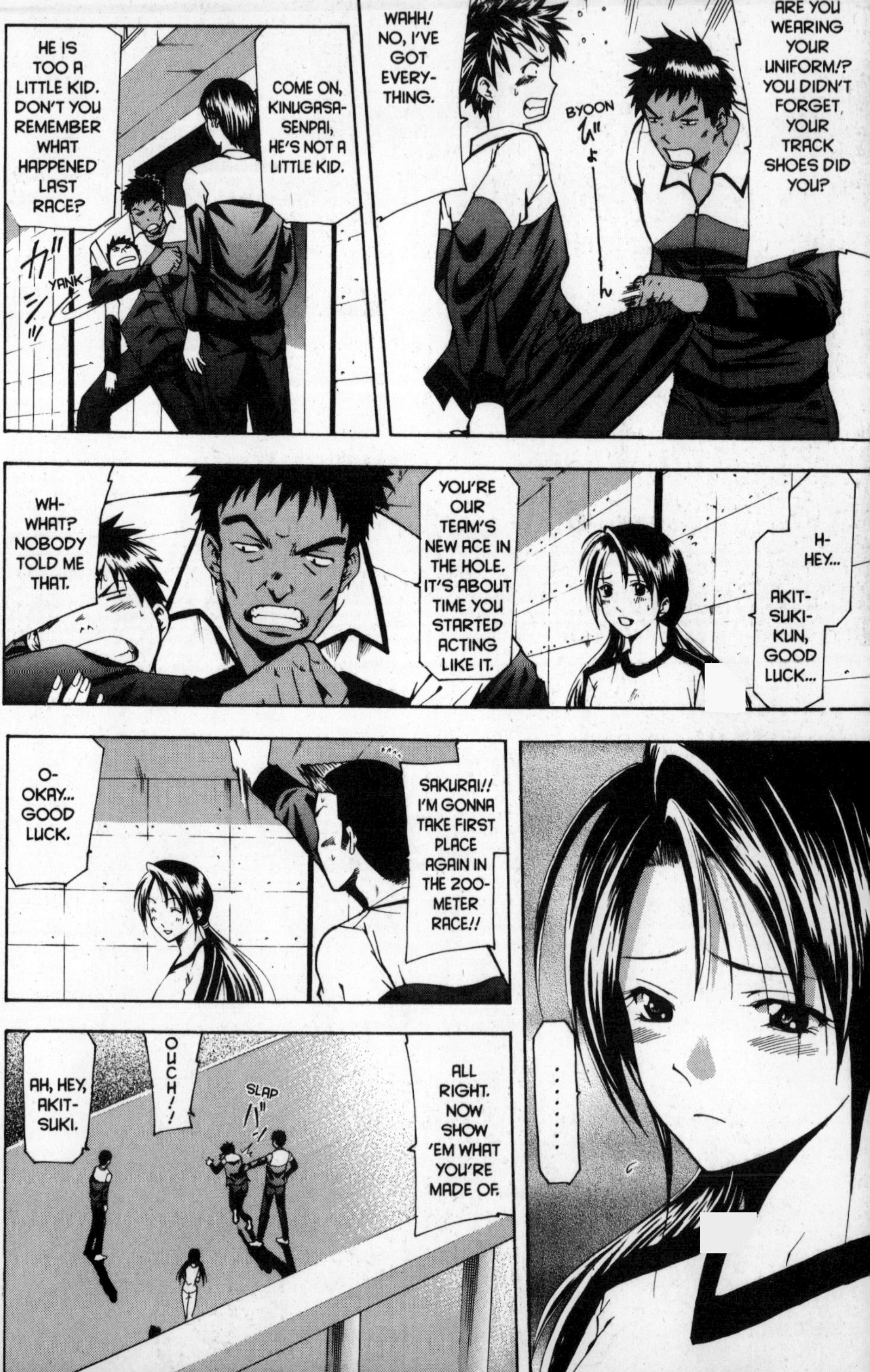
ARE YOU WEARING YOUR UNIFORM!? YOU DIDN'T FORGET YOUR TRACK SHOES DID YOU?
BYOON
WAHH! NO, I'VE GOT EVERY-THING.
COME ON, KINUGASA-SENPAI, HE'S NOT A LITTLE KID.
HE IS TOO A LITTLE KID. DON'T YOU REMEMBER WHAT HAPPENED LAST RACE?
YANK
H-HEY...
AKIT-SUKI-KUN, GOOD LUCK...
YOU'RE OUR TEAM'S NEW ACE IN THE HOLE. IT'S ABOUT TIME YOU STARTED ACTING LIKE IT.
WH-WHAT? NOBODY TOLD ME THAT.
......
SAKURAI!! I'M GONNA TAKE FIRST PLACE AGAIN IN THE 200-METER RACE!!
O-OKAY... GOOD LUCK.
ALL RIGHT. NOW SHOW 'EM WHAT YOU'RE MADE OF.
OUCH!!
SLAP
AH, HEY, AKIT-SUKI.

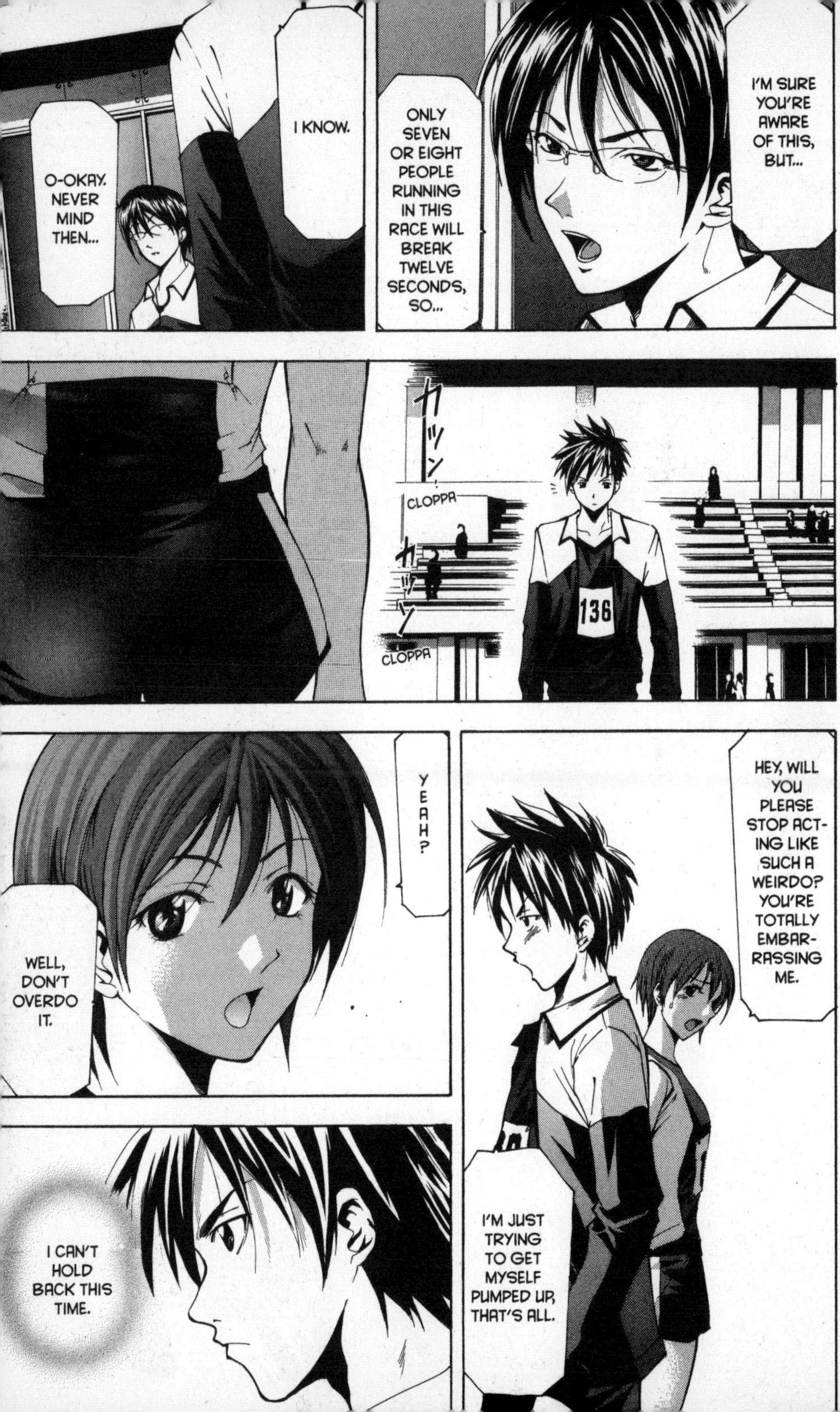
I'M SURE YOU'RE AWARE OF THIS, BUT...
ONLY SEVEN OR EIGHT PEOPLE RUNNING IN THIS RACE WILL BREAK TWELVE SECONDS, SO...
I KNOW.
O-OKAY. NEVER MIND THEN...
CLOPPA
CLOPPA
HEY, WILL YOU PLEASE STOP ACT-ING LIKE SUCH A WEIRDO? YOU'RE TOTALLY EMBAR-RASSING ME.
I'M JUST TRYING TO GET MYSELF PUMPED UP, THAT'S ALL.
YEAH?
WELL, DON'T OVERDO IT.
I CAN'T HOLD BACK THIS TIME.

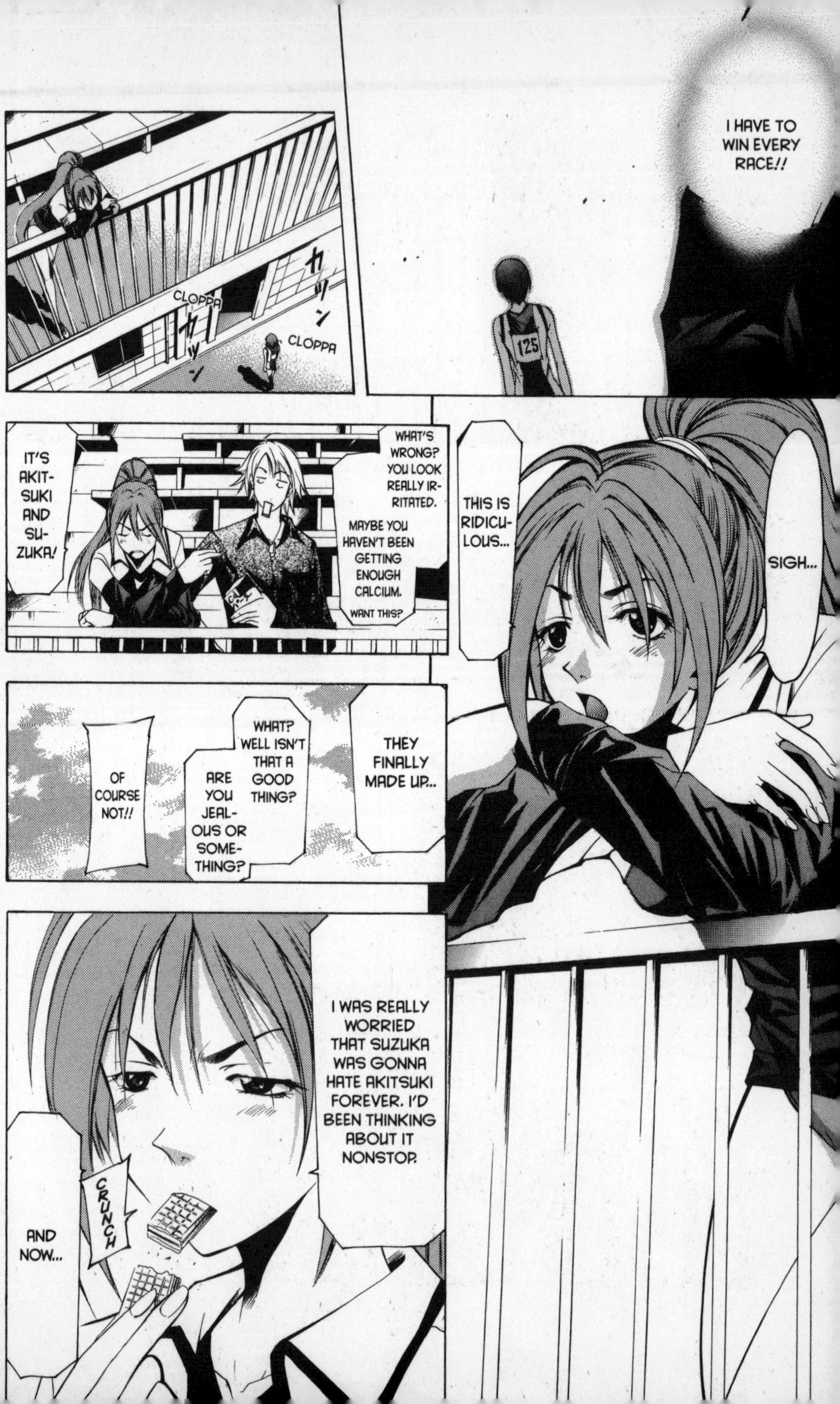

I HAVE TO WIN EVERY RACE!!
カッン
CLOPPA
カッ
CLOPPA
SIGH...
THIS IS RIDICULOUS...
WHAT'S WRONG? YOU LOOK REALLY IRRITATED.
MAYBE YOU HAVEN'T BEEN GETTING ENOUGH CALCIUM.
WANT THIS?
IT'S AKITSUKI AND SUZUKA!
THEY FINALLY MADE UP...
WHAT? WELL ISN'T THAT A GOOD THING?
ARE YOU JEALOUS OR SOMETHING?
OF COURSE NOT!!
I WAS REALLY WORRIED THAT SUZUKA WAS GONNA HATE AKITSUKI FOREVER. I'D BEEN THINKING ABOUT IT NONSTOP.
CRUNCH
AND NOW...

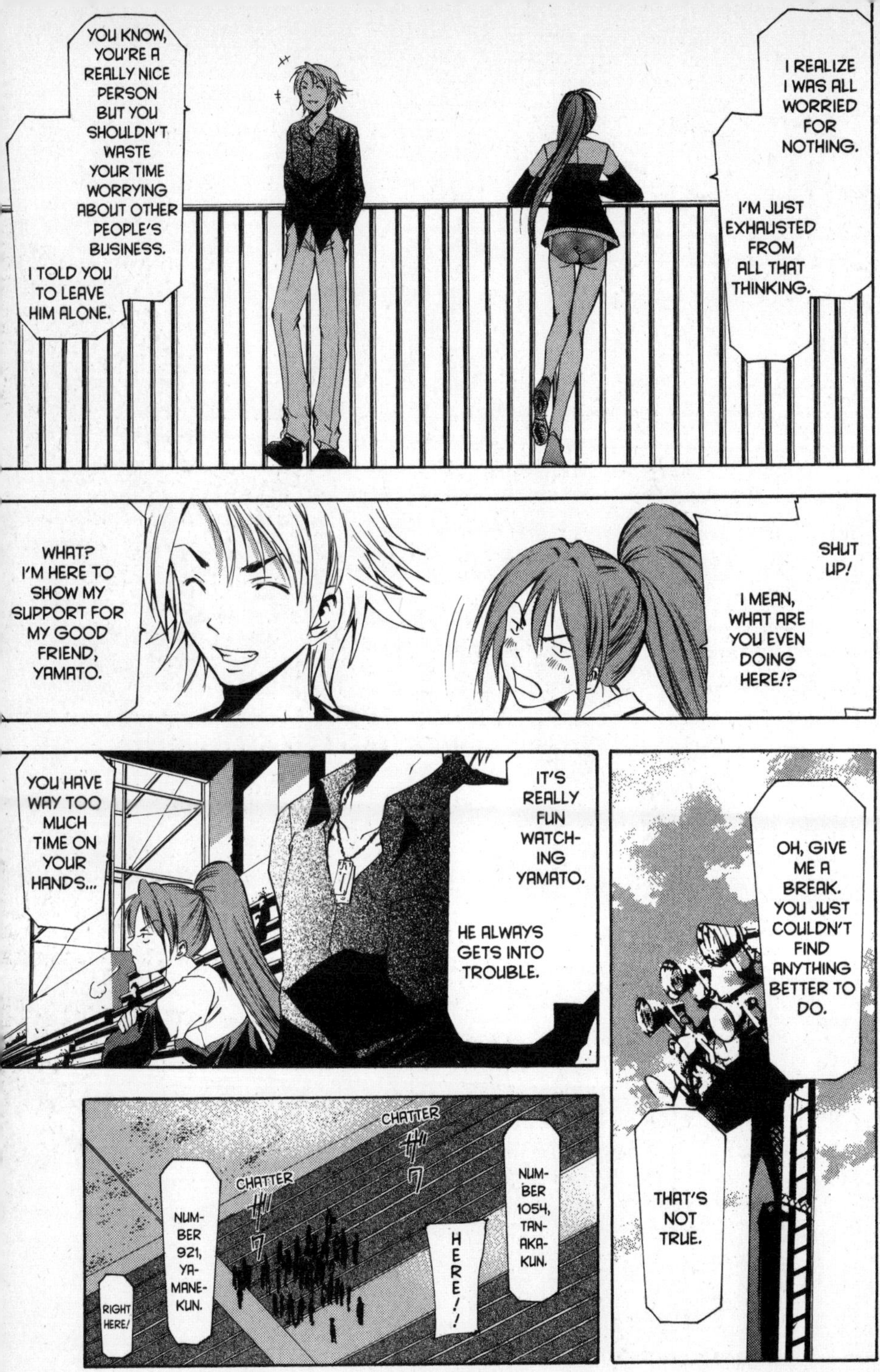
I REALIZE I WAS ALL WORRIED FOR NOTHING.
I'M JUST EXHAUSTED FROM ALL THAT THINKING.
YOU KNOW, YOU'RE A REALLY NICE PERSON BUT YOU SHOULDN'T WASTE YOUR TIME WORRYING ABOUT OTHER PEOPLE'S BUSINESS.
I TOLD YOU TO LEAVE HIM ALONE.
SHUT UP!
I MEAN, WHAT ARE YOU EVEN DOING HERE!?
WHAT? I'M HERE TO SHOW MY SUPPORT FOR MY GOOD FRIEND, YAMATO.
OH, GIVE ME A BREAK. YOU JUST COULDN'T FIND ANYTHING BETTER TO DO.
THAT'S NOT TRUE.
IT'S REALLY FUN WATCHING YAMATO.
HE ALWAYS GETS INTO TROUBLE.
YOU HAVE WAY TOO MUCH TIME ON YOUR HANDS...
CHATTER ザワ
NUMBER 1054, TANAKA-KUN.
HERE!!
CHATTER ザワ
NUMBER 921, YAMANE-KUN.
RIGHT HERE!

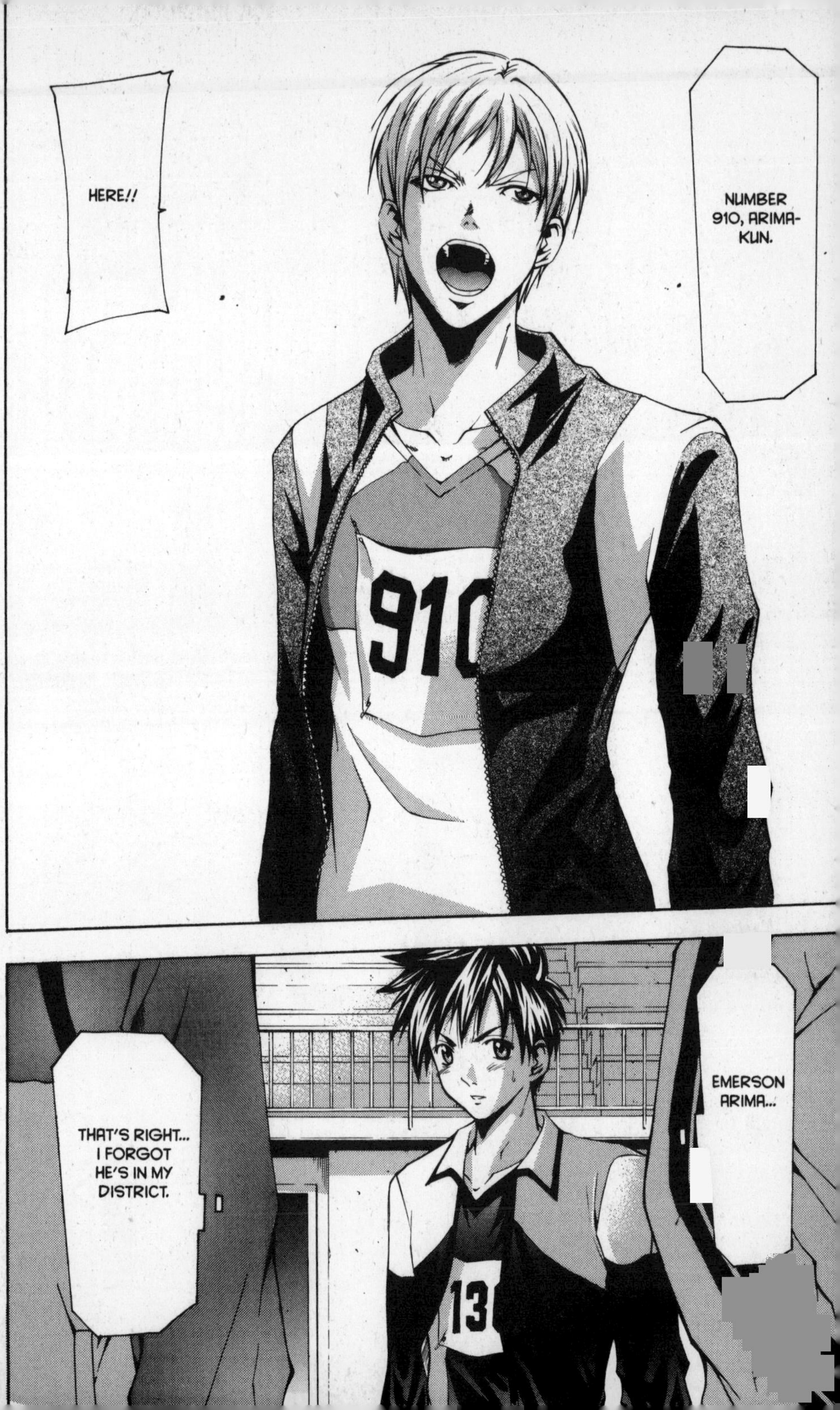
NUMBER 910, ARIMA-KUN.
HERE!!
EMERSON ARIMA...
THAT'S RIGHT... I FORGOT HE'S IN MY DISTRICT.

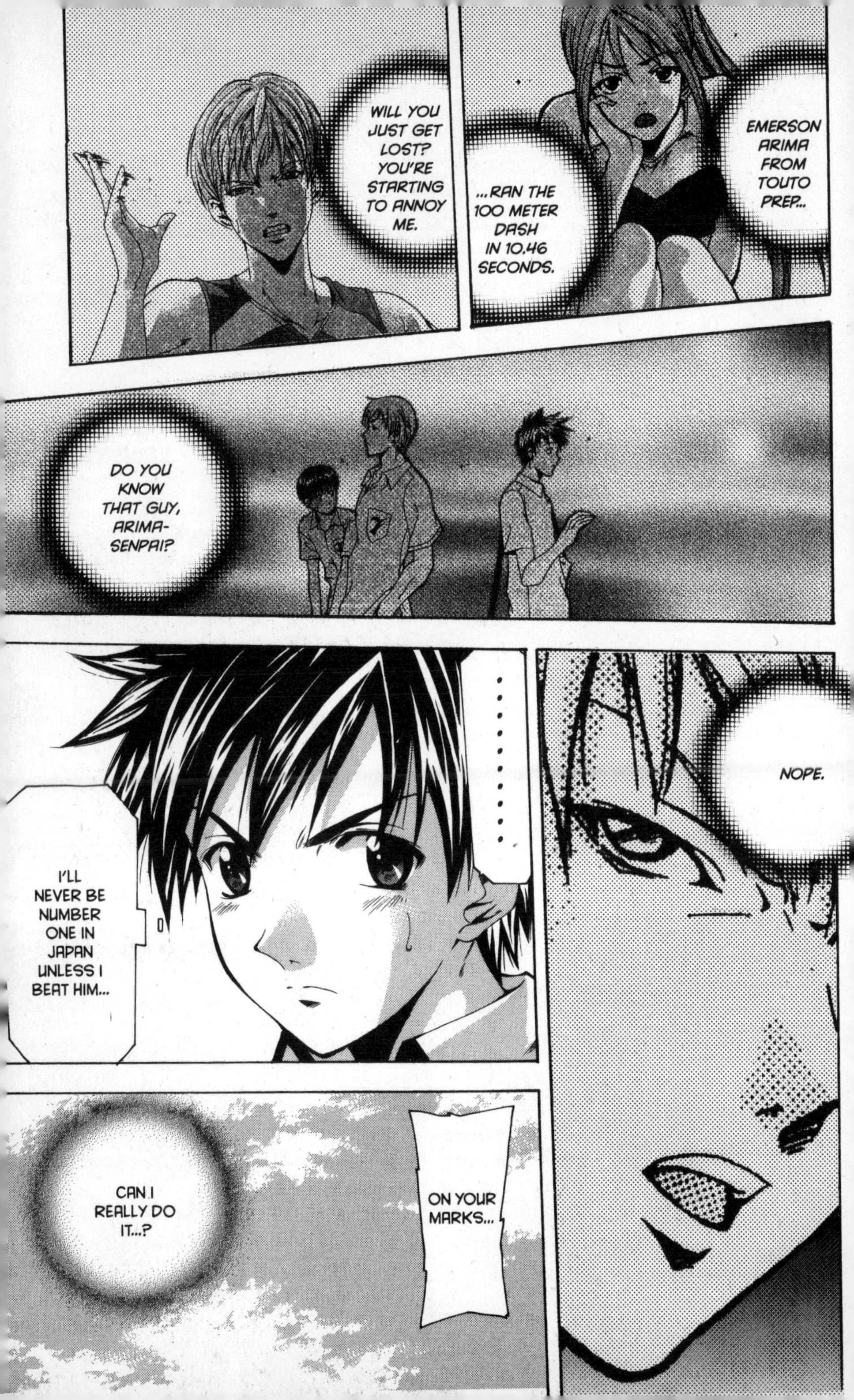
EMERSON ARIMA FROM TOUTO PREP...
...RAN THE 100 METER DASH IN 10.46 SECONDS.
WILL YOU JUST GET LOST? YOU'RE STARTING TO ANNOY ME.
DO YOU KNOW THAT GUY, ARIMA-SENPAI?
NOPE.
......
I'LL NEVER BE NUMBER ONE IN JAPAN UNLESS I BEAT HIM...
ON YOUR MARKS...
CAN I REALLY DO IT...?

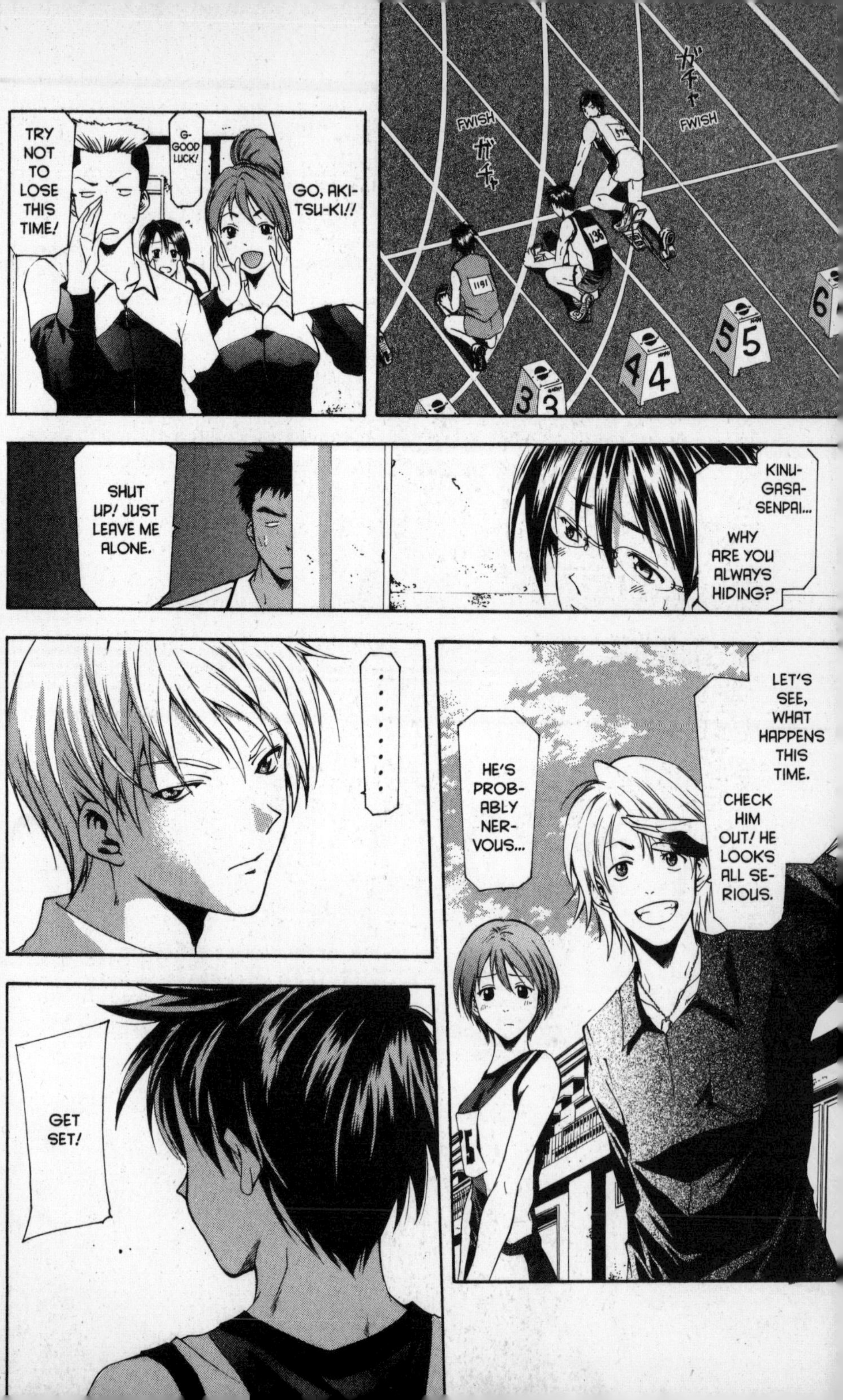
ガチャ
FWISH
FWISH
ガチャ
GO, AKI-TSU-KI!!
G-GOOD LUCK!
TRY NOT TO LOSE THIS TIME!
KINU-GASA-SENPAI...
WHY ARE YOU ALWAYS HIDING?
SHUT UP! JUST LEAVE ME ALONE.
LET'S SEE, WHAT HAPPENS THIS TIME.
CHECK HIM OUT! HE LOOKS ALL SE-RIOUS.
HE'S PROB-ABLY NER-VOUS...
......
GET SET!

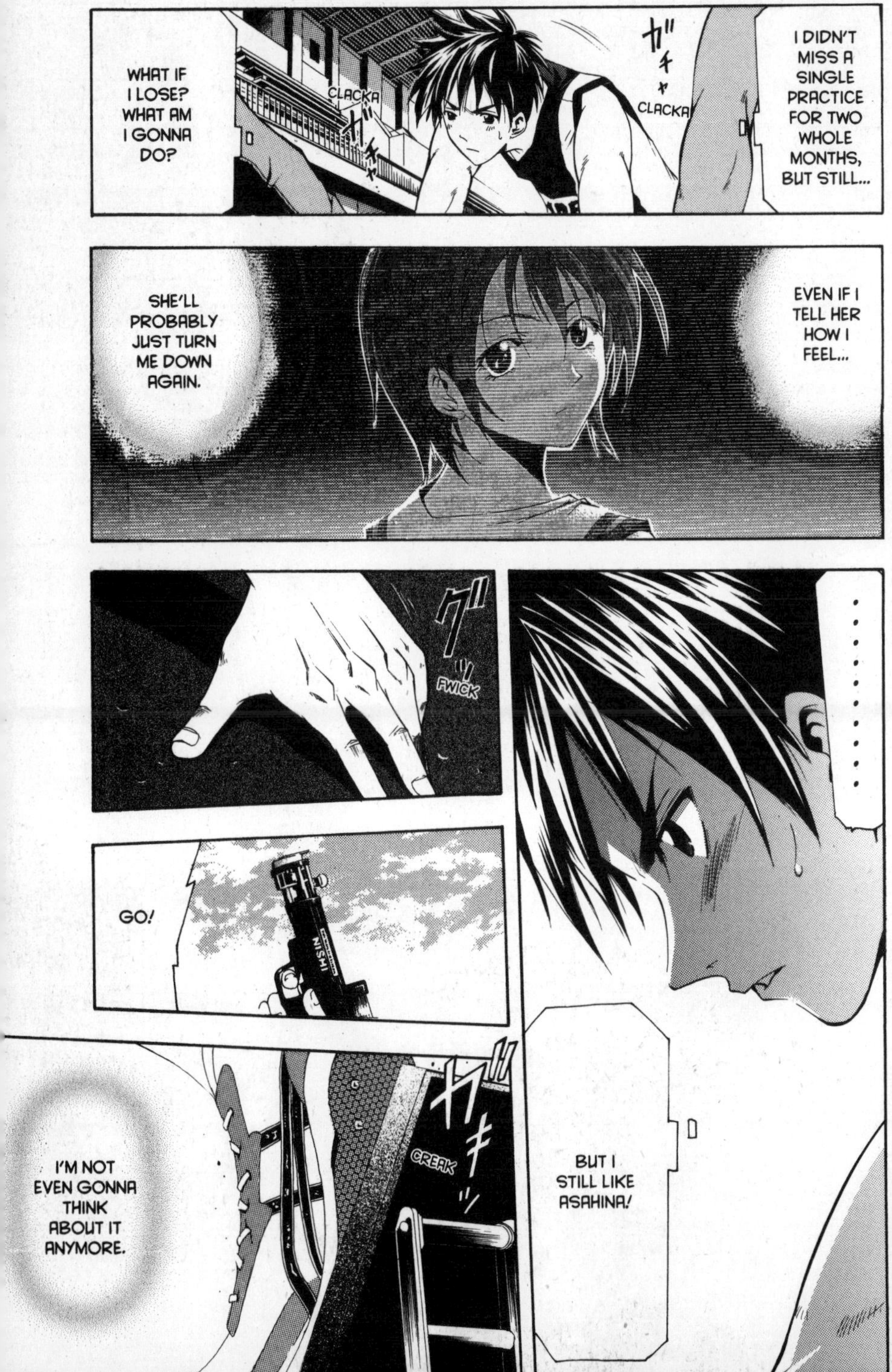
I DIDN'T MISS A SINGLE PRACTICE FOR TWO WHOLE MONTHS, BUT STILL...
CLACKA
CLACKA
WHAT IF I LOSE? WHAT AM I GONNA DO?
EVEN IF I TELL HER HOW I FEEL...
SHE'LL PROBABLY JUST TURN ME DOWN AGAIN.
......
FWICK
GO!
BUT I STILL LIKE ASAHINA!
CREAK
I'M NOT EVEN GONNA THINK ABOUT IT ANYMORE.

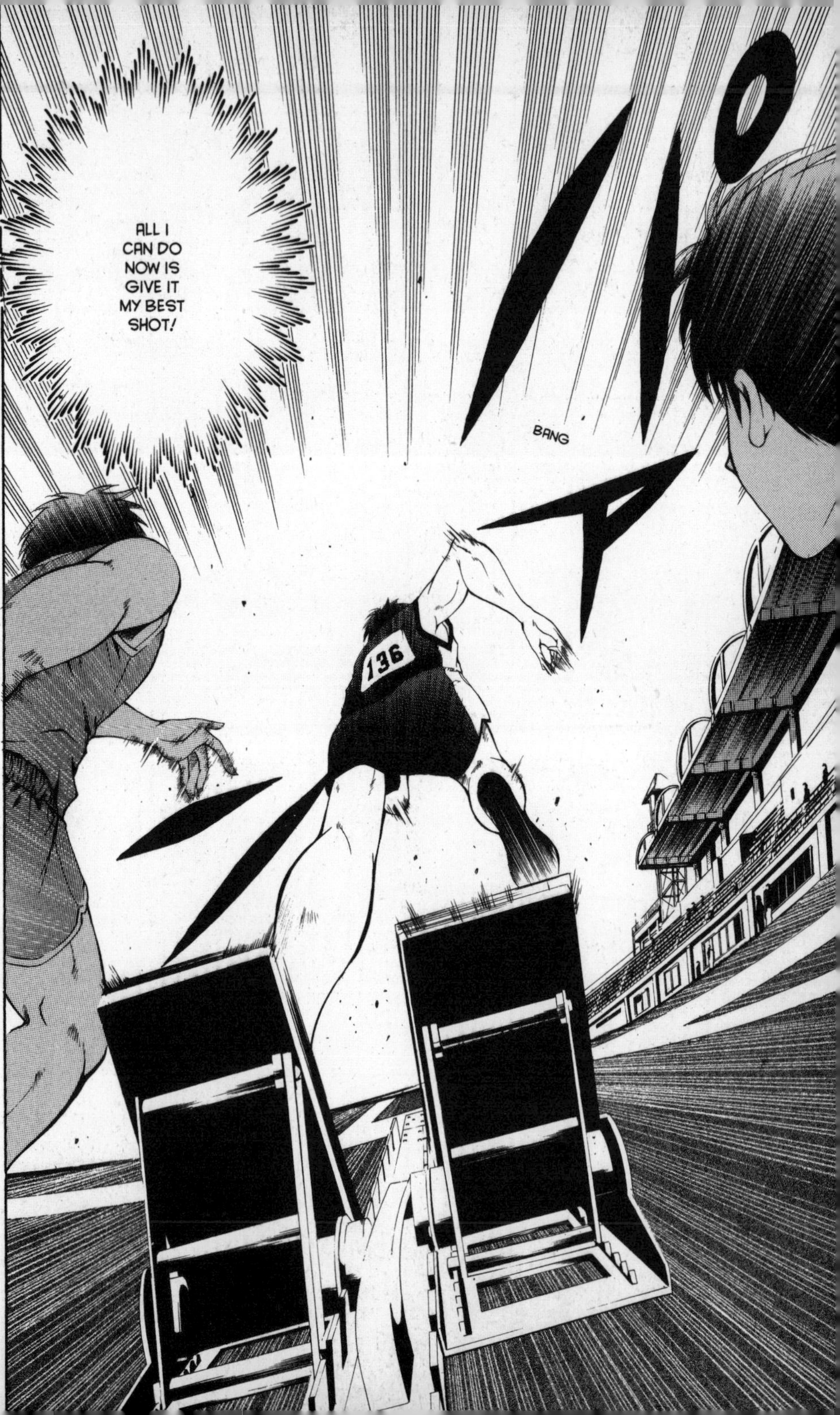
BANG
ALL I CAN DO NOW IS GIVE IT MY BEST SHOT!

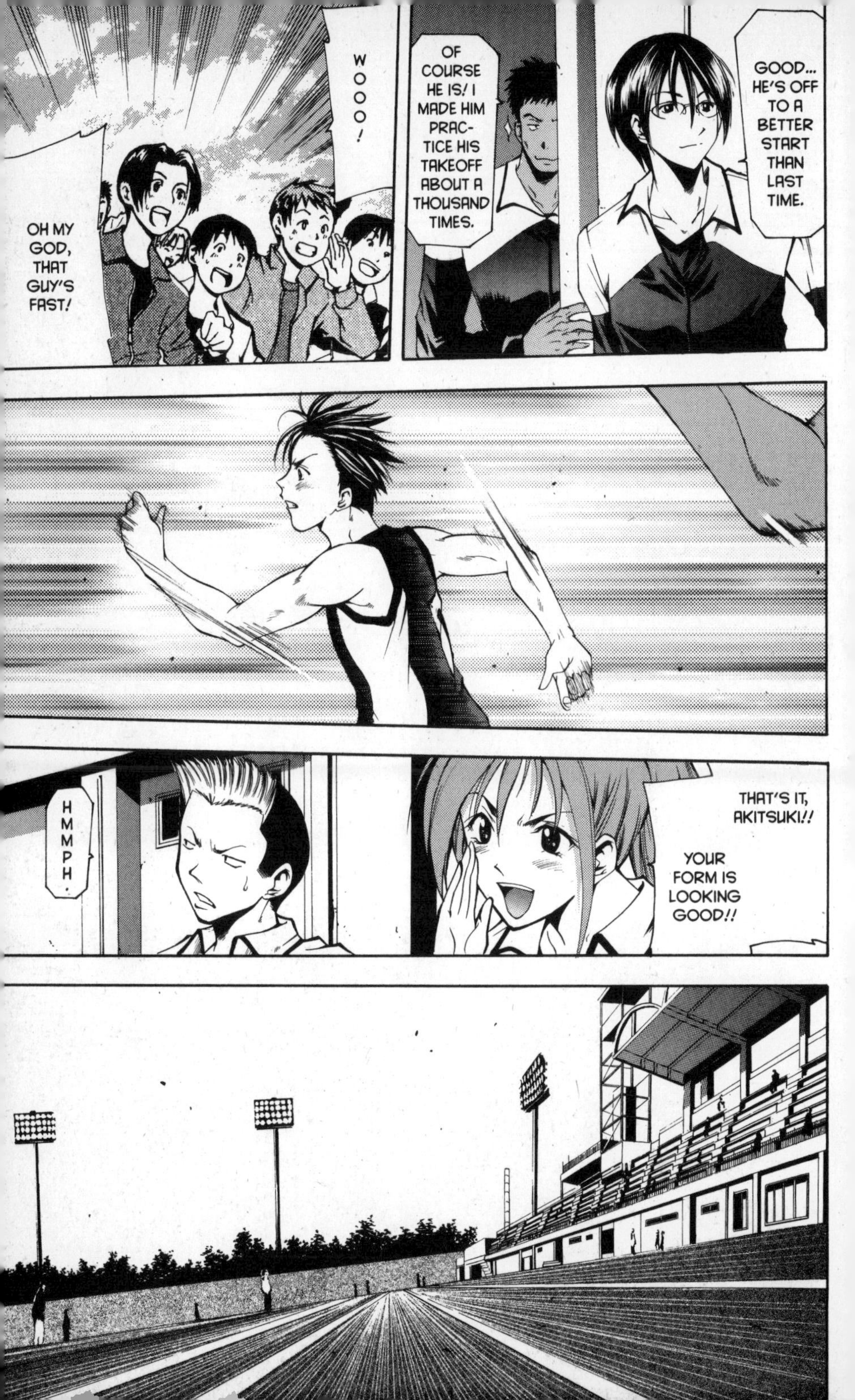
GOOD... HE'S OFF TO A BETTER START THAN LAST TIME.
OF COURSE HE IS! I MADE HIM PRACTICE HIS TAKEOFF ABOUT A THOUSAND TIMES.
WOOOO!
OH MY GOD, THAT GUY'S FAST!
THAT'S IT, AKITSUKI!!
YOUR FORM IS LOOKING GOOD!!
HMMPH.

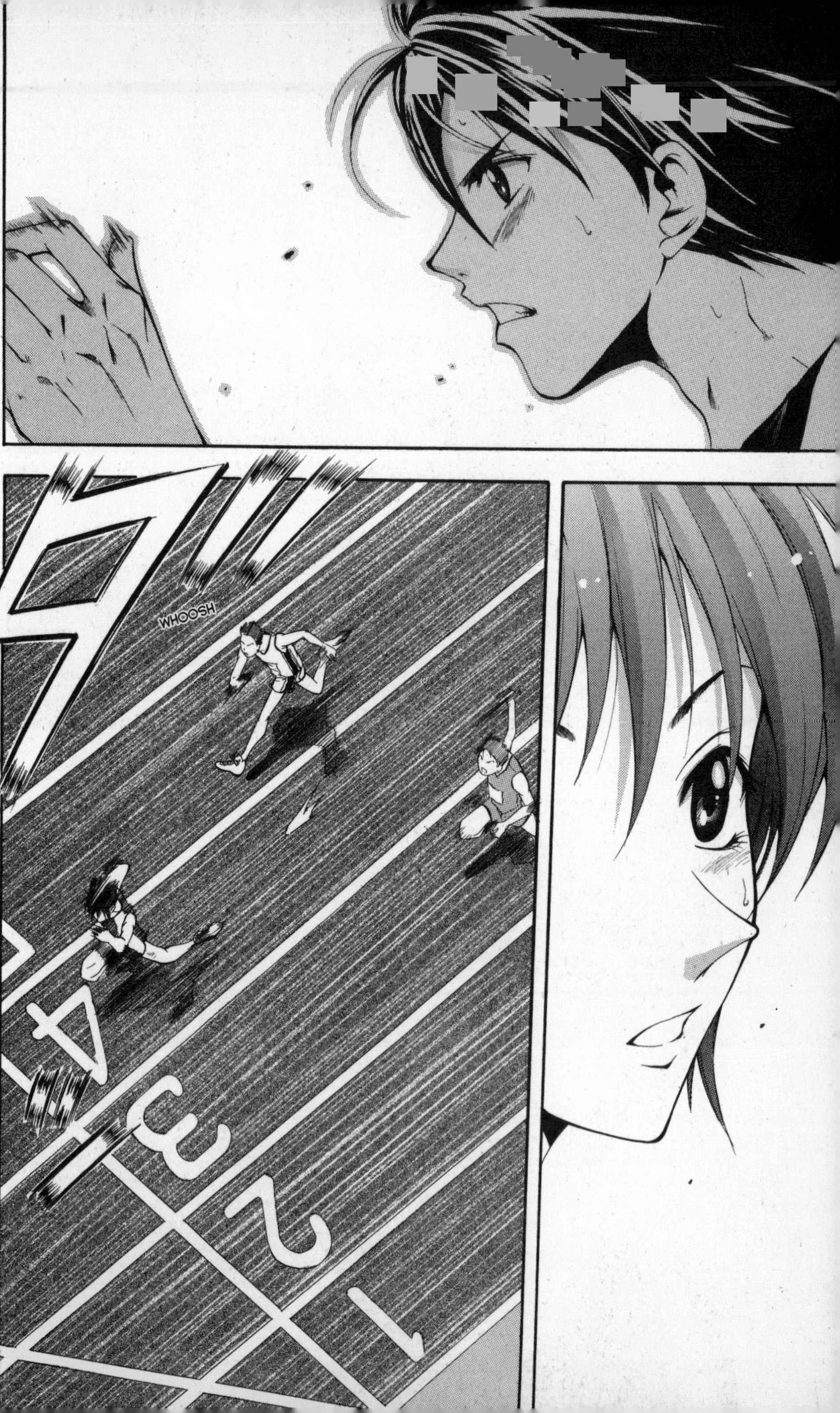
WHOOSH

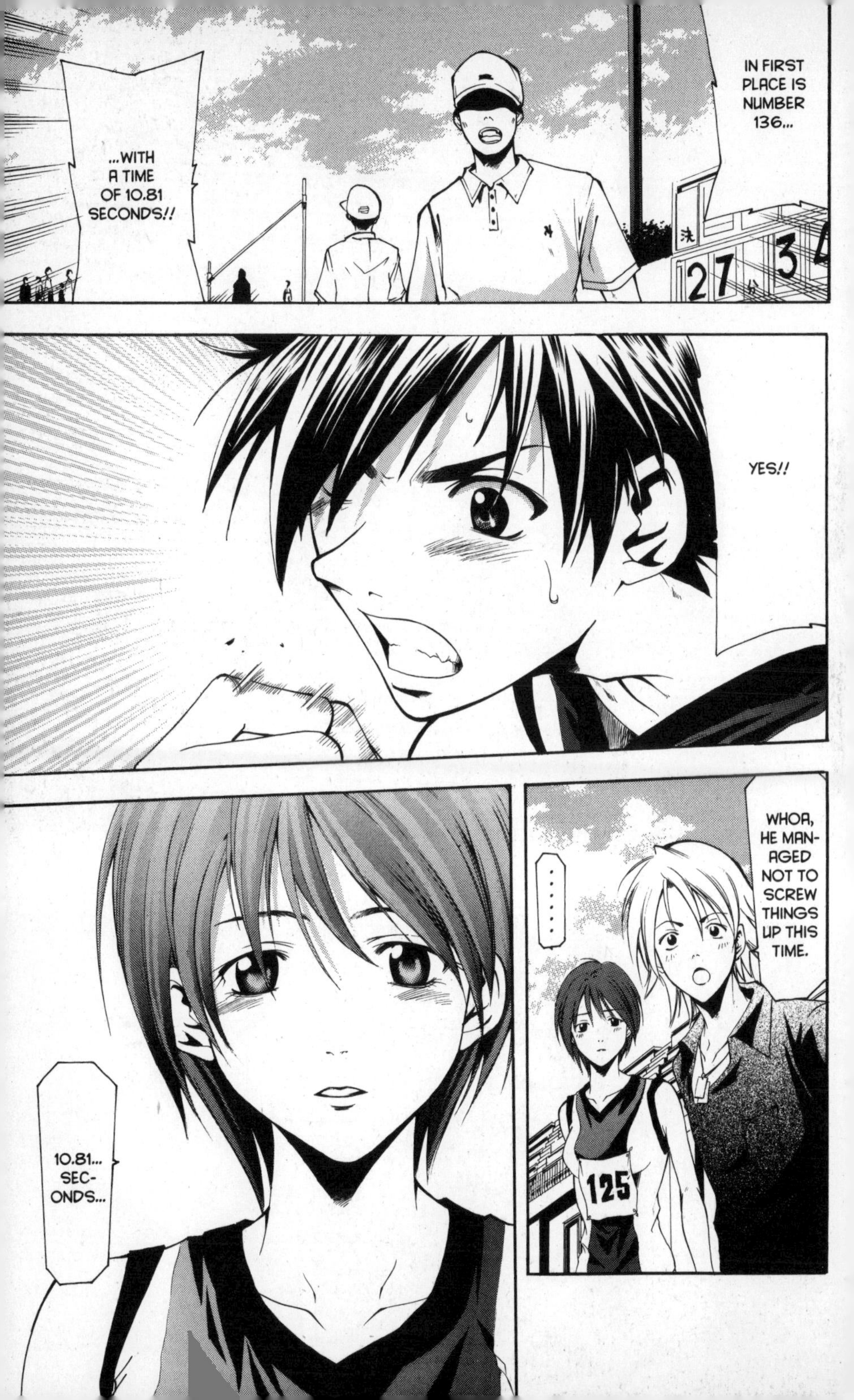
IN FIRST PLACE IS NUMBER 136...
...WITH A TIME OF 10.81 SECONDS!!
YES!!
WHOA, HE MAN-AGED NOT TO SCREW THINGS UP THIS TIME.
......
10.81... SEC-ONDS...

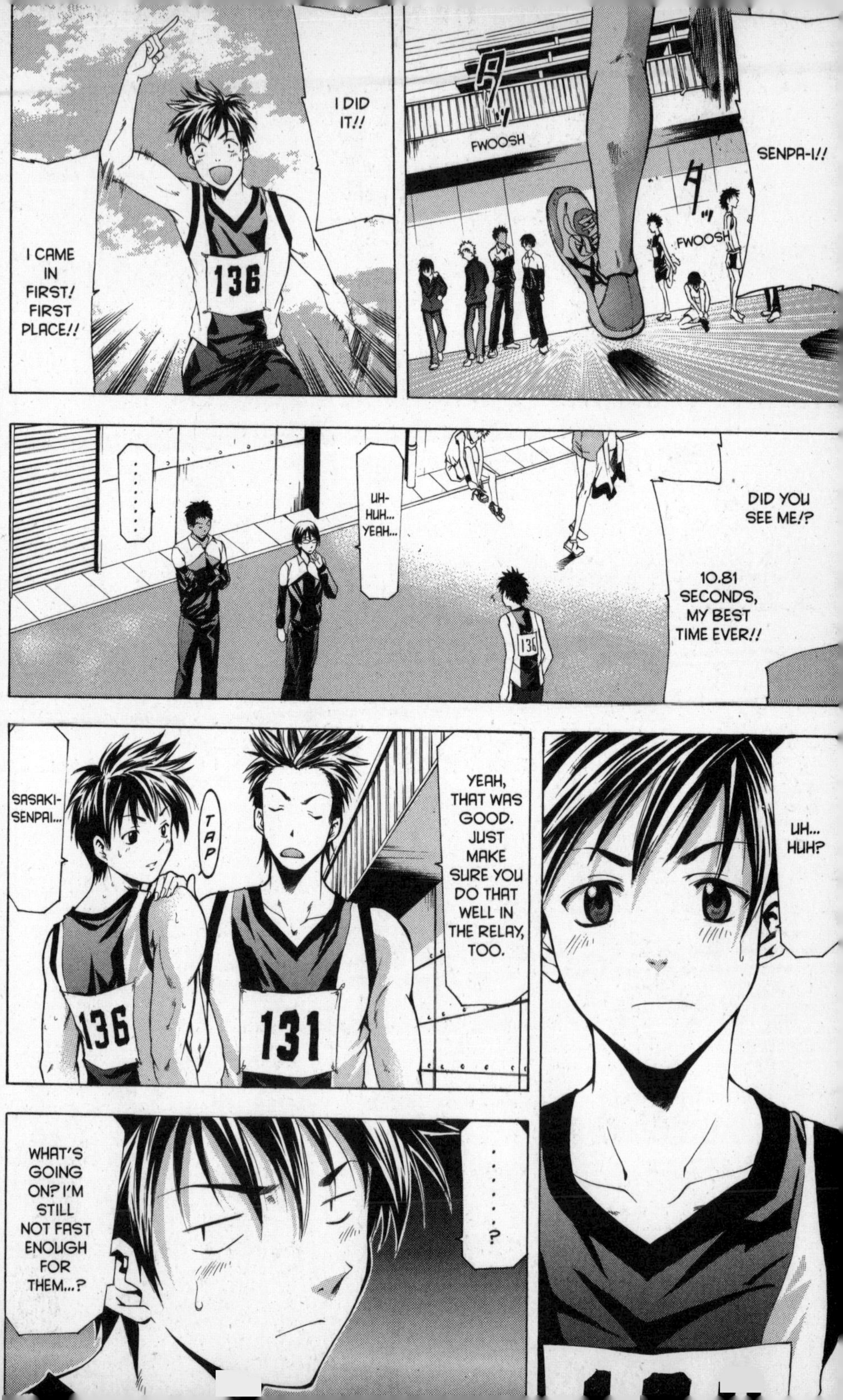
FWOOSH
SENPA-I!!
FWOOSH
I DID IT!!
I CAME IN FIRST! FIRST PLACE!!
DID YOU SEE ME!?
10.81 SECONDS, MY BEST TIME EVER!!
UH-HUH... YEAH...
....
UH... HUH?
YEAH, THAT WAS GOOD. JUST MAKE SURE YOU DO THAT WELL IN THE RELAY, TOO.
TAP
SASAKI-SENPAI...
......?
WHAT'S GOING ON? I'M STILL NOT FAST ENOUGH FOR THEM...?

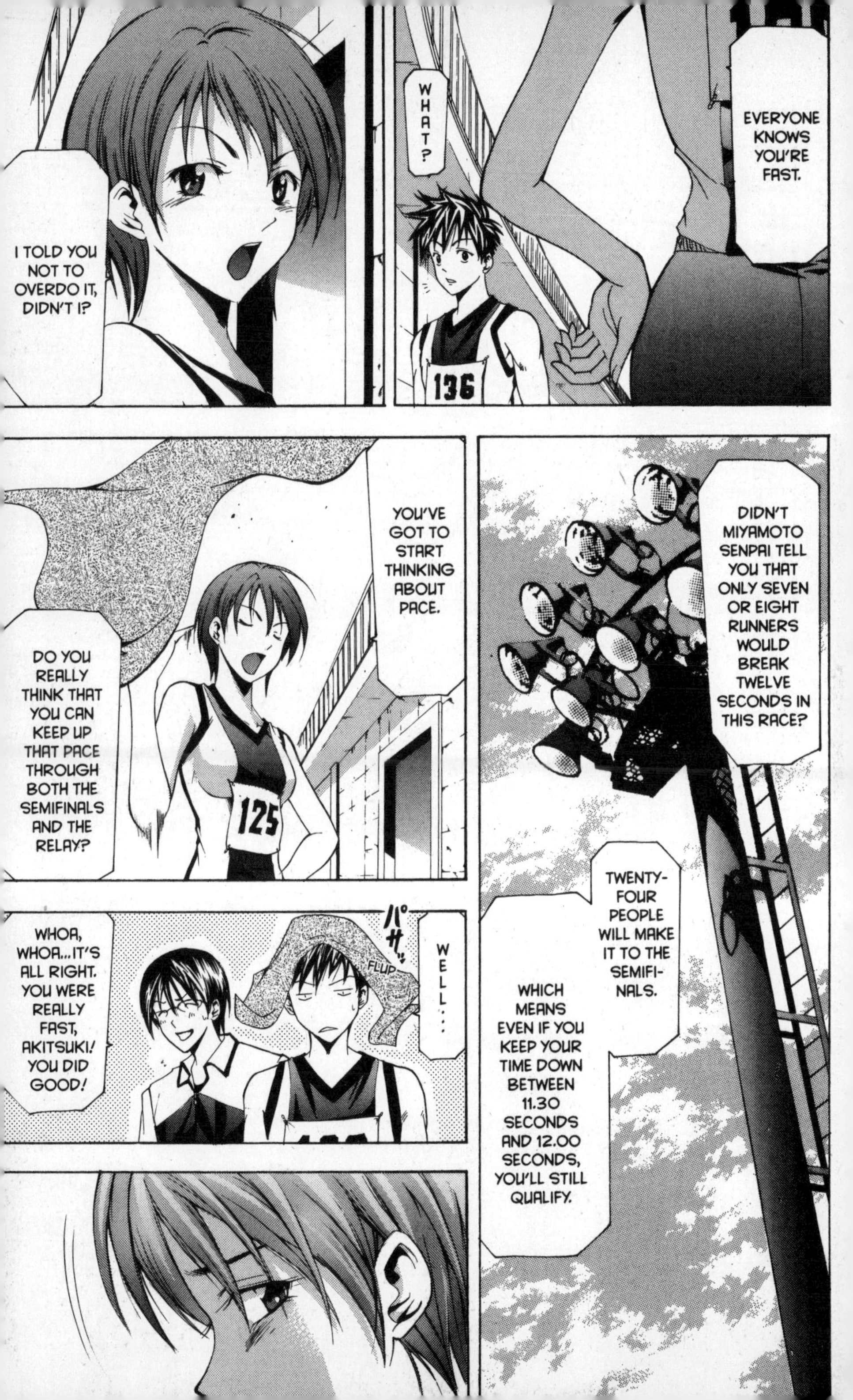
EVERYONE KNOWS YOU'RE FAST.
WHAT?
I TOLD YOU NOT TO OVERDO IT, DIDN'T I?
DIDN'T MIYAMOTO SENPAI TELL YOU THAT ONLY SEVEN OR EIGHT RUNNERS WOULD BREAK TWELVE SECONDS IN THIS RACE?
TWENTY-FOUR PEOPLE WILL MAKE IT TO THE SEMIFINALS.
WHICH MEANS EVEN IF YOU KEEP YOUR TIME DOWN BETWEEN 11.30 SECONDS AND 12.00 SECONDS, YOU'LL STILL QUALIFY.
YOU'VE GOT TO START THINKING ABOUT PACE.
DO YOU REALLY THINK THAT YOU CAN KEEP UP THAT PACE THROUGH BOTH THE SEMIFINALS AND THE RELAY?
WELL...
パサッ
FLUP
WHOA, WHOA...IT'S ALL RIGHT. YOU WERE REALLY FAST, AKITSUKI! YOU DID GOOD!

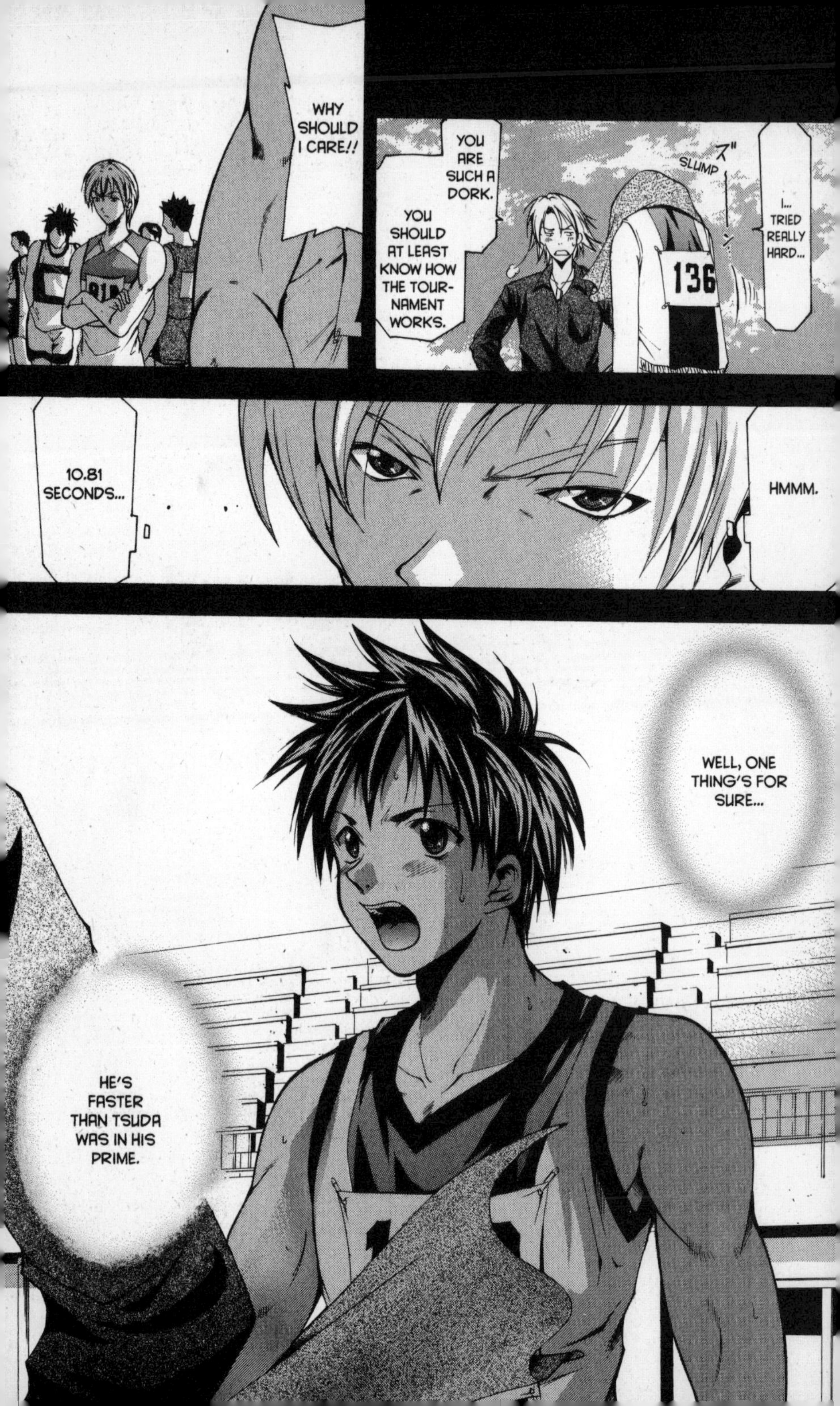
ズ
SLUMP
I... TRIED REALLY HARD...
YOU ARE SUCH A DORK.
YOU SHOULD AT LEAST KNOW HOW THE TOUR-NAMENT WORKS.
WHY SHOULD I CARE!!
HMMM.
10.81 SECONDS...
WELL, ONE THING'S FOR SURE...
HE'S FASTER THAN TSUDA WAS IN HIS PRIME.

SUZUKA

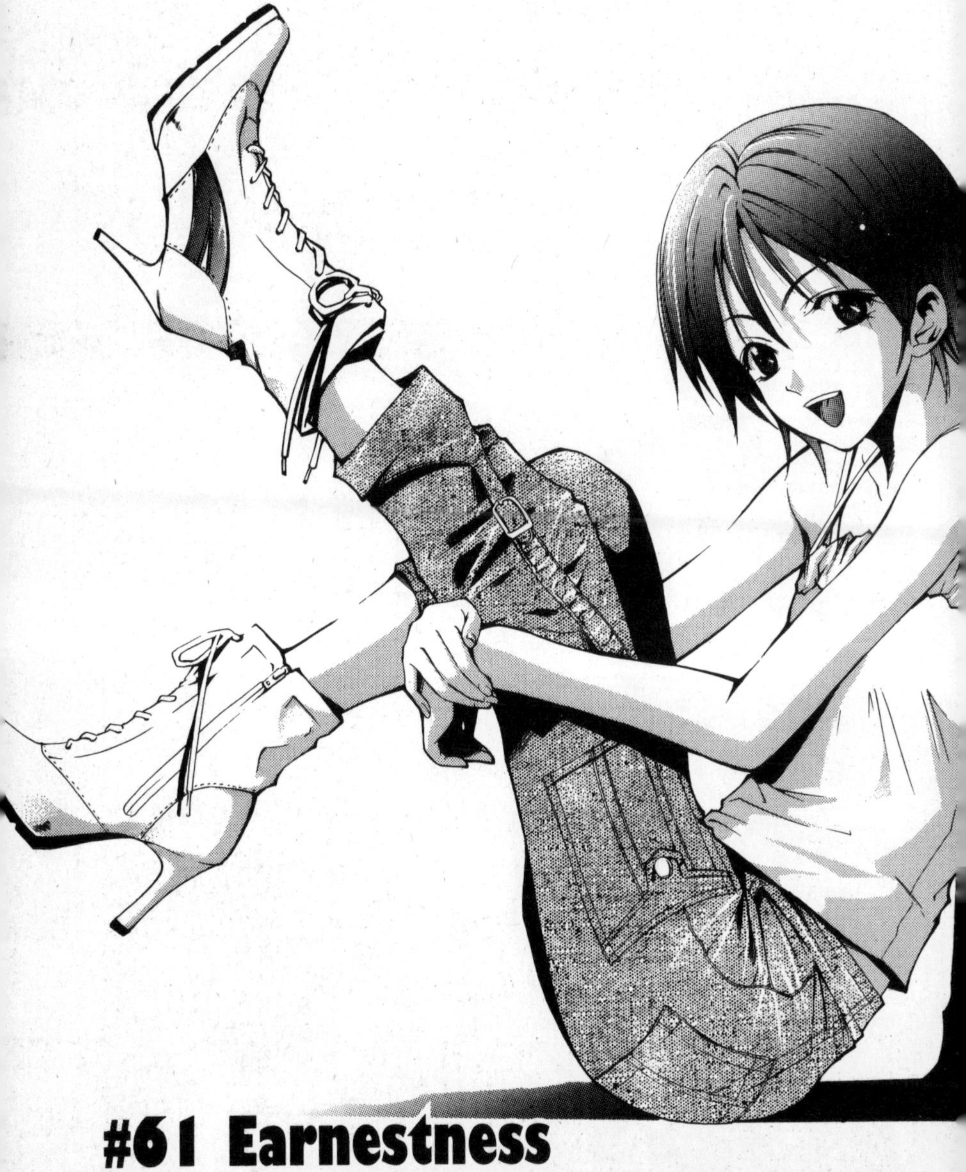

#61 Earnestness

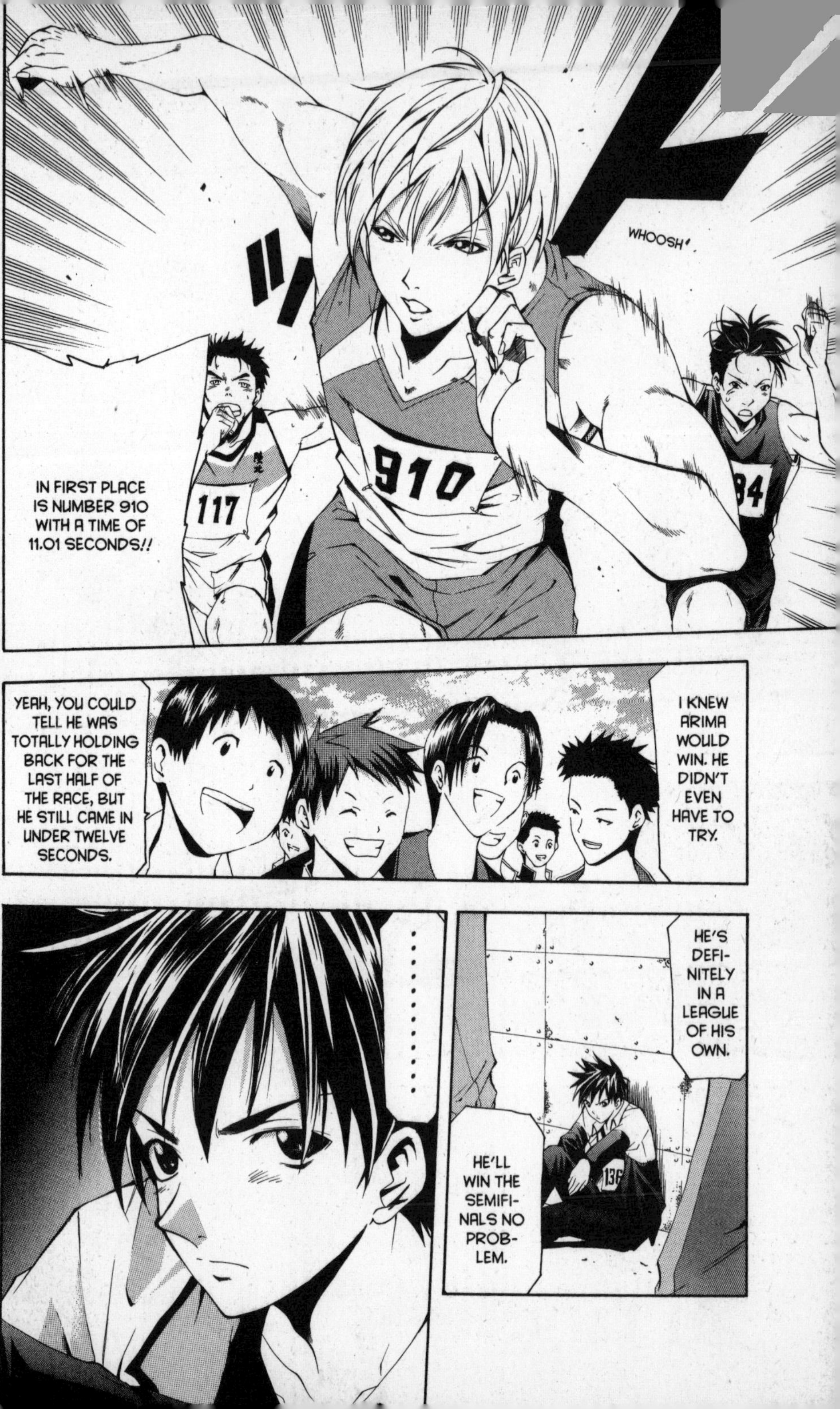
WHOOSH
IN FIRST PLACE IS NUMBER 910 WITH A TIME OF 11.01 SECONDS!!
I KNEW ARIMA WOULD WIN. HE DIDN'T EVEN HAVE TO TRY.
YEAH, YOU COULD TELL HE WAS TOTALLY HOLDING BACK FOR THE LAST HALF OF THE RACE, BUT HE STILL CAME IN UNDER TWELVE SECONDS.
HE'S DEFINITELY IN A LEAGUE OF HIS OWN.
HE'LL WIN THE SEMIFINALS NO PROBLEM.
......

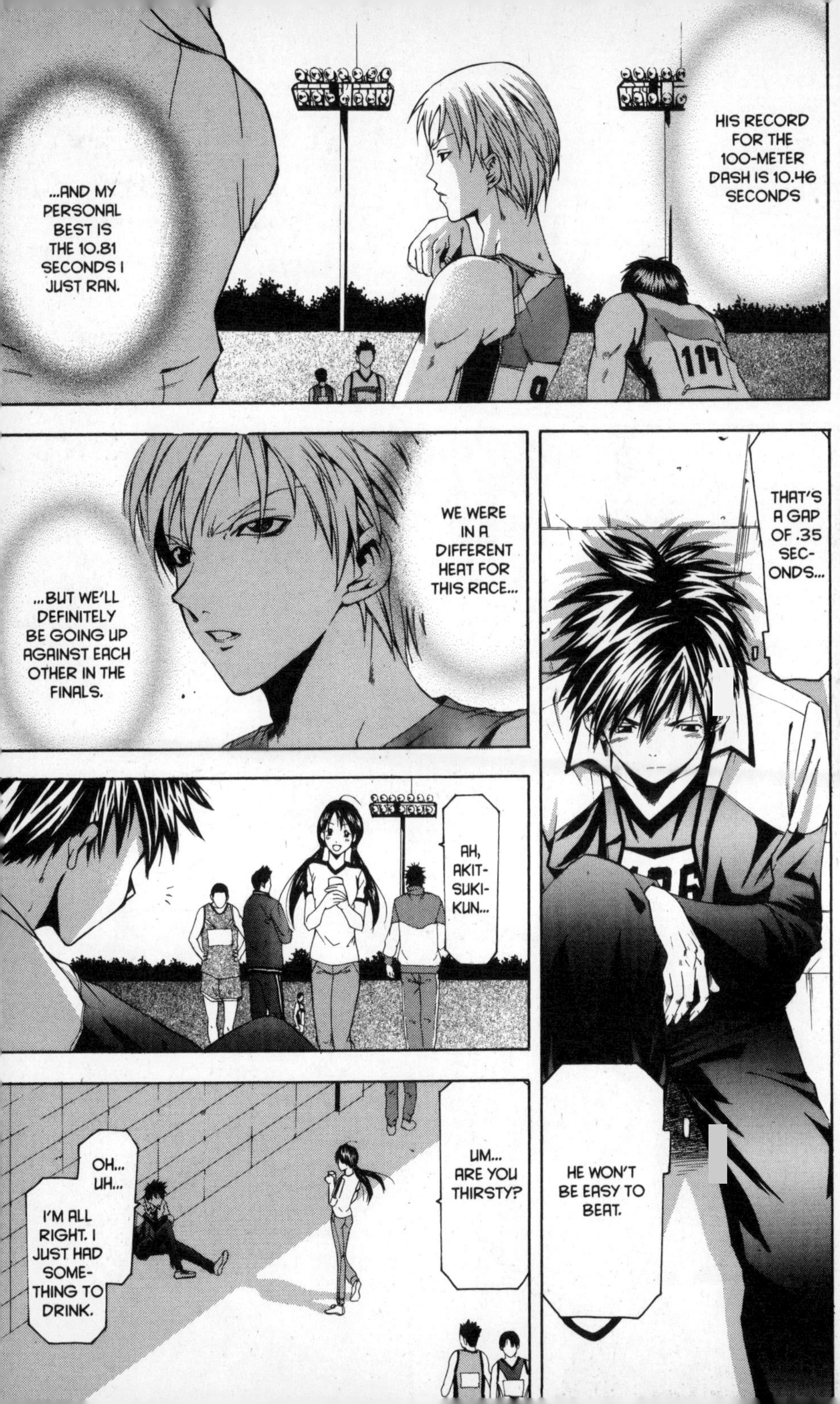
HIS RECORD FOR THE 100-METER DASH IS 10.46 SECONDS
...AND MY PERSONAL BEST IS THE 10.81 SECONDS I JUST RAN.
THAT'S A GAP OF .35 SECONDS...
HE WON'T BE EASY TO BEAT.
WE WERE IN A DIFFERENT HEAT FOR THIS RACE...
...BUT WE'LL DEFINITELY BE GOING UP AGAINST EACH OTHER IN THE FINALS.
AH, AKITSUKI-KUN...
UM... ARE YOU THIRSTY?
OH... UH...
I'M ALL RIGHT. I JUST HAD SOMETHING TO DRINK.

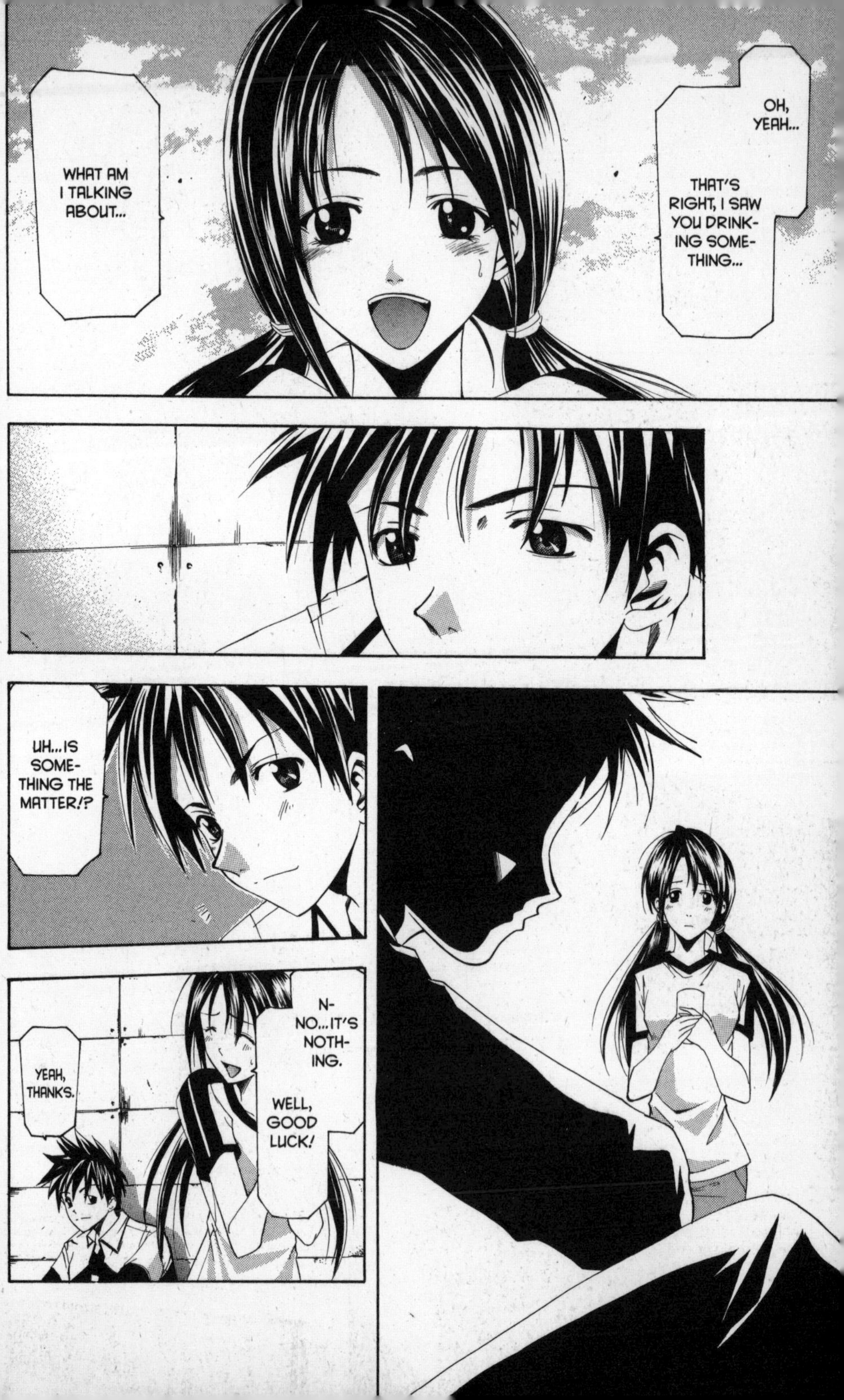
OH, YEAH...
THAT'S RIGHT, I SAW YOU DRINKING SOMETHING...
WHAT AM I TALKING ABOUT...
UH...IS SOMETHING THE MATTER!?
N-NO...IT'S NOTHING.
WELL, GOOD LUCK!
YEAH, THANKS.

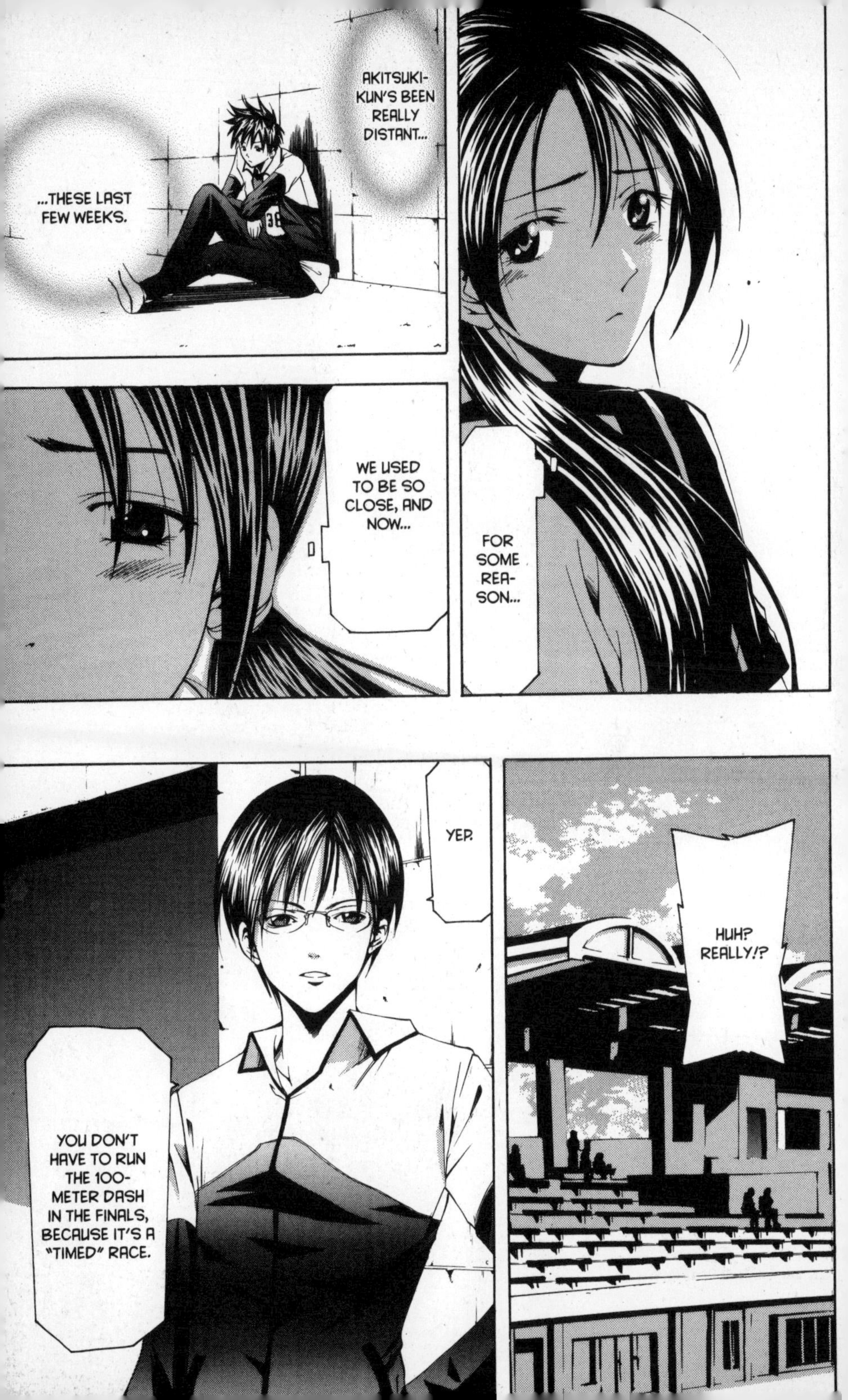
AKITSUKI-KUN'S BEEN REALLY DISTANT...
...THESE LAST FEW WEEKS.
FOR SOME REA-SON...
WE USED TO BE SO CLOSE, AND NOW...
HUH? REALLY!?
YEP.
YOU DON'T HAVE TO RUN THE 100-METER DASH IN THE FINALS, BECAUSE IT'S A "TIMED" RACE.

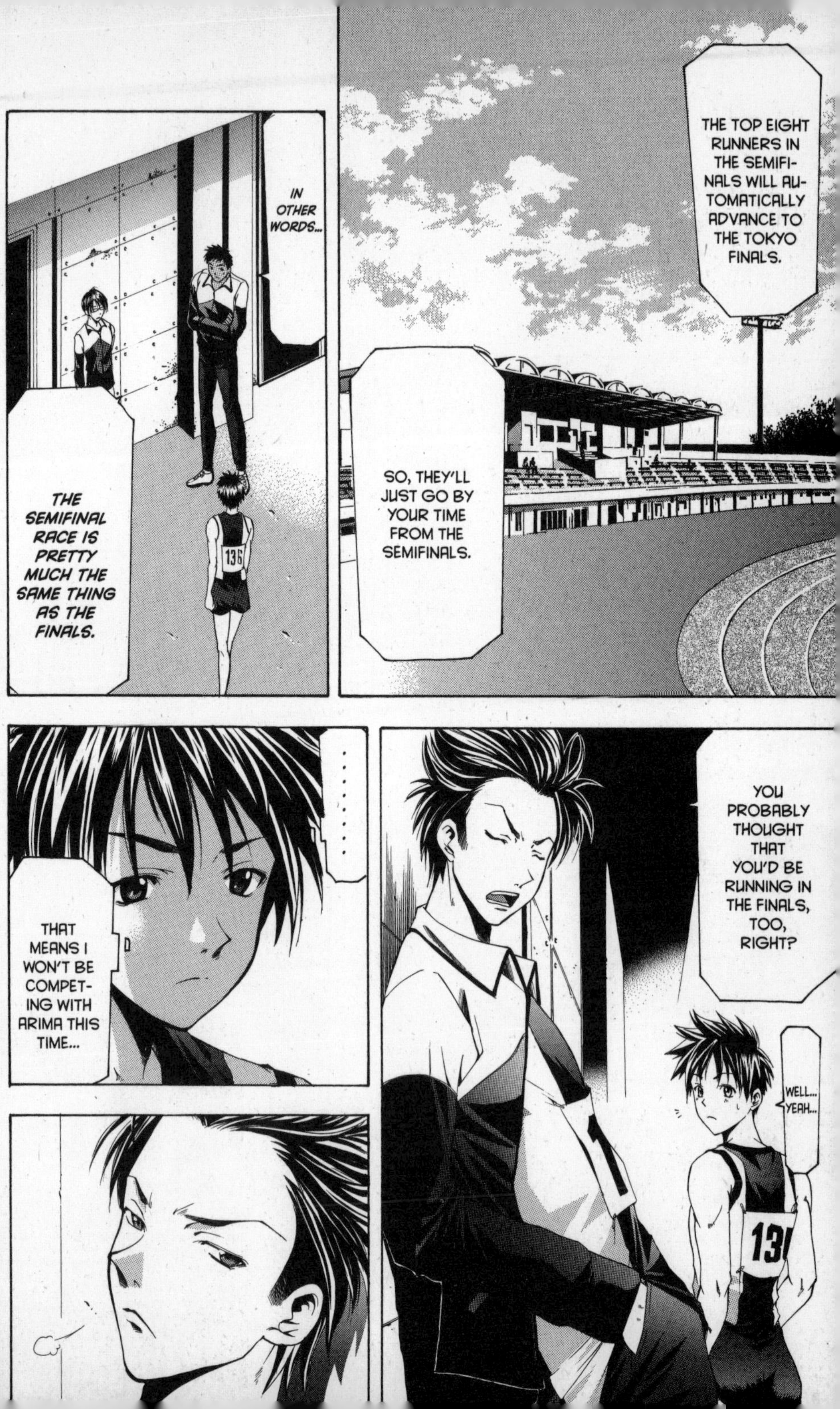
THE TOP EIGHT RUNNERS IN THE SEMIFI-NALS WILL AU-TOMATICALLY ADVANCE TO THE TOKYO FINALS.
SO, THEY'LL JUST GO BY YOUR TIME FROM THE SEMIFINALS.
IN OTHER WORDS...
THE SEMIFINAL RACE IS PRETTY MUCH THE SAME THING AS THE FINALS.
YOU PROBABLY THOUGHT THAT YOU'D BE RUNNING IN THE FINALS, TOO, RIGHT?
WELL... YEAH...
......
THAT MEANS I WON'T BE COMPET-ING WITH ARIMA THIS TIME...

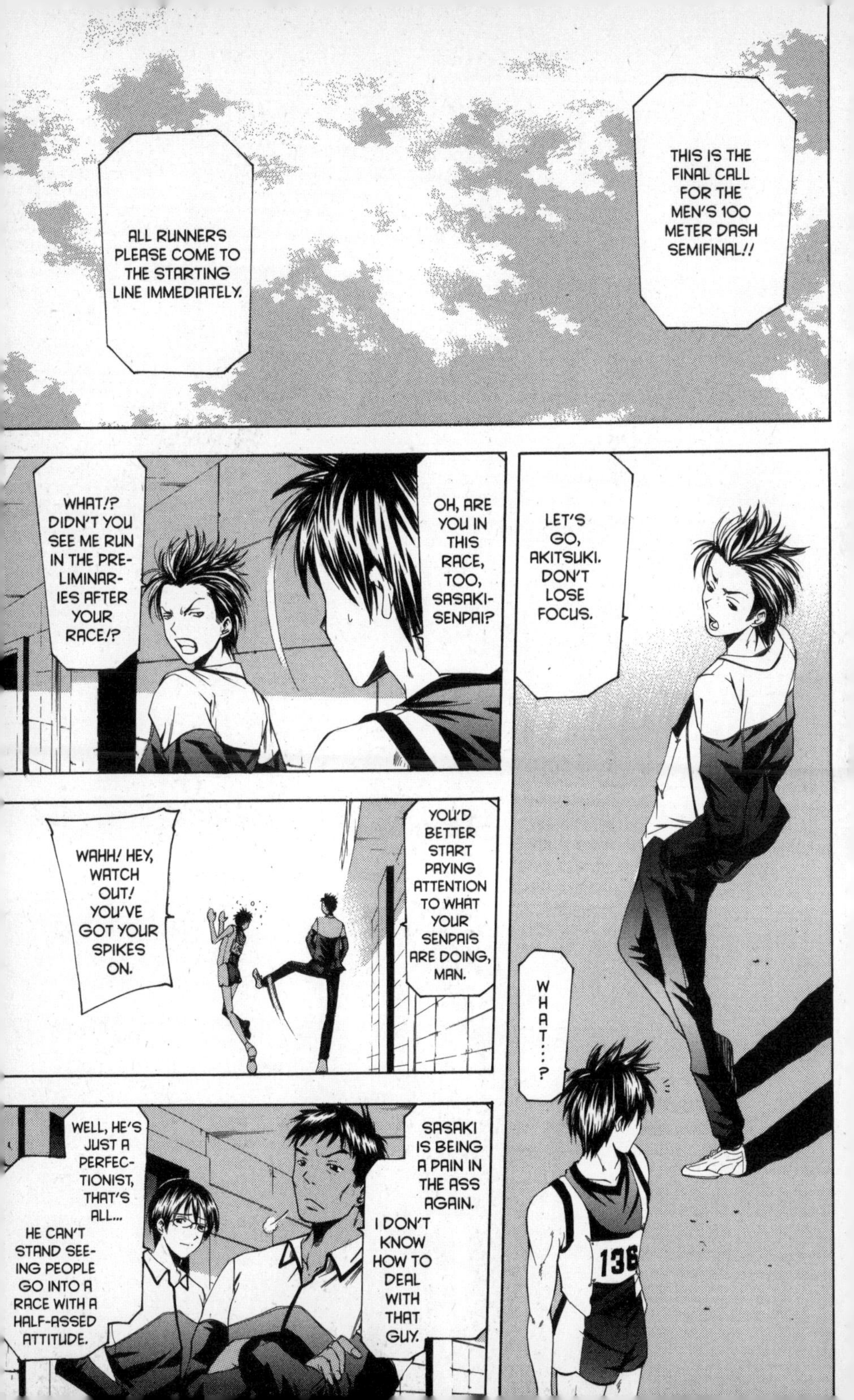
THIS IS THE FINAL CALL FOR THE MEN'S 100 METER DASH SEMIFINAL!!
ALL RUNNERS PLEASE COME TO THE STARTING LINE IMMEDIATELY.
LET'S GO, AKITSUKI. DON'T LOSE FOCUS.
WHAT...?
OH, ARE YOU IN THIS RACE, TOO, SASAKI-SENPAI?
WHAT!? DIDN'T YOU SEE ME RUN IN THE PRELIMINARIES AFTER YOUR RACE!?
YOU'D BETTER START PAYING ATTENTION TO WHAT YOUR SENPAIS ARE DOING, MAN.
WAHH! HEY, WATCH OUT! YOU'VE GOT YOUR SPIKES ON.
SASAKI IS BEING A PAIN IN THE ASS AGAIN.
I DON'T KNOW HOW TO DEAL WITH THAT GUY.
WELL, HE'S JUST A PERFECTIONIST, THAT'S ALL...
HE CAN'T STAND SEEING PEOPLE GO INTO A RACE WITH A HALF-ASSED ATTITUDE.
136

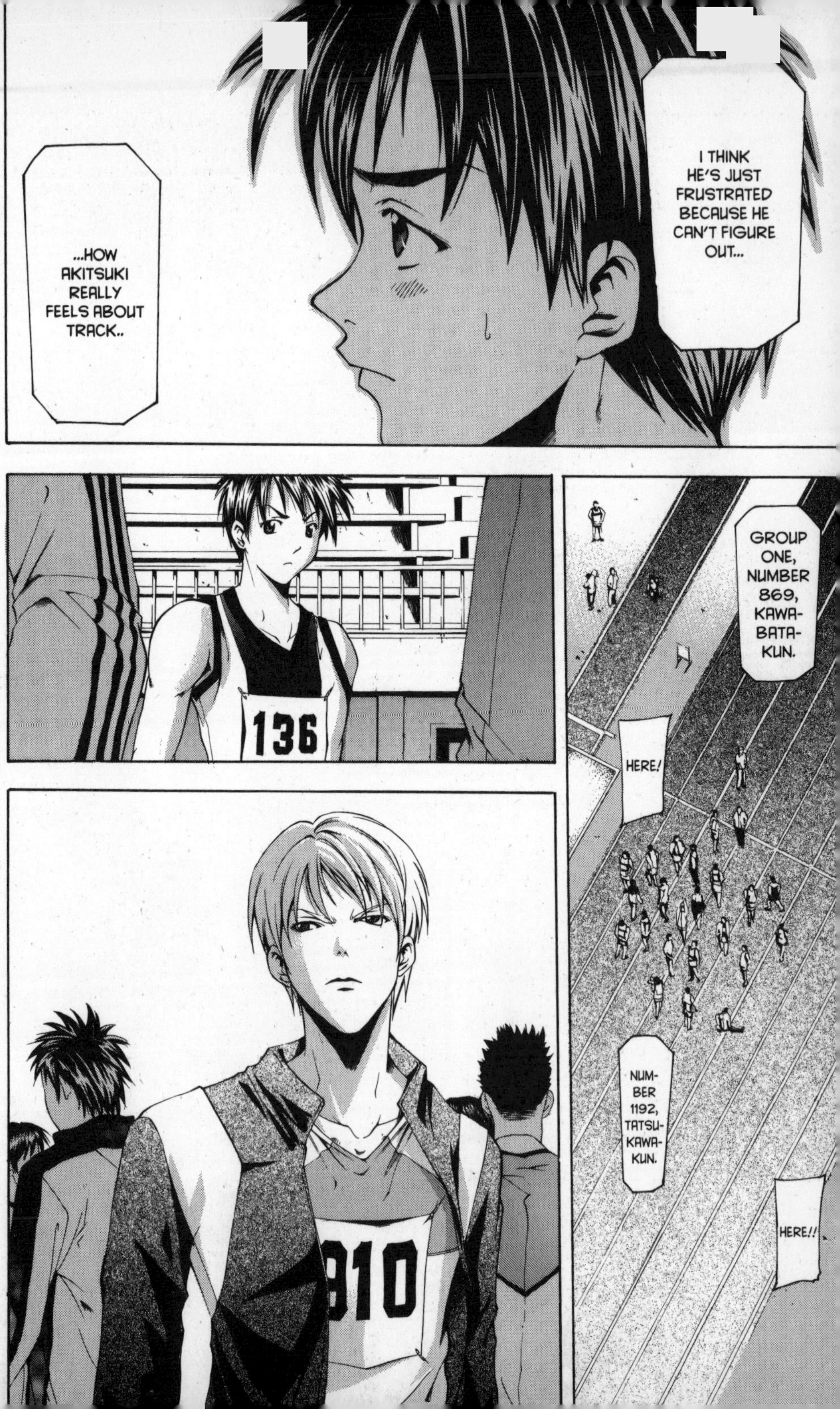
I THINK HE'S JUST FRUSTRATED BECAUSE HE CAN'T FIGURE OUT...
...HOW AKITSUKI REALLY FEELS ABOUT TRACK..
GROUP ONE, NUMBER 869, KAWA-BATA-KUN.
HERE!
NUMBER 1192, TATSU-KAWA-KUN.
HERE!!

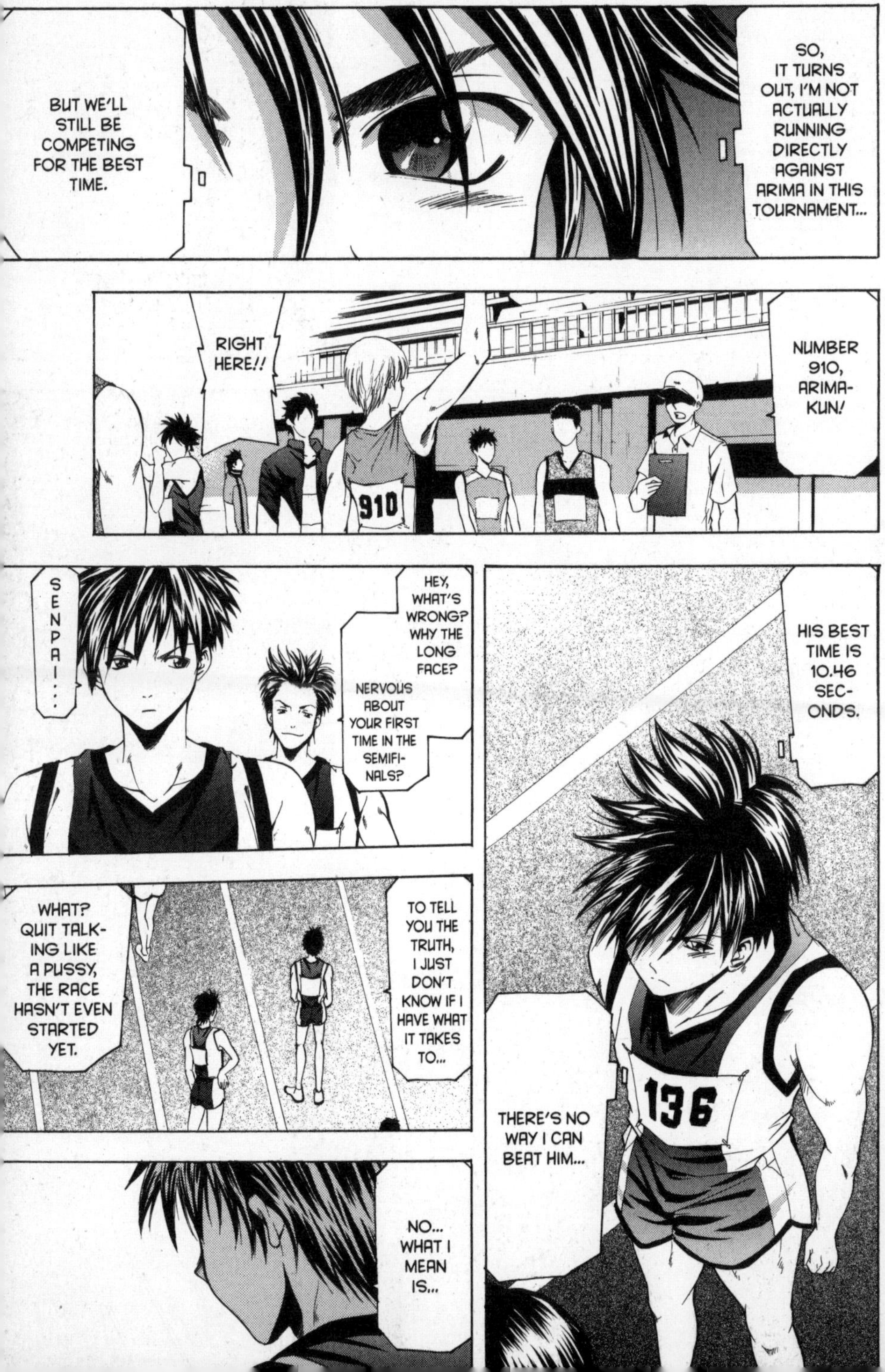
SO, IT TURNS OUT, I'M NOT ACTUALLY RUNNING DIRECTLY AGAINST ARIMA IN THIS TOURNAMENT...
BUT WE'LL STILL BE COMPETING FOR THE BEST TIME.
NUMBER 910, ARIMA-KUN!
RIGHT HERE!!
910
HIS BEST TIME IS 10.46 SEC-ONDS.
THERE'S NO WAY I CAN BEAT HIM...
136
HEY, WHAT'S WRONG? WHY THE LONG FACE?
NERVOUS ABOUT YOUR FIRST TIME IN THE SEMIFI-NALS?
SENPAI...
TO TELL YOU THE TRUTH, I JUST DON'T KNOW IF I HAVE WHAT IT TAKES TO...
WHAT? QUIT TALK-ING LIKE A PUSSY, THE RACE HASN'T EVEN STARTED YET.
NO... WHAT I MEAN IS...

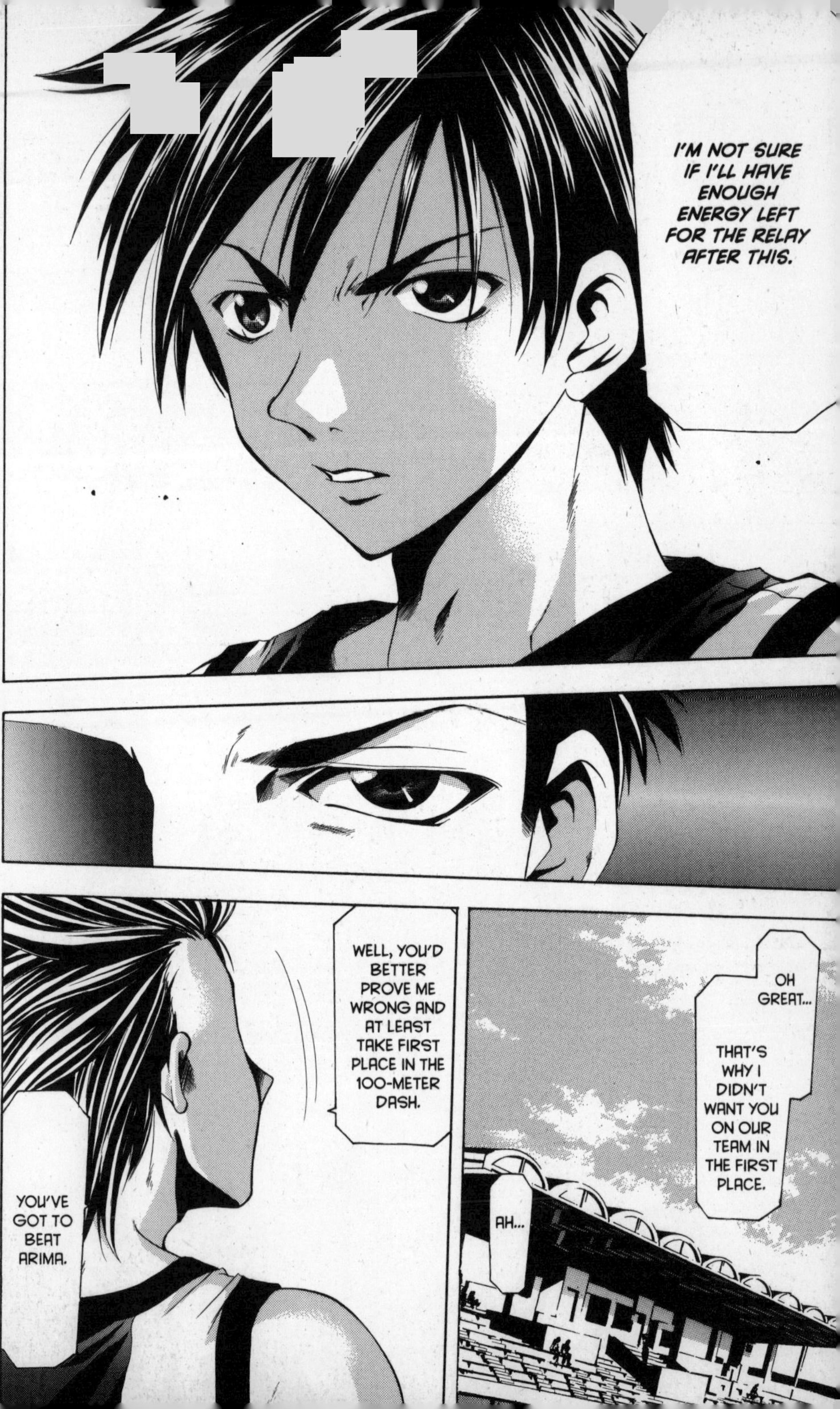
I'M NOT SURE IF I'LL HAVE ENOUGH ENERGY LEFT FOR THE RELAY AFTER THIS.
OH GREAT...
THAT'S WHY I DIDN'T WANT YOU ON OUR TEAM IN THE FIRST PLACE.
AH...
WELL, YOU'D BETTER PROVE ME WRONG AND AT LEAST TAKE FIRST PLACE IN THE 100-METER DASH.
YOU'VE GOT TO BEAT ARIMA.

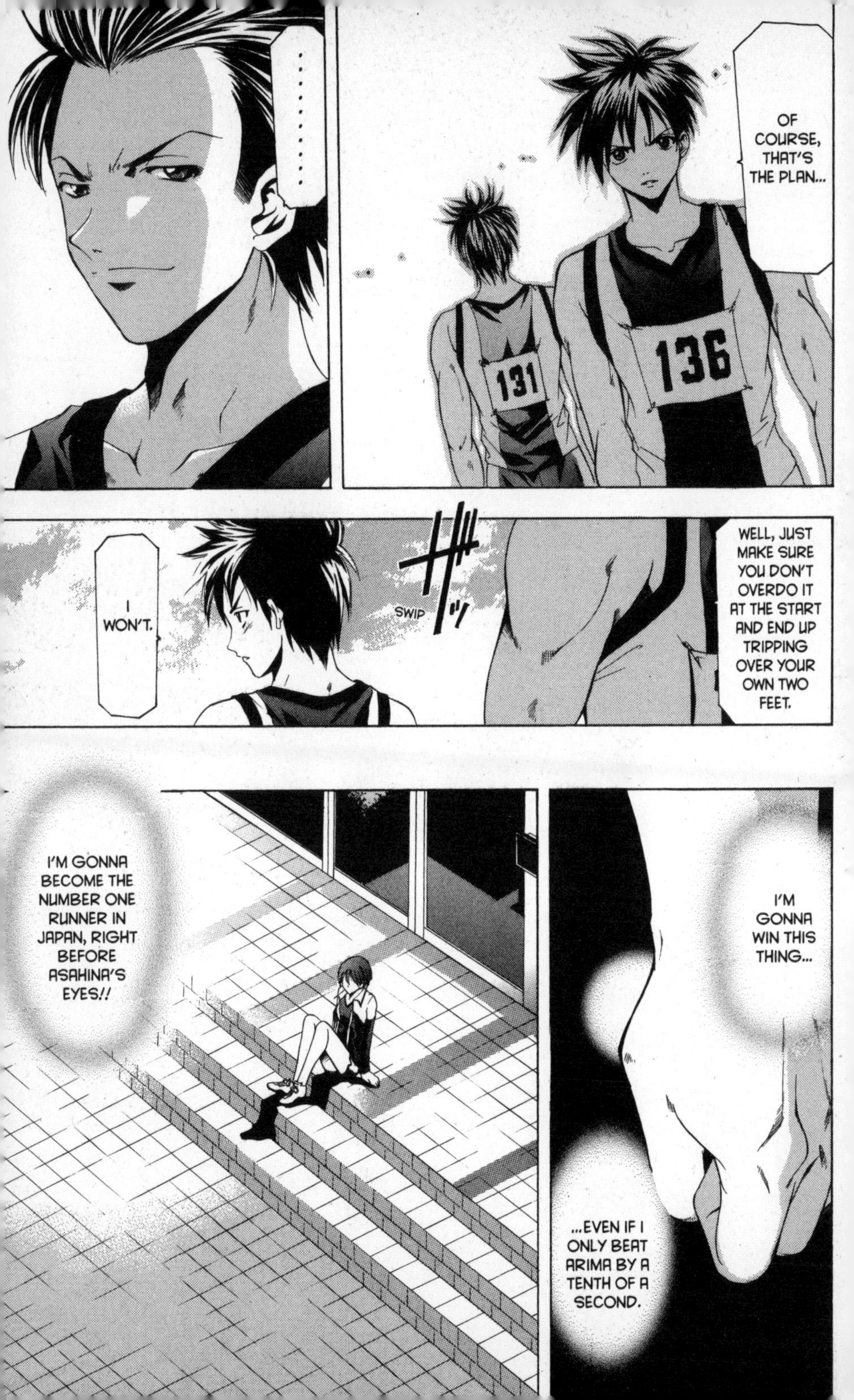

OF COURSE, THAT'S THE PLAN...
136
131
......
WELL, JUST MAKE SURE YOU DON'T OVERDO IT AT THE START AND END UP TRIPPING OVER YOUR OWN TWO FEET.
SWIP
I WON'T.
I'M GONNA WIN THIS THING...
...EVEN IF I ONLY BEAT ARIMA BY A TENTH OF A SECOND.
I'M GONNA BECOME THE NUMBER ONE RUNNER IN JAPAN, RIGHT BEFORE ASAHINA'S EYES!!

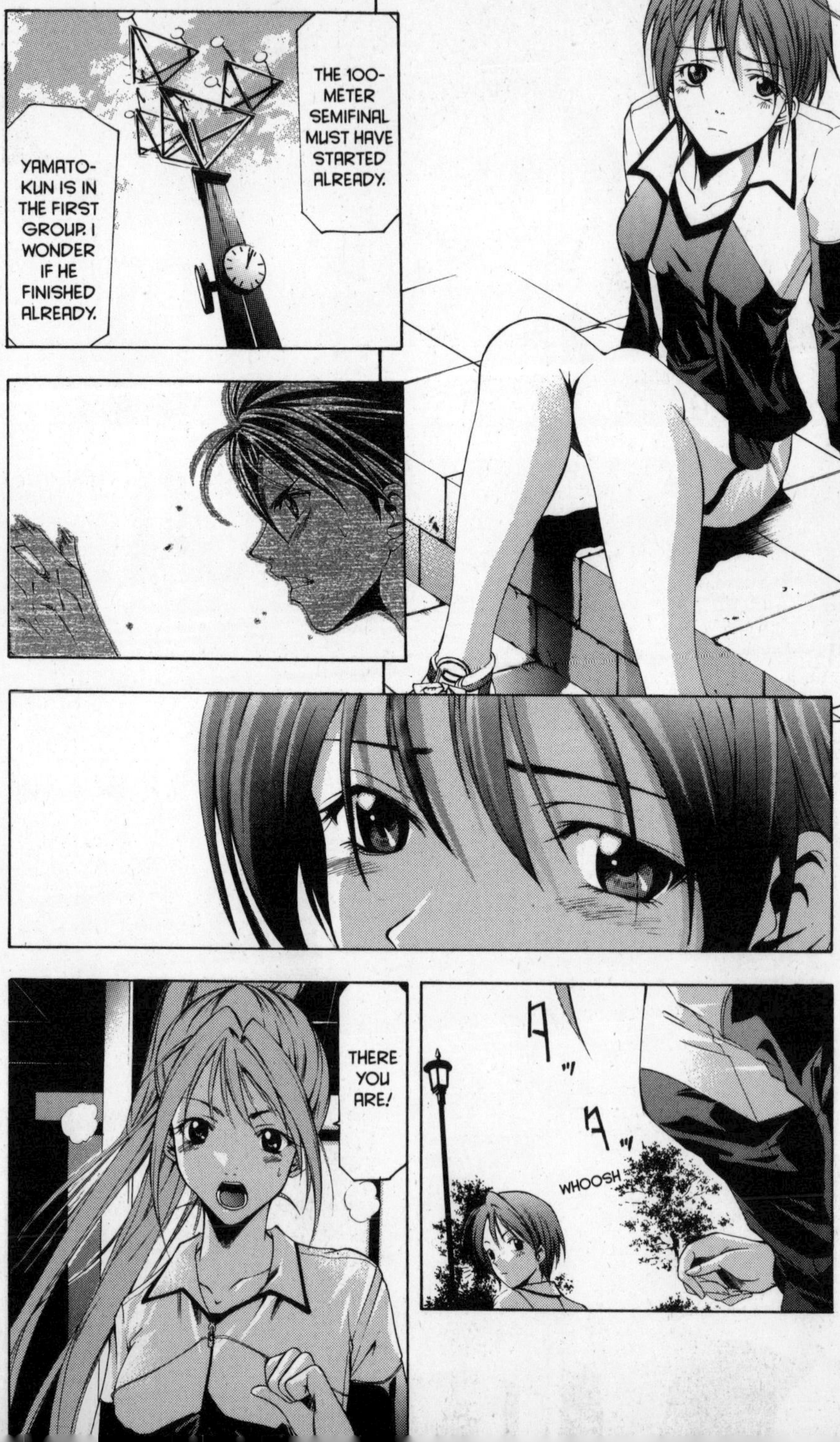
THE 100-METER SEMIFINAL MUST HAVE STARTED ALREADY.
YAMATO-KUN IS IN THE FIRST GROUP. I WONDER IF HE FINISHED ALREADY.
タッ
タッ
WHOOSH
THERE YOU ARE!

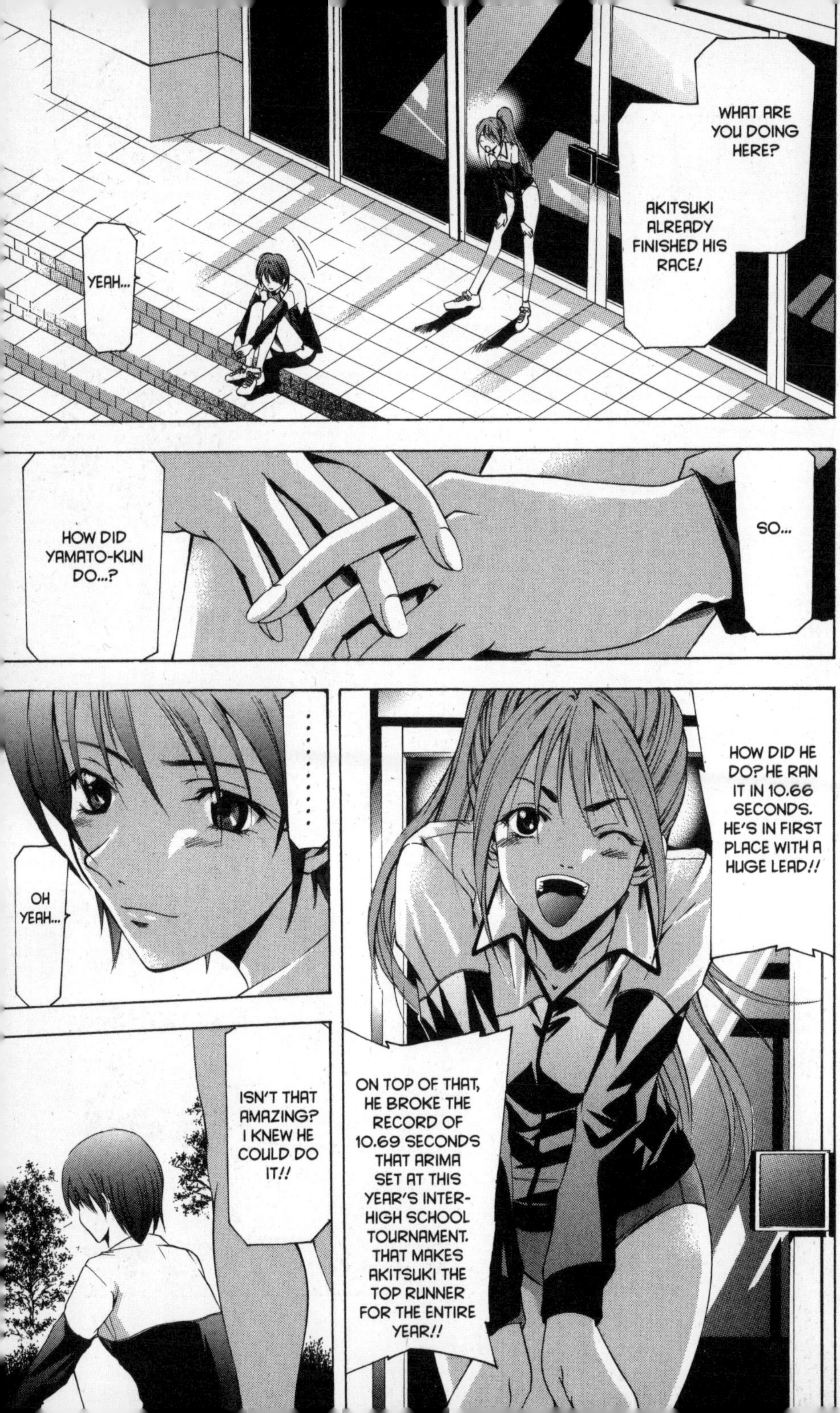
WHAT ARE YOU DOING HERE?
AKITSUKI ALREADY FINISHED HIS RACE!
YEAH...
SO...
HOW DID YAMATO-KUN DO...?
HOW DID HE DO? HE RAN IT IN 10.66 SECONDS. HE'S IN FIRST PLACE WITH A HUGE LEAD!!
ON TOP OF THAT, HE BROKE THE RECORD OF 10.69 SECONDS THAT ARIMA SET AT THIS YEAR'S INTER-HIGH SCHOOL TOURNAMENT. THAT MAKES AKITSUKI THE TOP RUNNER FOR THE ENTIRE YEAR!!
......
OH YEAH...
ISN'T THAT AMAZING? I KNEW HE COULD DO IT!!

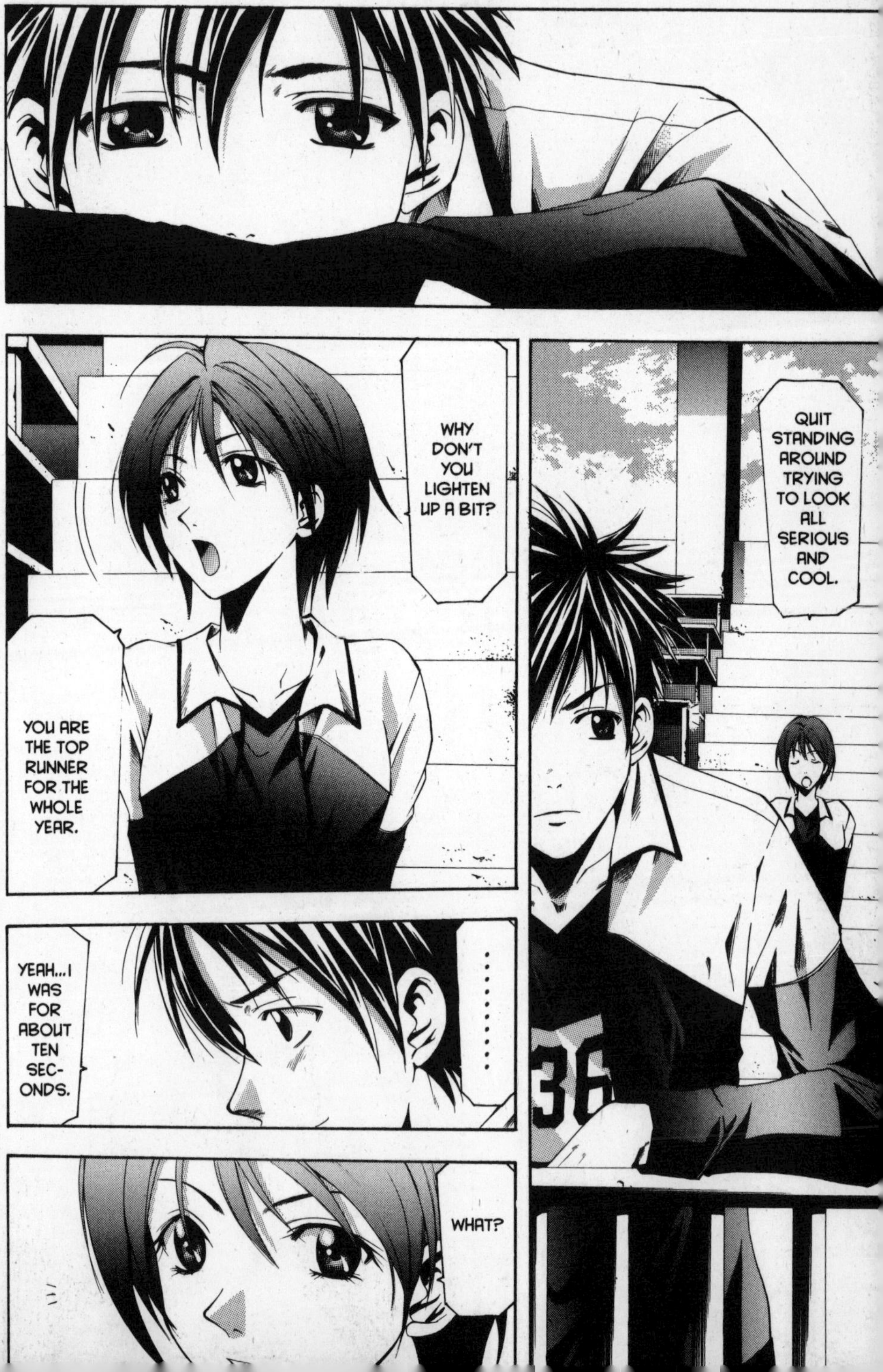
QUIT STANDING AROUND TRYING TO LOOK ALL SERIOUS AND COOL.
WHY DON'T YOU LIGHTEN UP A BIT?
YOU ARE THE TOP RUNNER FOR THE WHOLE YEAR.
....
YEAH...I WAS FOR ABOUT TEN SEC-ONDS.
WHAT?

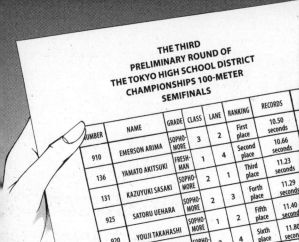

NUMBER	NAME	GRADE	CLASS	LANE	RANKING	RECORDS
			3	2	First place	10.50 seconds
910	EMERSON ARIMA	SOPHO-MORE			Second place	10.66 seconds
136	YAMATO AKITSUKI	FRESH-MAN	1	4	Third place	11.23 seconds
131	KAZUYUKI SASAKI	SOPHO-MORE	2	1	Forth place	11.29 seconds
925	SATORU UEHARA	SOPHO-MORE	2	3	Fifth place	11.40 second
920	YOUJI TAKAHASHI	SOPHO-MORE	1	2	Sixth place	11.80 secon
1392	SHINJI KUWATA	SOPHO-MORE	3	4	Seventh place	12
		SOPHO-	1	3		

Table title:

THE THIRD PRELIMINARY ROUND OF THE TOKYO HIGH SCHOOL DISTRICT CHAMPIONSHIPS 100-METER SEMIFINALS

LOOK...

THAT JERK BLEW ME AWAY!

HUH? SO YOU CAME IN SEC-OND?

B-BUT STILL, IT'S AMAZING. 10.66 SECONDS!!

THAT MEANS YOU'RE IN SECOND PLACE FOR THE INTER HIGH. BESIDES, YOU STILL MADE IT INTO THE TOKYO HIGH SCHOOL DISTRICT CHAMPION-SHIPS.

UM... WELL...

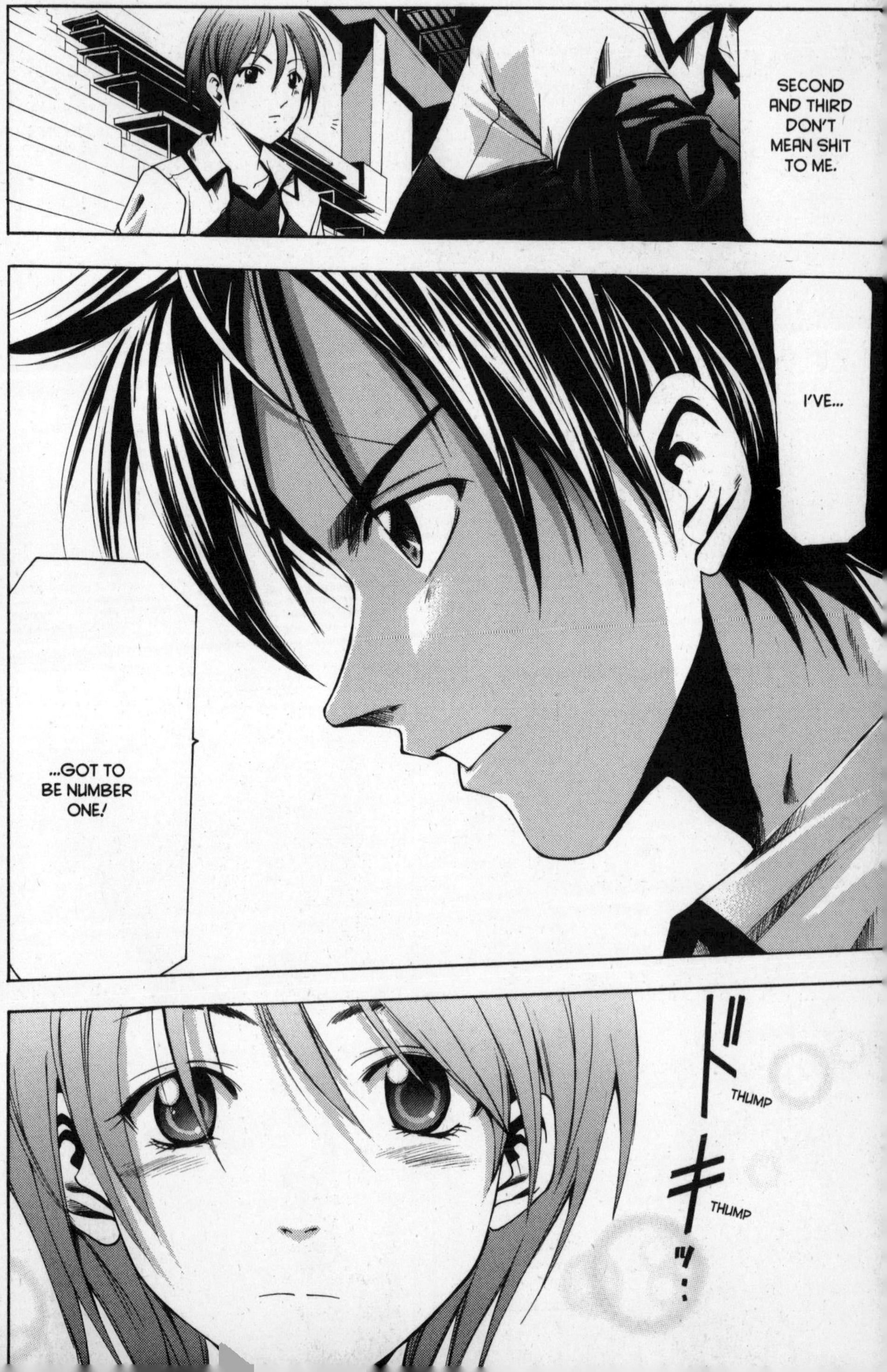
SECOND AND THIRD DON'T MEAN SHIT TO ME.
I'VE...
...GOT TO BE NUMBER ONE!
ドキッ..
THUMP
THUMP

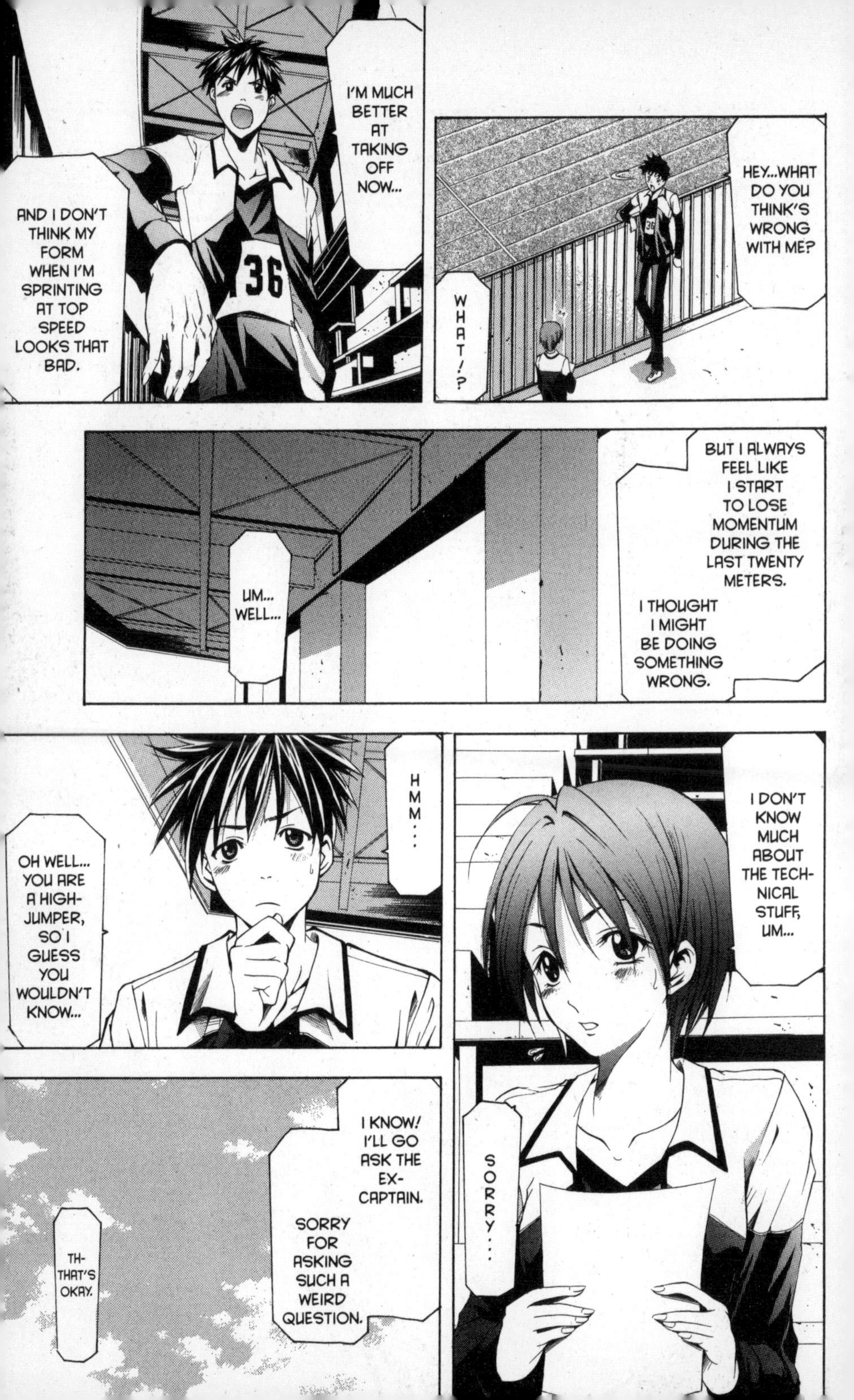
HEY...WHAT DO YOU THINK'S WRONG WITH ME?
WHAT!?
I'M MUCH BETTER AT TAKING OFF NOW...
AND I DON'T THINK MY FORM WHEN I'M SPRINTING AT TOP SPEED LOOKS THAT BAD.
BUT I ALWAYS FEEL LIKE I START TO LOSE MOMENTUM DURING THE LAST TWENTY METERS.
I THOUGHT I MIGHT BE DOING SOMETHING WRONG.
UM... WELL...
I DON'T KNOW MUCH ABOUT THE TECH-NICAL STUFF, UM...
SORRY...
HMM...
OH WELL... YOU ARE A HIGH-JUMPER, SO I GUESS YOU WOULDN'T KNOW...
I KNOW! I'LL GO ASK THE EX-CAPTAIN.
SORRY FOR ASKING SUCH A WEIRD QUESTION.
TH-THAT'S OKAY.

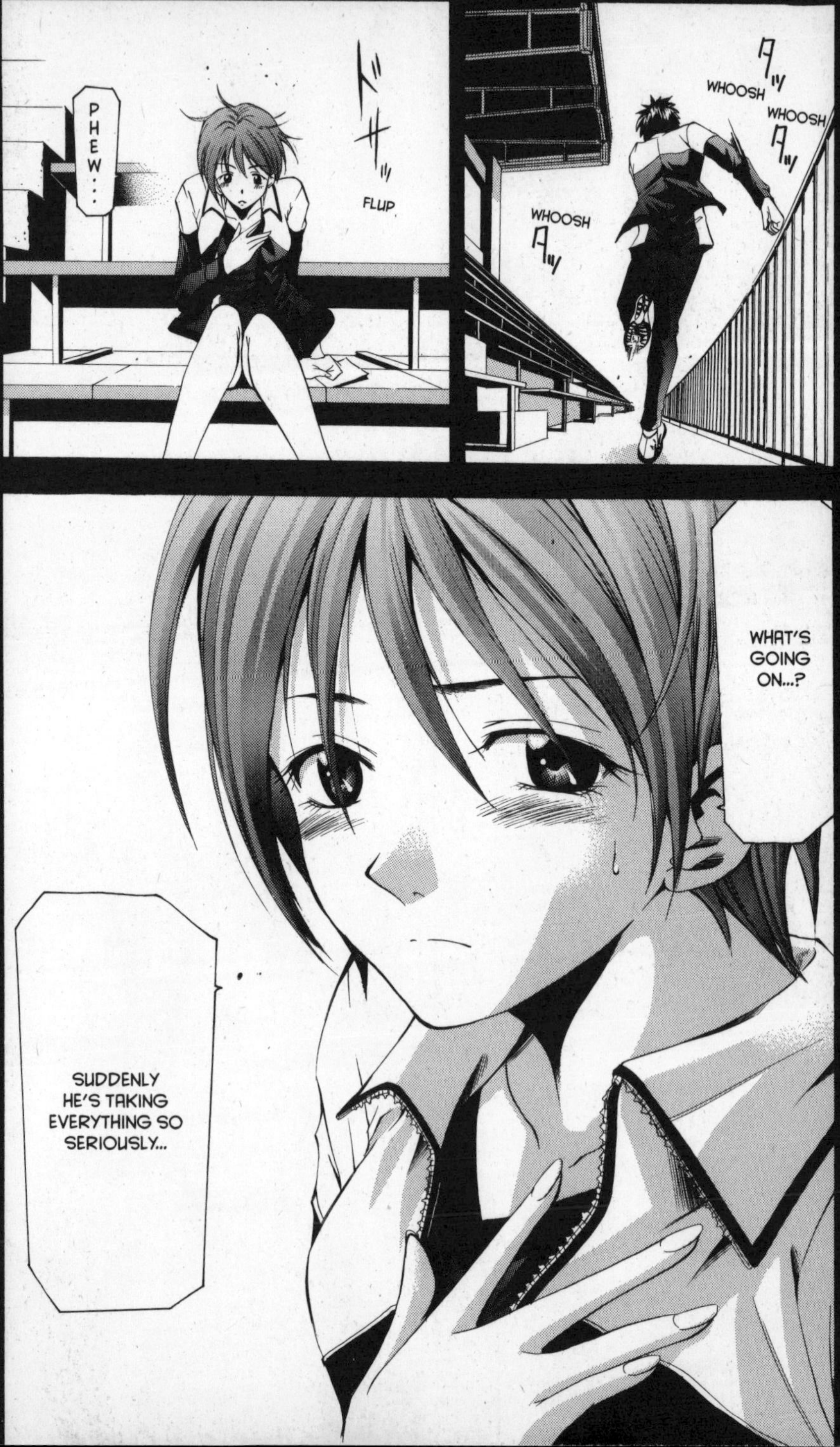

タッ
WHOOSH
WHOOSH
タッ
WHOOSH
タッ
PHEW...
ドサッ
FLUP
WHAT'S GOING ON...?
SUDDENLY HE'S TAKING EVERYTHING SO SERIOUSLY...

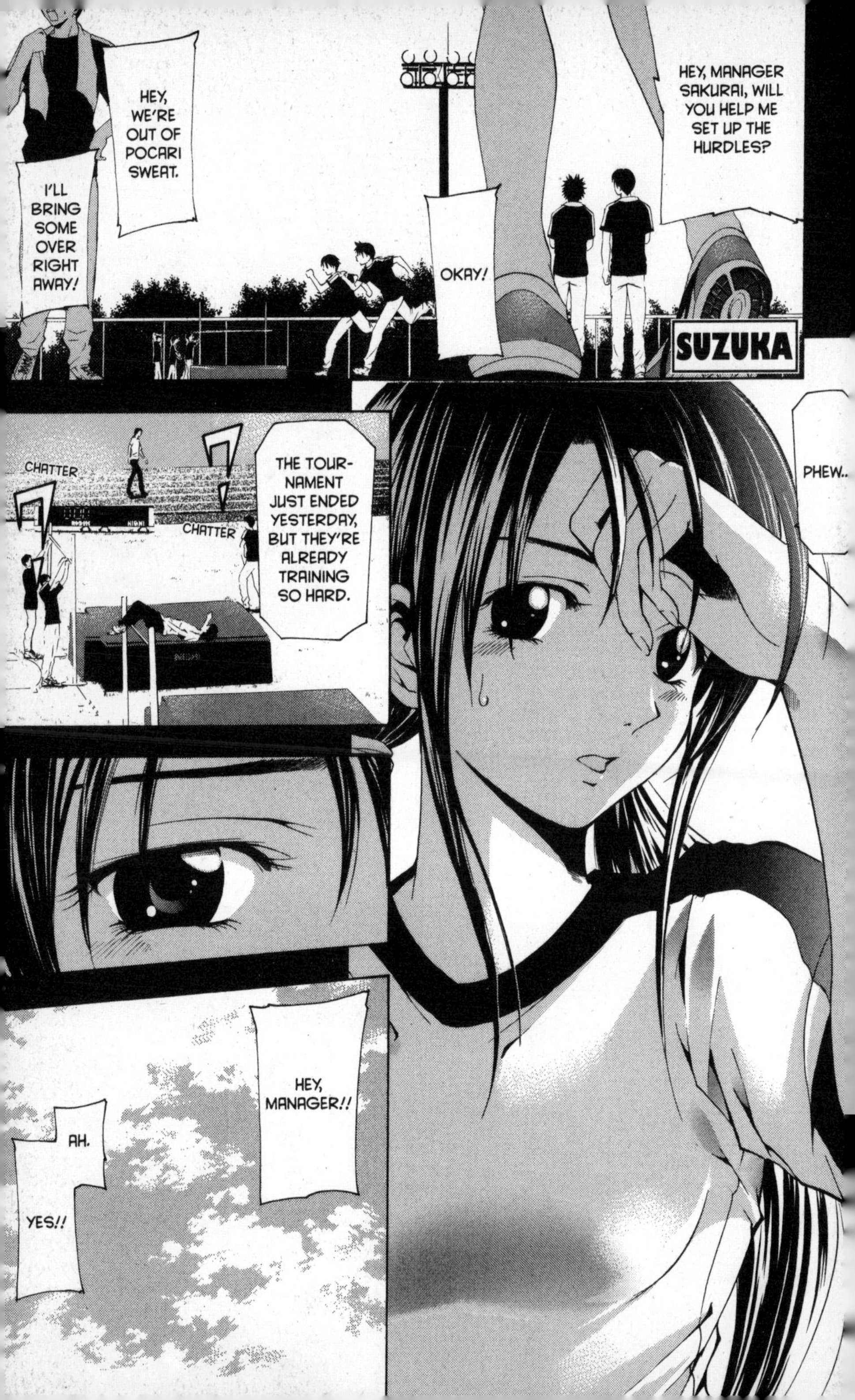
HEY, MANAGER SAKURAI, WILL YOU HELP ME SET UP THE HURDLES?
OKAY!
HEY, WE'RE OUT OF POCARI SWEAT.
I'LL BRING SOME OVER RIGHT AWAY!
SUZUKA
PHEW..
THE TOUR-NAMENT JUST ENDED YESTERDAY, BUT THEY'RE ALREADY TRAINING SO HARD.
CHATTER
CHATTER
HEY, MANAGER!!
AH.
YES!!

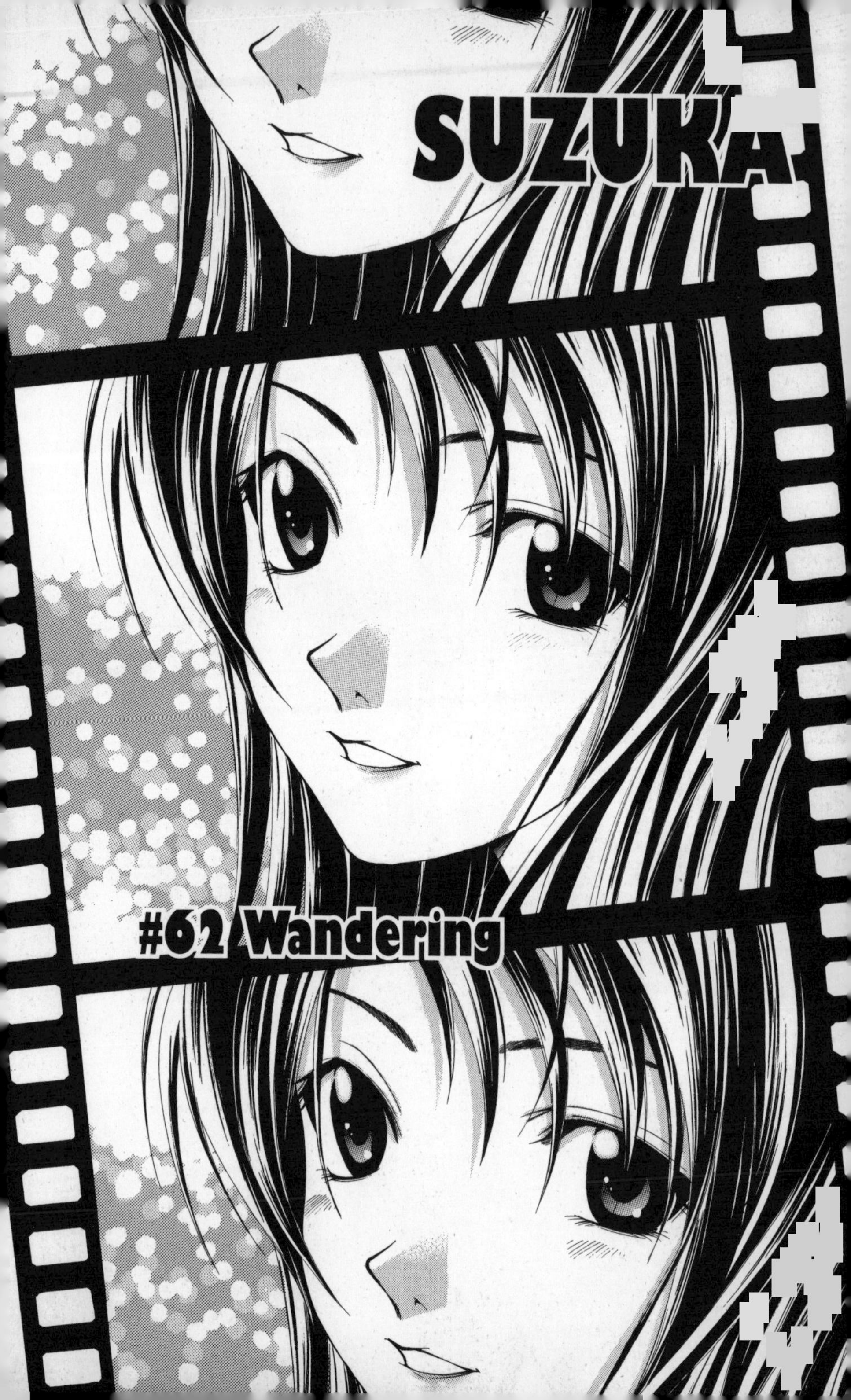
SUZUKA
#62 Wandering

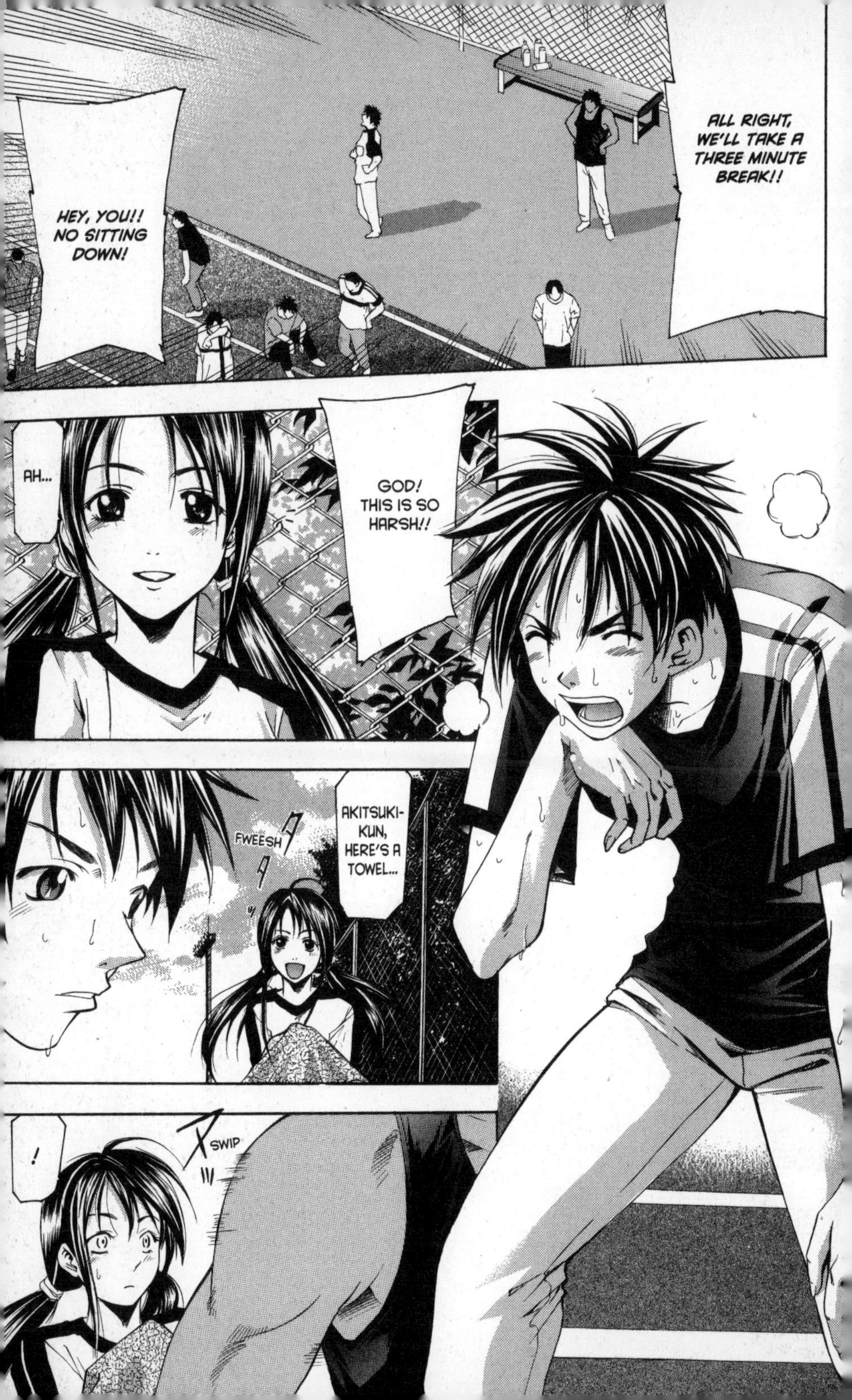
ALL RIGHT, WE'LL TAKE A THREE MINUTE BREAK!!
HEY, YOU!! NO SITTING DOWN!
GOD! THIS IS SO HARSH!!
AH...
AKITSUKI-KUN, HERE'S A TOWEL...
FWEESH
SWIP
!

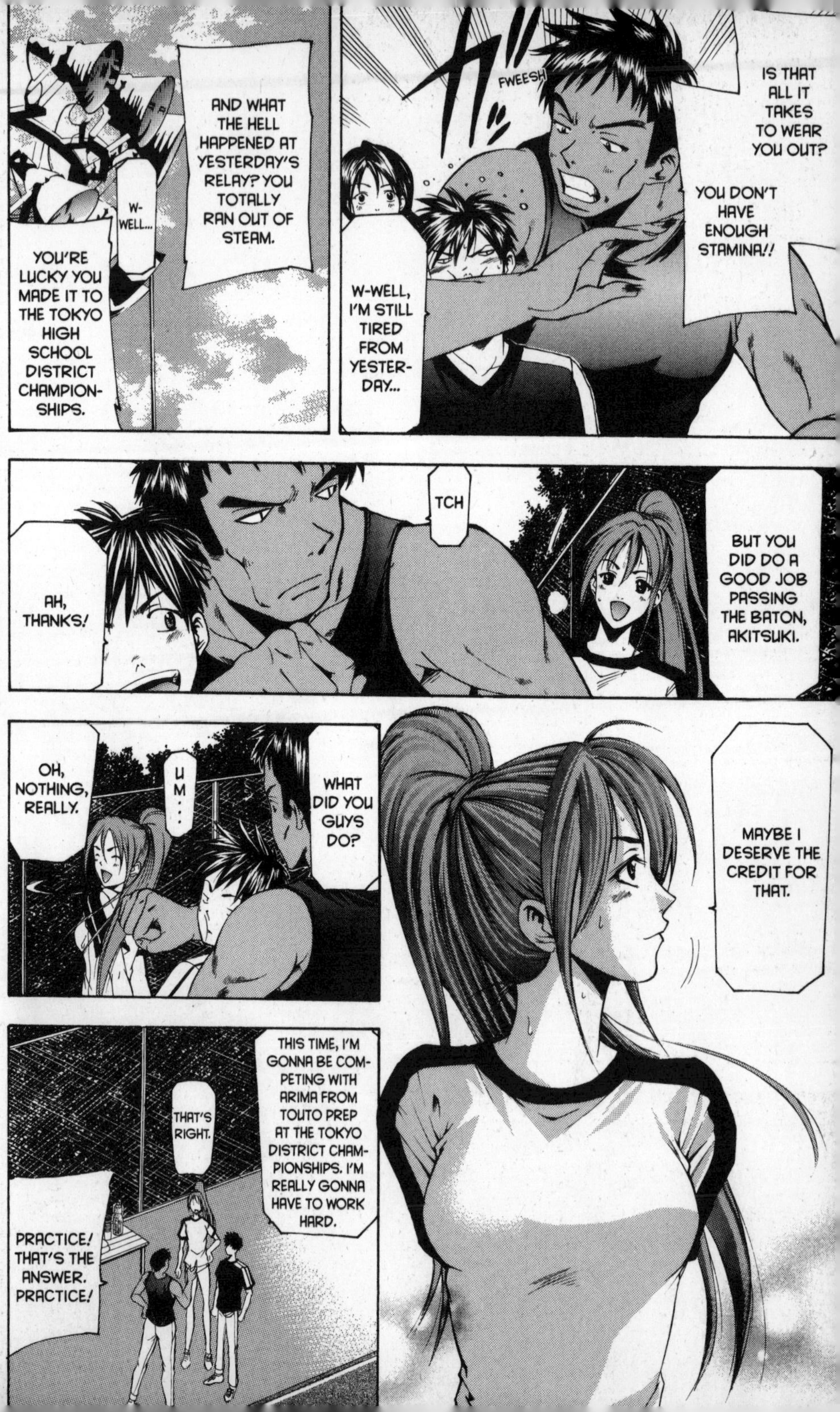
FWEESH
IS THAT ALL IT TAKES TO WEAR YOU OUT?
YOU DON'T HAVE ENOUGH STAMINA!!
W-WELL, I'M STILL TIRED FROM YESTER-DAY...
AND WHAT THE HELL HAPPENED AT YESTERDAY'S RELAY? YOU TOTALLY RAN OUT OF STEAM.
W-WELL...
YOU'RE LUCKY YOU MADE IT TO THE TOKYO HIGH SCHOOL DISTRICT CHAMPION-SHIPS.
BUT YOU DID DO A GOOD JOB PASSING THE BATON, AKITSUKI.
TCH
AH, THANKS!
MAYBE I DESERVE THE CREDIT FOR THAT.
WHAT DID YOU GUYS DO?
UM...
OH, NOTHING, REALLY.
THIS TIME, I'M GONNA BE COM-PETING WITH ARIMA FROM TOUTO PREP AT THE TOKYO DISTRICT CHAM-PIONSHIPS. I'M REALLY GONNA HAVE TO WORK HARD.
THAT'S RIGHT.
PRACTICE! THAT'S THE ANSWER. PRACTICE!

SUZUKA TOPPED THE PRELIMINARIES...

I'VE GOTTA HANG IN THERE, TOO...

I DON'T KNOW WHY, BUT...

I'M STARTING TO FEEL LIKE AKITSUKI-KUN IS LEAVING ME BEHIND.

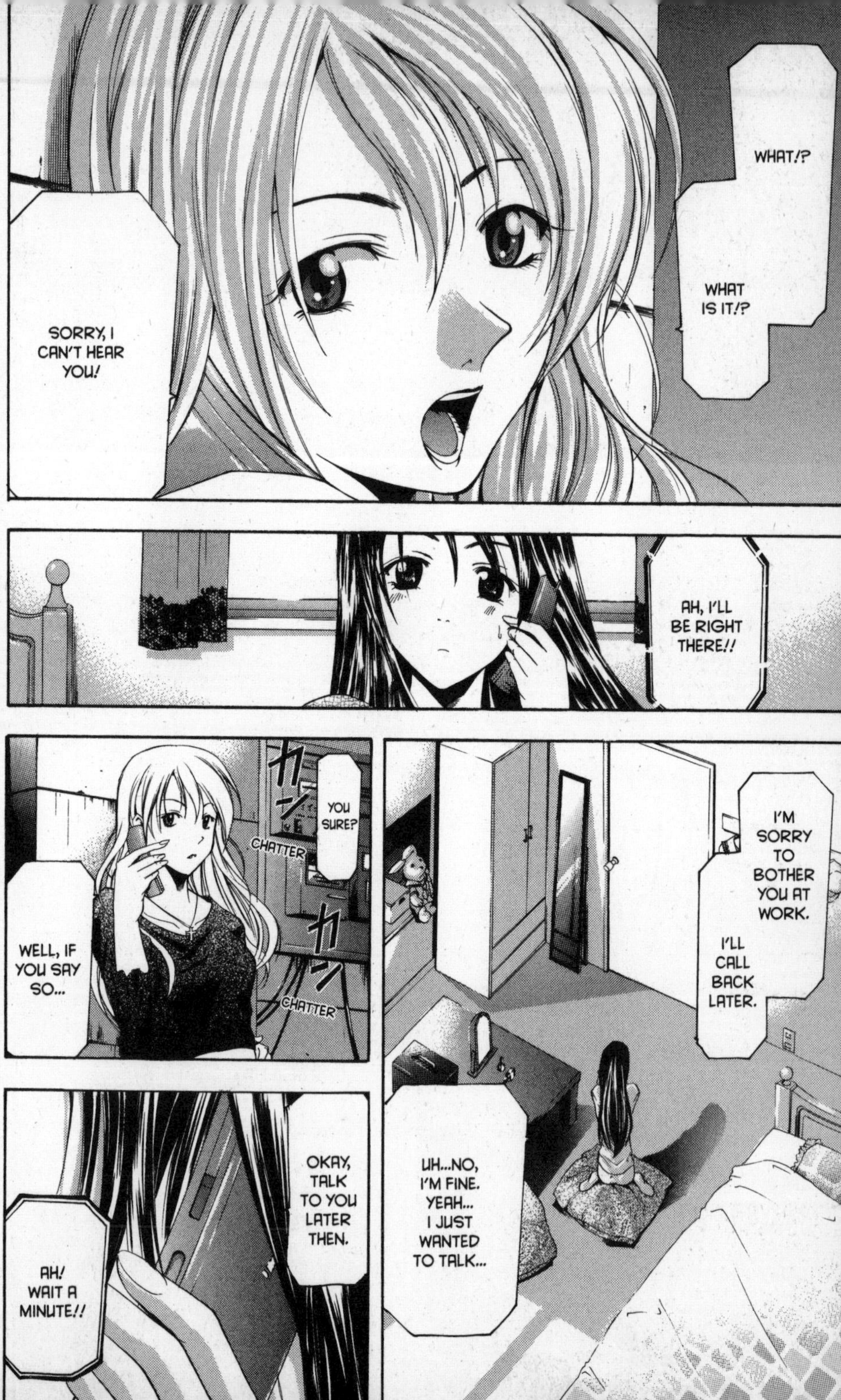
WHAT!?
WHAT IS IT!?
SORRY, I CAN'T HEAR YOU!
AH, I'LL BE RIGHT THERE!!
I'M SORRY TO BOTHER YOU AT WORK.
I'LL CALL BACK LATER.
UH...NO, I'M FINE. YEAH... I JUST WANTED TO TALK...
YOU SURE?
CHATTER
WELL, IF YOU SAY SO...
CHATTER
OKAY, TALK TO YOU LATER THEN.
AH! WAIT A MINUTE!!

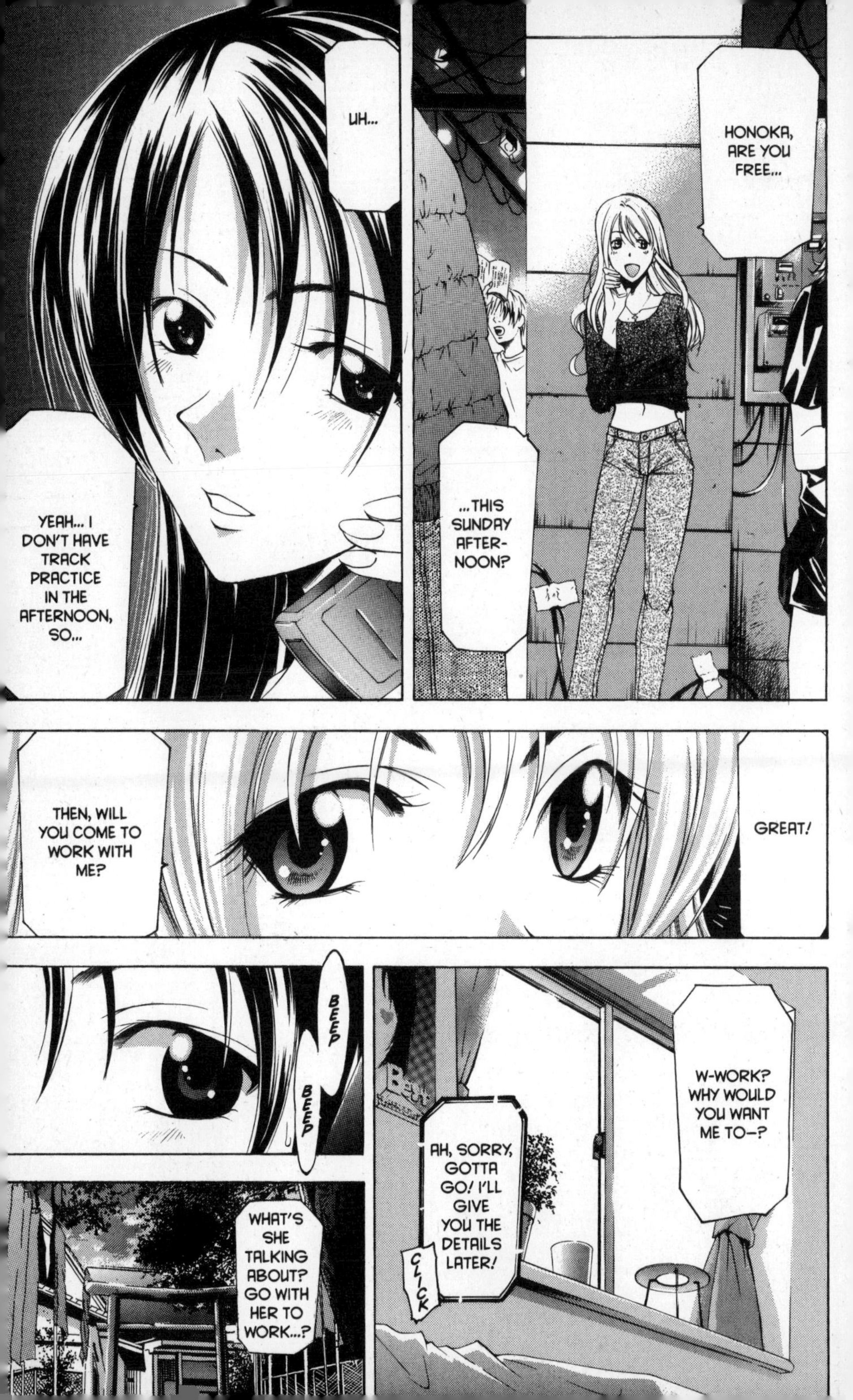
HONOKA, ARE YOU FREE...
...THIS SUNDAY AFTERNOON?
UH...
YEAH... I DON'T HAVE TRACK PRACTICE IN THE AFTERNOON, SO...
GREAT!
THEN, WILL YOU COME TO WORK WITH ME?
W-WORK? WHY WOULD YOU WANT ME TO—?
AH, SORRY, GOTTA GO! I'LL GIVE YOU THE DETAILS LATER!
CLICK
BEEP
BEEP
WHAT'S SHE TALKING ABOUT? GO WITH HER TO WORK...?

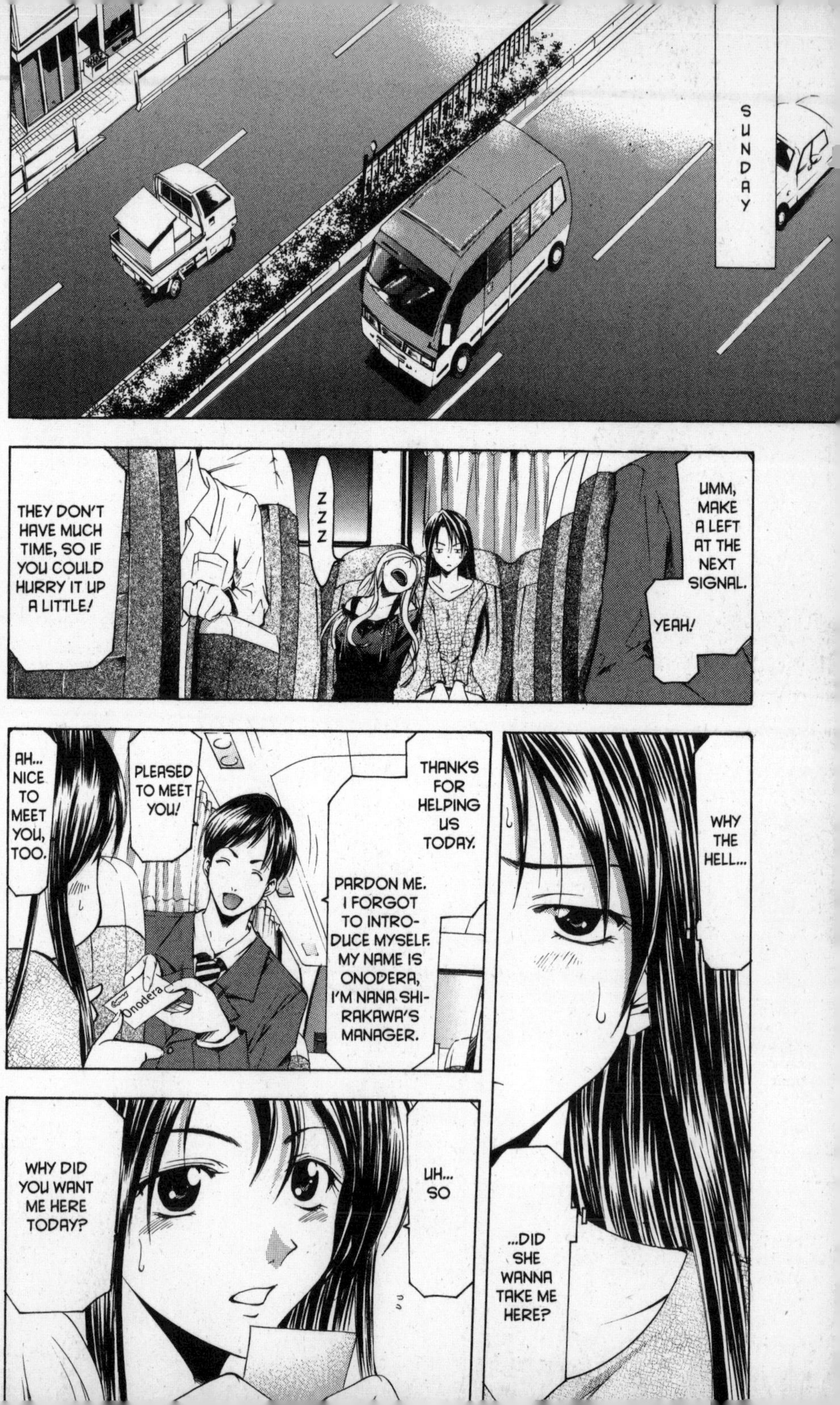
SUNDAY
UMM, MAKE A LEFT AT THE NEXT SIGNAL.
YEAH!
ZZZ
THEY DON'T HAVE MUCH TIME, SO IF YOU COULD HURRY IT UP A LITTLE!
WHY THE HELL...
...DID SHE WANNA TAKE ME HERE?
THANKS FOR HELPING US TODAY.
PARDON ME. I FORGOT TO INTRO-DUCE MYSELF. MY NAME IS ONODERA, I'M NANA SHI-RAKAWA'S MANAGER.
PLEASED TO MEET YOU!
AH... NICE TO MEET YOU, TOO.
Onodera
UH... SO
WHY DID YOU WANT ME HERE TODAY?

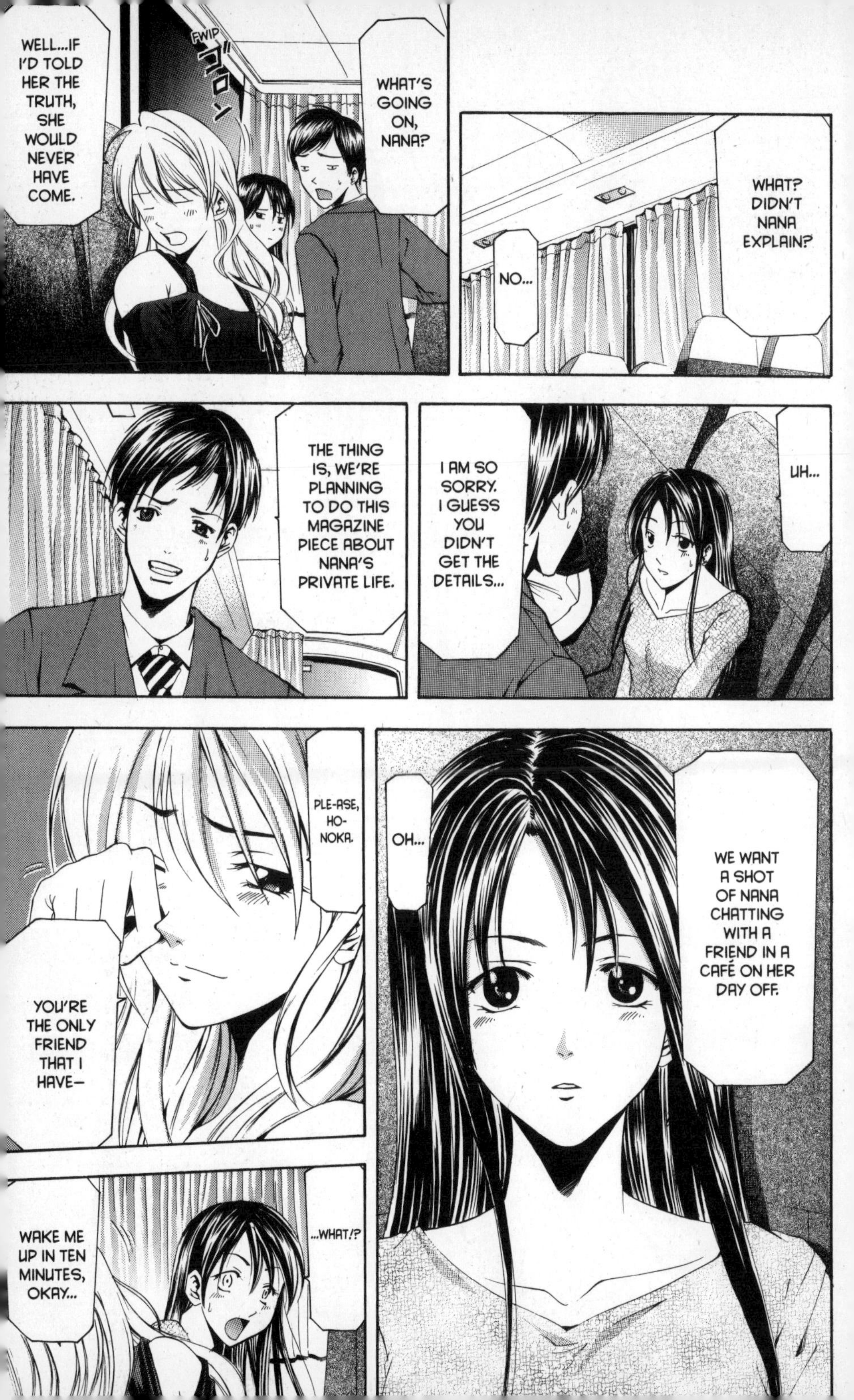
WHAT'S GOING ON, NANA?
FWIP
WELL...IF I'D TOLD HER THE TRUTH, SHE WOULD NEVER HAVE COME.
WHAT? DIDN'T NANA EXPLAIN?
NO...
UH...
I AM SO SORRY. I GUESS YOU DIDN'T GET THE DETAILS...
THE THING IS, WE'RE PLANNING TO DO THIS MAGAZINE PIECE ABOUT NANA'S PRIVATE LIFE.
WE WANT A SHOT OF NANA CHATTING WITH A FRIEND IN A CAFÉ ON HER DAY OFF.
OH...
PLE-ASE, HO-NOKA.
YOU'RE THE ONLY FRIEND THAT I HAVE—
...WHAT!?
WAKE ME UP IN TEN MINUTES, OKAY...

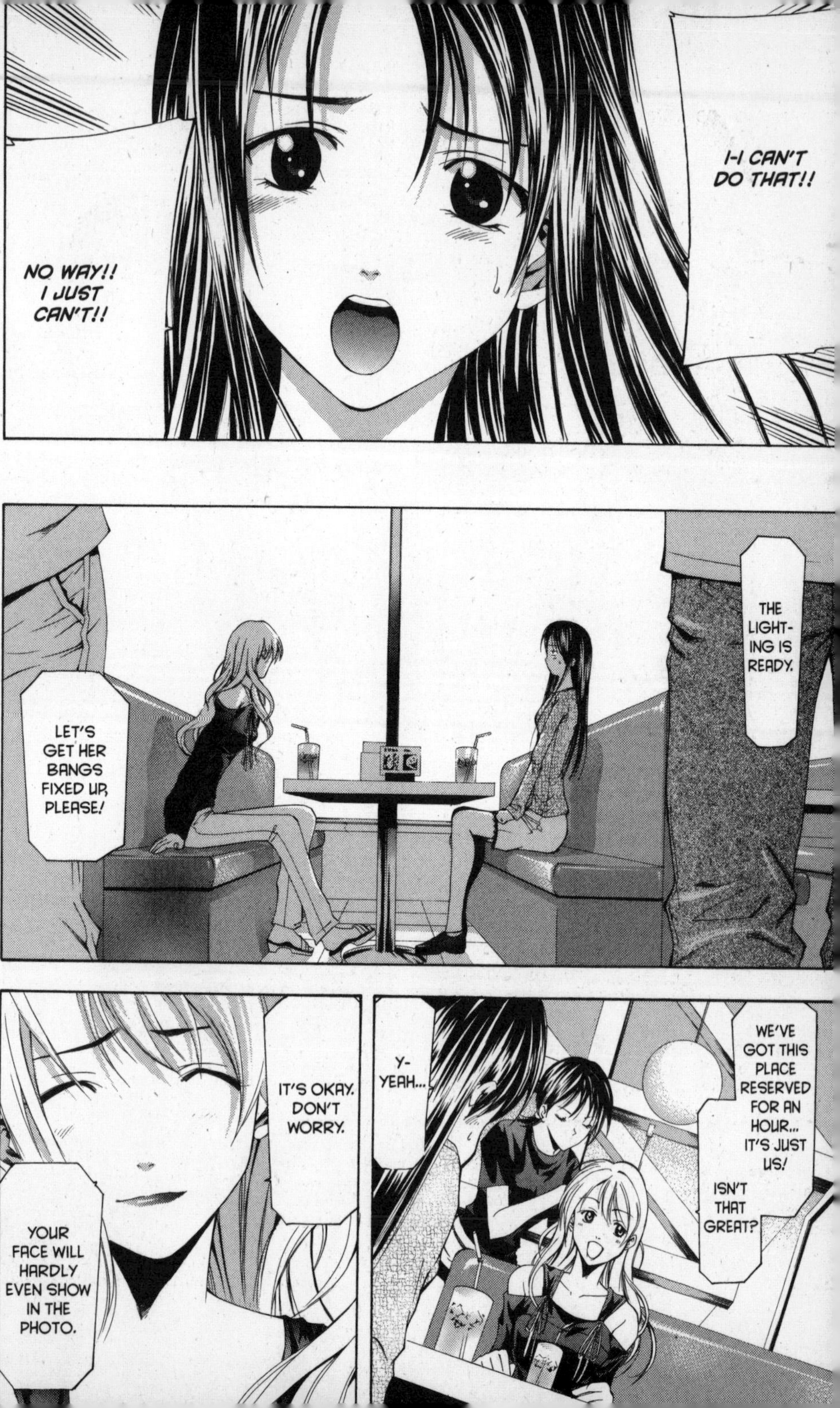
I-I CAN'T DO THAT!!
NO WAY!! I JUST CAN'T!!
THE LIGHT-ING IS READY.
LET'S GET HER BANGS FIXED UP, PLEASE!
WE'VE GOT THIS PLACE RESERVED FOR AN HOUR... IT'S JUST US!
ISN'T THAT GREAT?
Y-YEAH...
IT'S OKAY. DON'T WORRY.
YOUR FACE WILL HARDLY EVEN SHOW IN THE PHOTO.

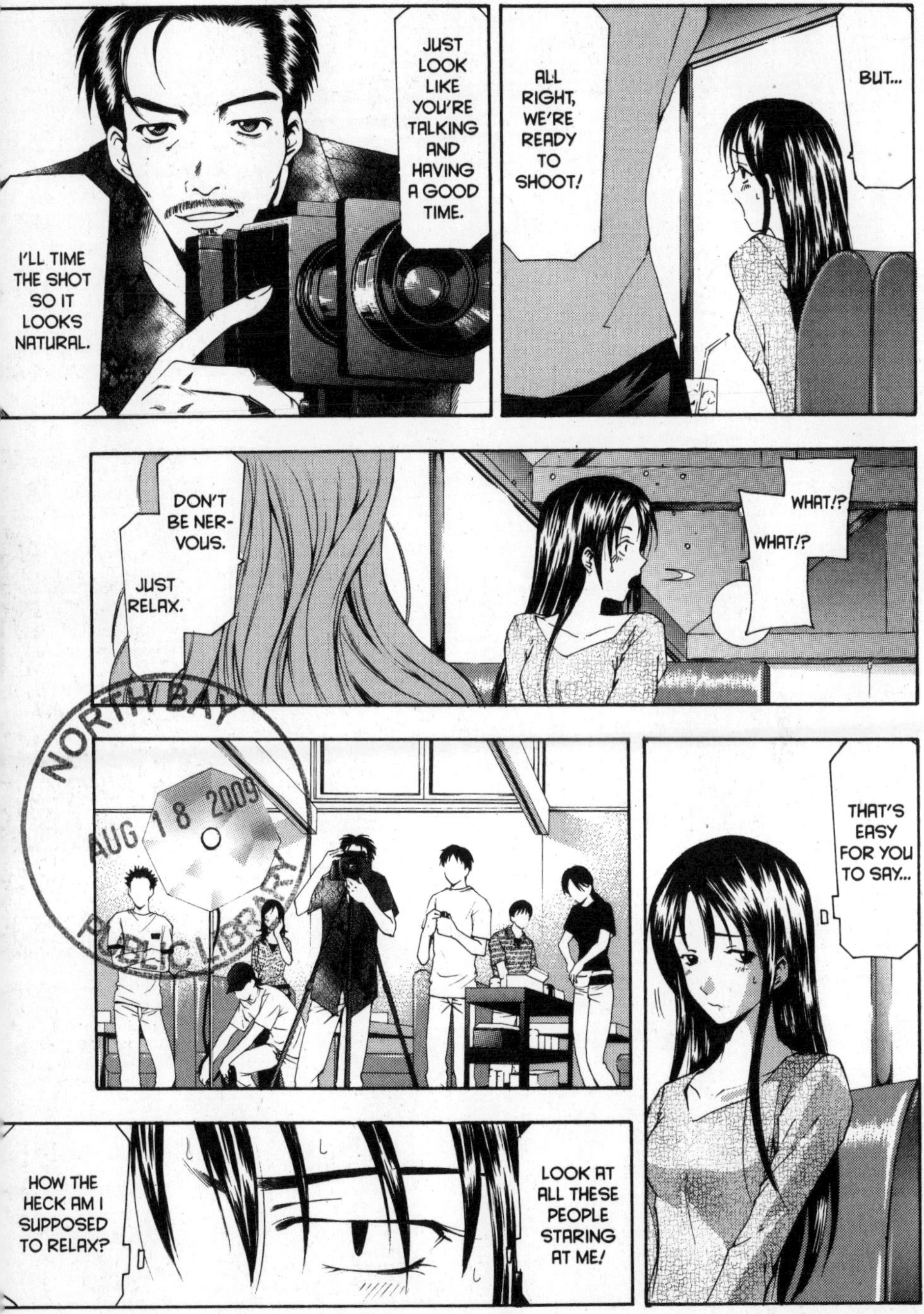
BUT...
ALL RIGHT, WE'RE READY TO SHOOT!
JUST LOOK LIKE YOU'RE TALKING AND HAVING A GOOD TIME.
I'LL TIME THE SHOT SO IT LOOKS NATURAL.
WHAT!?
WHAT!?
DON'T BE NERVOUS.
JUST RELAX.
THAT'S EASY FOR YOU TO SAY...
LOOK AT ALL THESE PEOPLE STARING AT ME!
HOW THE HECK AM I SUPPOSED TO RELAX?

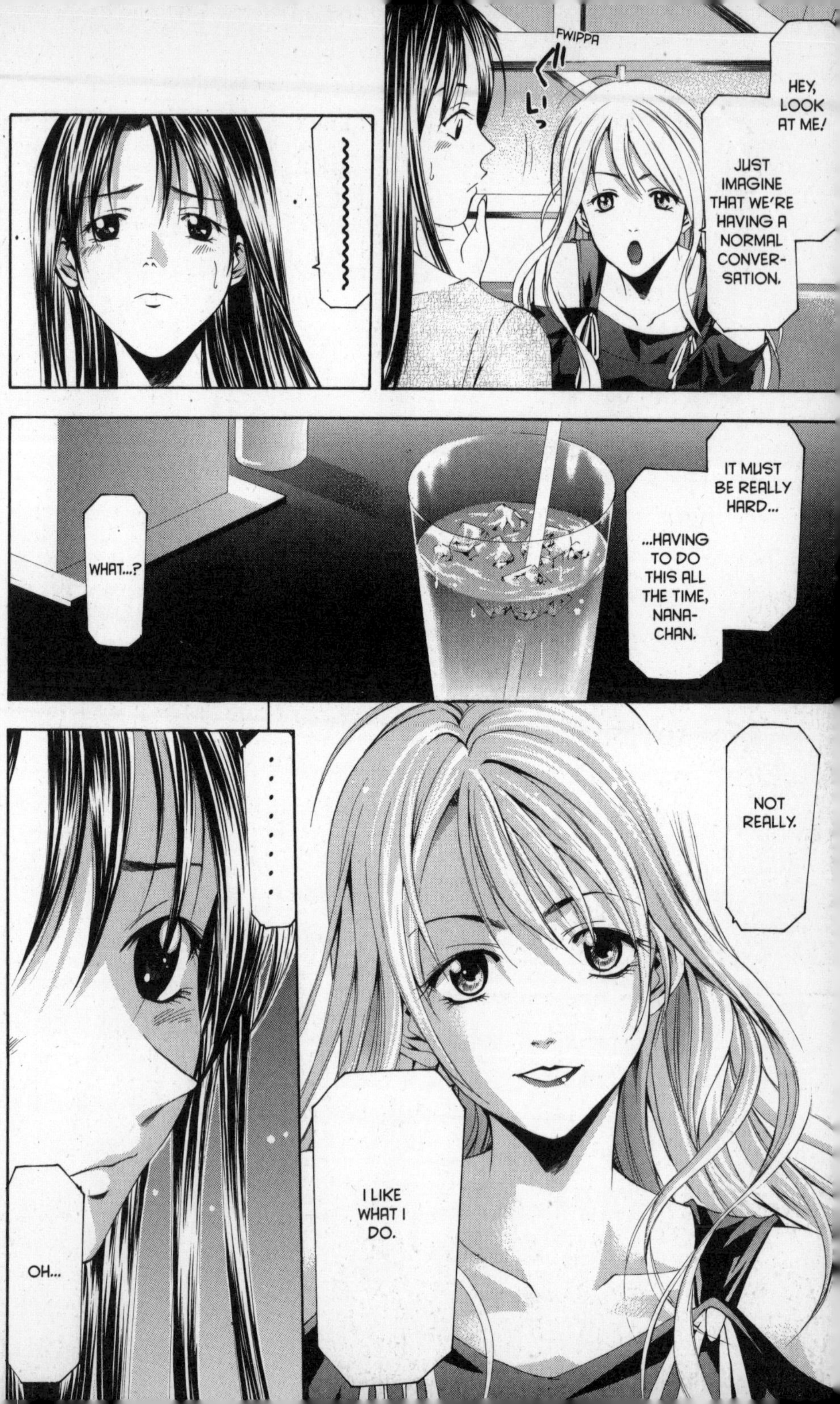
FWIPPA
HEY, LOOK AT ME!
JUST IMAGINE THAT WE'RE HAVING A NORMAL CONVERSATION.
IT MUST BE REALLY HARD...
...HAVING TO DO THIS ALL THE TIME, NANA-CHAN.
WHAT...?
NOT REALLY.
I LIKE WHAT I DO.
......
OH...

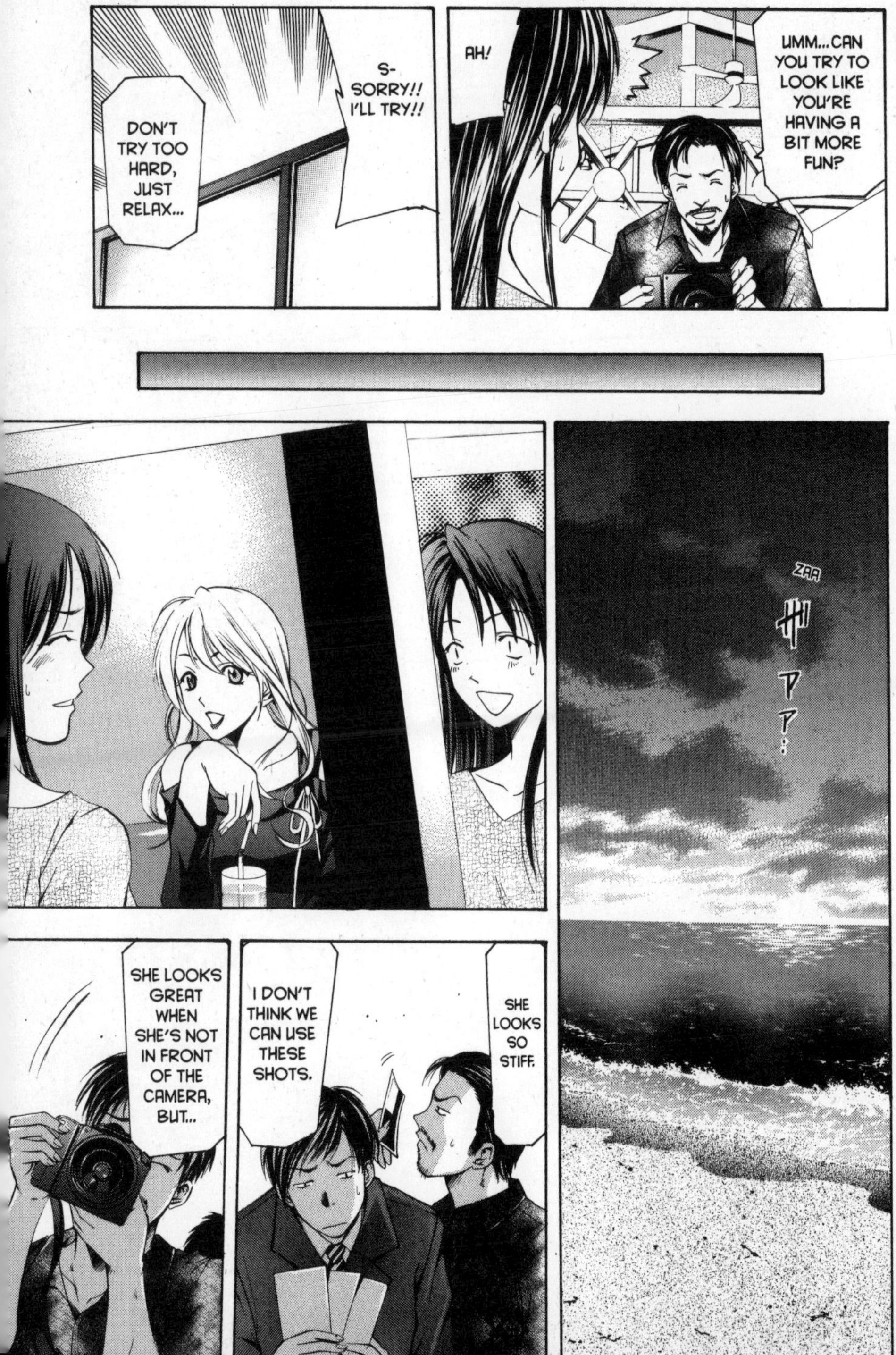
UMM...CAN YOU TRY TO LOOK LIKE YOU'RE HAVING A BIT MORE FUN?
AH!
S- SORRY!! I'LL TRY!!
DON'T TRY TOO HARD, JUST RELAX...
ZAA
ザァァ…
SHE LOOKS SO STIFF.
I DON'T THINK WE CAN USE THESE SHOTS.
SHE LOOKS GREAT WHEN SHE'S NOT IN FRONT OF THE CAMERA, BUT...

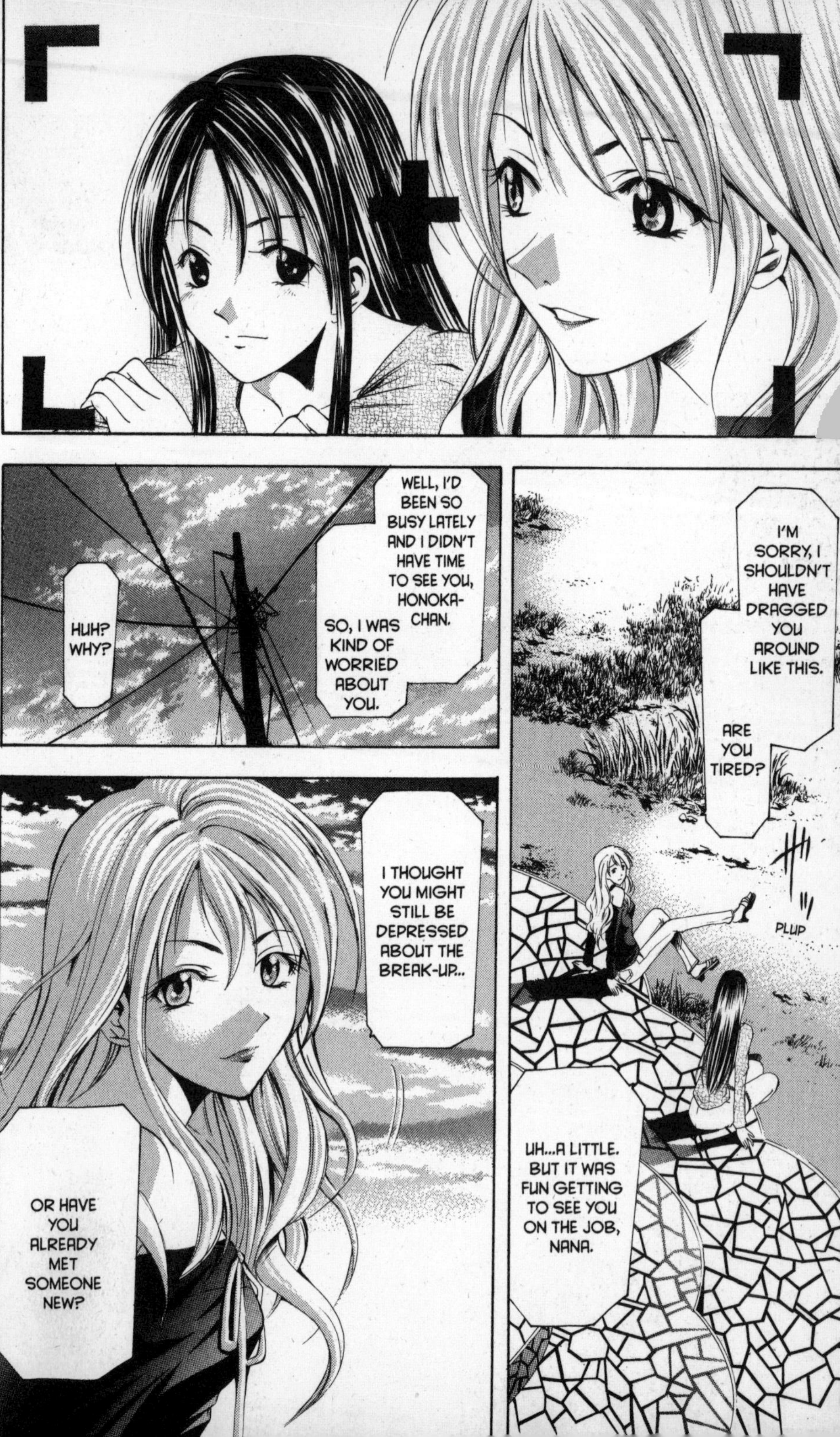
I'M SORRY, I SHOULDN'T HAVE DRAGGED YOU AROUND LIKE THIS.
ARE YOU TIRED?
PLUP
UH...A LITTLE. BUT IT WAS FUN GETTING TO SEE YOU ON THE JOB, NANA.
WELL, I'D BEEN SO BUSY LATELY AND I DIDN'T HAVE TIME TO SEE YOU, HONOKA-CHAN.
SO, I WAS KIND OF WORRIED ABOUT YOU.
HUH? WHY?
I THOUGHT YOU MIGHT STILL BE DEPRESSED ABOUT THE BREAK-UP...
OR HAVE YOU ALREADY MET SOMEONE NEW?

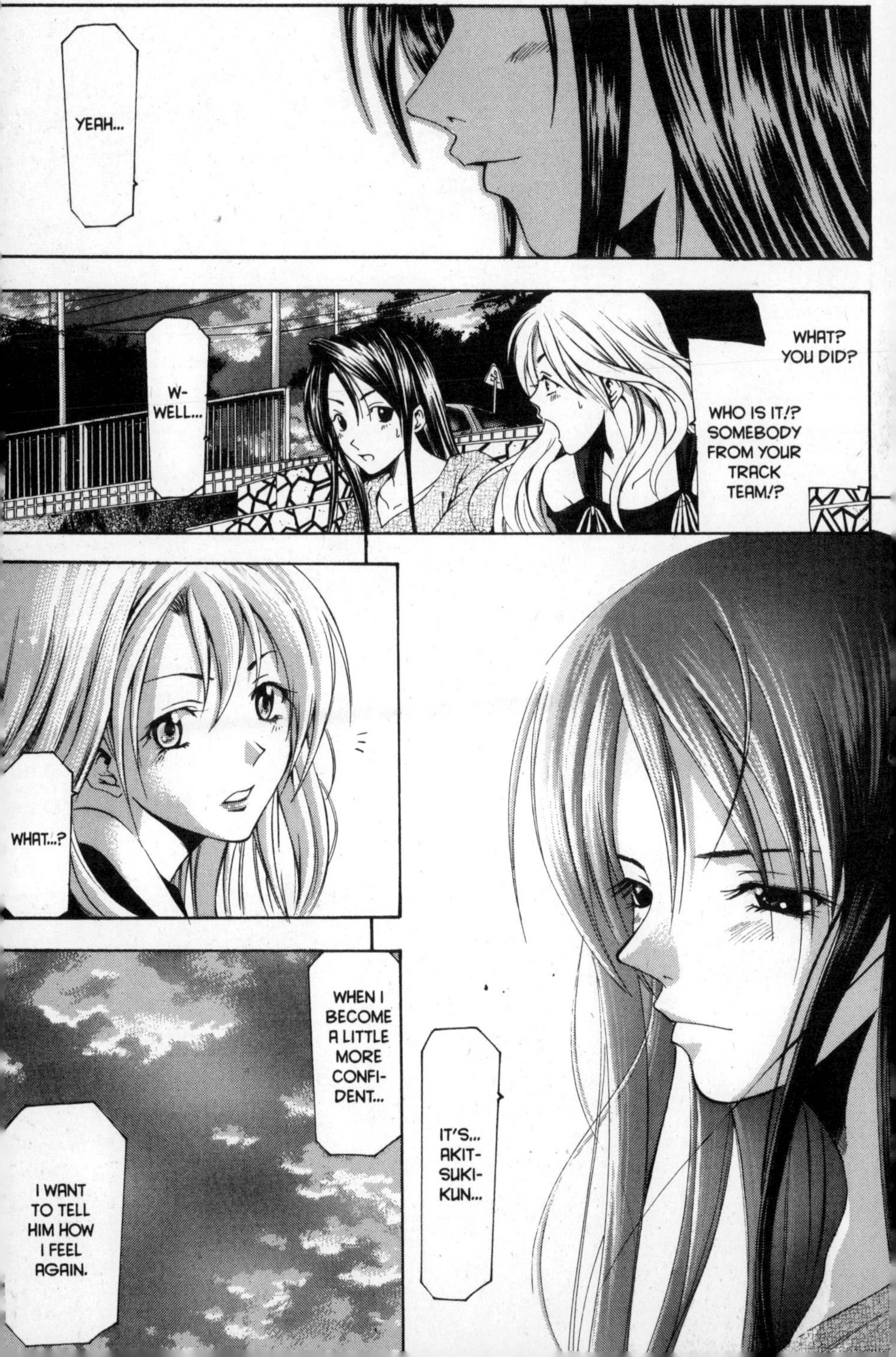
YEAH...
WHAT? YOU DID?
WHO IS IT!? SOMEBODY FROM YOUR TRACK TEAM!?
W-WELL...
IT'S... AKIT-SUKI-KUN...
WHAT...?
WHEN I BECOME A LITTLE MORE CONFI-DENT...
I WANT TO TELL HIM HOW I FEEL AGAIN.

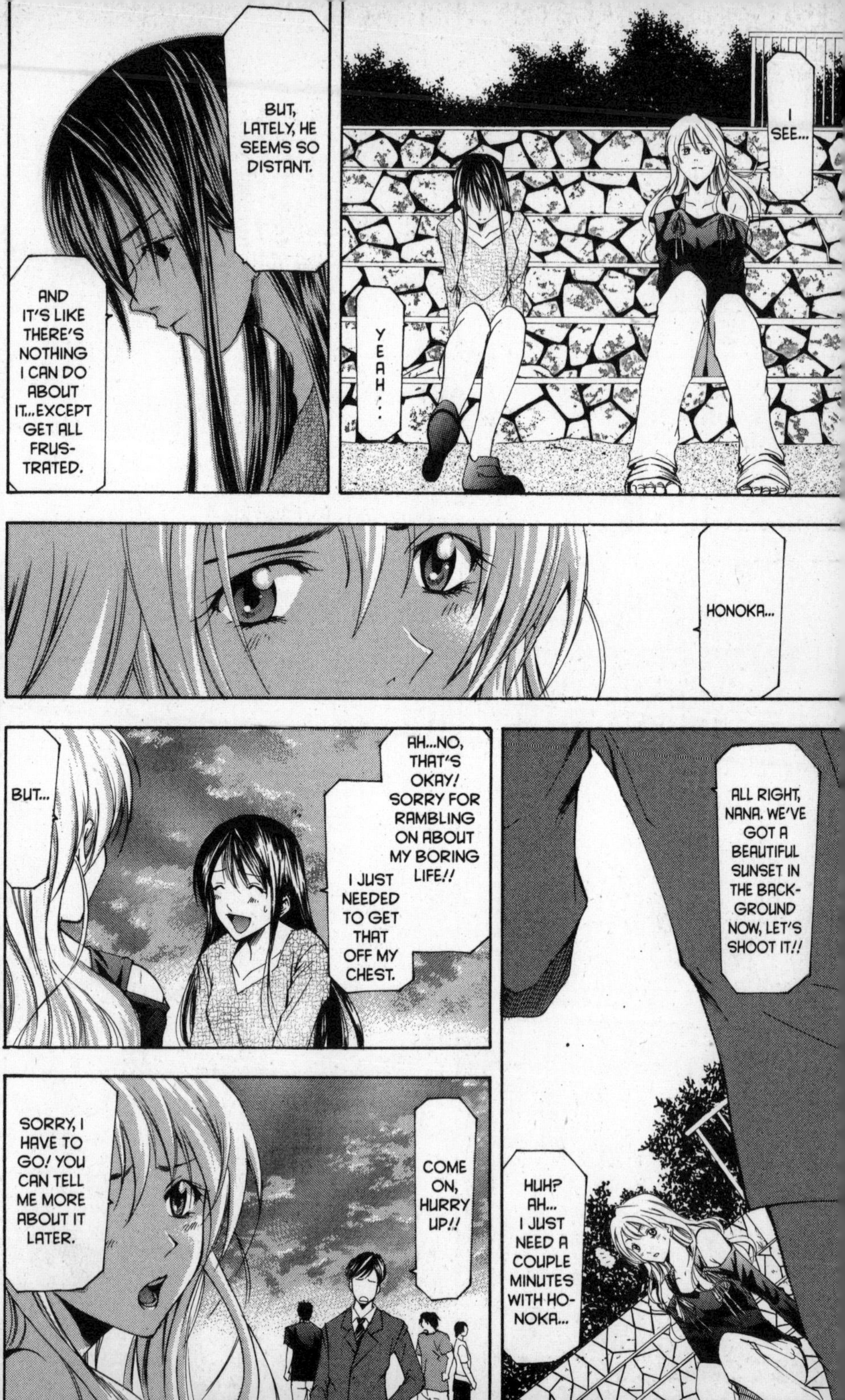

I SEE...
YEAH...
BUT, LATELY, HE SEEMS SO DISTANT.
AND IT'S LIKE THERE'S NOTHING I CAN DO ABOUT IT...EXCEPT GET ALL FRUS-TRATED.
HONOKA...
ALL RIGHT, NANA. WE'VE GOT A BEAUTIFUL SUNSET IN THE BACK-GROUND NOW, LET'S SHOOT IT!!
HUH? AH... I JUST NEED A COUPLE MINUTES WITH HO-NOKA...
AH...NO, THAT'S OKAY! SORRY FOR RAMBLING ON ABOUT MY BORING LIFE!!
I JUST NEEDED TO GET THAT OFF MY CHEST.
BUT...
COME ON, HURRY UP!!
SORRY, I HAVE TO GO! YOU CAN TELL ME MORE ABOUT IT LATER.

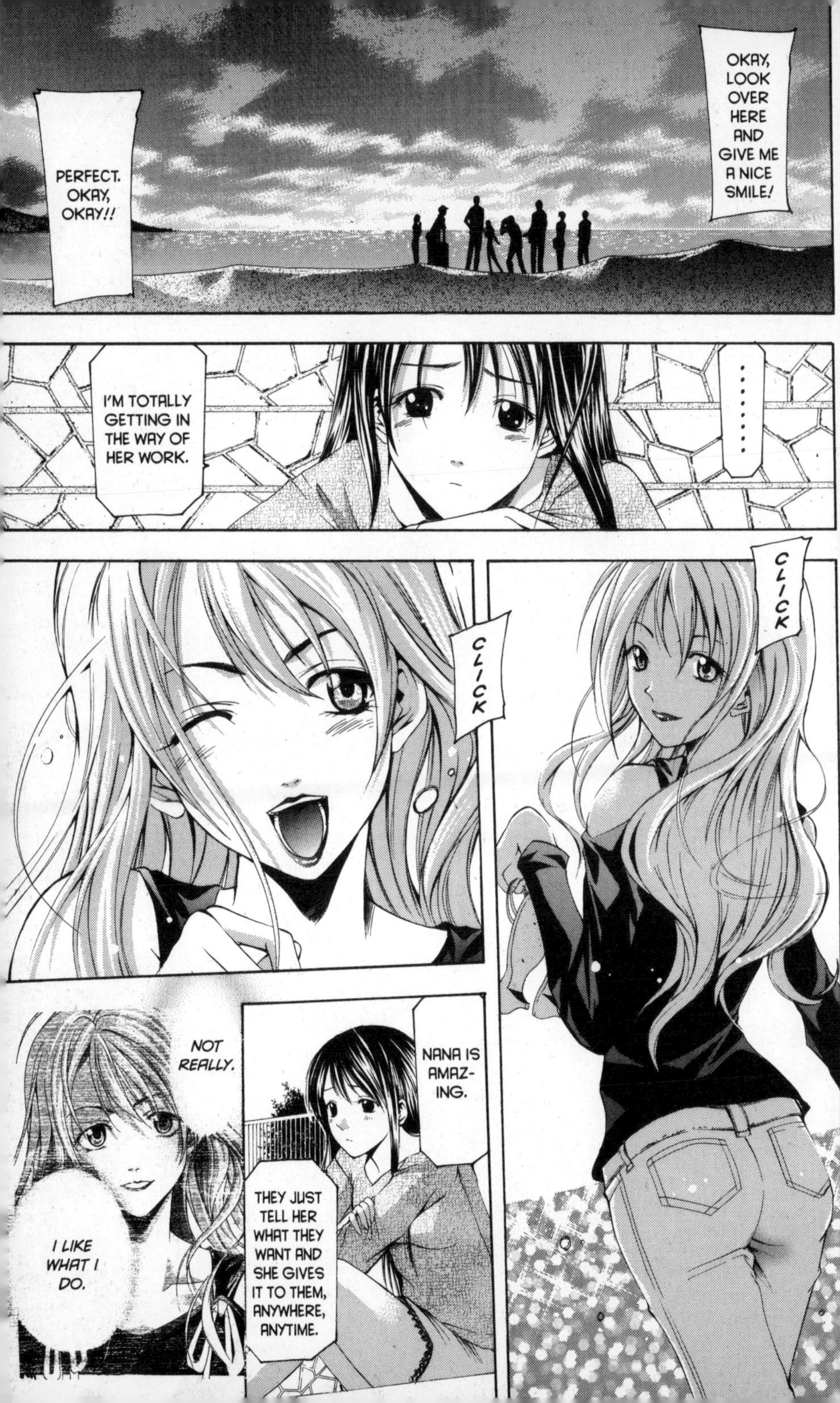
OKAY, LOOK OVER HERE AND GIVE ME A NICE SMILE!
PERFECT. OKAY, OKAY!!
......
I'M TOTALLY GETTING IN THE WAY OF HER WORK.
CLICK
CLICK
NANA IS AMAZ-ING.
THEY JUST TELL HER WHAT THEY WANT AND SHE GIVES IT TO THEM, ANYWHERE, ANYTIME.
NOT REALLY.
I LIKE WHAT I DO.

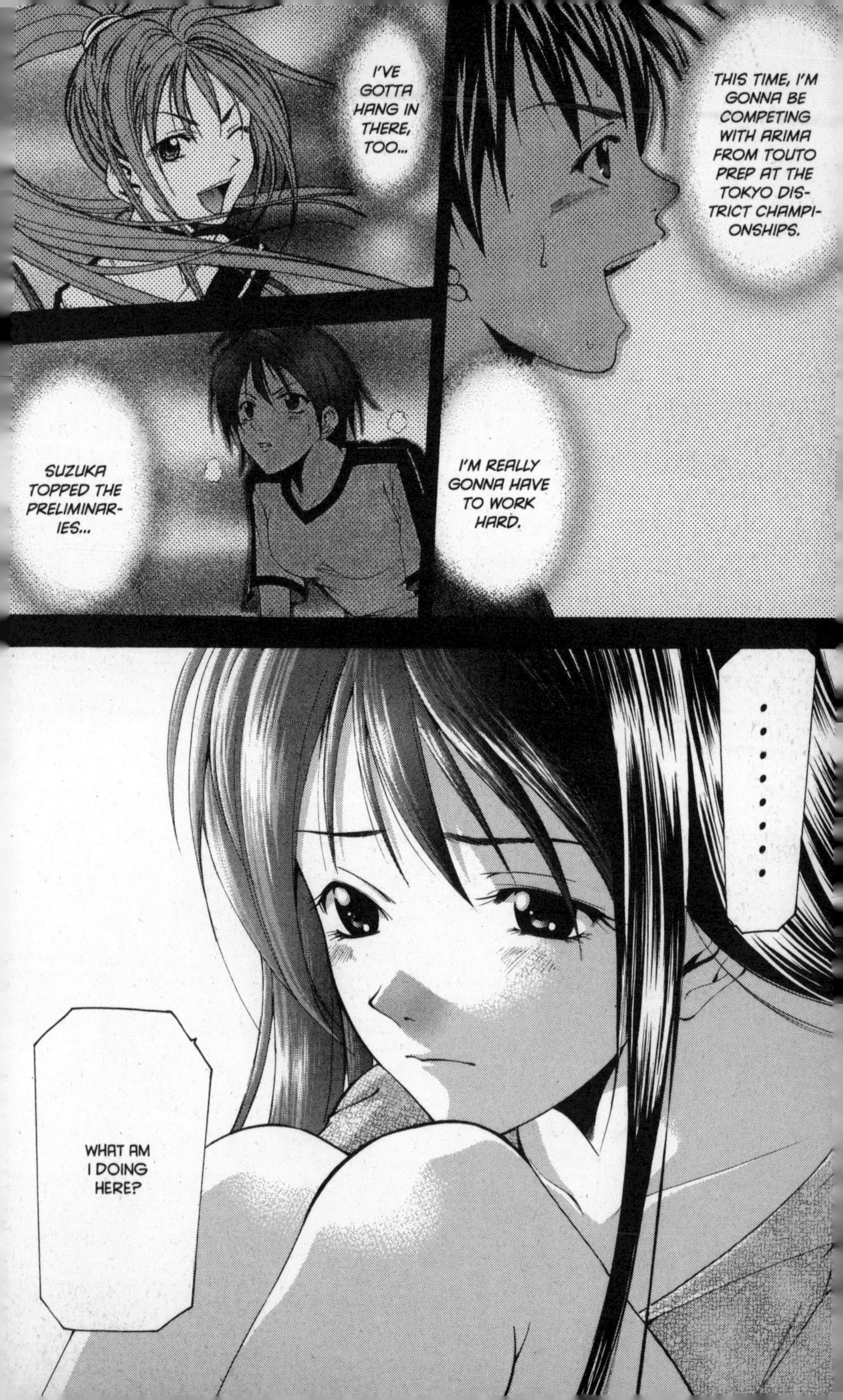
THIS TIME, I'M GONNA BE COMPETING WITH ARIMA FROM TOUTO PREP AT THE TOKYO DISTRICT CHAMPIONSHIPS.
I'M REALLY GONNA HAVE TO WORK HARD.
I'VE GOTTA HANG IN THERE, TOO...
SUZUKA TOPPED THE PRELIMINARIES...
....
WHAT AM I DOING HERE?

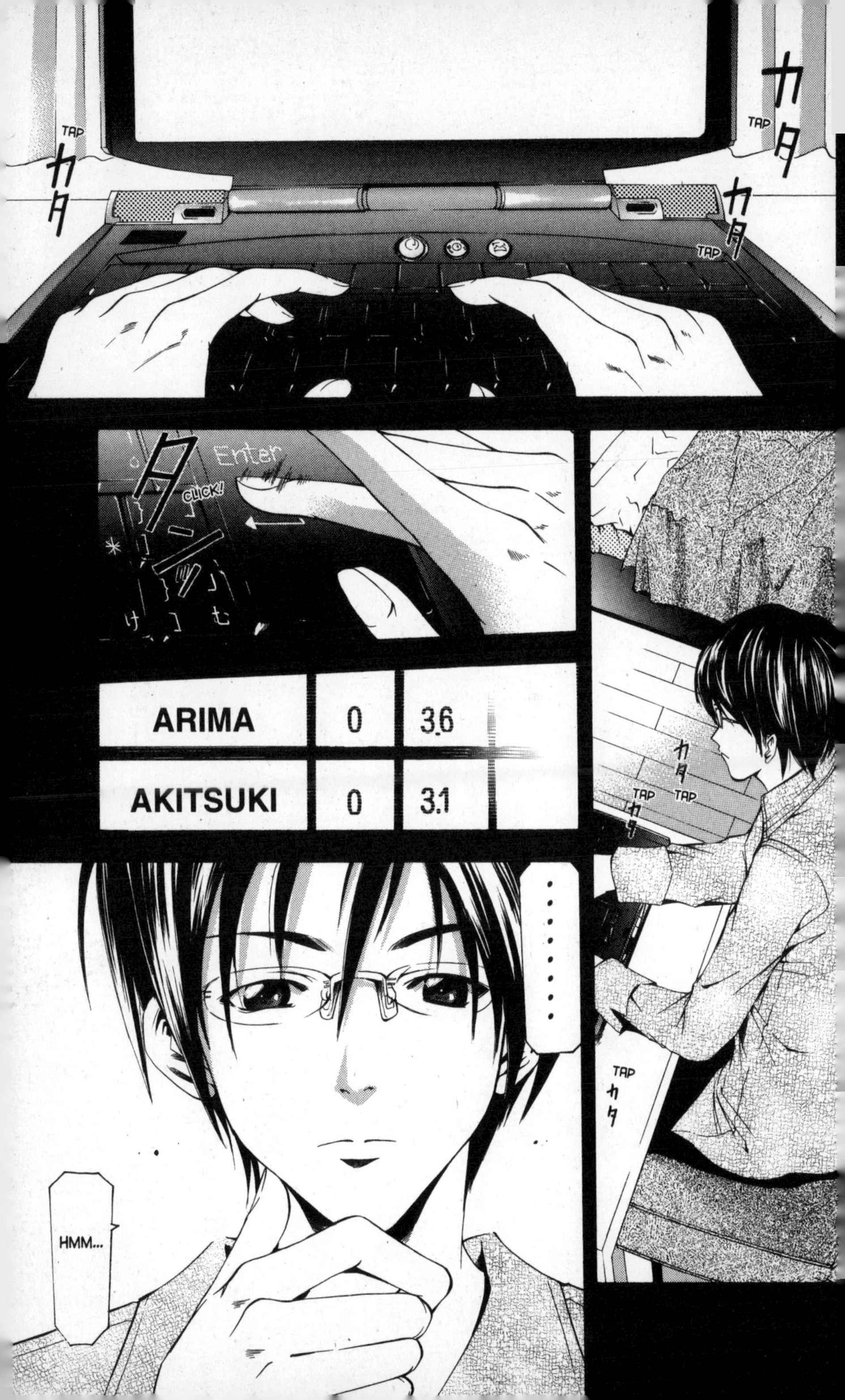
カタ
TAP
カタ
TAP
TAP
カタ
カタ
TAP
TAP
カタ
TAP
カタ
Enter
カ
CLICK!
ARIMA 0 3.6
AKITSUKI 0 3.1
......
HMM...

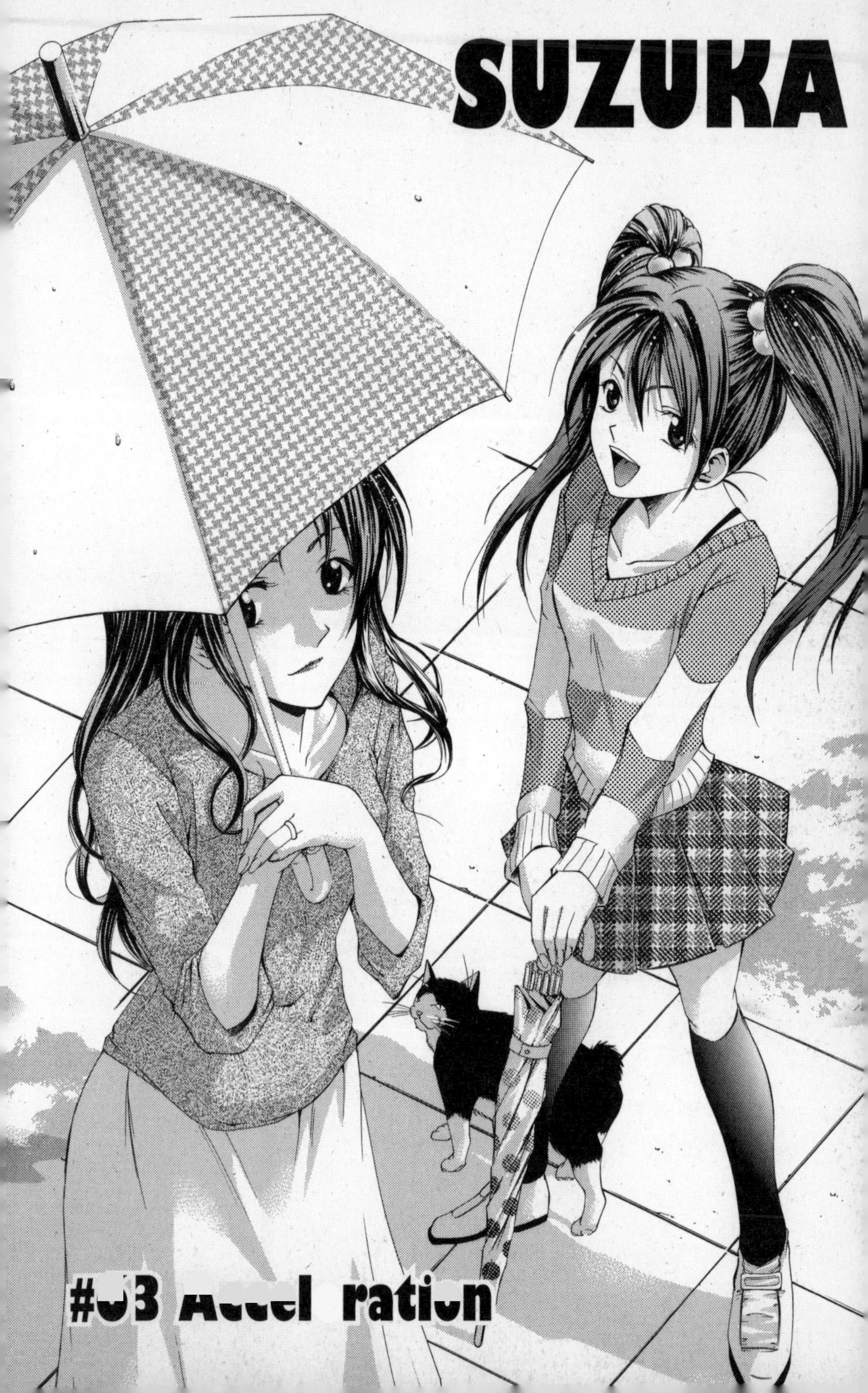
SUZUKA
#03 Acceleration

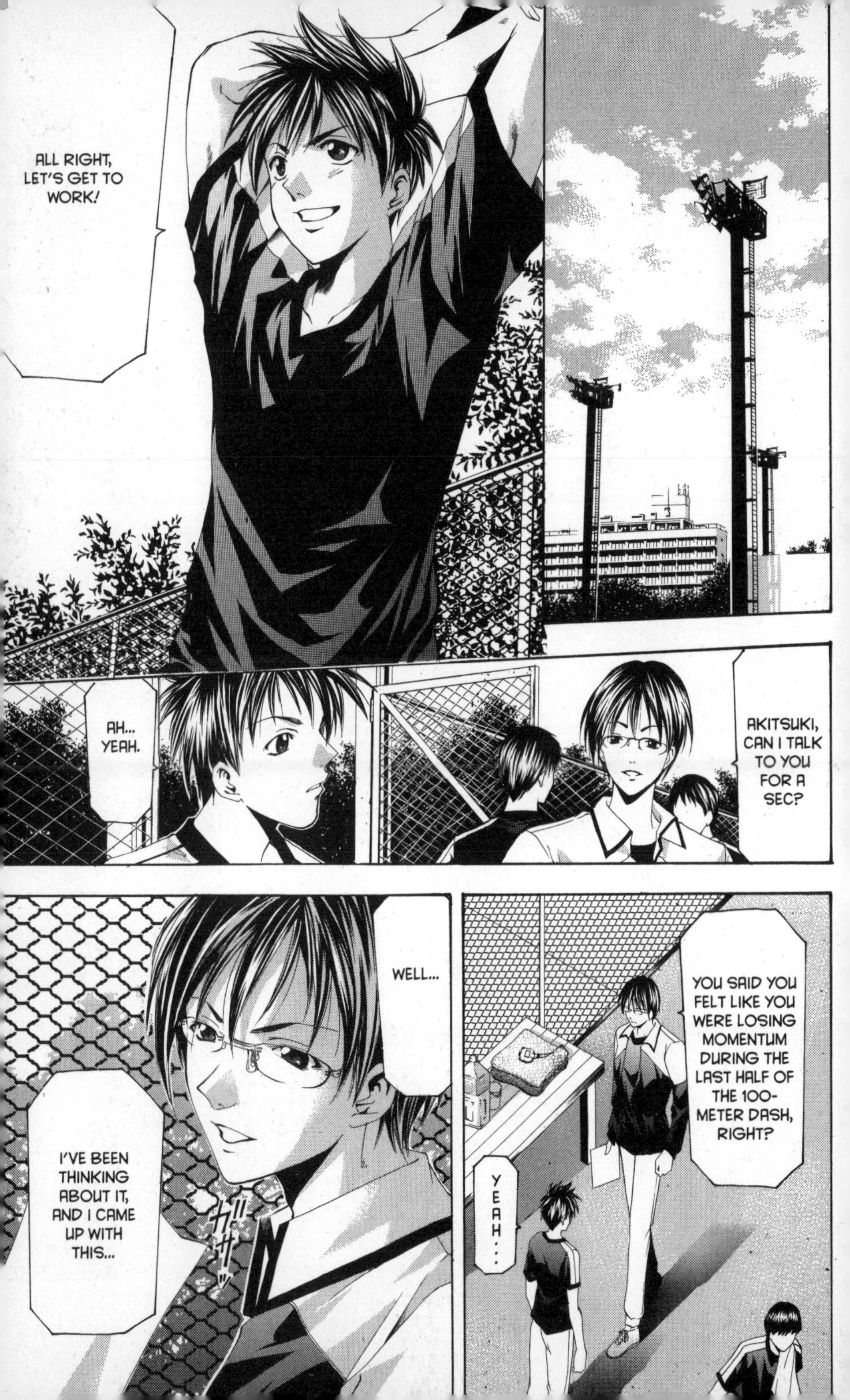
ALL RIGHT, LET'S GET TO WORK!
AKITSUKI, CAN I TALK TO YOU FOR A SEC?
AH... YEAH.
YOU SAID YOU FELT LIKE YOU WERE LOSING MOMENTUM DURING THE LAST HALF OF THE 100-METER DASH, RIGHT?
YEAH...
WELL...
I'VE BEEN THINKING ABOUT IT, AND I CAME UP WITH THIS...

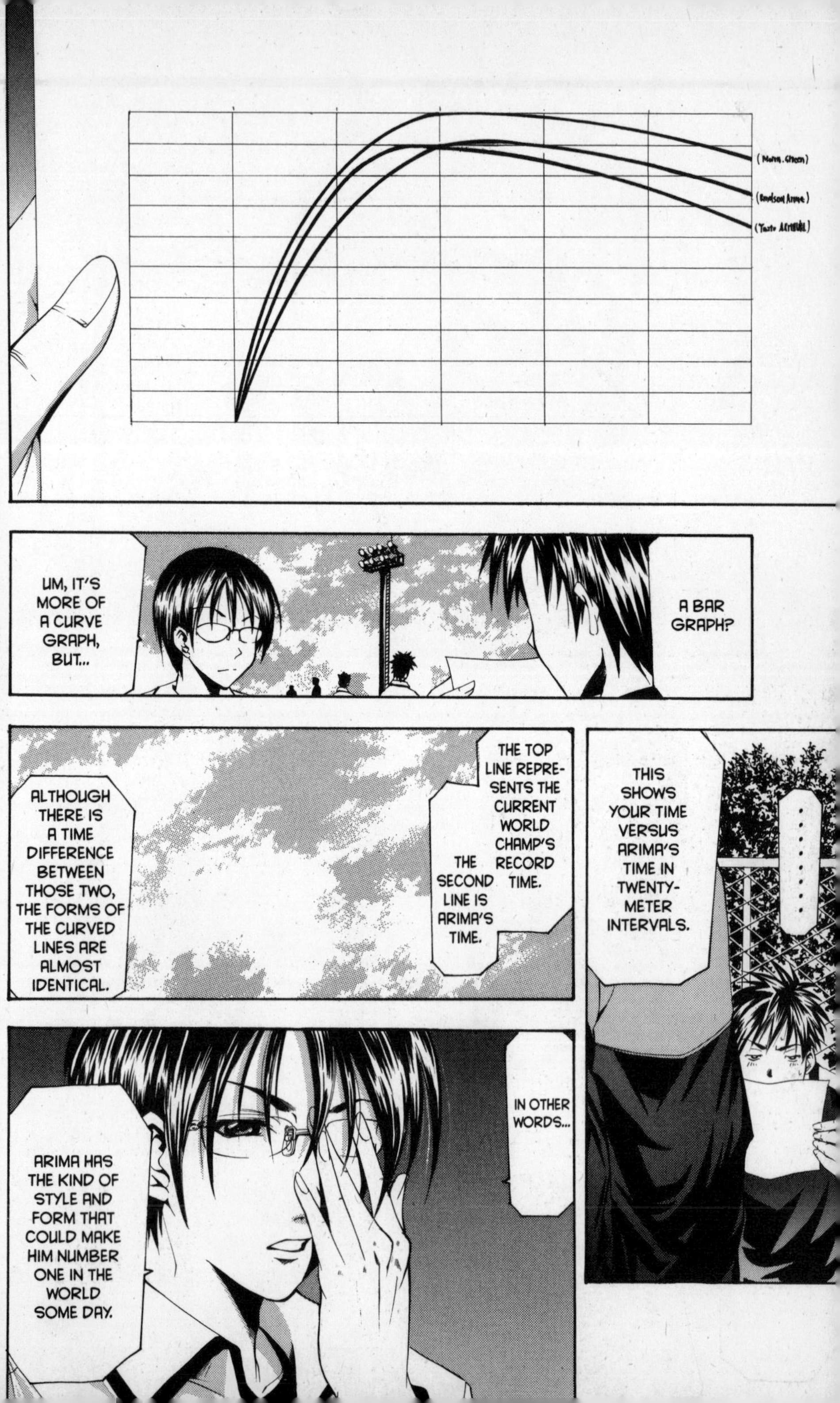
A BAR GRAPH?
UM, IT'S MORE OF A CURVE GRAPH, BUT...
THIS SHOWS YOUR TIME VERSUS ARIMA'S TIME IN TWENTY-METER INTERVALS.
......
THE TOP LINE REPRESENTS THE CURRENT WORLD CHAMP'S RECORD TIME.
THE SECOND LINE IS ARIMA'S TIME.
ALTHOUGH THERE IS A TIME DIFFERENCE BETWEEN THOSE TWO, THE FORMS OF THE CURVED LINES ARE ALMOST IDENTICAL.
IN OTHER WORDS...
ARIMA HAS THE KIND OF STYLE AND FORM THAT COULD MAKE HIM NUMBER ONE IN THE WORLD SOME DAY.

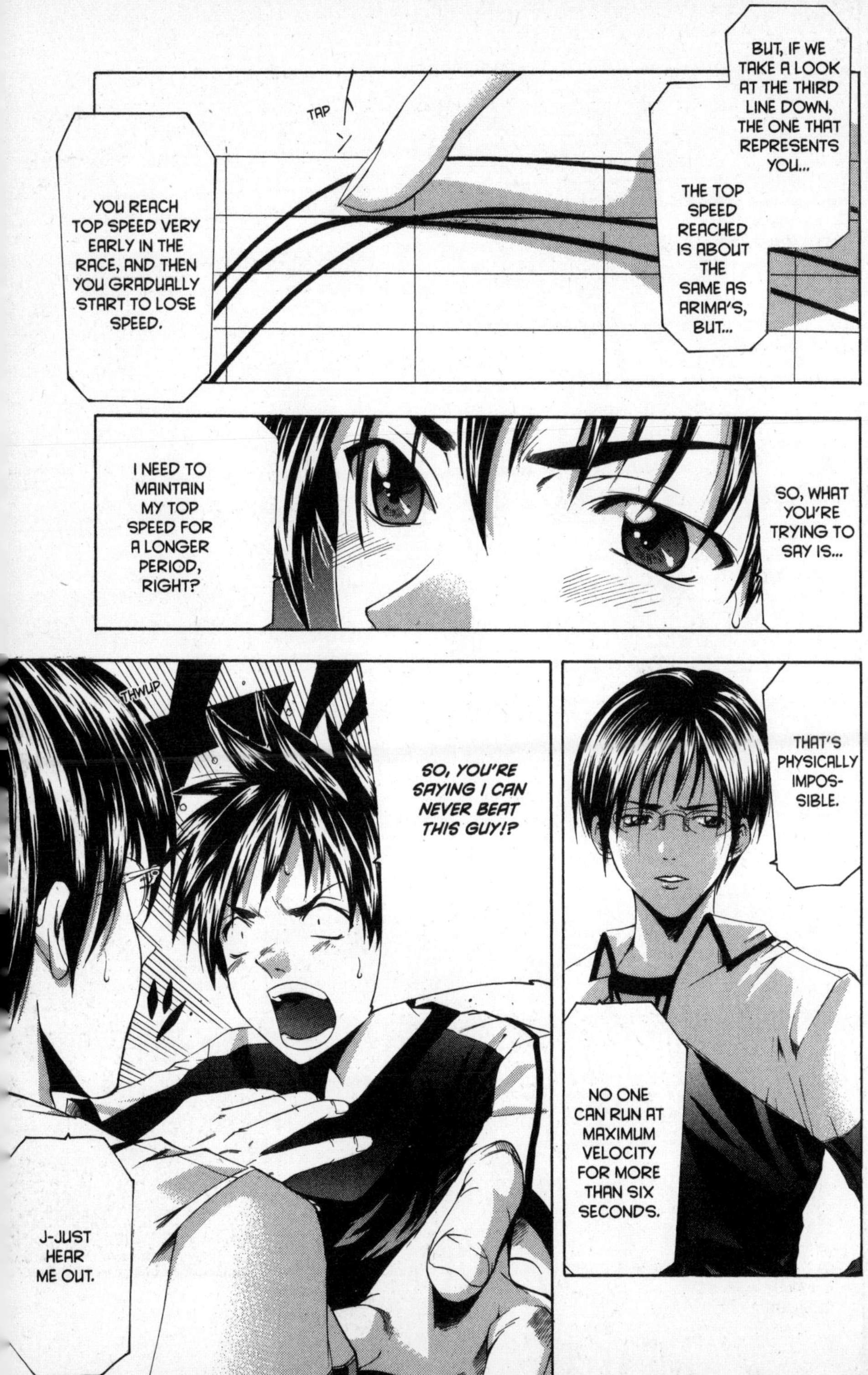
BUT, IF WE TAKE A LOOK AT THE THIRD LINE DOWN, THE ONE THAT REPRESENTS YOU...
THE TOP SPEED REACHED IS ABOUT THE SAME AS ARIMA'S, BUT...
TAP
YOU REACH TOP SPEED VERY EARLY IN THE RACE, AND THEN YOU GRADUALLY START TO LOSE SPEED.
SO, WHAT YOU'RE TRYING TO SAY IS...
I NEED TO MAINTAIN MY TOP SPEED FOR A LONGER PERIOD, RIGHT?
THAT'S PHYSICALLY IMPOS-SIBLE.
NO ONE CAN RUN AT MAXIMUM VELOCITY FOR MORE THAN SIX SECONDS.
THWUP
SO, YOU'RE SAYING I CAN NEVER BEAT THIS GUY!?
J-JUST HEAR ME OUT.

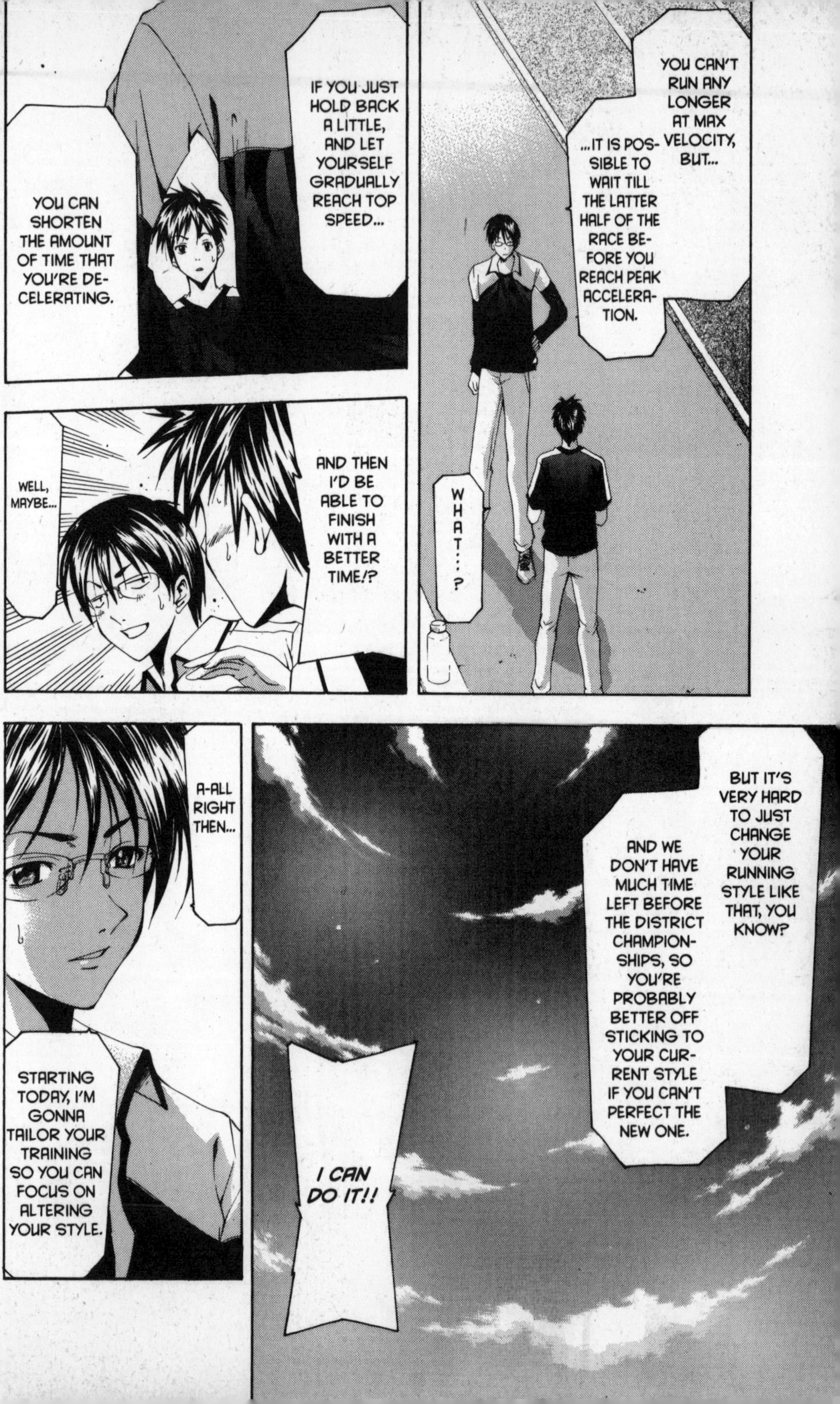
YOU CAN'T RUN ANY LONGER AT MAX VELOCITY, BUT...
...IT IS POSSIBLE TO WAIT TILL THE LATTER HALF OF THE RACE BEFORE YOU REACH PEAK ACCELERATION.
WHAT...?
IF YOU JUST HOLD BACK A LITTLE, AND LET YOURSELF GRADUALLY REACH TOP SPEED...
YOU CAN SHORTEN THE AMOUNT OF TIME THAT YOU'RE DECELERATING.
AND THEN I'D BE ABLE TO FINISH WITH A BETTER TIME!?
WELL, MAYBE...
BUT IT'S VERY HARD TO JUST CHANGE YOUR RUNNING STYLE LIKE THAT, YOU KNOW?
AND WE DON'T HAVE MUCH TIME LEFT BEFORE THE DISTRICT CHAMPIONSHIPS, SO YOU'RE PROBABLY BETTER OFF STICKING TO YOUR CURRENT STYLE IF YOU CAN'T PERFECT THE NEW ONE.
I CAN DO IT!!
A-ALL RIGHT THEN...
STARTING TODAY, I'M GONNA TAILOR YOUR TRAINING SO YOU CAN FOCUS ON ALTERING YOUR STYLE.

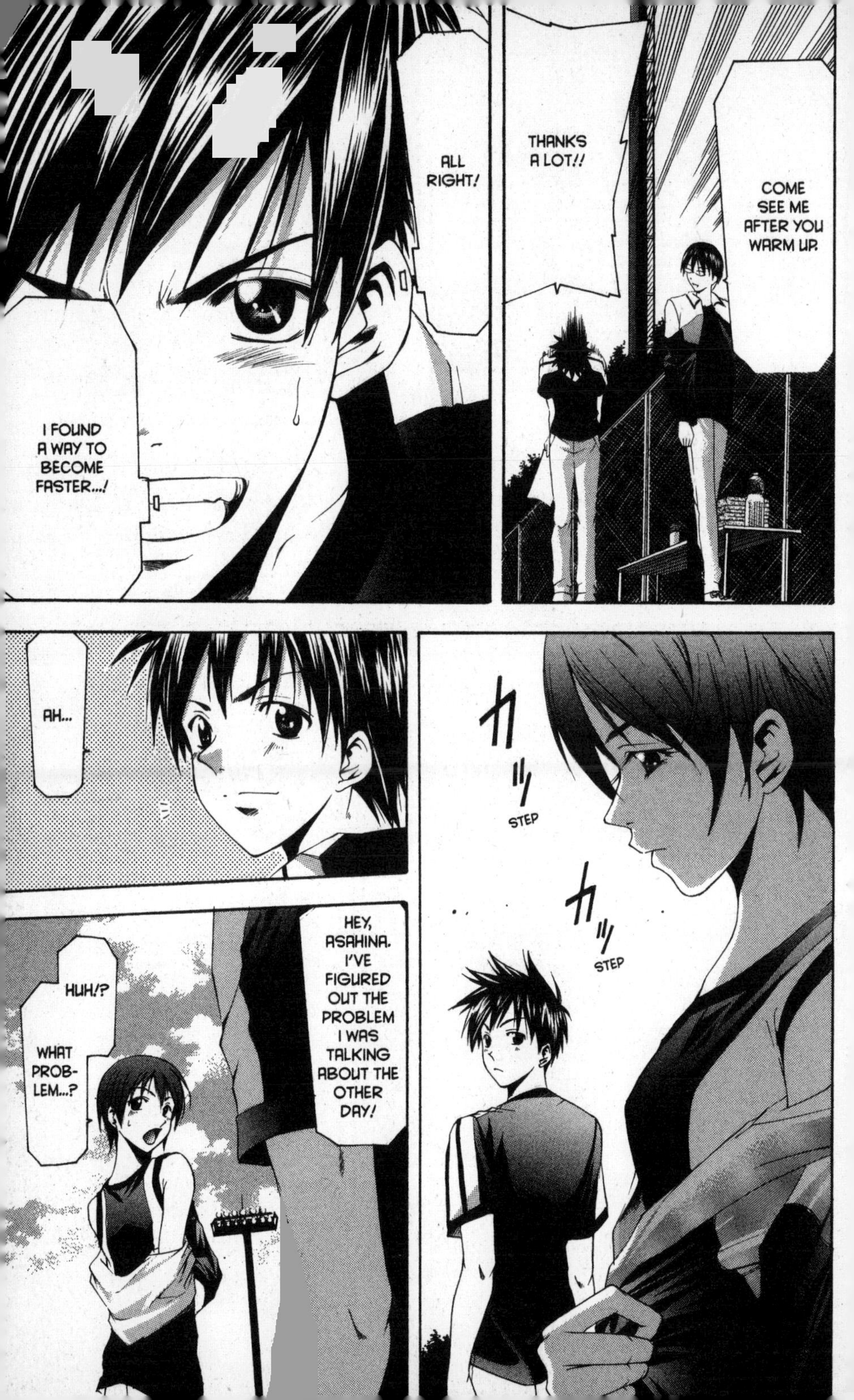

COME SEE ME AFTER YOU WARM UP.
THANKS A LOT!!
ALL RIGHT!
I FOUND A WAY TO BECOME FASTER...!
カッ
STEP
カッ
STEP
AH...
HEY, ASAHINA. I'VE FIGURED OUT THE PROBLEM I WAS TALKING ABOUT THE OTHER DAY!
HUH!?
WHAT PROB-LEM...?

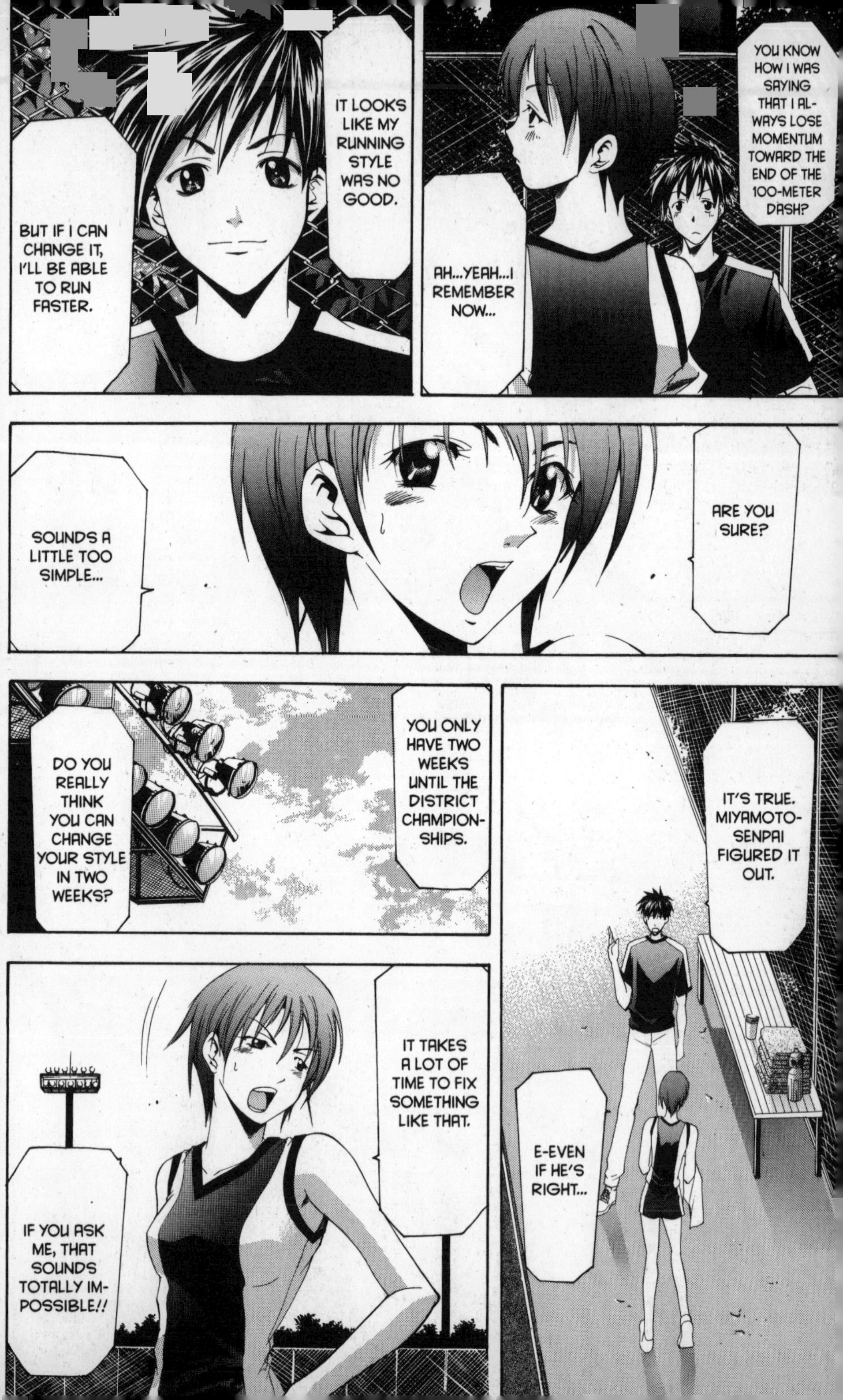
YOU KNOW HOW I WAS SAYING THAT I AL-WAYS LOSE MOMENTUM TOWARD THE END OF THE 100-METER DASH?
AH...YEAH...I REMEMBER NOW...
IT LOOKS LIKE MY RUNNING STYLE WAS NO GOOD.
BUT IF I CAN CHANGE IT, I'LL BE ABLE TO RUN FASTER.
ARE YOU SURE?
SOUNDS A LITTLE TOO SIMPLE...
IT'S TRUE. MIYAMOTO-SENPAI FIGURED IT OUT.
E-EVEN IF HE'S RIGHT...
YOU ONLY HAVE TWO WEEKS UNTIL THE DISTRICT CHAMPION-SHIPS.
DO YOU REALLY THINK YOU CAN CHANGE YOUR STYLE IN TWO WEEKS?
IT TAKES A LOT OF TIME TO FIX SOMETHING LIKE THAT.
IF YOU ASK ME, THAT SOUNDS TOTALLY IM-POSSIBLE!!

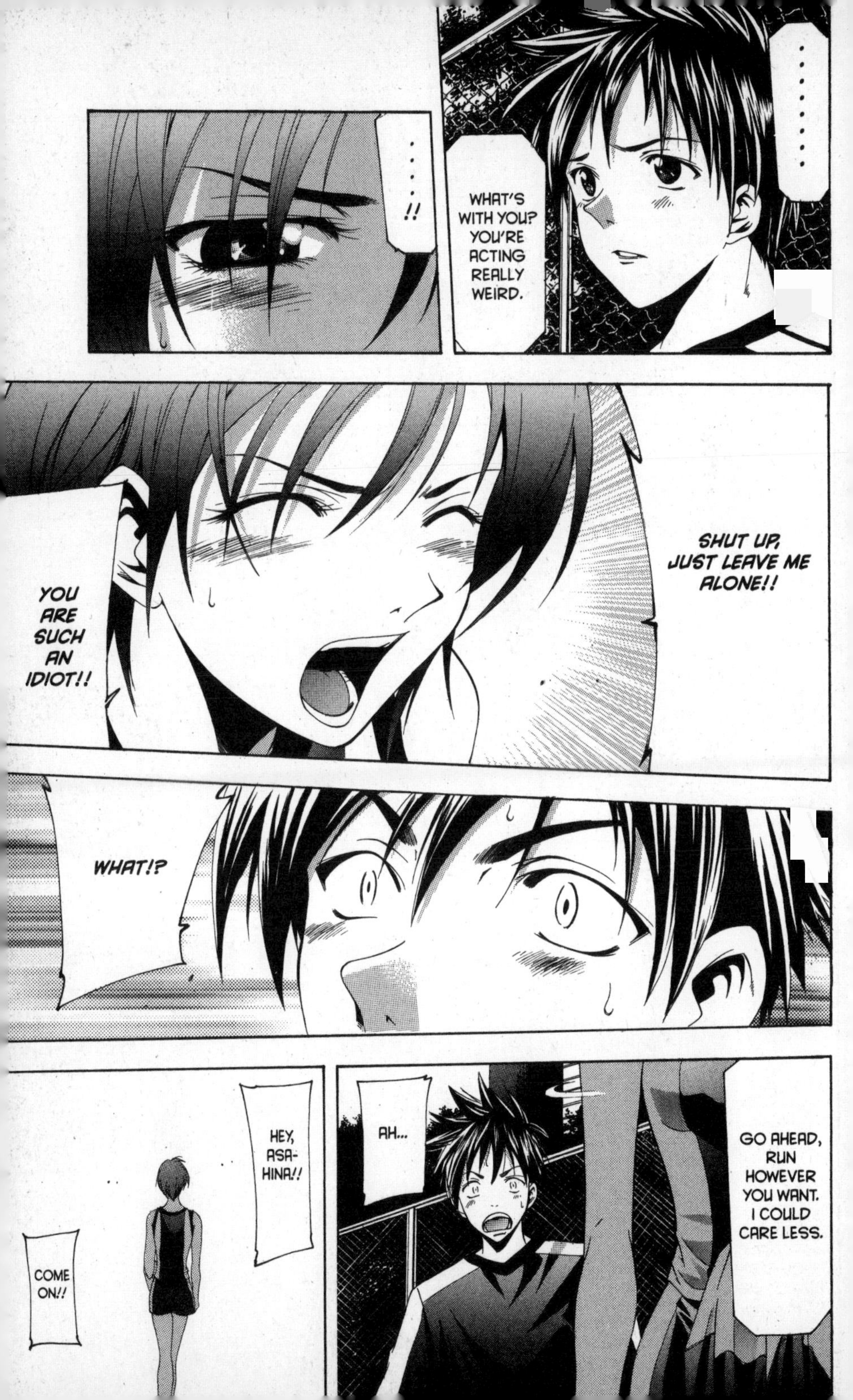
......
WHAT'S WITH YOU? YOU'RE ACTING REALLY WEIRD.
......!!
SHUT UP, JUST LEAVE ME ALONE!!
YOU ARE SUCH AN IDIOT!!
WHAT!?
GO AHEAD, RUN HOWEVER YOU WANT. I COULD CARE LESS.
AH...
HEY, ASA-HINA!!
COME ON!!

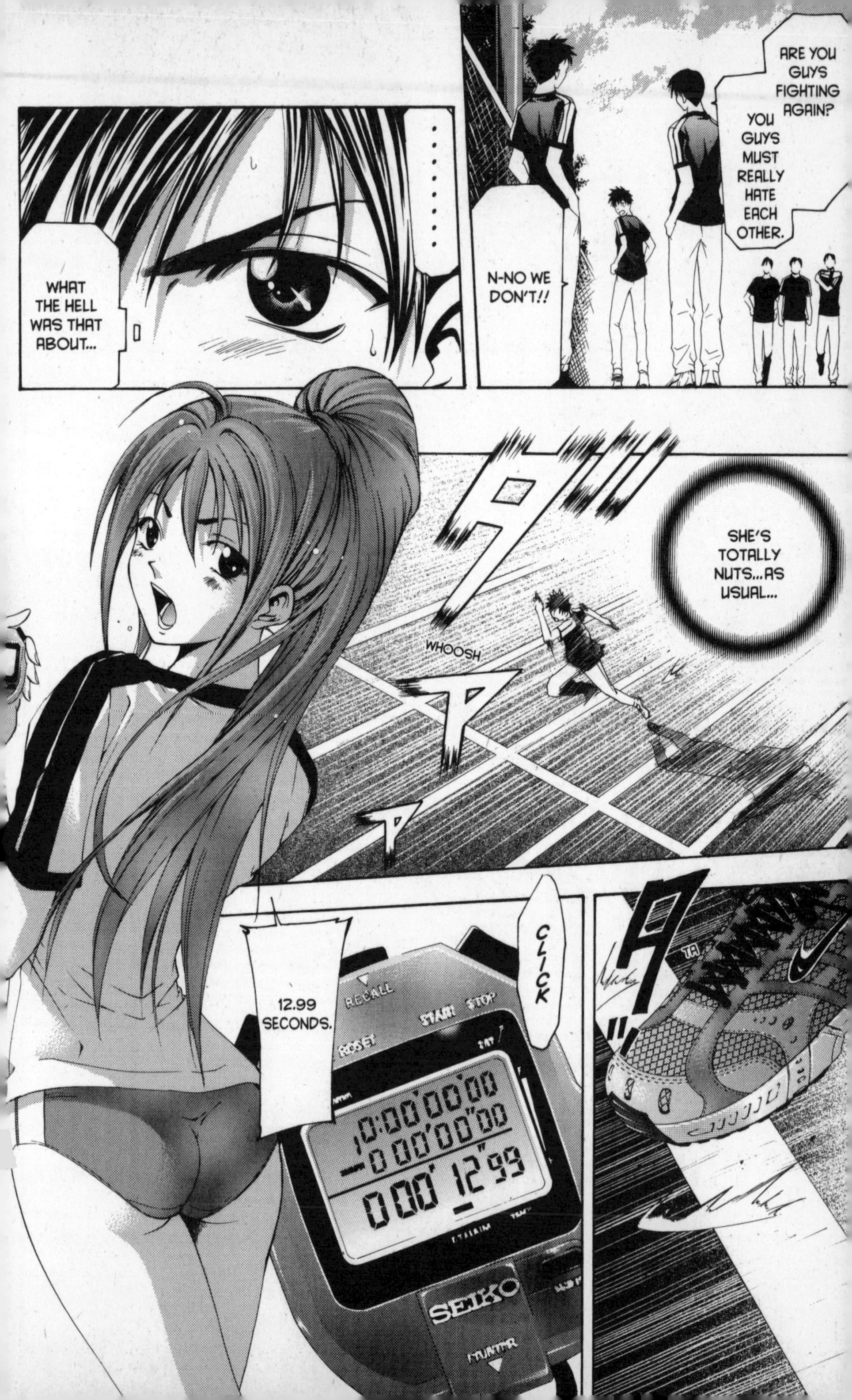
ARE YOU GUYS FIGHTING AGAIN?
YOU GUYS MUST REALLY HATE EACH OTHER.
N-NO WE DON'T!!
......
WHAT THE HELL WAS THAT ABOUT...
SHE'S TOTALLY NUTS...AS USUAL...
WHOOSH
TA
CLICK
12.99 SECONDS.

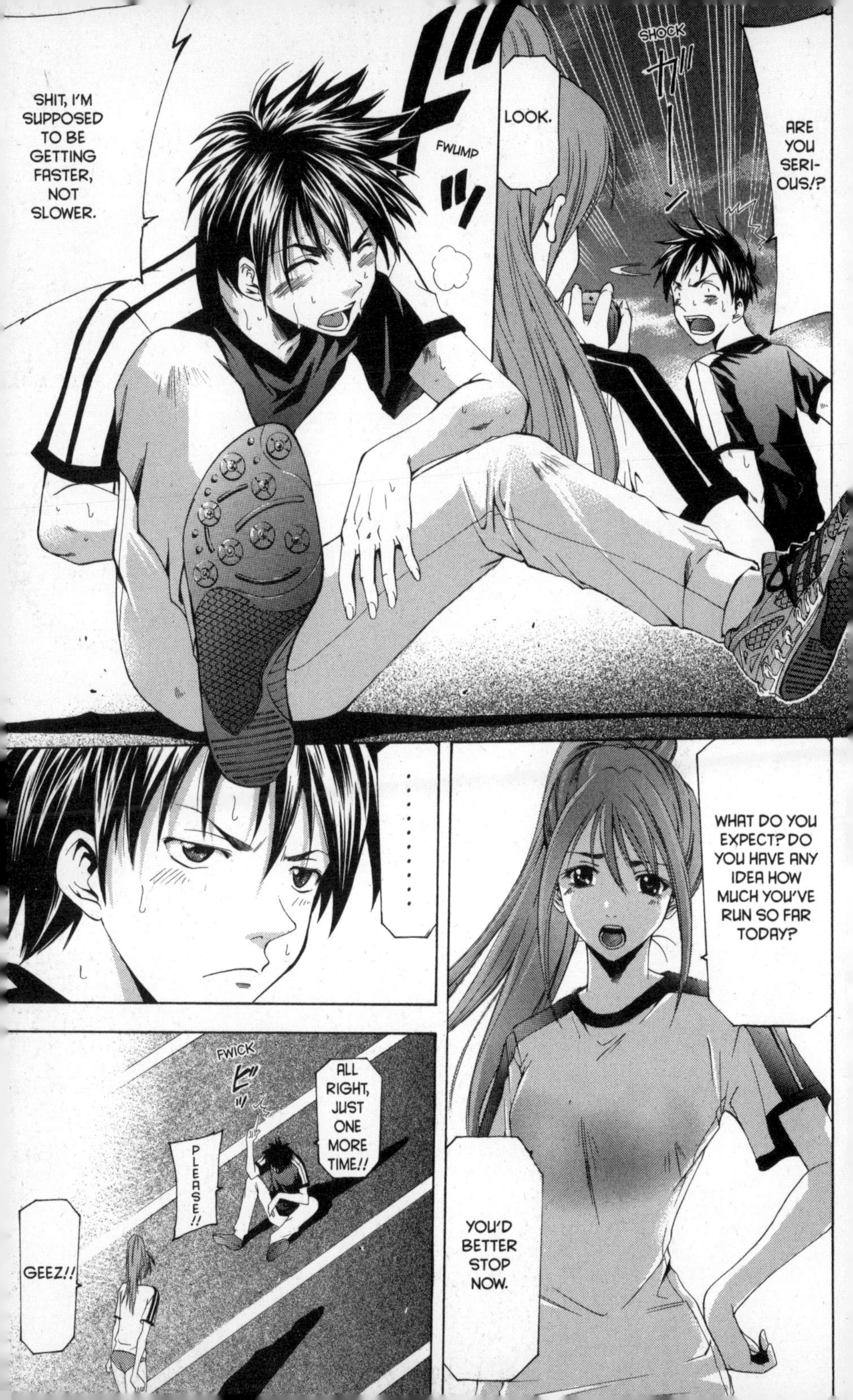
SHOCK
ARE YOU SERI-OUS!?
LOOK.
FWUMP
SHIT, I'M SUPPOSED TO BE GETTING FASTER, NOT SLOWER.
WHAT DO YOU EXPECT? DO YOU HAVE ANY IDEA HOW MUCH YOU'VE RUN SO FAR TODAY?
YOU'D BETTER STOP NOW.
......
FWICK
ALL RIGHT, JUST ONE MORE TIME!!
PLEASE!!
GEEZ!!

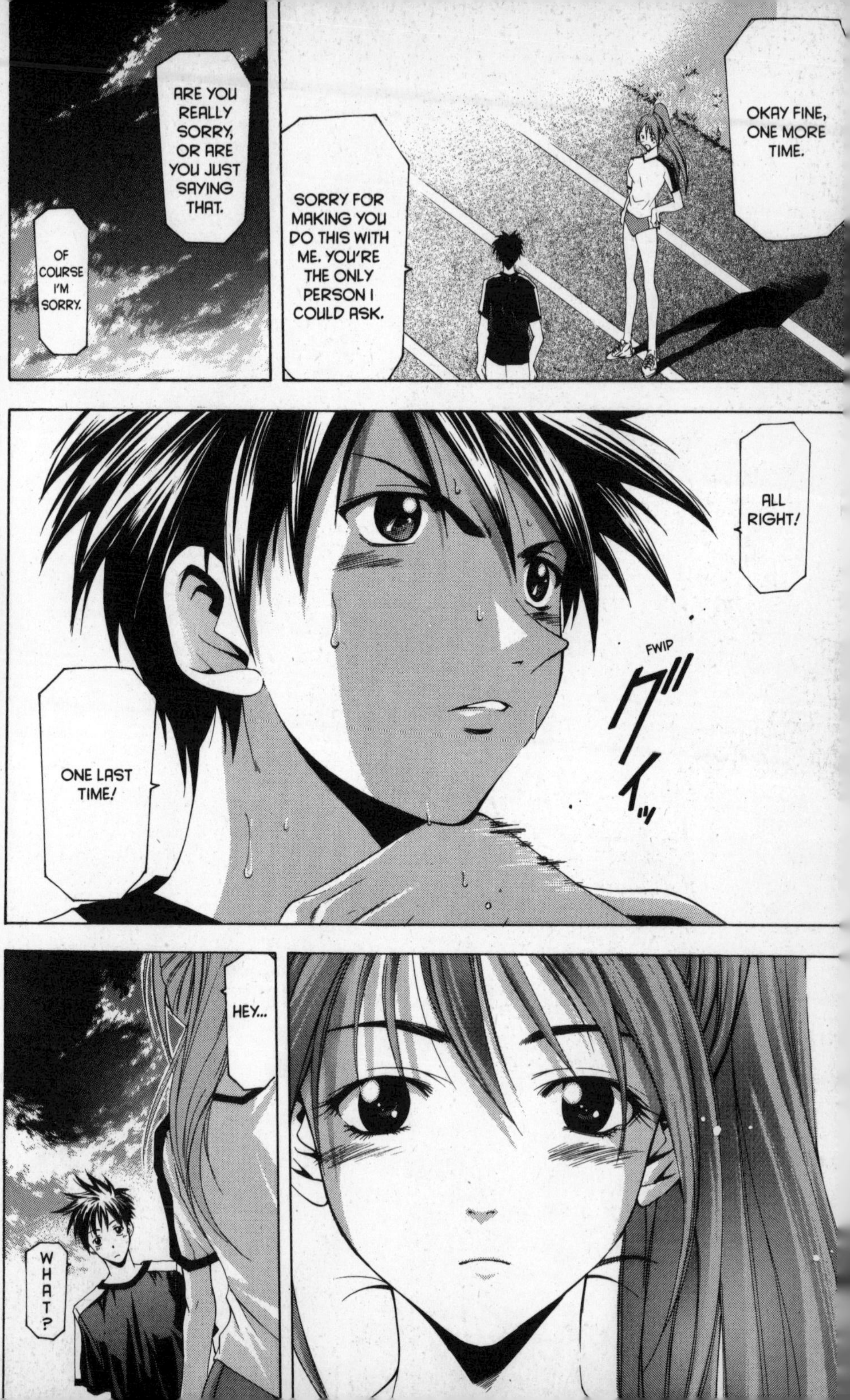
OKAY FINE, ONE MORE TIME.
SORRY FOR MAKING YOU DO THIS WITH ME. YOU'RE THE ONLY PERSON I COULD ASK.
ARE YOU REALLY SORRY, OR ARE YOU JUST SAYING THAT.
OF COURSE I'M SORRY.
ALL RIGHT!
FWIP
グイッ
ONE LAST TIME!
HEY...
WHAT?

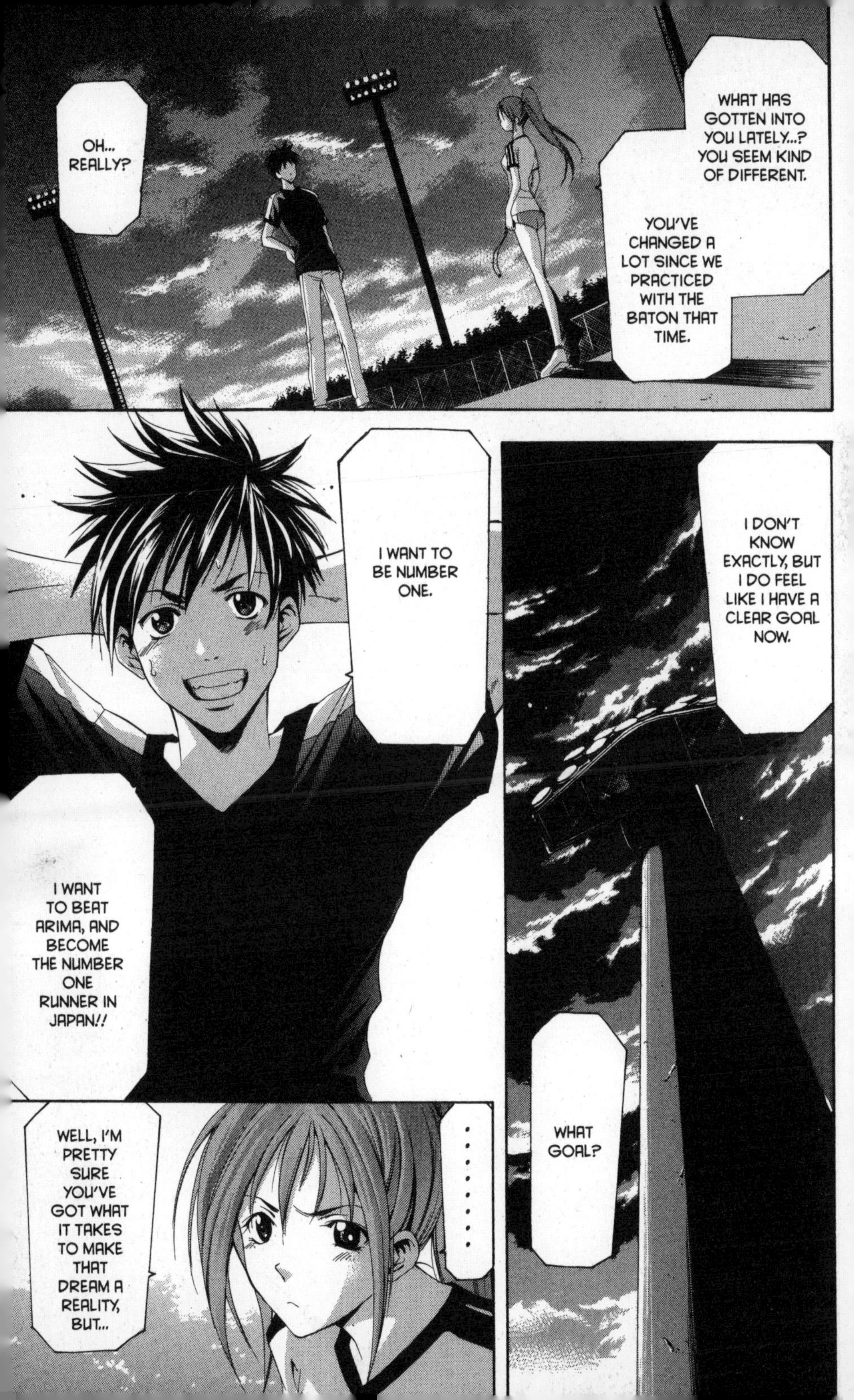
WHAT HAS GOTTEN INTO YOU LATELY...? YOU SEEM KIND OF DIFFERENT.
YOU'VE CHANGED A LOT SINCE WE PRACTICED WITH THE BATON THAT TIME.
OH... REALLY?
I DON'T KNOW EXACTLY, BUT I DO FEEL LIKE I HAVE A CLEAR GOAL NOW.
WHAT GOAL?
I WANT TO BE NUMBER ONE.
I WANT TO BEAT ARIMA, AND BECOME THE NUMBER ONE RUNNER IN JAPAN!!
......
WELL, I'M PRETTY SURE YOU'VE GOT WHAT IT TAKES TO MAKE THAT DREAM A REALITY, BUT...

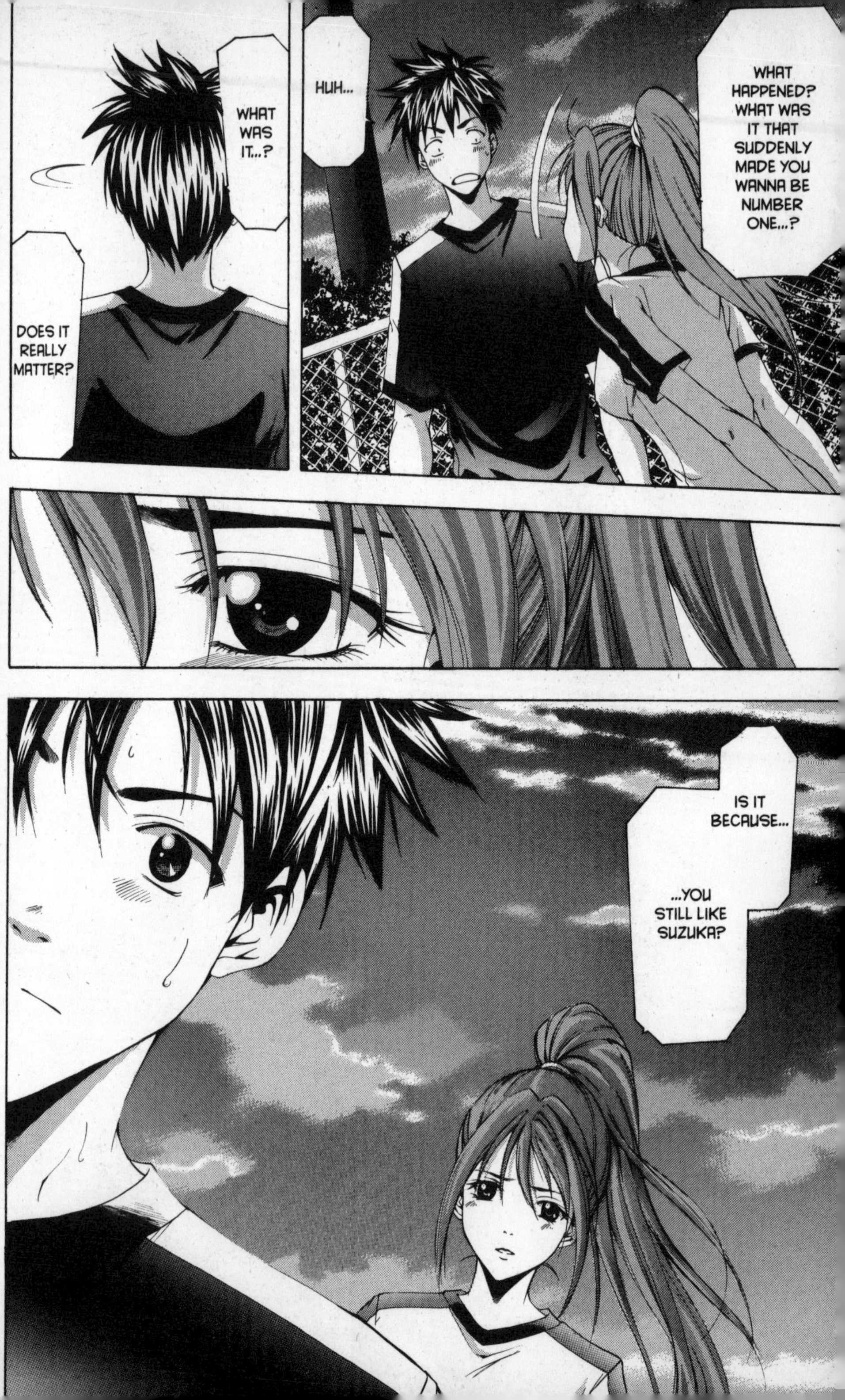
WHAT HAPPENED? WHAT WAS IT THAT SUDDENLY MADE YOU WANNA BE NUMBER ONE...?
HUH...
WHAT WAS IT...?
DOES IT REALLY MATTER?
IS IT BECAUSE...
...YOU STILL LIKE SUZUKA?

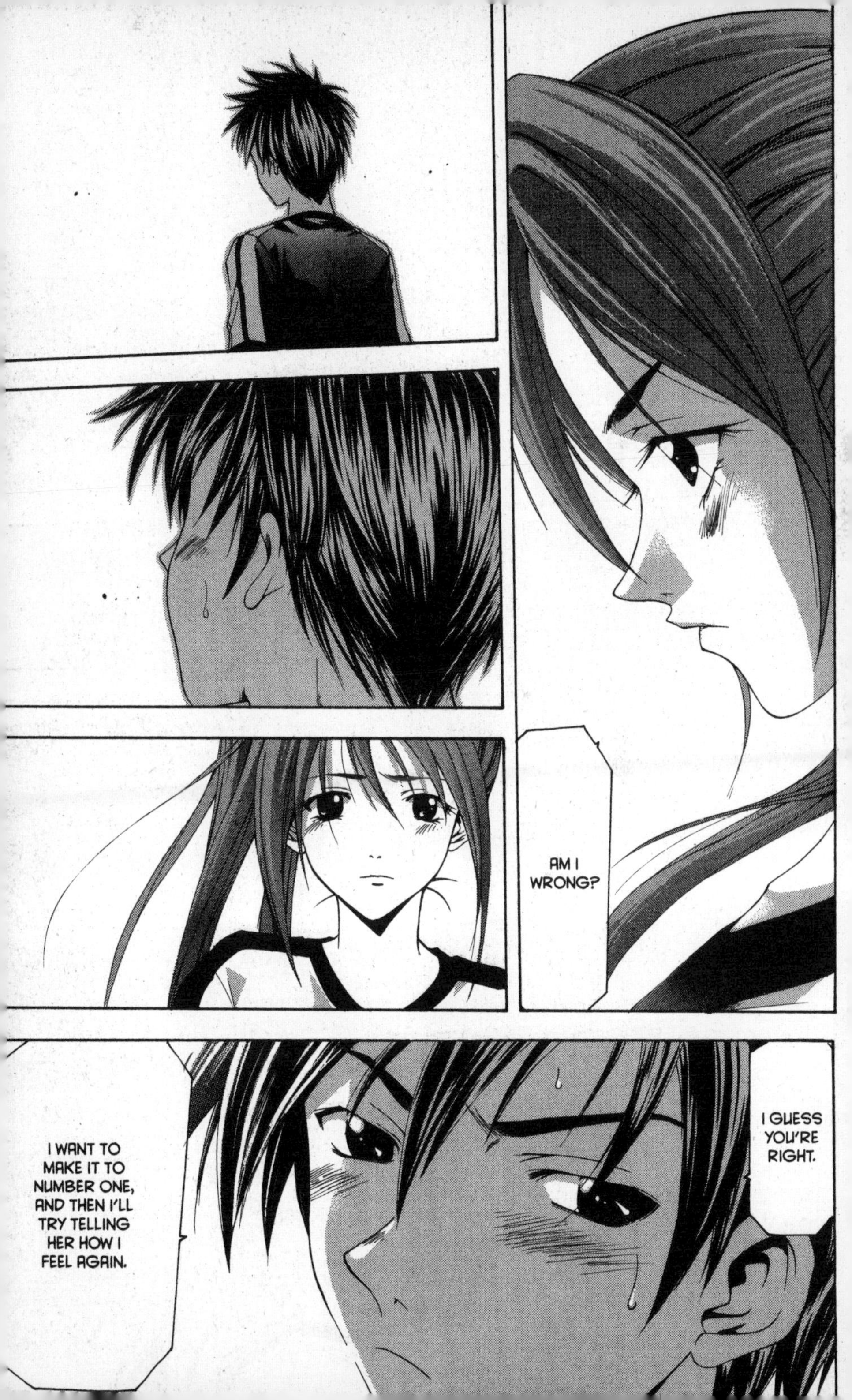
AM I WRONG?
I GUESS YOU'RE RIGHT.
I WANT TO MAKE IT TO NUMBER ONE, AND THEN I'LL TRY TELLING HER HOW I FEEL AGAIN.

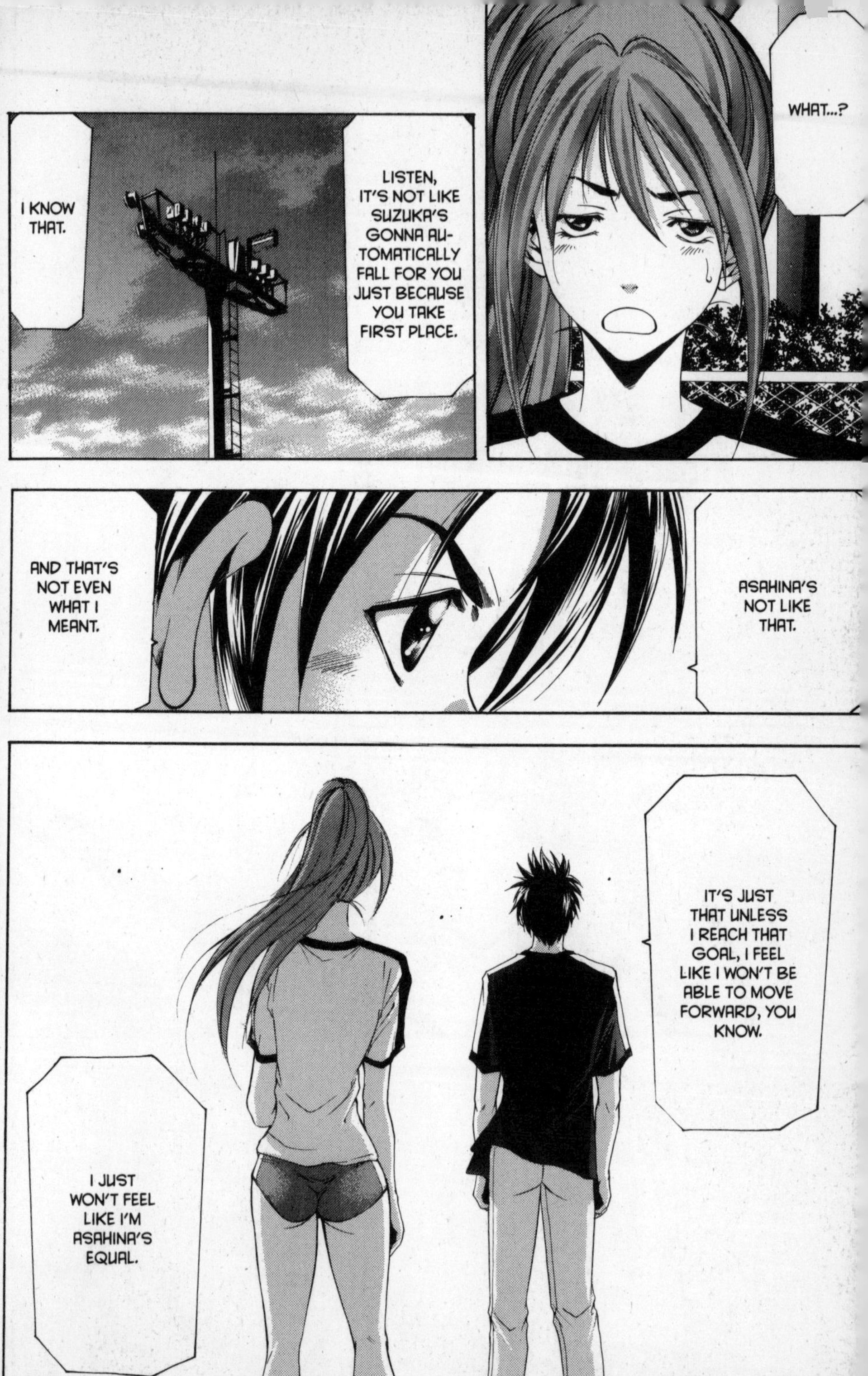
WHAT...?
LISTEN, IT'S NOT LIKE SUZUKA'S GONNA AU-TOMATICALLY FALL FOR YOU JUST BECAUSE YOU TAKE FIRST PLACE.
I KNOW THAT.
ASAHINA'S NOT LIKE THAT.
AND THAT'S NOT EVEN WHAT I MEANT.
IT'S JUST THAT UNLESS I REACH THAT GOAL, I FEEL LIKE I WON'T BE ABLE TO MOVE FORWARD, YOU KNOW.
I JUST WON'T FEEL LIKE I'M ASAHINA'S EQUAL.

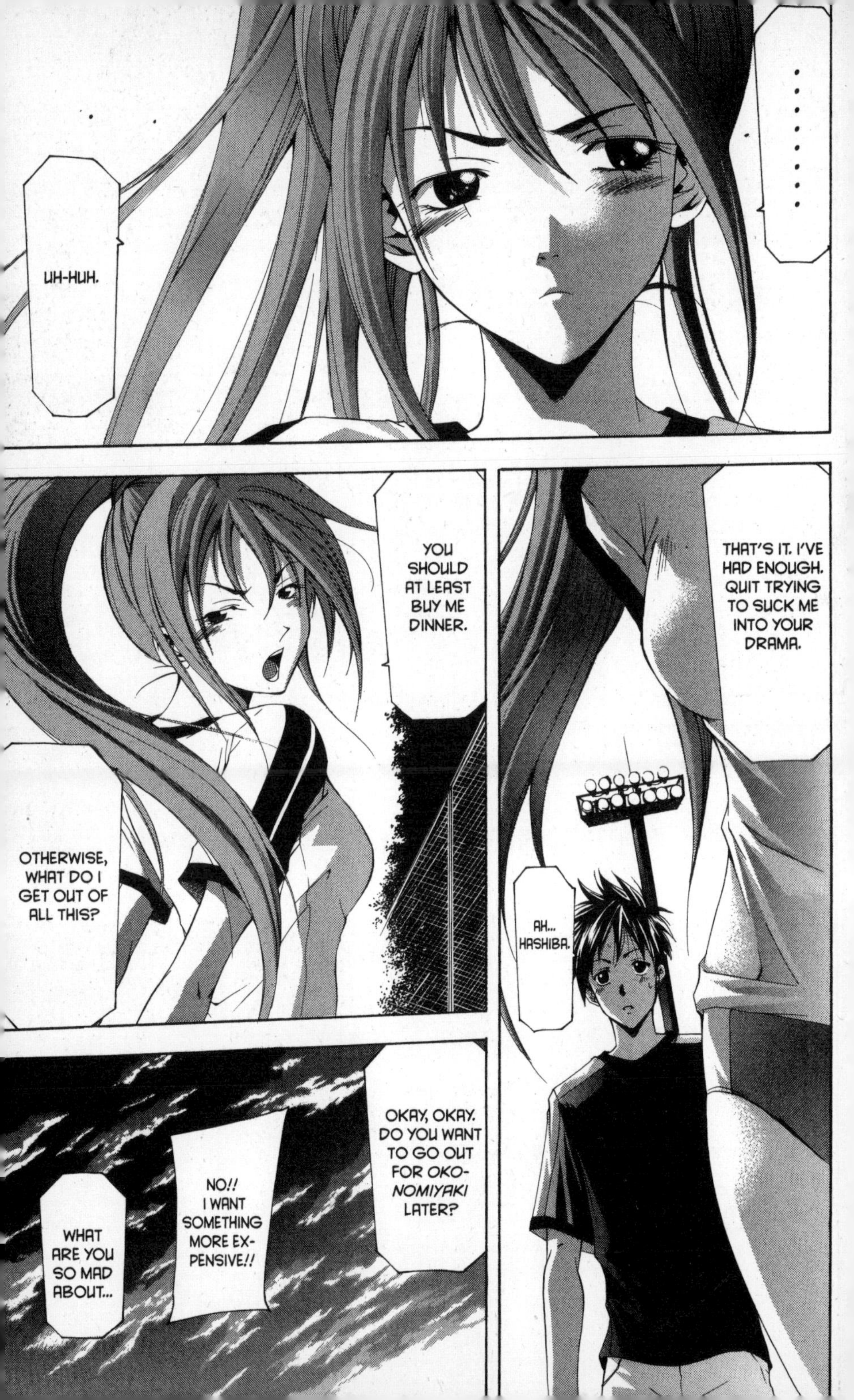
......
UH-HUH.
THAT'S IT. I'VE HAD ENOUGH. QUIT TRYING TO SUCK ME INTO YOUR DRAMA.
AH... HASHIBA.
YOU SHOULD AT LEAST BUY ME DINNER.
OTHERWISE, WHAT DO I GET OUT OF ALL THIS?
OKAY, OKAY. DO YOU WANT TO GO OUT FOR *OKONOMIYAKI* LATER?
NO!! I WANT SOMETHING MORE EXPENSIVE!!
WHAT ARE YOU SO MAD ABOUT...

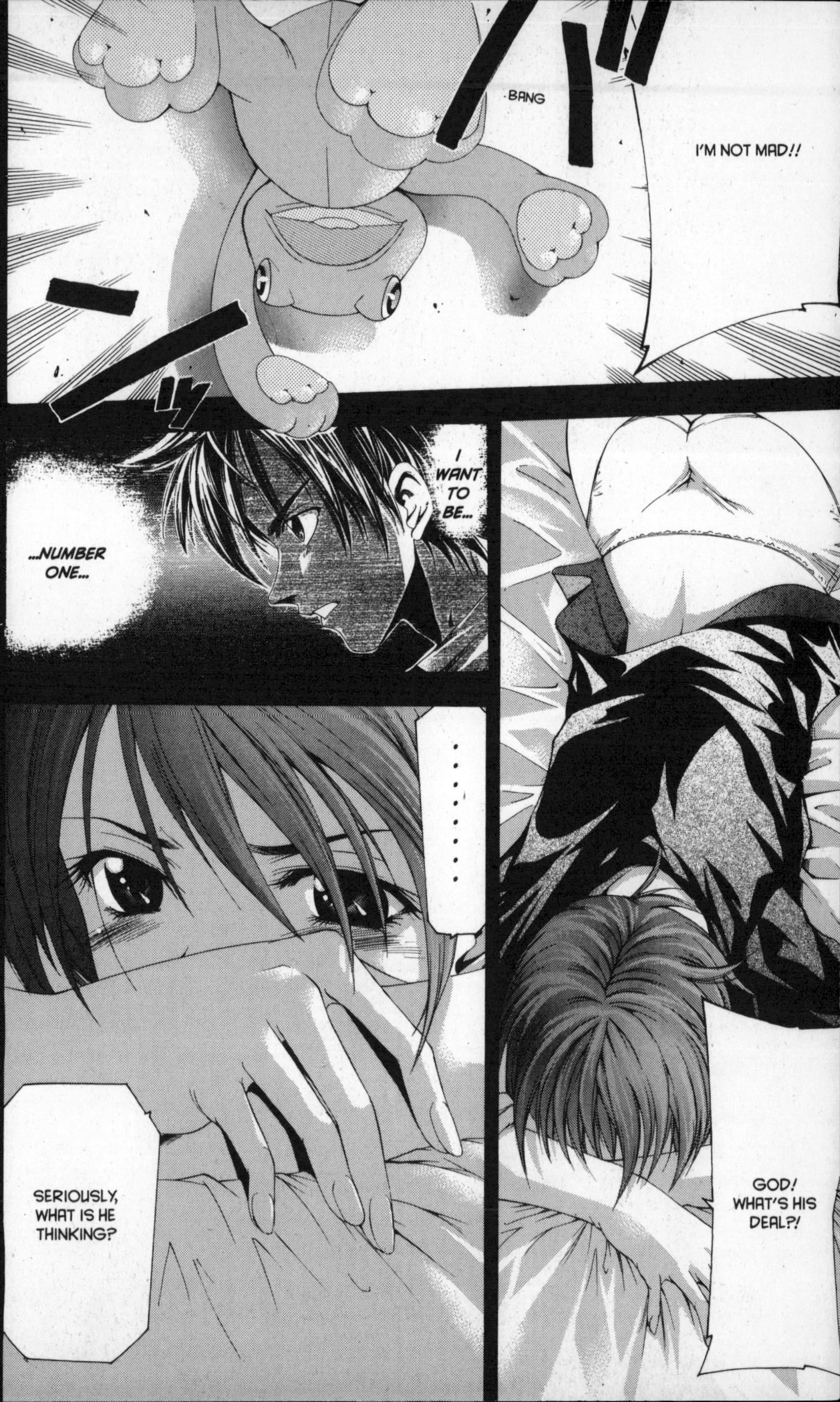
I'M NOT MAD!!
BANG
GOD! WHAT'S HIS DEAL?!
I WANT TO BE...
...NUMBER ONE...
....
SERIOUSLY, WHAT IS HE THINKING?

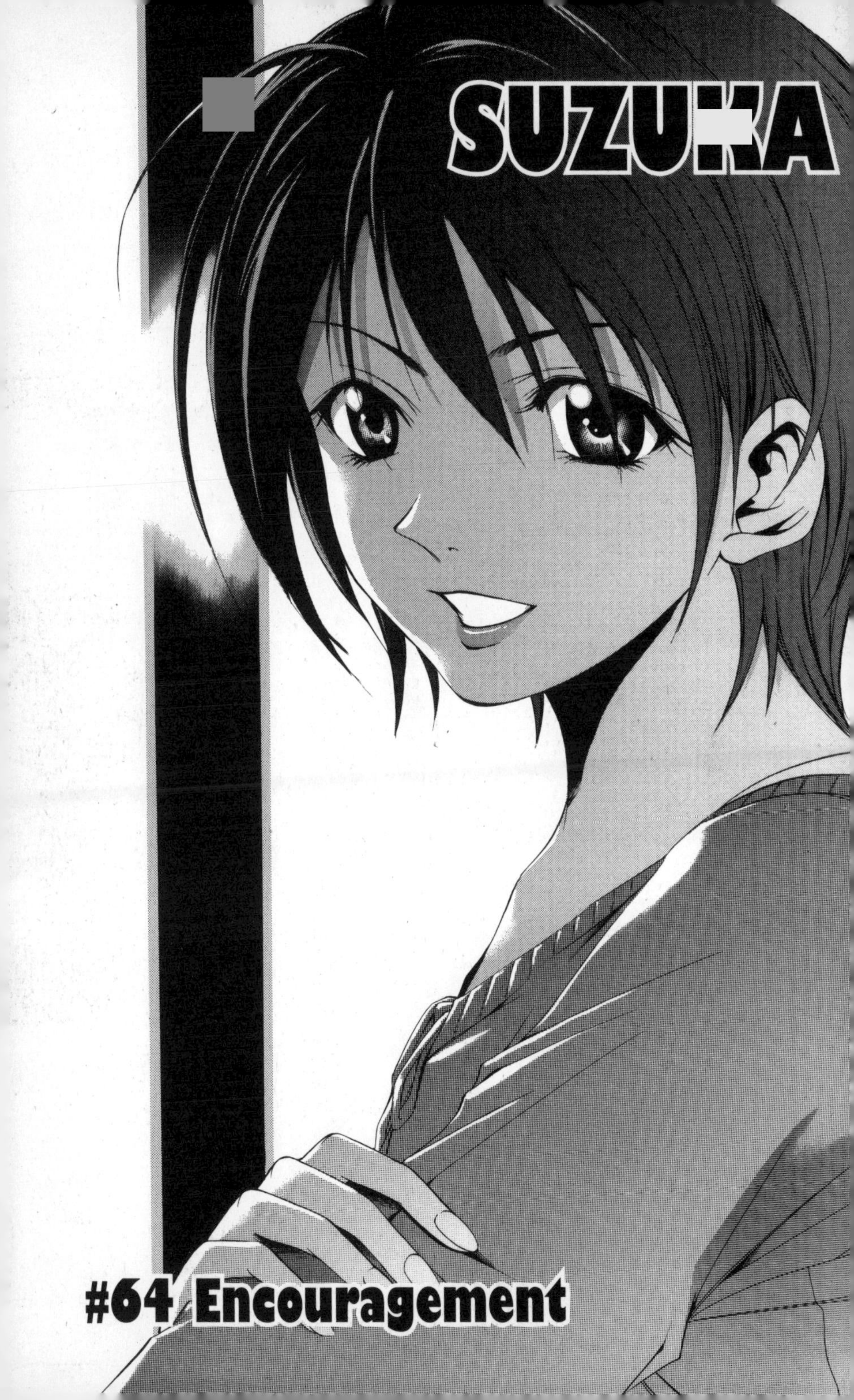
SUZUKA
#64 Encouragement

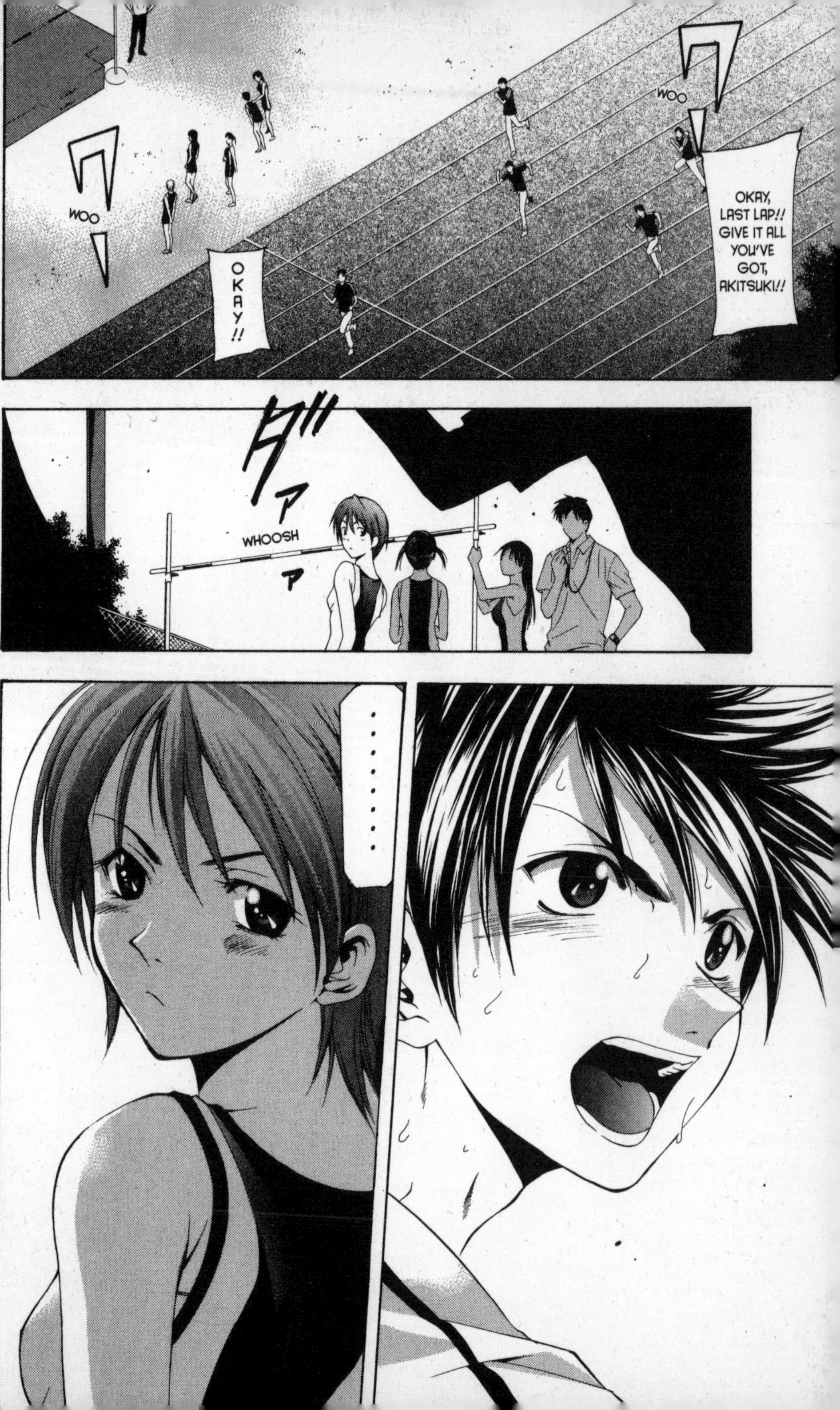
WOO
OKAY, LAST LAP!! GIVE IT ALL YOU'VE GOT, AKITSUKI!!
OKAY!!
WOO
WHOOSH
......

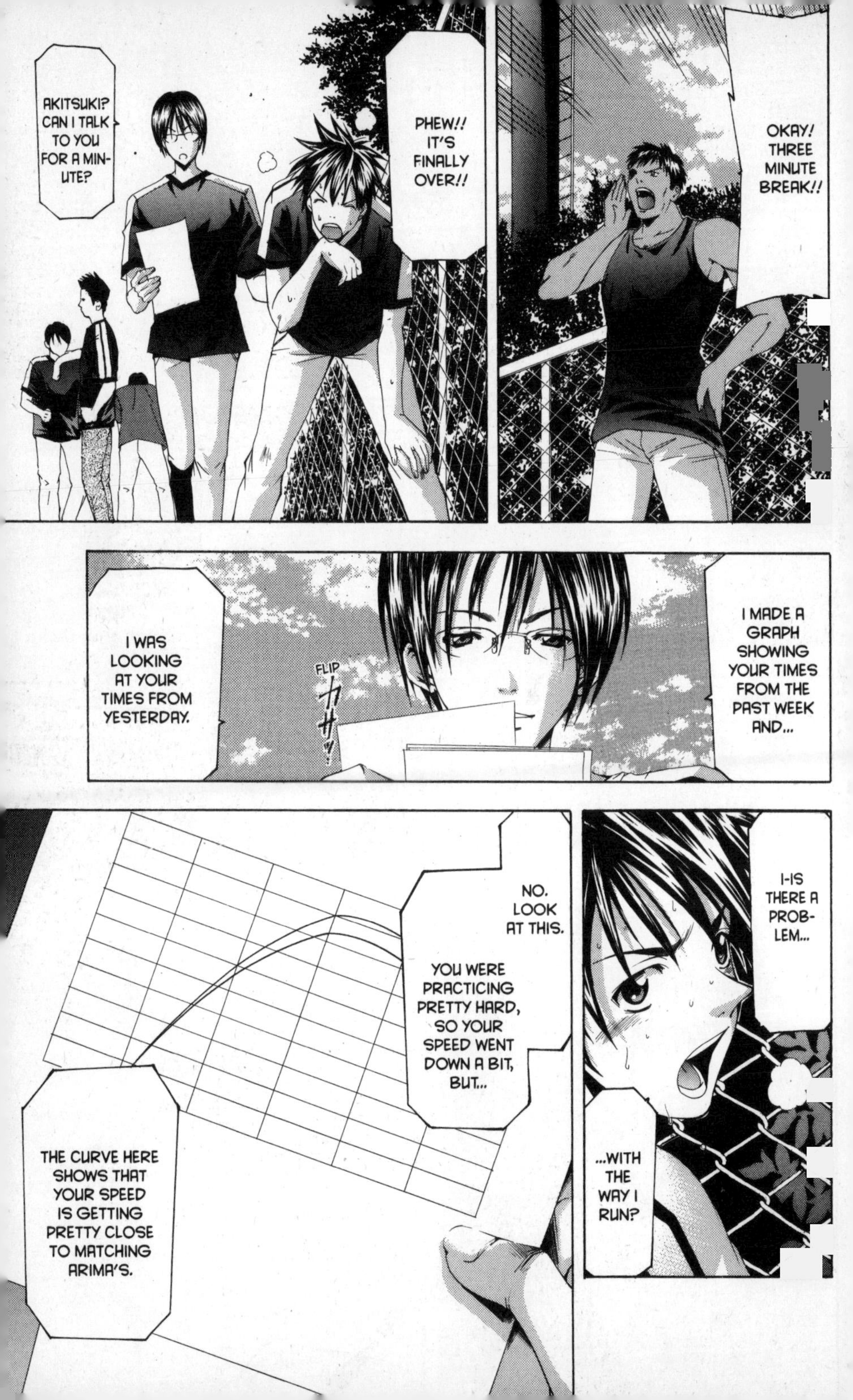

OKAY! THREE MINUTE BREAK!!
PHEW!! IT'S FINALLY OVER!!
AKITSUKI? CAN I TALK TO YOU FOR A MIN-UTE?
I MADE A GRAPH SHOWING YOUR TIMES FROM THE PAST WEEK AND...
FLIP
カサッ
I WAS LOOKING AT YOUR TIMES FROM YESTERDAY.
I-IS THERE A PROB-LEM...
...WITH THE WAY I RUN?
NO. LOOK AT THIS.
YOU WERE PRACTICING PRETTY HARD, SO YOUR SPEED WENT DOWN A BIT, BUT...
THE CURVE HERE SHOWS THAT YOUR SPEED IS GETTING PRETTY CLOSE TO MATCHING ARIMA'S.

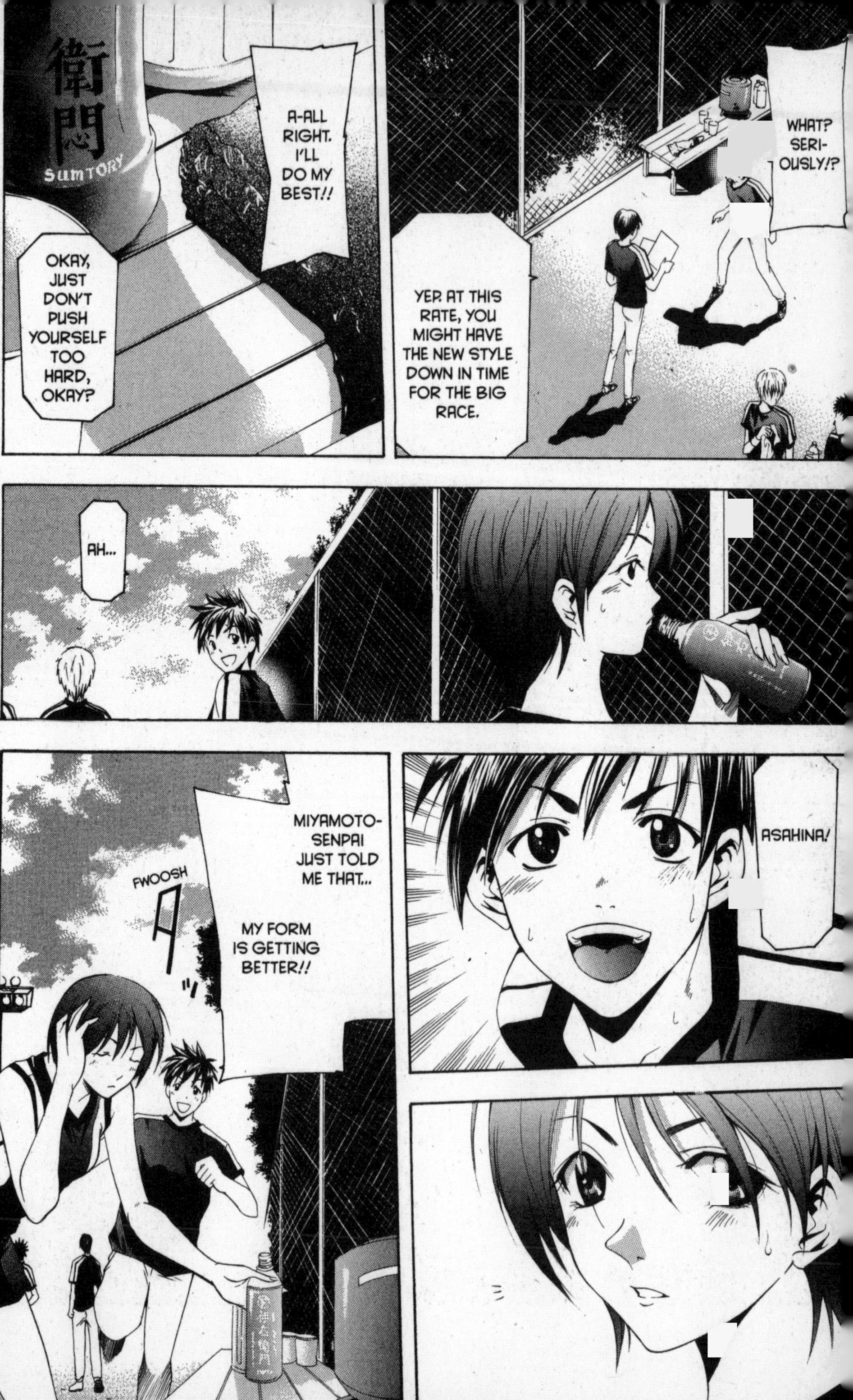
WHAT? SERI-OUSLY!?
YEP. AT THIS RATE, YOU MIGHT HAVE THE NEW STYLE DOWN IN TIME FOR THE BIG RACE.
A-ALL RIGHT. I'LL DO MY BEST!!
衛悶
SUMTORY
OKAY, JUST DON'T PUSH YOURSELF TOO HARD, OKAY?
AH...
ASAHINA!
MIYAMOTO-SENPAI JUST TOLD ME THAT...
MY FORM IS GETTING BETTER!!
FWOOSH

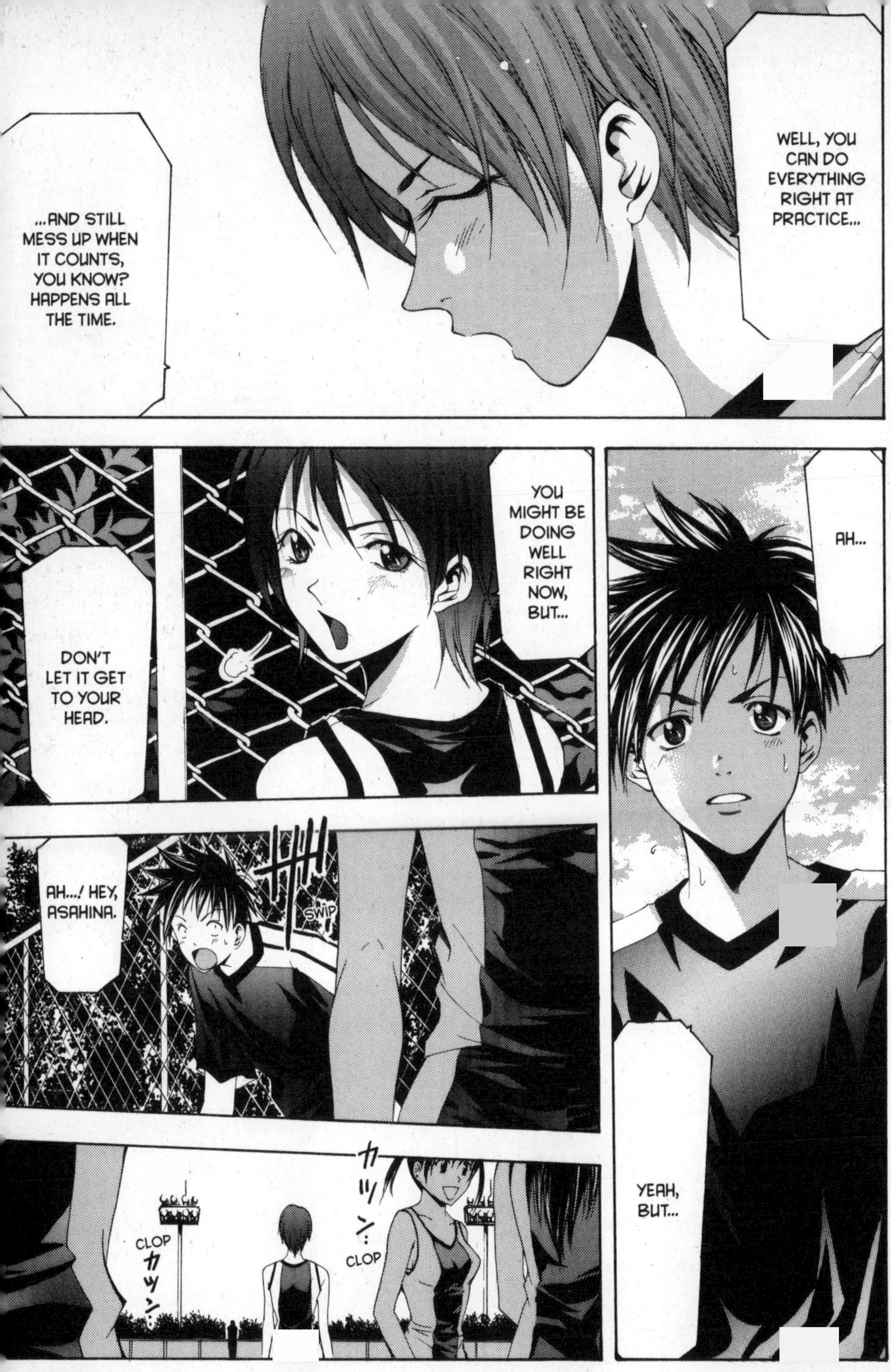
WELL, YOU CAN DO EVERYTHING RIGHT AT PRACTICE...
...AND STILL MESS UP WHEN IT COUNTS, YOU KNOW? HAPPENS ALL THE TIME.
AH...
YEAH, BUT...
YOU MIGHT BE DOING WELL RIGHT NOW, BUT...
DON'T LET IT GET TO YOUR HEAD.
SWIP
AH...! HEY, ASAHINA.
カッン
CLOP
CLOP
カッン

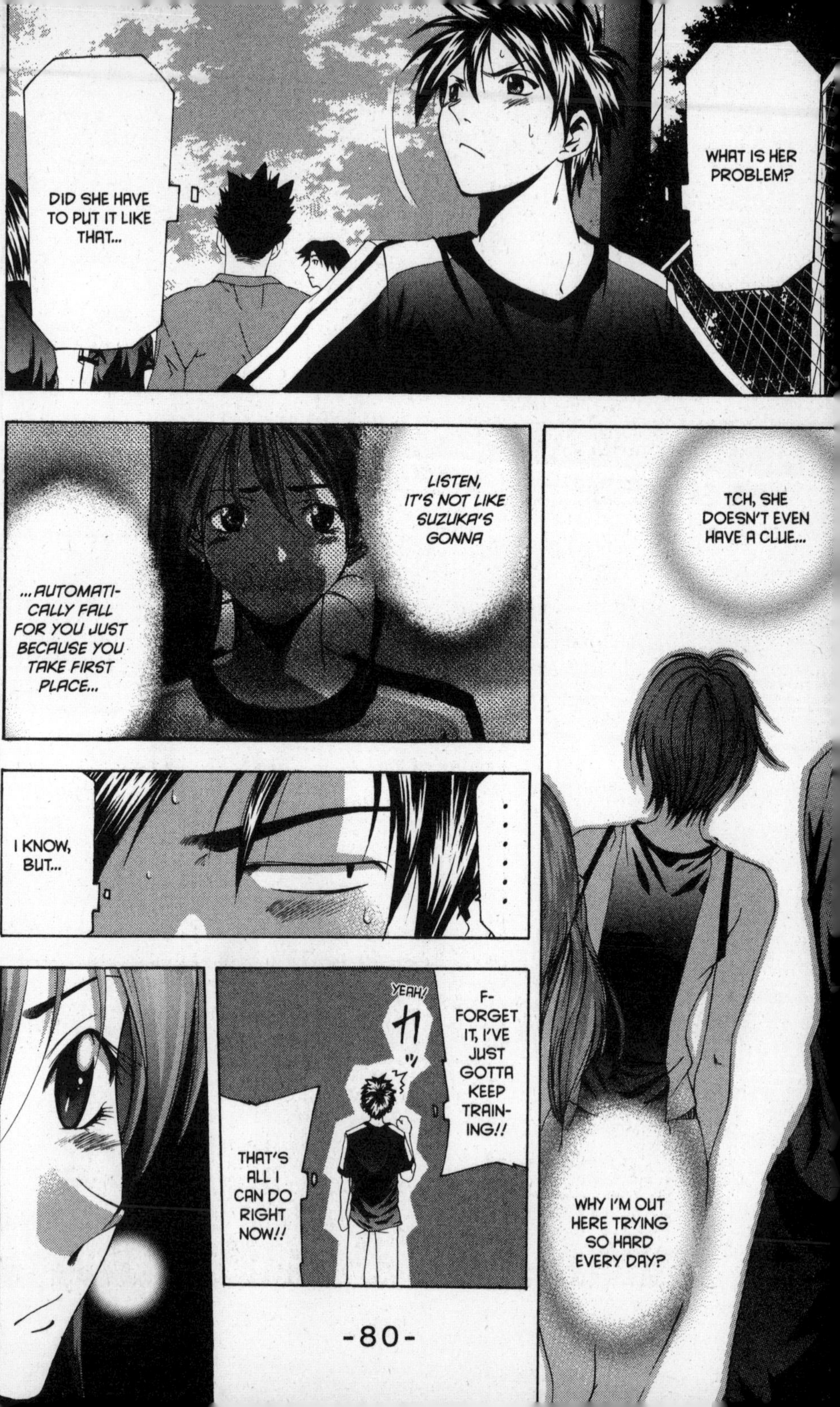
WHAT IS HER PROBLEM?
DID SHE HAVE TO PUT IT LIKE THAT...
TCH, SHE DOESN'T EVEN HAVE A CLUE...
WHY I'M OUT HERE TRYING SO HARD EVERY DAY?
LISTEN, IT'S NOT LIKE SUZUKA'S GONNA
...AUTOMATI-CALLY FALL FOR YOU JUST BECAUSE YOU TAKE FIRST PLACE...
......
I KNOW, BUT...
F-FORGET IT, I'VE JUST GOTTA KEEP TRAIN-ING!!
YEAH!
THAT'S ALL I CAN DO RIGHT NOW!!

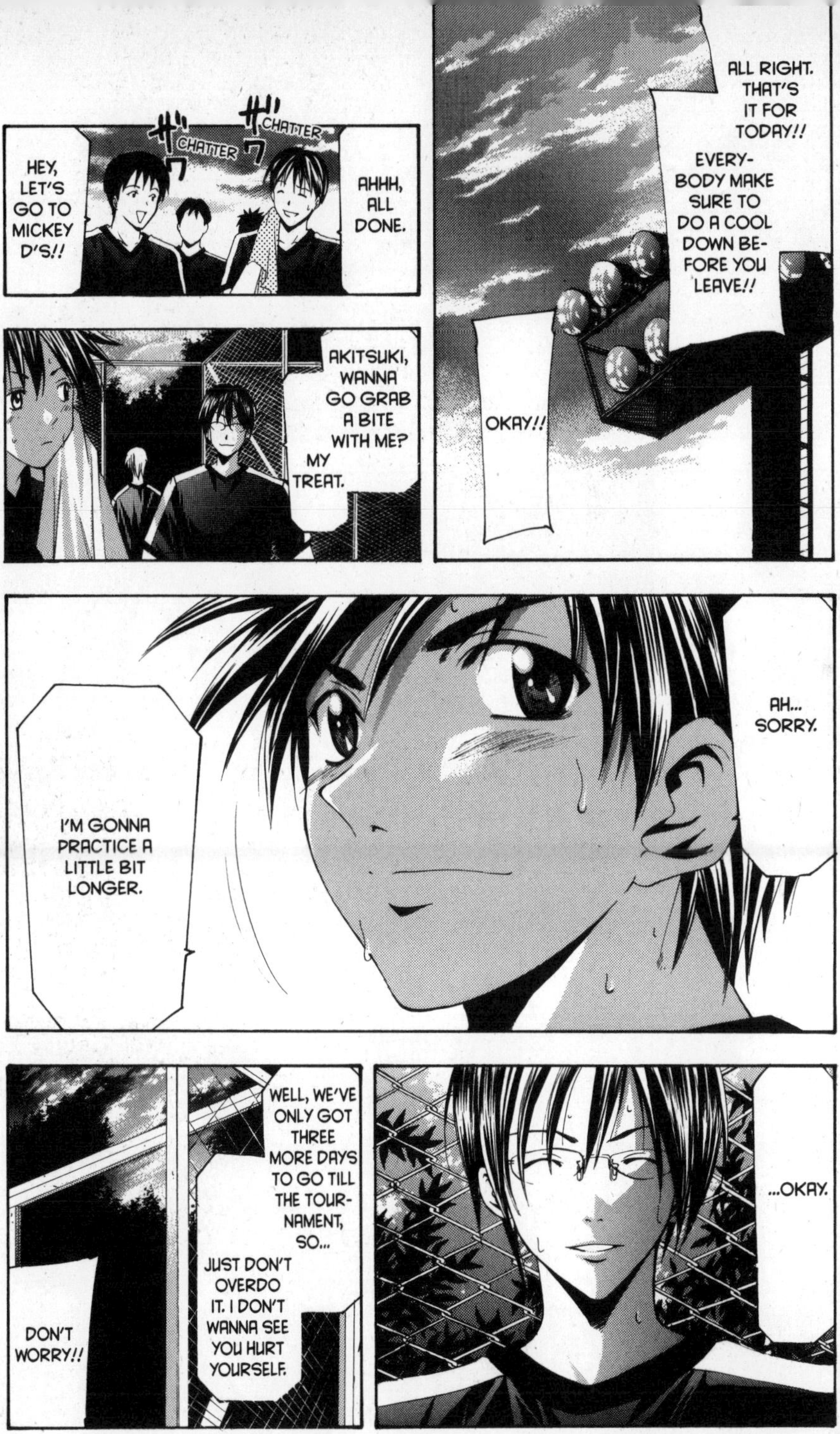
ALL RIGHT. THAT'S IT FOR TODAY!!
EVERY-BODY MAKE SURE TO DO A COOL DOWN BE-FORE YOU LEAVE!!
OKAY!!
ザワ CHATTER
ザワ CHATTER
AHHH, ALL DONE.
HEY, LET'S GO TO MICKEY D'S!!
AKITSUKI, WANNA GO GRAB A BITE WITH ME?
MY TREAT.
AH... SORRY.
I'M GONNA PRACTICE A LITTLE BIT LONGER.
...OKAY.
WELL, WE'VE ONLY GOT THREE MORE DAYS TO GO TILL THE TOUR-NAMENT, SO...
JUST DON'T OVERDO IT. I DON'T WANNA SEE YOU HURT YOURSELF.
DON'T WORRY!!

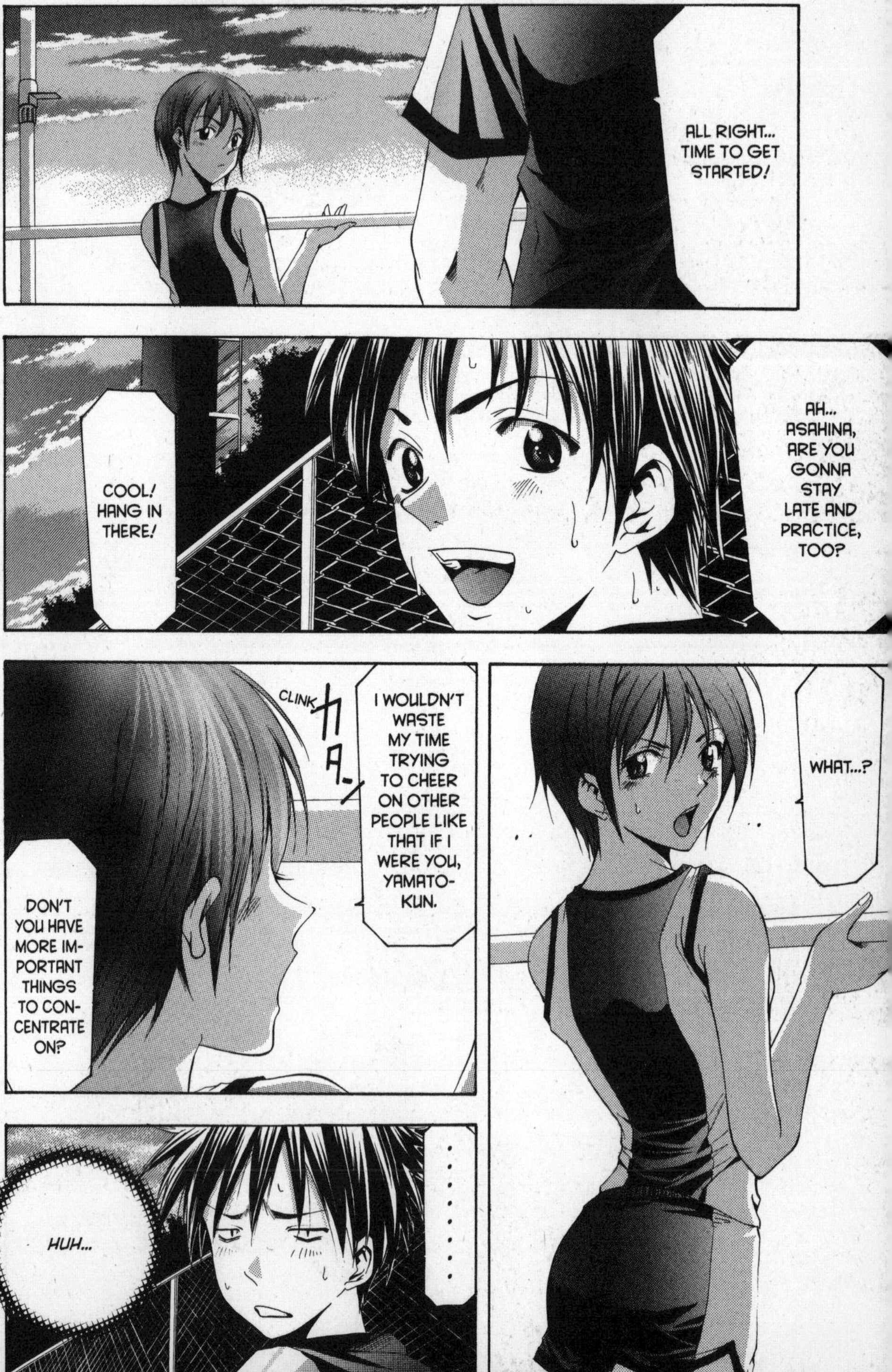
ALL RIGHT... TIME TO GET STARTED!
AH... ASAHINA, ARE YOU GONNA STAY LATE AND PRACTICE, TOO?
COOL! HANG IN THERE!
WHAT...?
CLINK
I WOULDN'T WASTE MY TIME TRYING TO CHEER ON OTHER PEOPLE LIKE THAT IF I WERE YOU, YAMATO-KUN.
DON'T YOU HAVE MORE IM-PORTANT THINGS TO CON-CENTRATE ON?
......
HUH...

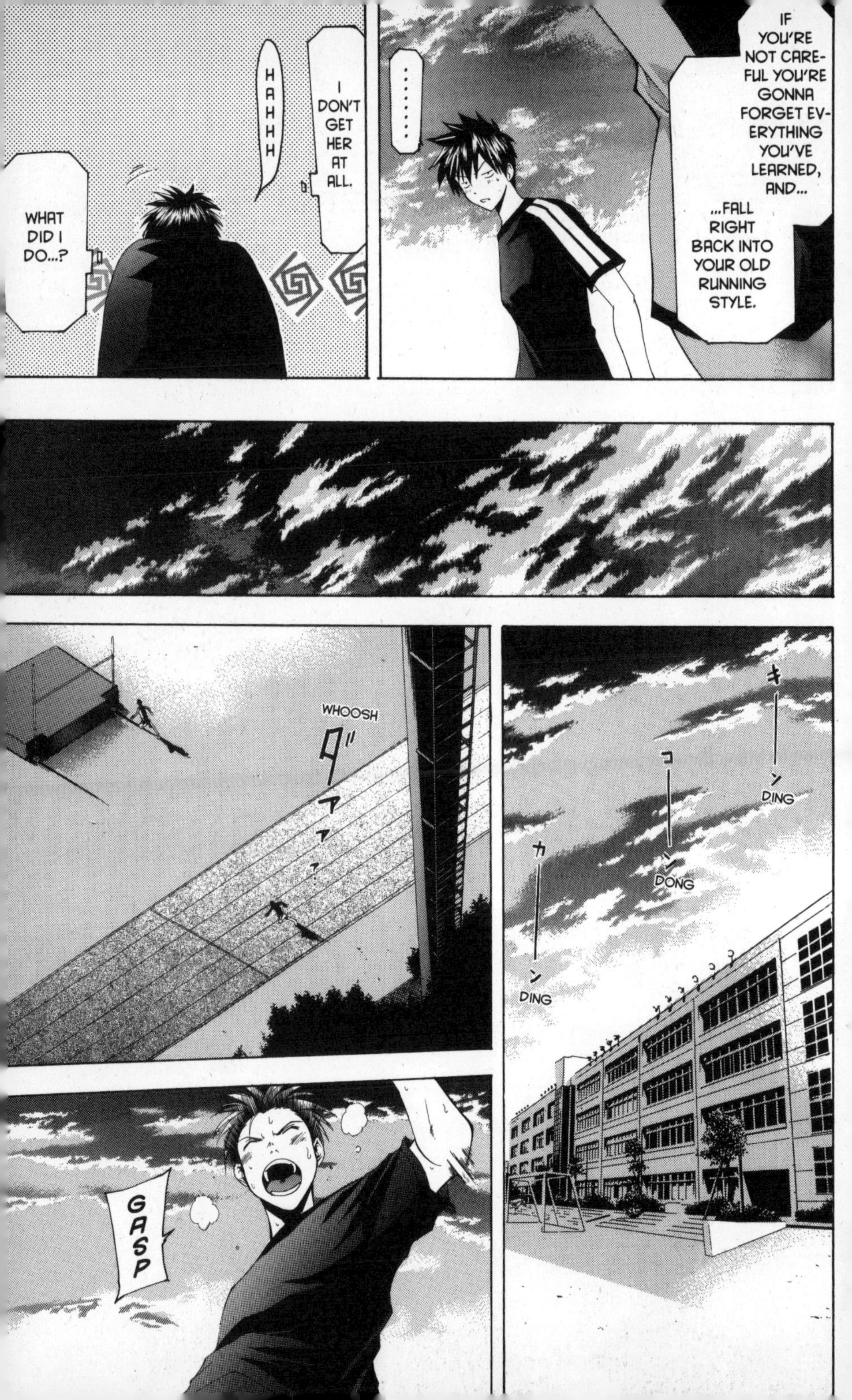
IF YOU'RE NOT CARE-FUL YOU'RE GONNA FORGET EV-ERYTHING YOU'VE LEARNED, AND...
...FALL RIGHT BACK INTO YOUR OLD RUNNING STYLE.
....
I DON'T GET HER AT ALL.
HAHHHH
WHAT DID I DO...?
キーン
DING
コーン
DONG
カーン
DING
WHOOSH
ダァァァ
GASP

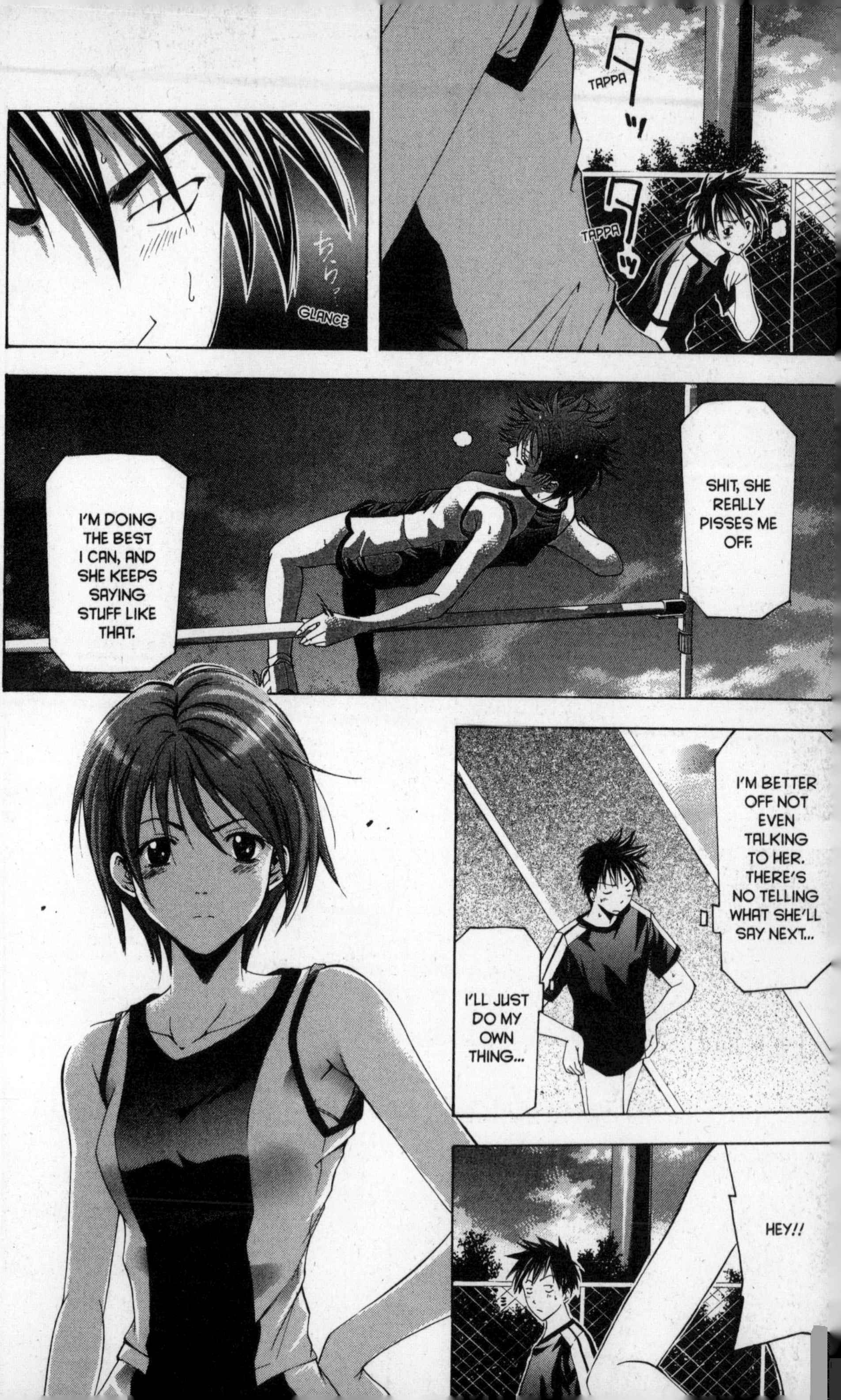
タッ
TAPPA
タッ
TAPPA
ちらっ
GLANCE
SHIT, SHE REALLY PISSES ME OFF.
I'M DOING THE BEST I CAN, AND SHE KEEPS SAYING STUFF LIKE THAT.
I'M BETTER OFF NOT EVEN TALKING TO HER. THERE'S NO TELLING WHAT SHE'LL SAY NEXT...
I'LL JUST DO MY OWN THING...
HEY!!

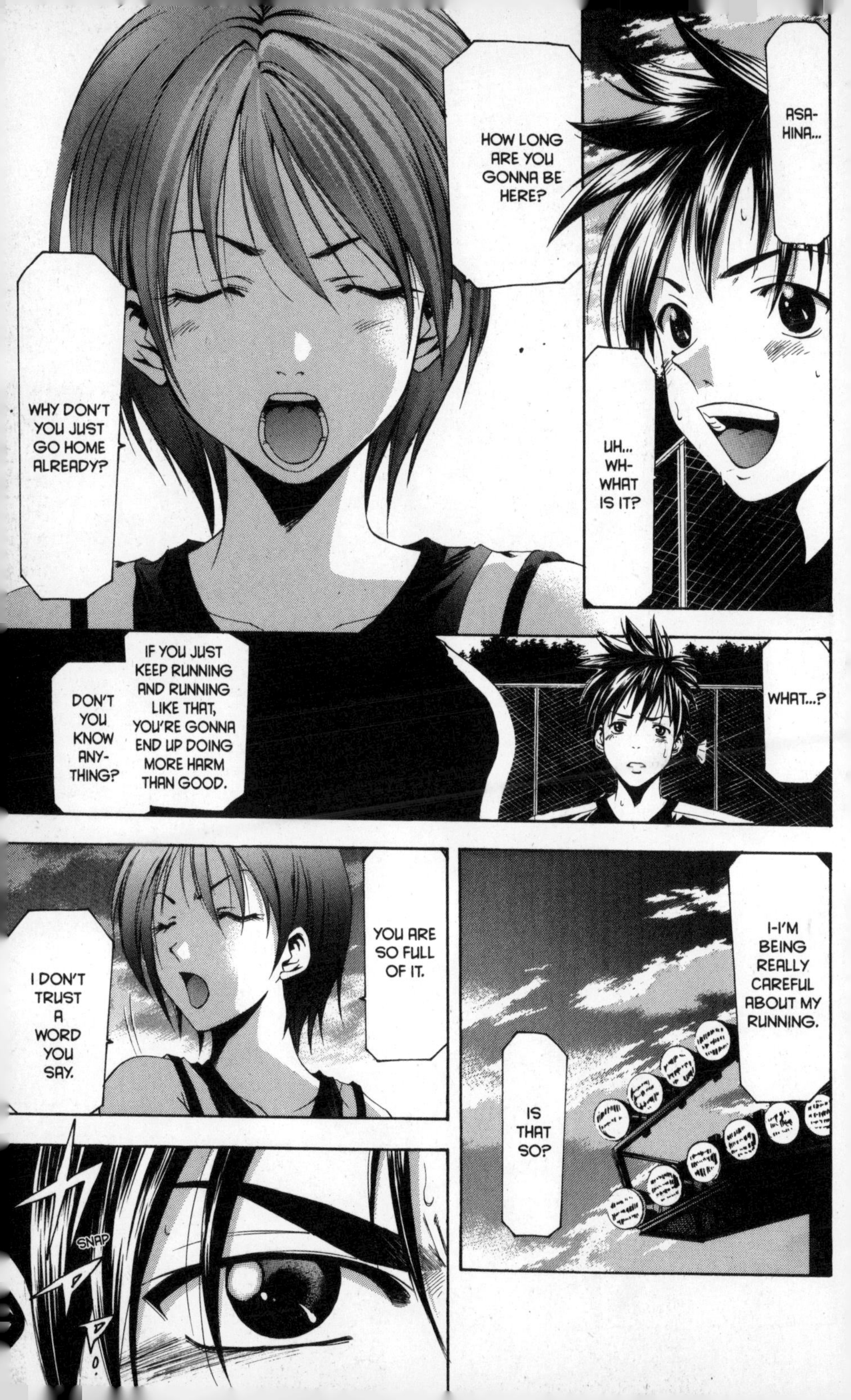
ASA-HINA...
UH... WH-WHAT IS IT?
HOW LONG ARE YOU GONNA BE HERE?
WHY DON'T YOU JUST GO HOME ALREADY?
WHAT...?
IF YOU JUST KEEP RUNNING AND RUNNING LIKE THAT, YOU'RE GONNA END UP DOING MORE HARM THAN GOOD.
DON'T YOU KNOW ANY-THING?
I-I'M BEING REALLY CAREFUL ABOUT MY RUNNING.
IS THAT SO?
YOU ARE SO FULL OF IT.
I DON'T TRUST A WORD YOU SAY.
SNAP

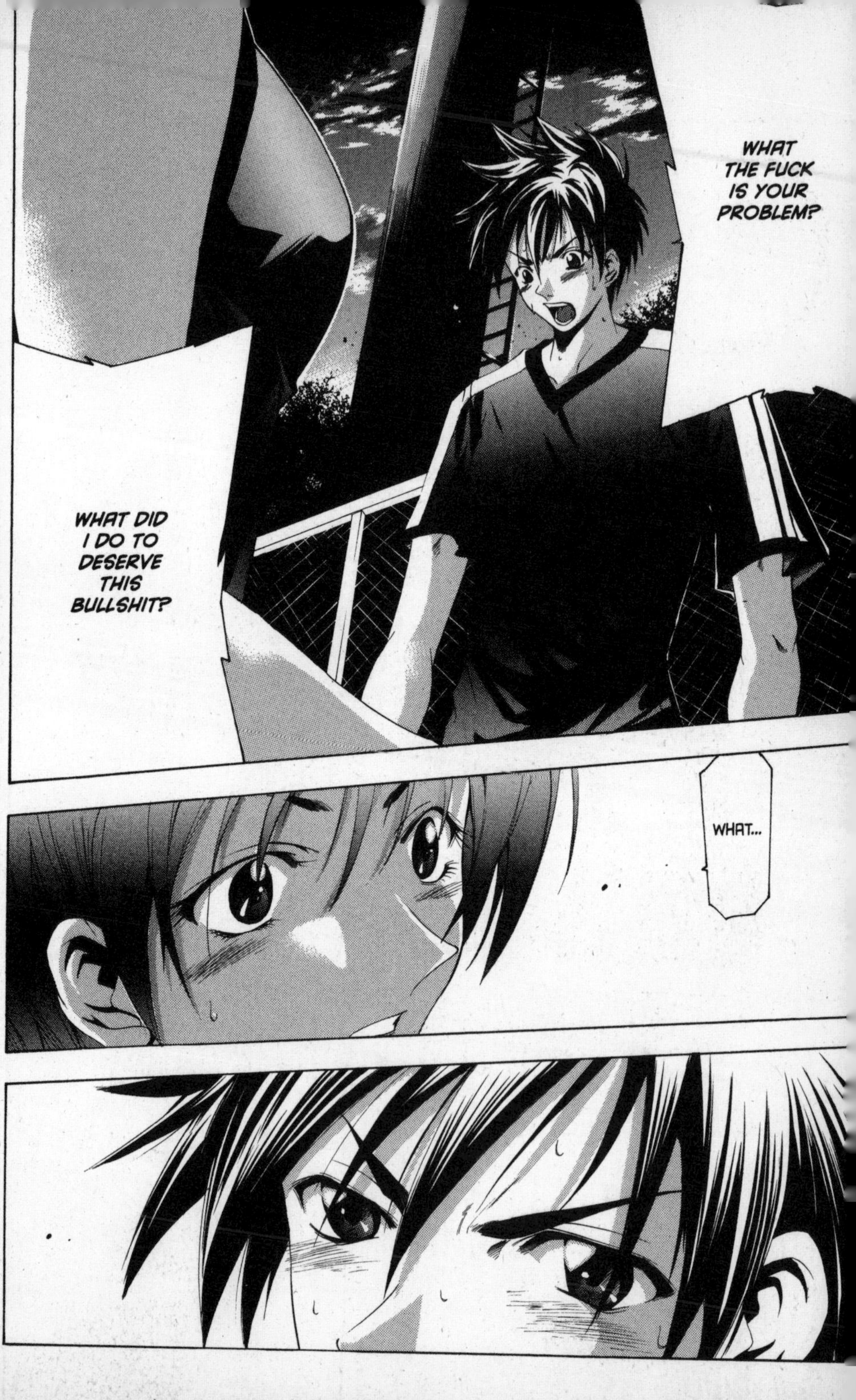
WHAT THE FUCK IS YOUR PROBLEM?
WHAT DID I DO TO DESERVE THIS BULLSHIT?
WHAT...
...
...

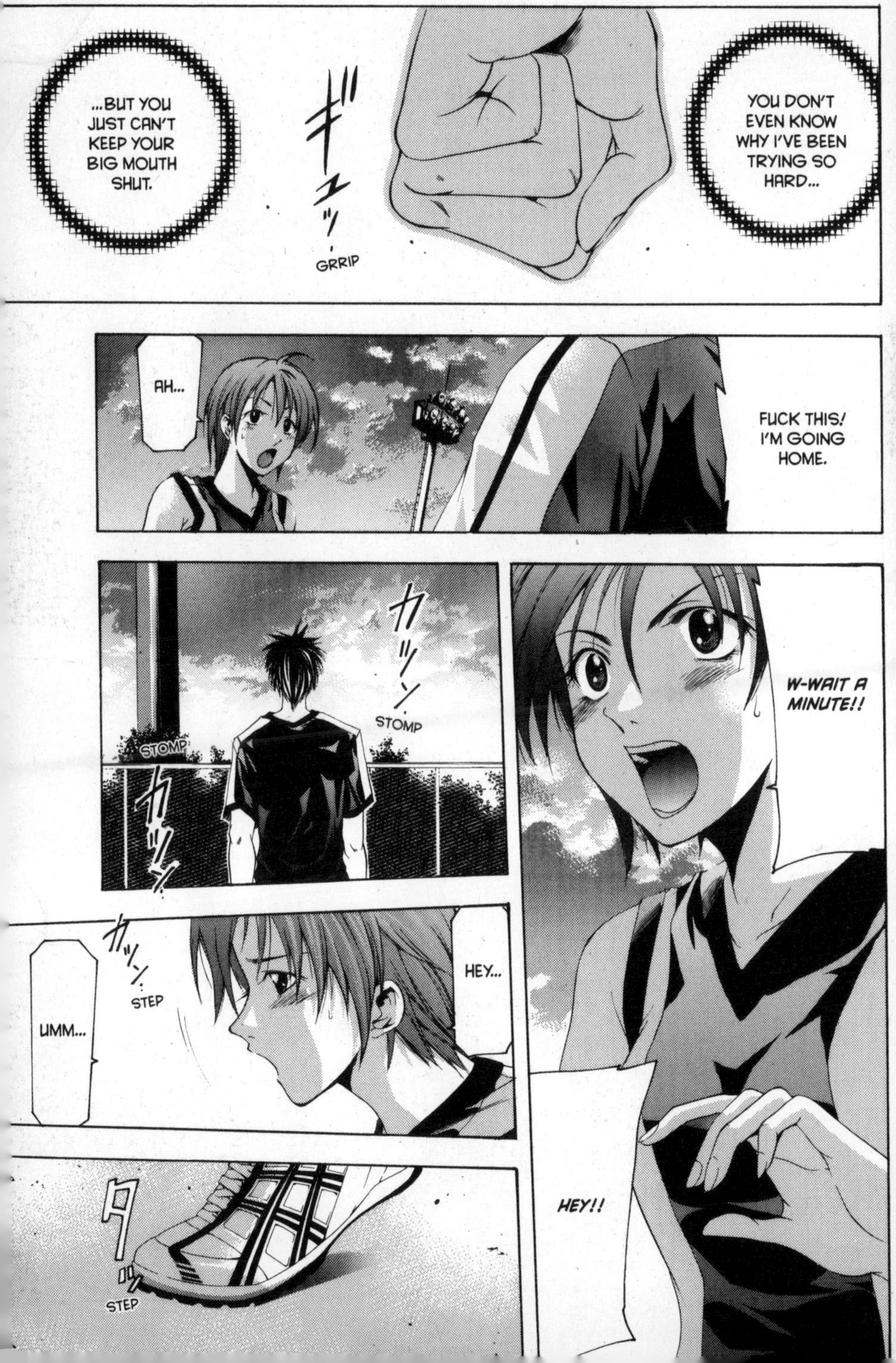
YOU DON'T EVEN KNOW WHY I'VE BEEN TRYING SO HARD...
GRRIP
...BUT YOU JUST CAN'T KEEP YOUR BIG MOUTH SHUT.
FUCK THIS! I'M GOING HOME.
AH...
W-WAIT A MINUTE!!
HEY!!
STOMP
STOMP
HEY...
STEP
UMM...
STEP

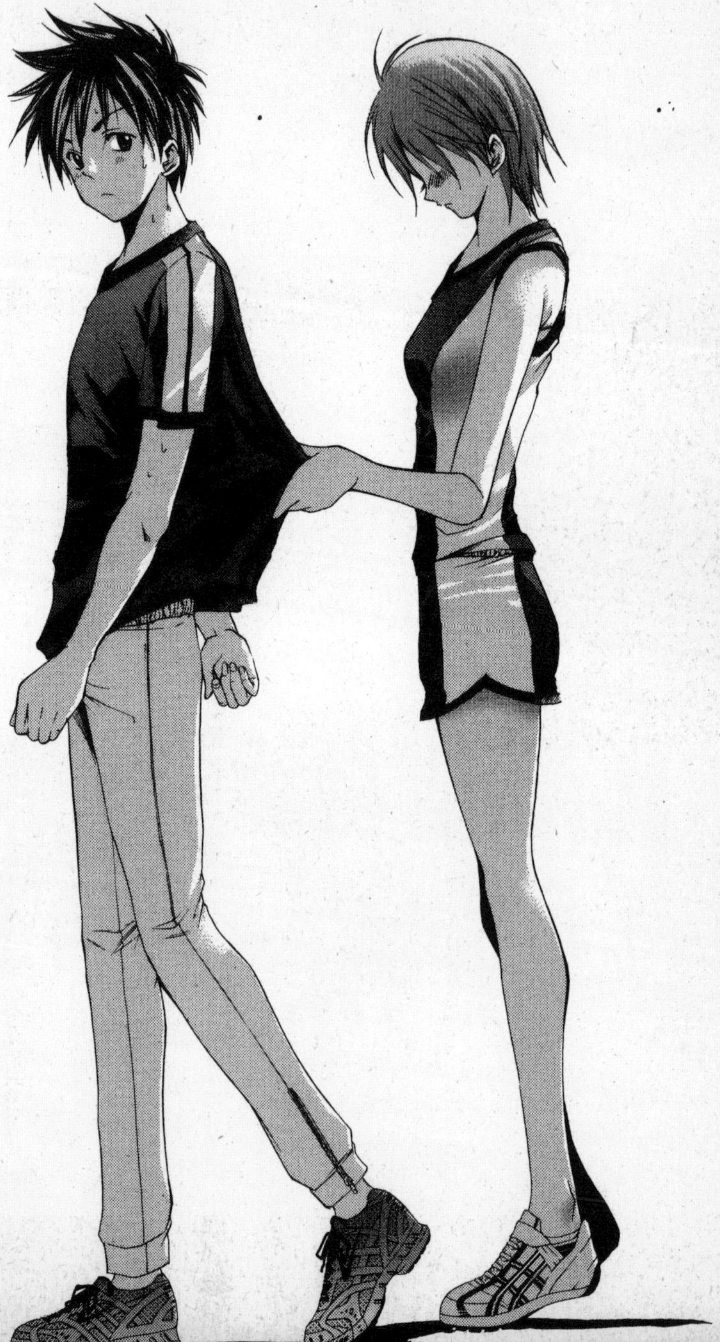

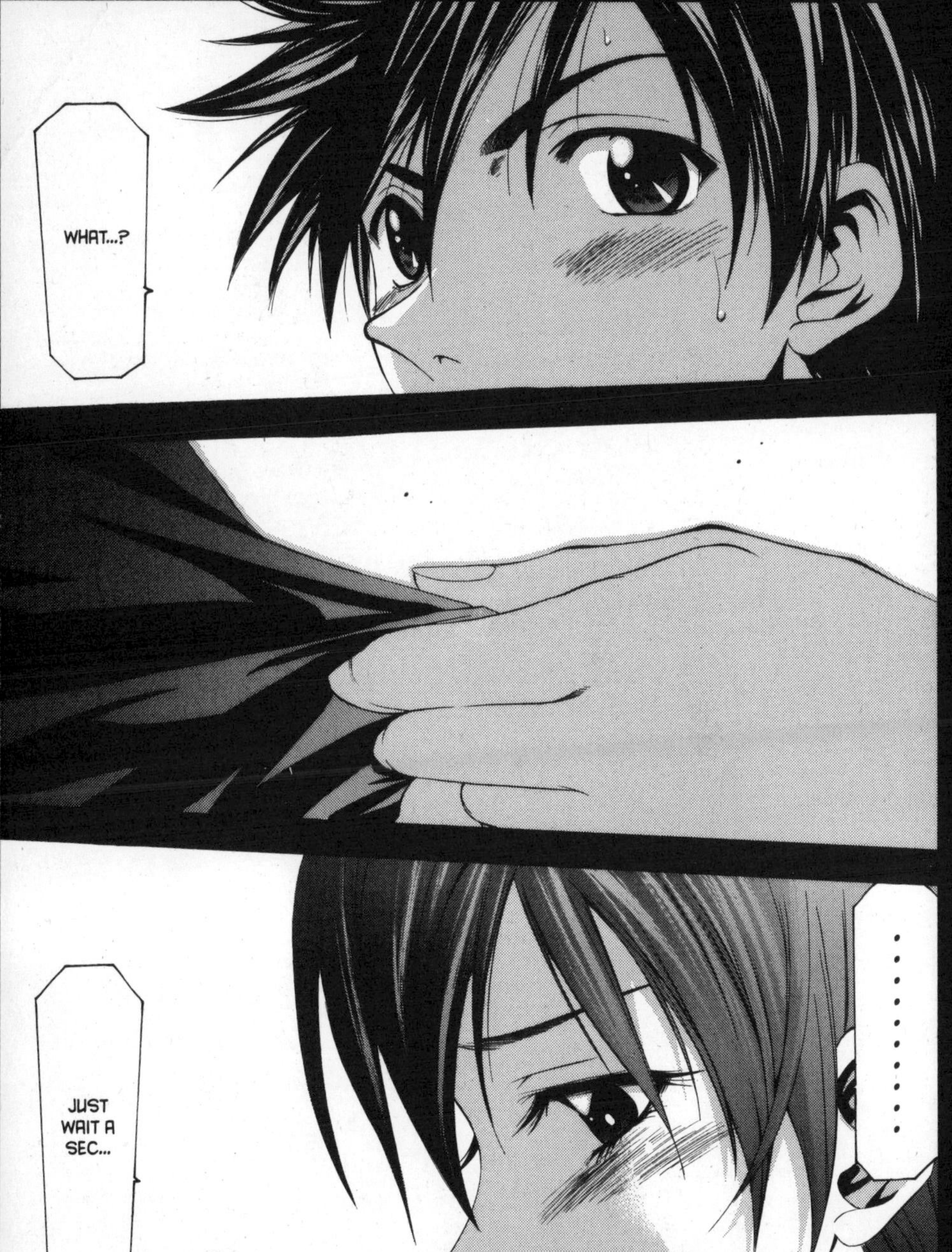
WHAT...?
....
JUST WAIT A SEC...

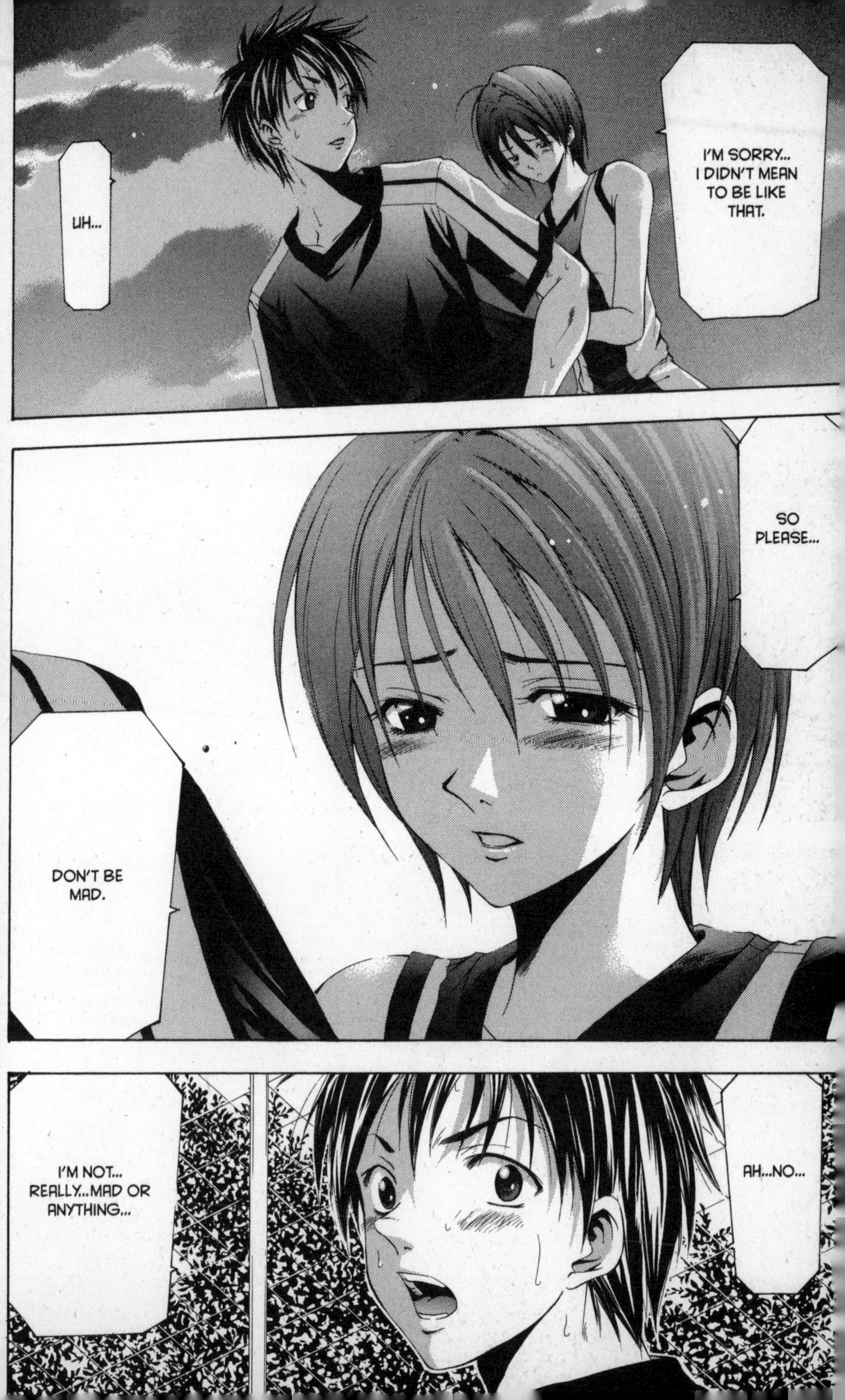
I'M SORRY... I DIDN'T MEAN TO BE LIKE THAT.
UH...
SO PLEASE...
DON'T BE MAD.
AH...NO...
I'M NOT... REALLY...MAD OR ANYTHING...

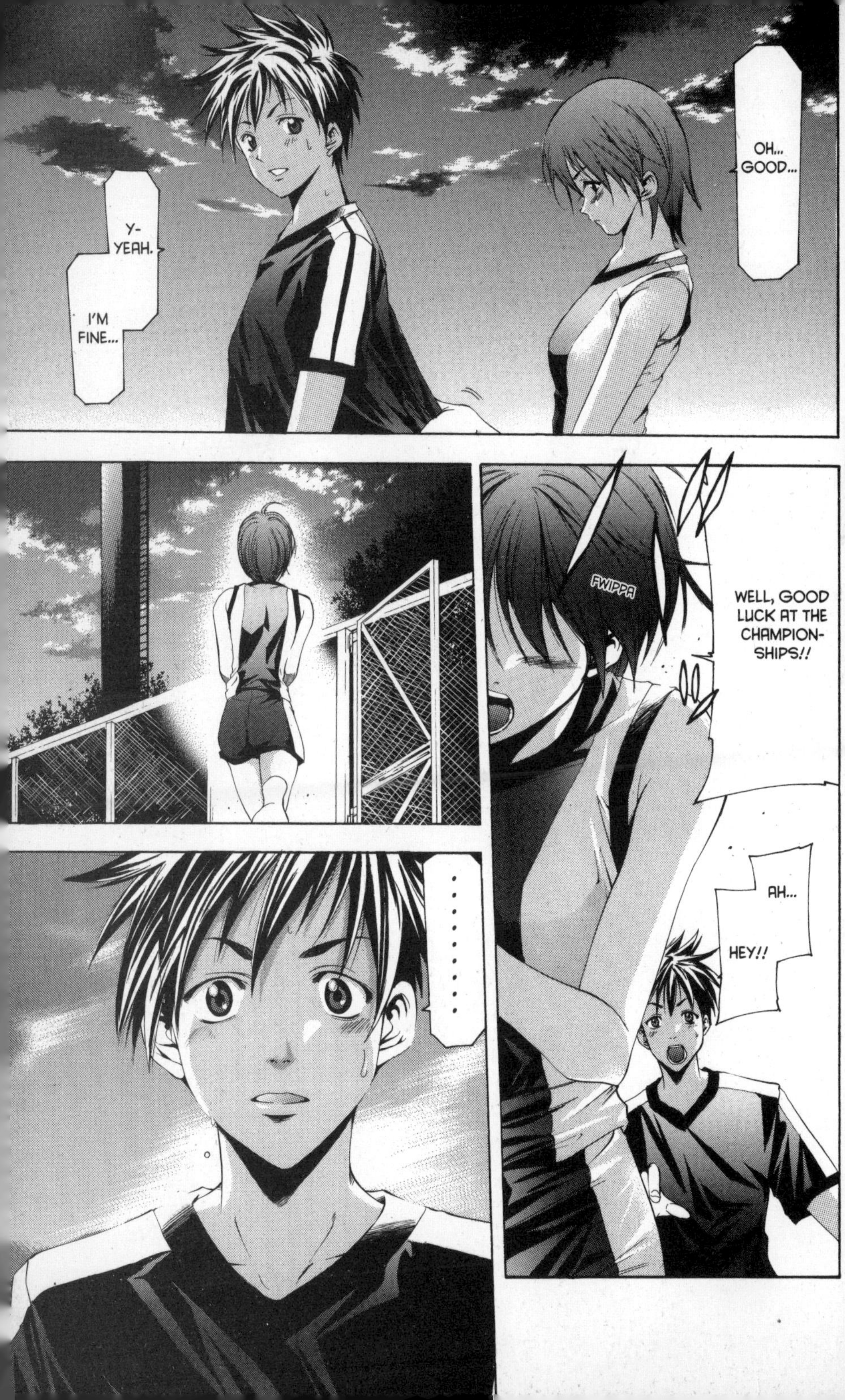
OH... GOOD...
Y- YEAH.
I'M FINE...
FWIPPA
WELL, GOOD LUCK AT THE CHAMPION-SHIPS!!
AH...
HEY!!
....

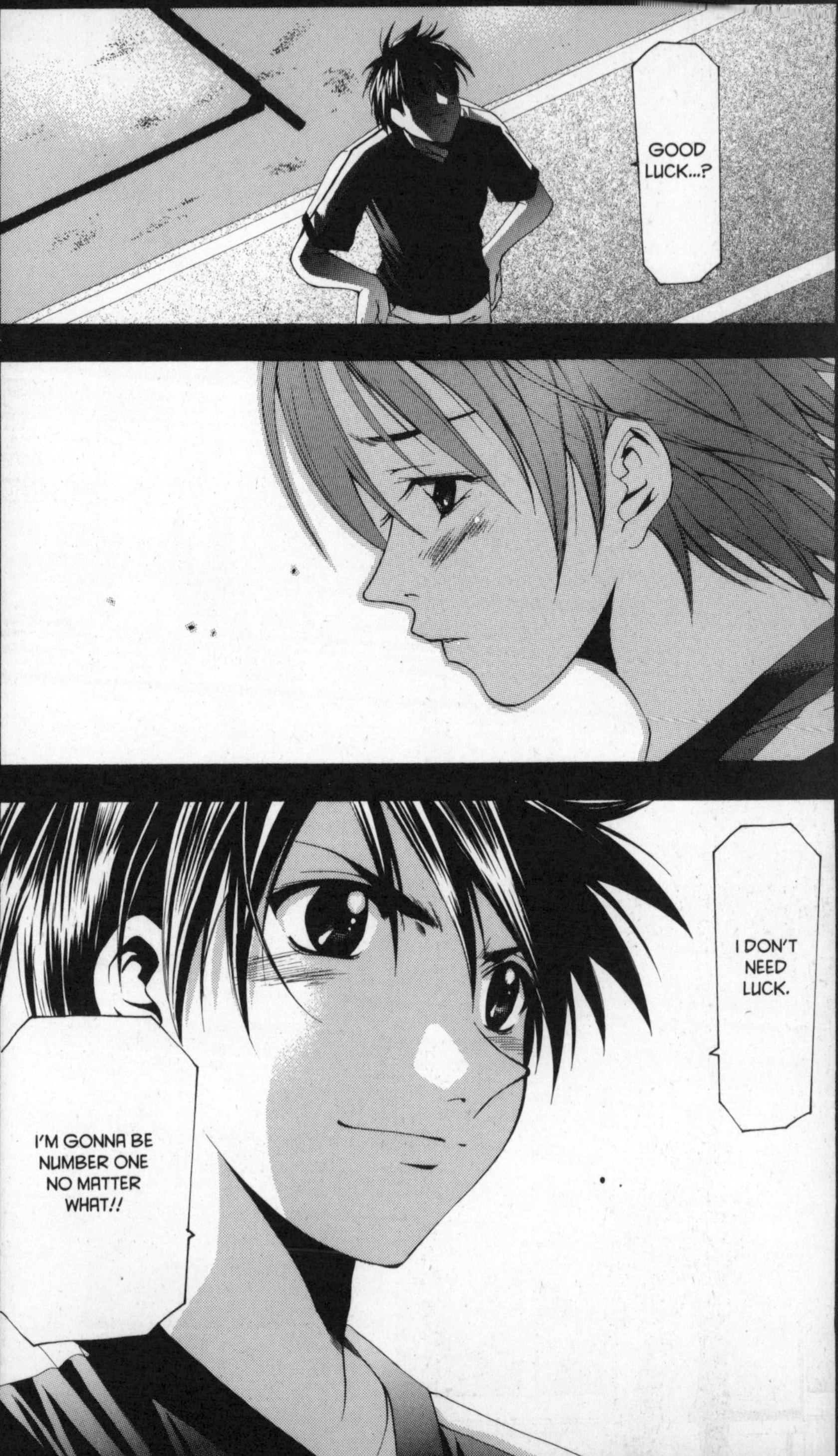
GOOD LUCK...?
I DON'T NEED LUCK.
I'M GONNA BE NUMBER ONE NO MATTER WHAT!!

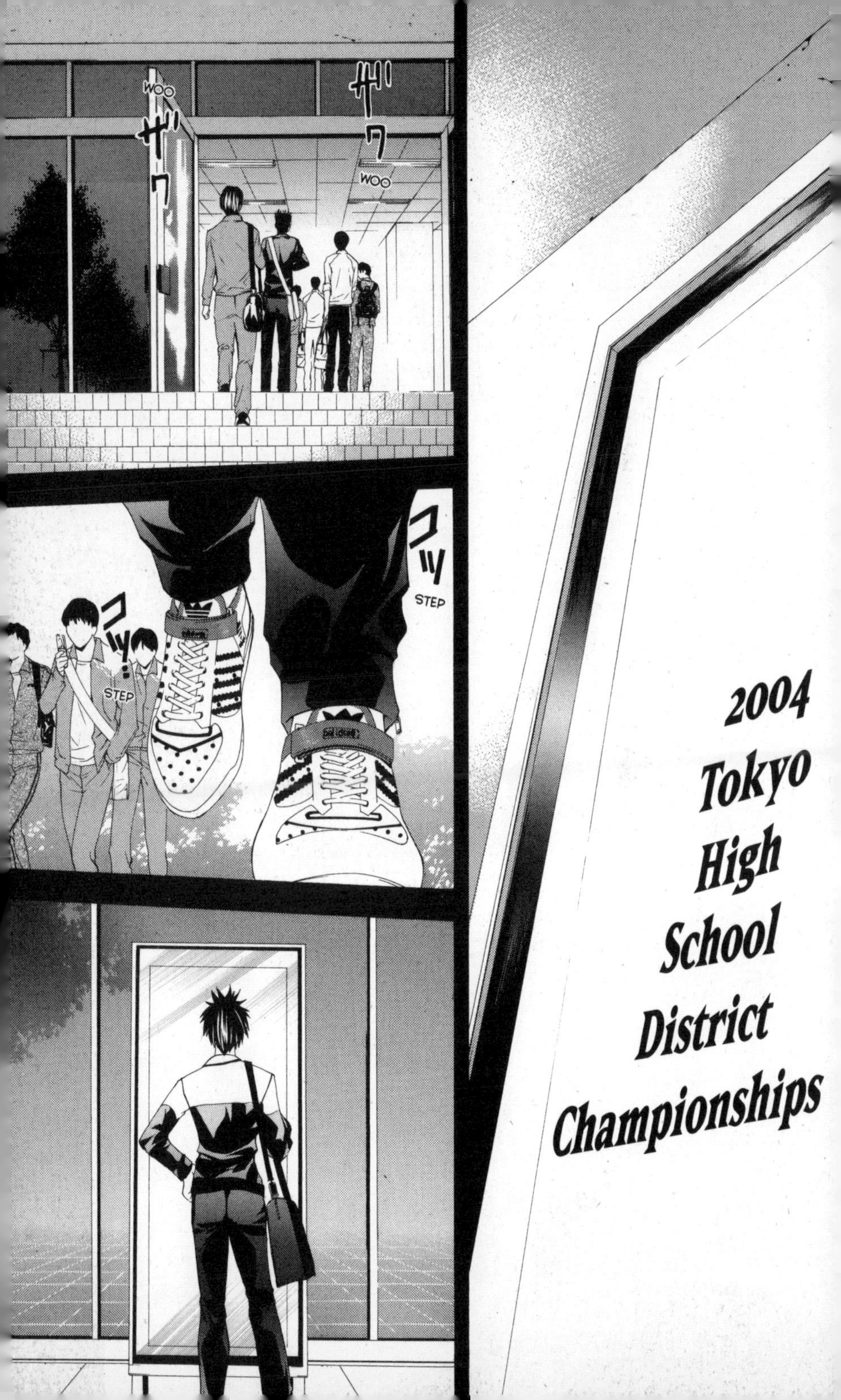
2004 Tokyo High School District Championships
ザワ
WOO
WOO
ザワ
コッ
STEP
コッ
STEP

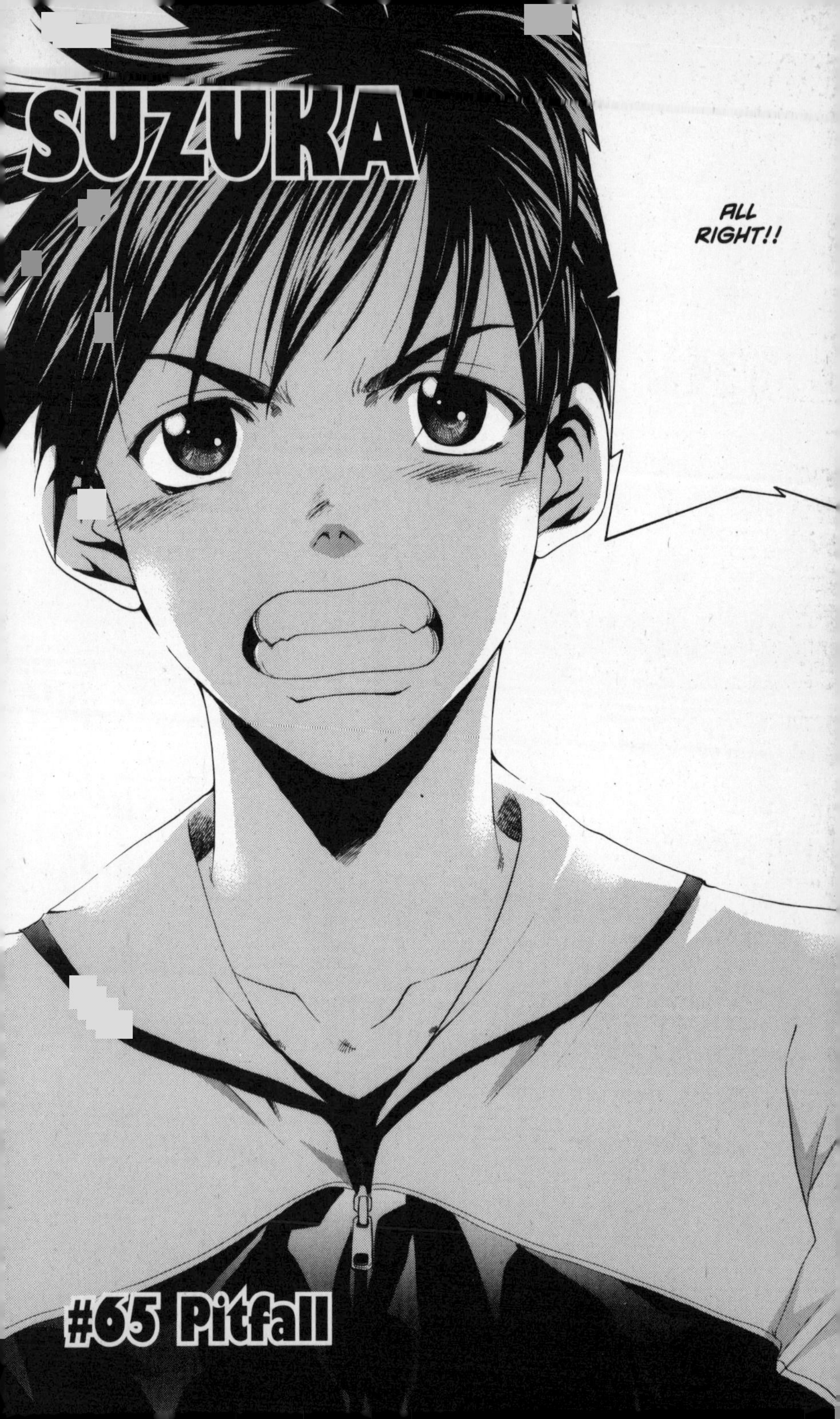
SUZUKA
ALL RIGHT!!
#65 Pitfall

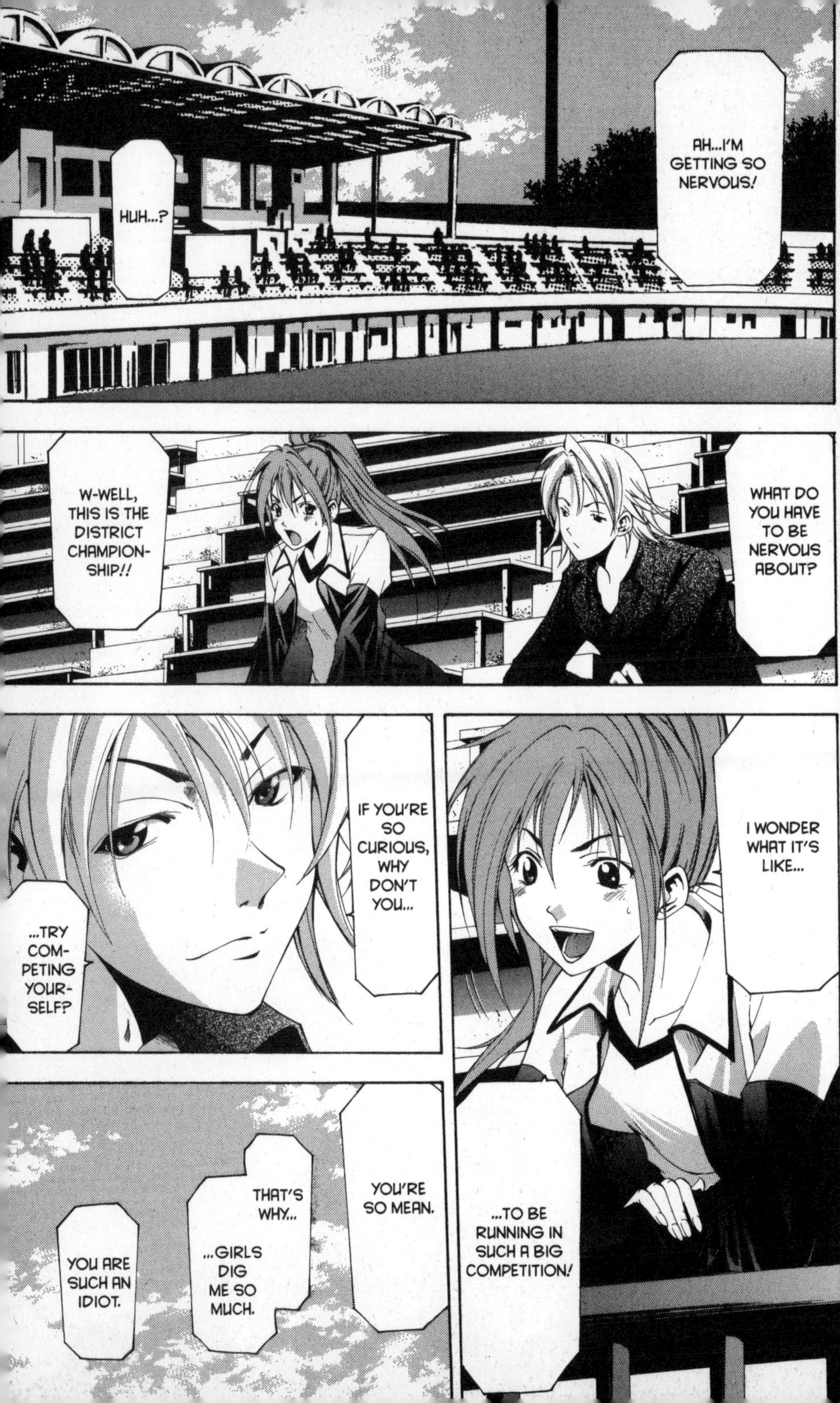
AH...I'M GETTING SO NERVOUS!
HUH...?
WHAT DO YOU HAVE TO BE NERVOUS ABOUT?
W-WELL, THIS IS THE DISTRICT CHAMPIONSHIP!!
I WONDER WHAT IT'S LIKE...
...TO BE RUNNING IN SUCH A BIG COMPETITION!
IF YOU'RE SO CURIOUS, WHY DON'T YOU...
...TRY COMPETING YOURSELF?
YOU'RE SO MEAN.
THAT'S WHY...
...GIRLS DIG ME SO MUCH.
YOU ARE SUCH AN IDIOT.

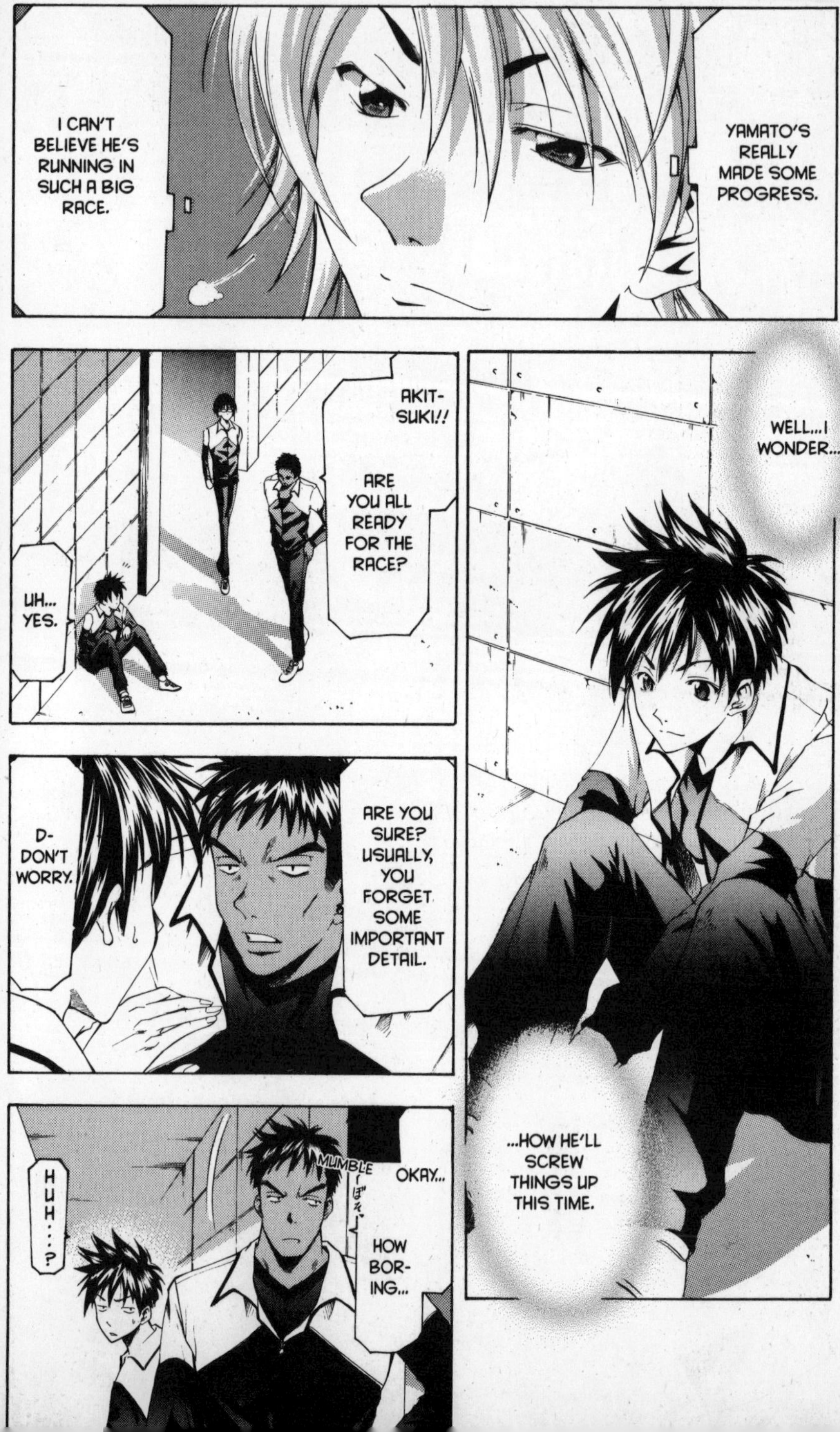
YAMATO'S REALLY MADE SOME PROGRESS.
I CAN'T BELIEVE HE'S RUNNING IN SUCH A BIG RACE.
WELL...I WONDER...
...HOW HE'LL SCREW THINGS UP THIS TIME.
AKIT-SUKI!!
ARE YOU ALL READY FOR THE RACE?
UH... YES.
ARE YOU SURE? USUALLY, YOU FORGET SOME IMPORTANT DETAIL.
D-DON'T WORRY.
OKAY...
MUMBLE
HOW BOR-ING...
HUH...?

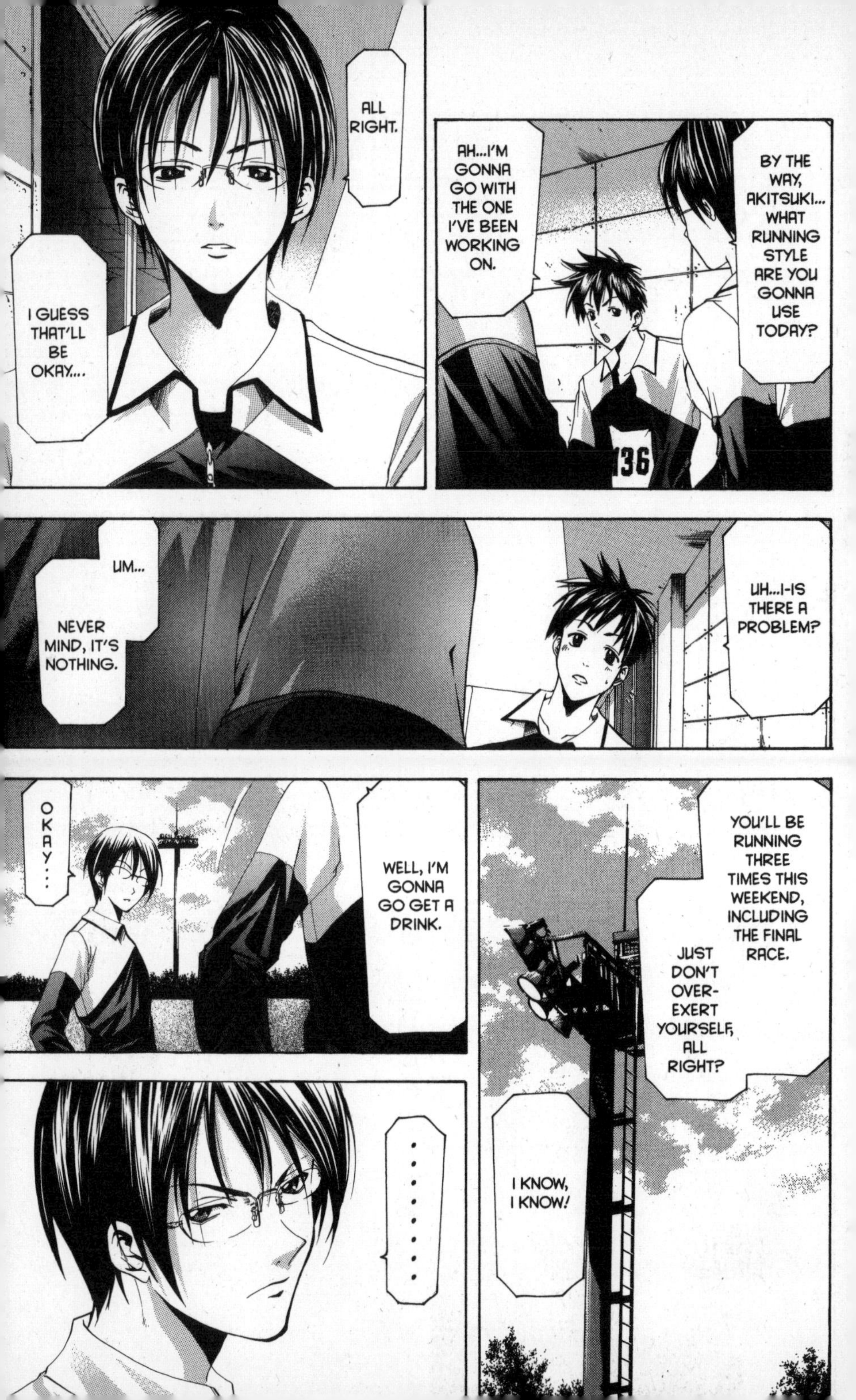
BY THE WAY, AKITSUKI... WHAT RUNNING STYLE ARE YOU GONNA USE TODAY?
AH...I'M GONNA GO WITH THE ONE I'VE BEEN WORKING ON.
136
ALL RIGHT.
I GUESS THAT'LL BE OKAY....
UH...I-IS THERE A PROBLEM?
UM...
NEVER MIND, IT'S NOTHING.
YOU'LL BE RUNNING THREE TIMES THIS WEEKEND, INCLUDING THE FINAL RACE.
JUST DON'T OVER-EXERT YOURSELF, ALL RIGHT?
I KNOW, I KNOW!
WELL, I'M GONNA GO GET A DRINK.
OKAY...
....

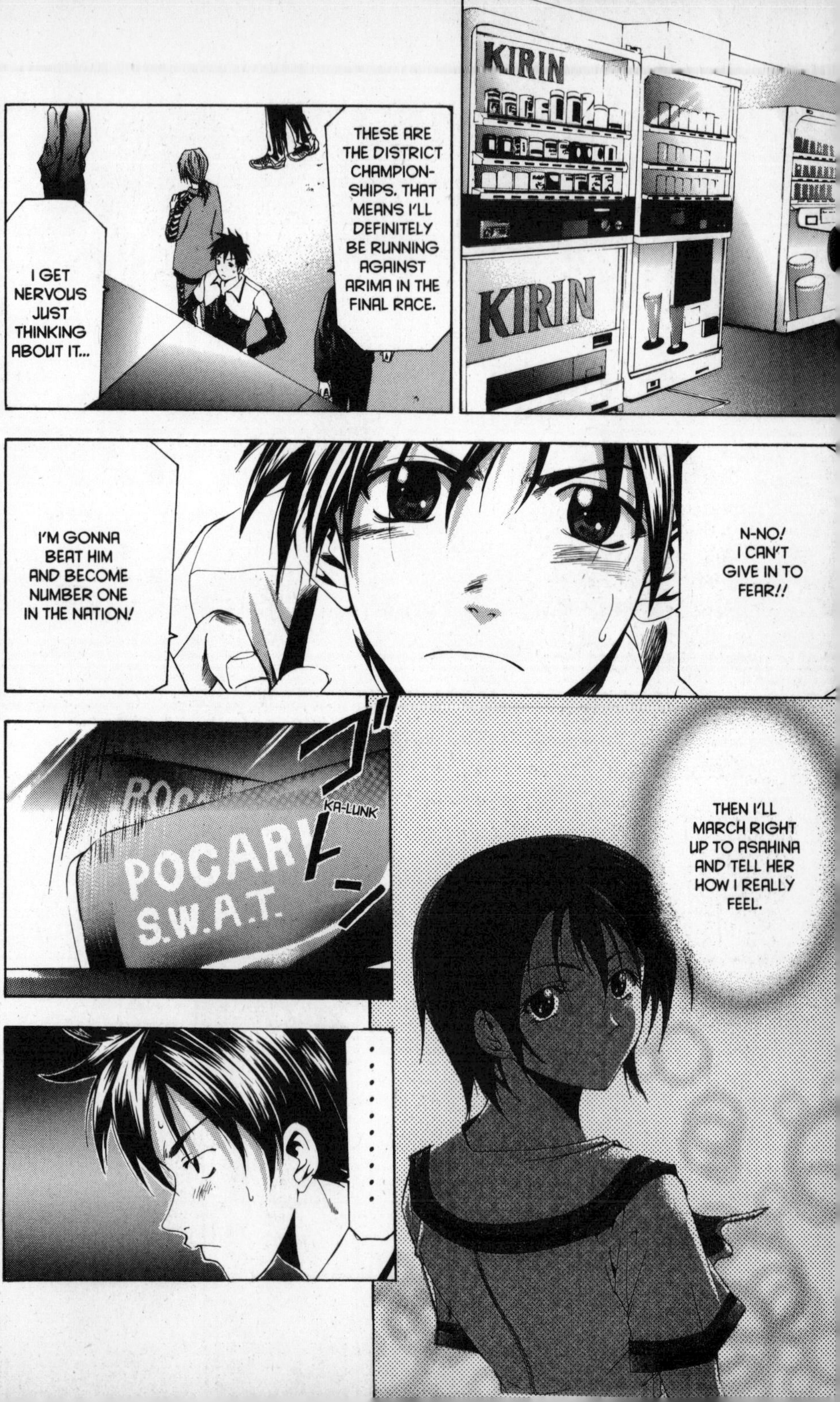
KIRIN
KIRIN
THESE ARE THE DISTRICT CHAMPIONSHIPS. THAT MEANS I'LL DEFINITELY BE RUNNING AGAINST ARIMA IN THE FINAL RACE.
I GET NERVOUS JUST THINKING ABOUT IT...
N-NO! I CAN'T GIVE IN TO FEAR!!
I'M GONNA BEAT HIM AND BECOME NUMBER ONE IN THE NATION!
THEN I'LL MARCH RIGHT UP TO ASAHINA AND TELL HER HOW I REALLY FEEL.
KA-LUNK
POCARI S.W.A.T.
....

...SHE DOESN'T TURN ME DOWN AGAIN.

SHUDDER ズーン...

I JUST HOPE...

I'M SORRY... I DIDN'T MEAN TO BE LIKE THAT...

SO PLEASE... DON'T BE MAD.

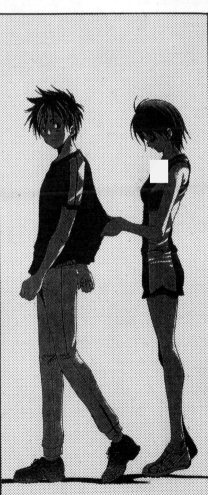

FWIPPA

WELL, GOOD LUCK AT THE CHAMPION-SHIPS!!

...THANKS.

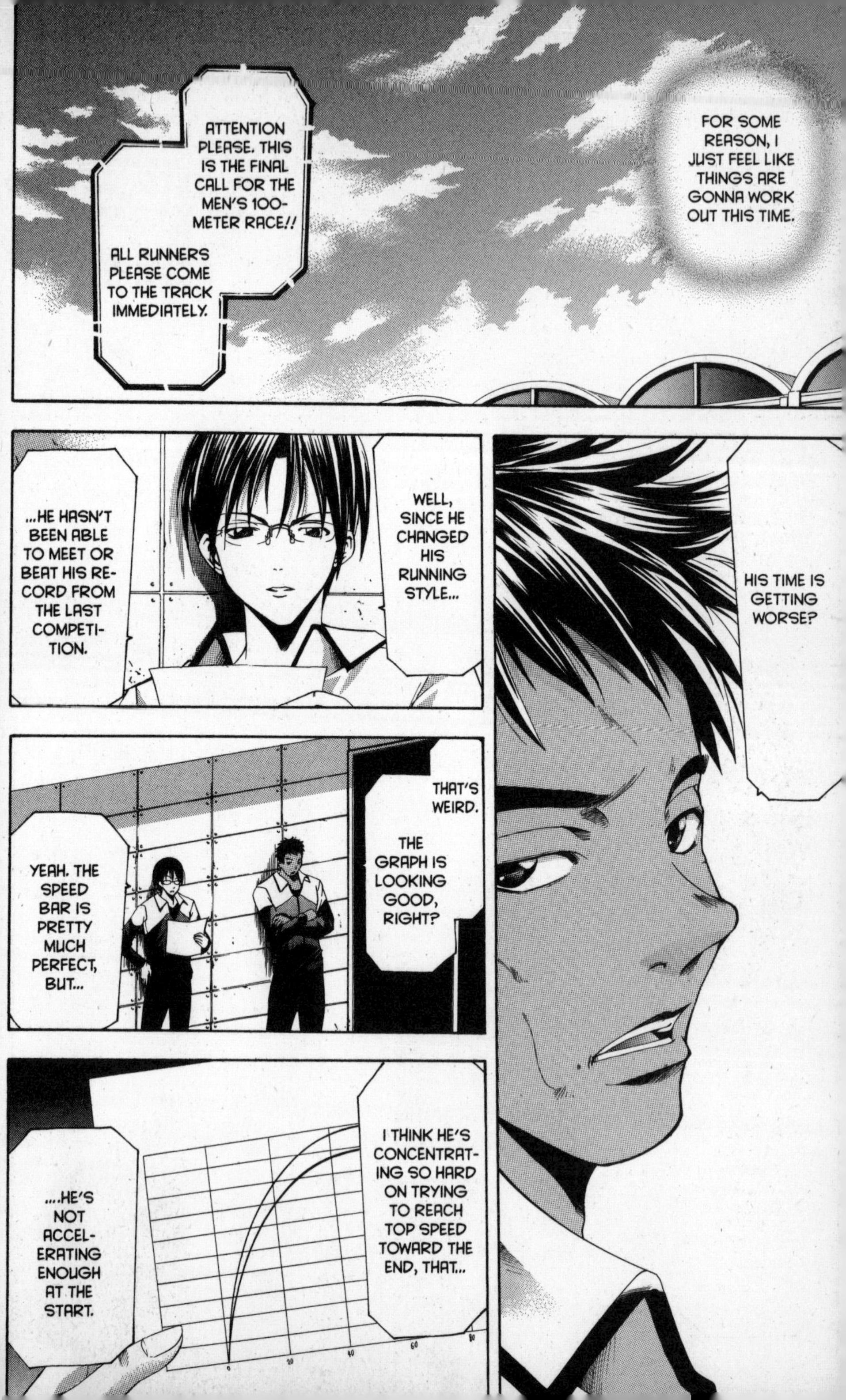
FOR SOME REASON, I JUST FEEL LIKE THINGS ARE GONNA WORK OUT THIS TIME.
ATTENTION PLEASE. THIS IS THE FINAL CALL FOR THE MEN'S 100-METER RACE!!
ALL RUNNERS PLEASE COME TO THE TRACK IMMEDIATELY.
HIS TIME IS GETTING WORSE?
WELL, SINCE HE CHANGED HIS RUNNING STYLE...
...HE HASN'T BEEN ABLE TO MEET OR BEAT HIS RE-CORD FROM THE LAST COMPETI-TION.
THAT'S WEIRD.
THE GRAPH IS LOOKING GOOD, RIGHT?
YEAH. THE SPEED BAR IS PRETTY MUCH PERFECT, BUT...
I THINK HE'S CONCENTRAT-ING SO HARD ON TRYING TO REACH TOP SPEED TOWARD THE END, THAT...
....HE'S NOT ACCEL-ERATING ENOUGH AT THE START.
0 20 40 60 80

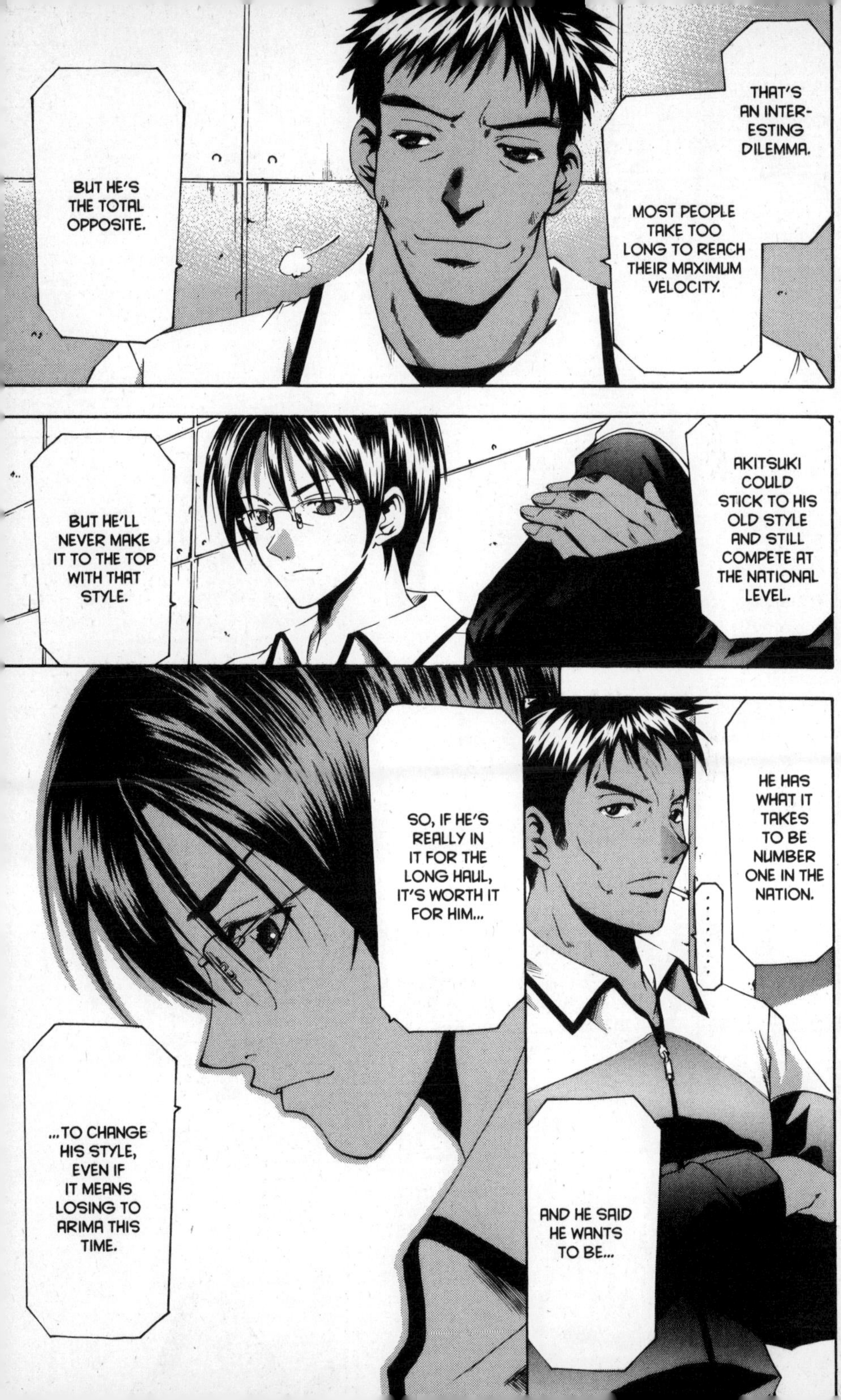
THAT'S AN INTER-ESTING DILEMMA.
MOST PEOPLE TAKE TOO LONG TO REACH THEIR MAXIMUM VELOCITY.
BUT HE'S THE TOTAL OPPOSITE.
AKITSUKI COULD STICK TO HIS OLD STYLE AND STILL COMPETE AT THE NATIONAL LEVEL.
BUT HE'LL NEVER MAKE IT TO THE TOP WITH THAT STYLE.
HE HAS WHAT IT TAKES TO BE NUMBER ONE IN THE NATION.
....
AND HE SAID HE WANTS TO BE...
SO, IF HE'S REALLY IN IT FOR THE LONG HAUL, IT'S WORTH IT FOR HIM...
...TO CHANGE HIS STYLE, EVEN IF IT MEANS LOSING TO ARIMA THIS TIME.

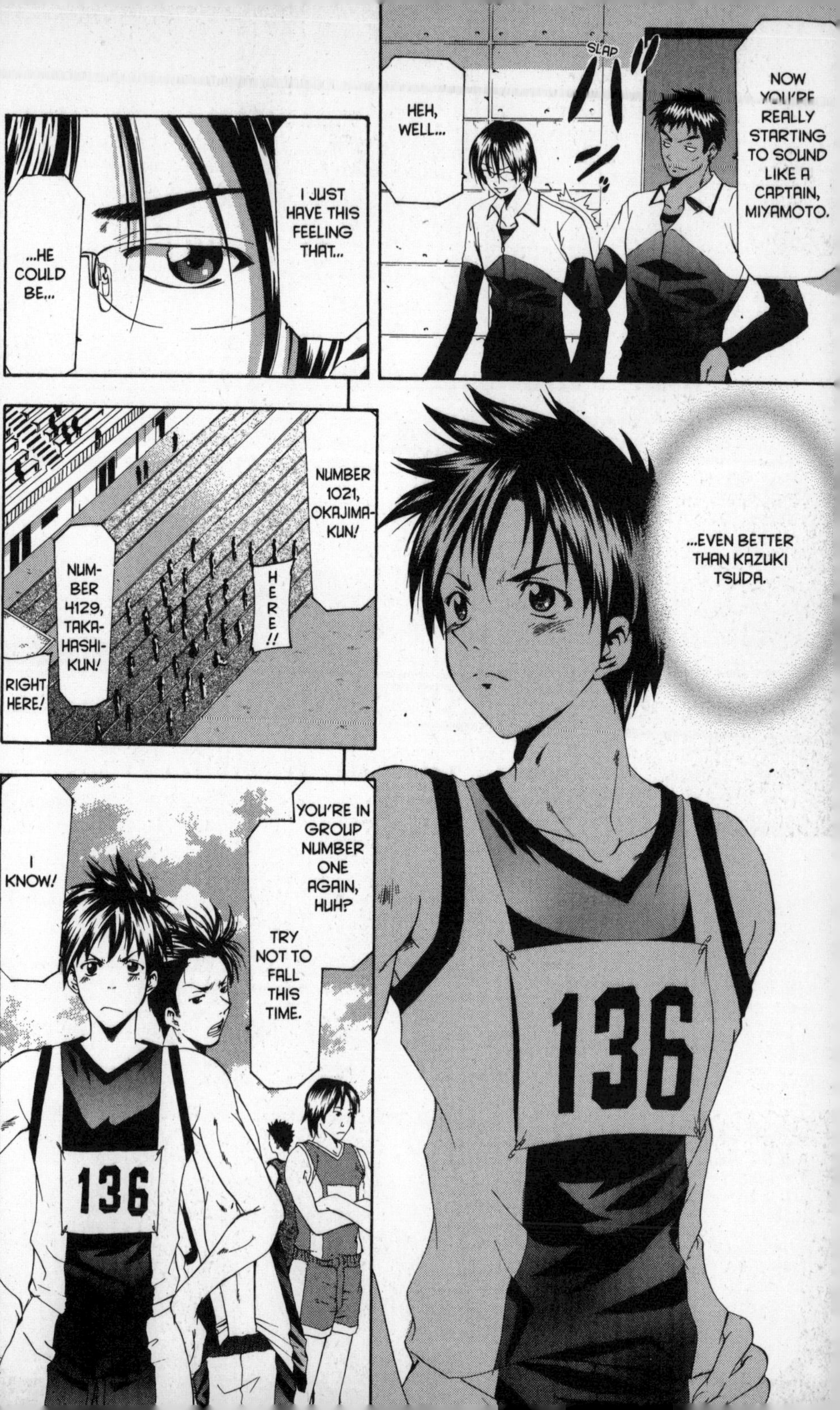

NOW YOU'RE REALLY STARTING TO SOUND LIKE A CAPTAIN, MIYAMOTO.
SLAP
HEH, WELL...
I JUST HAVE THIS FEELING THAT...
...HE COULD BE...
...EVEN BETTER THAN KAZUKI TSUDA.
136
NUMBER 1021, OKAJIMA-KUN!
HERE!!
NUMBER 4129, TAKAHASHI-KUN!
RIGHT HERE!
YOU'RE IN GROUP NUMBER ONE AGAIN, HUH?
TRY NOT TO FALL THIS TIME.
I KNOW!
136

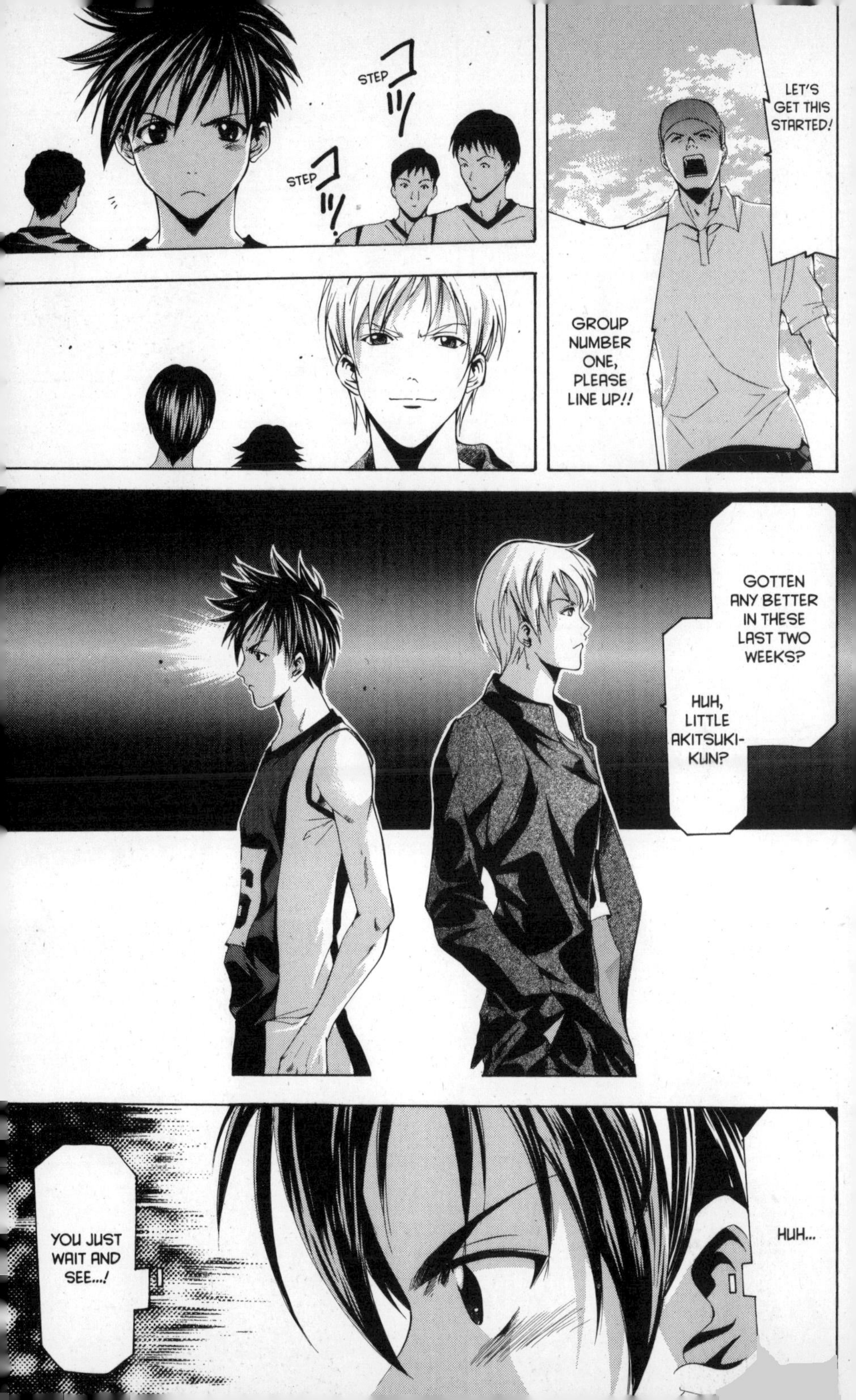
LET'S GET THIS STARTED!
GROUP NUMBER ONE, PLEASE LINE UP!!
STEP
コツ
STEP
コツ!
GOTTEN ANY BETTER IN THESE LAST TWO WEEKS?
HUH, LITTLE AKITSUKI-KUN?
HUH...
YOU JUST WAIT AND SEE...!

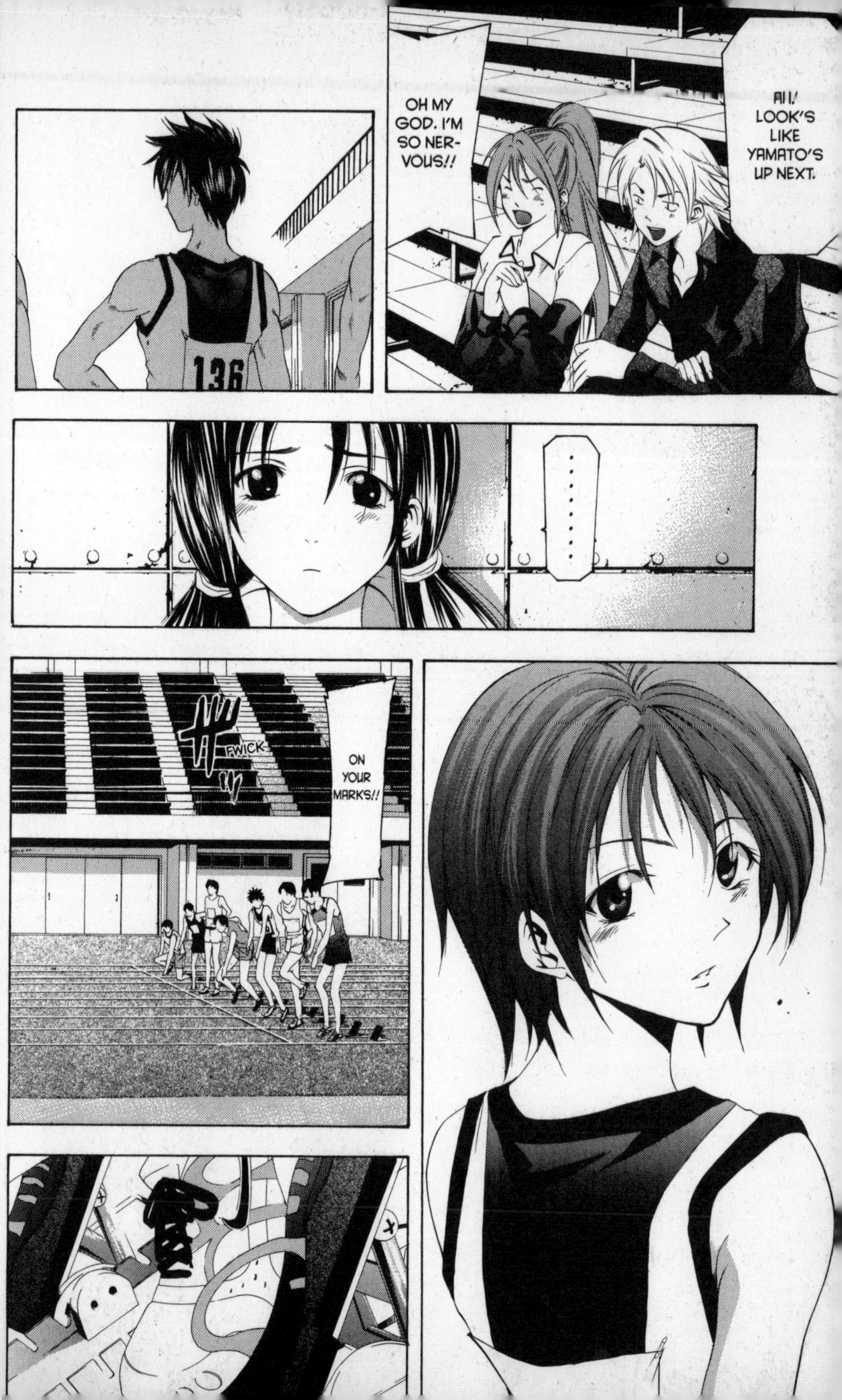
AH! LOOK'S LIKE YAMATO'S UP NEXT.
OH MY GOD. I'M SO NER-VOUS!!
......
ON YOUR MARKS!!
FWICK

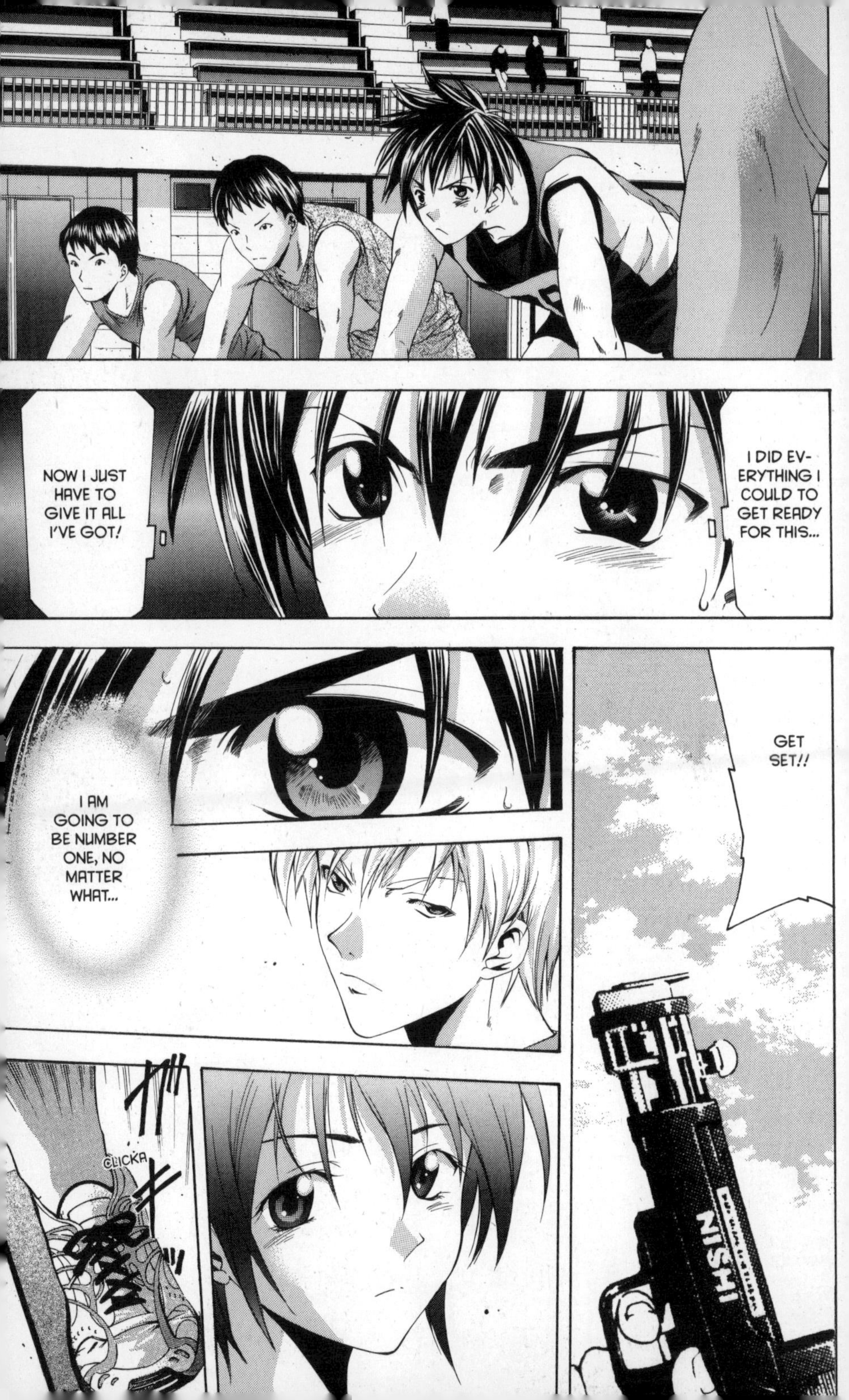
I DID EV-ERYTHING I COULD TO GET READY FOR THIS...
NOW I JUST HAVE TO GIVE IT ALL I'VE GOT!
GET SET!!
NISHI
I AM GOING TO BE NUMBER ONE, NO MATTER WHAT...
CLICKA

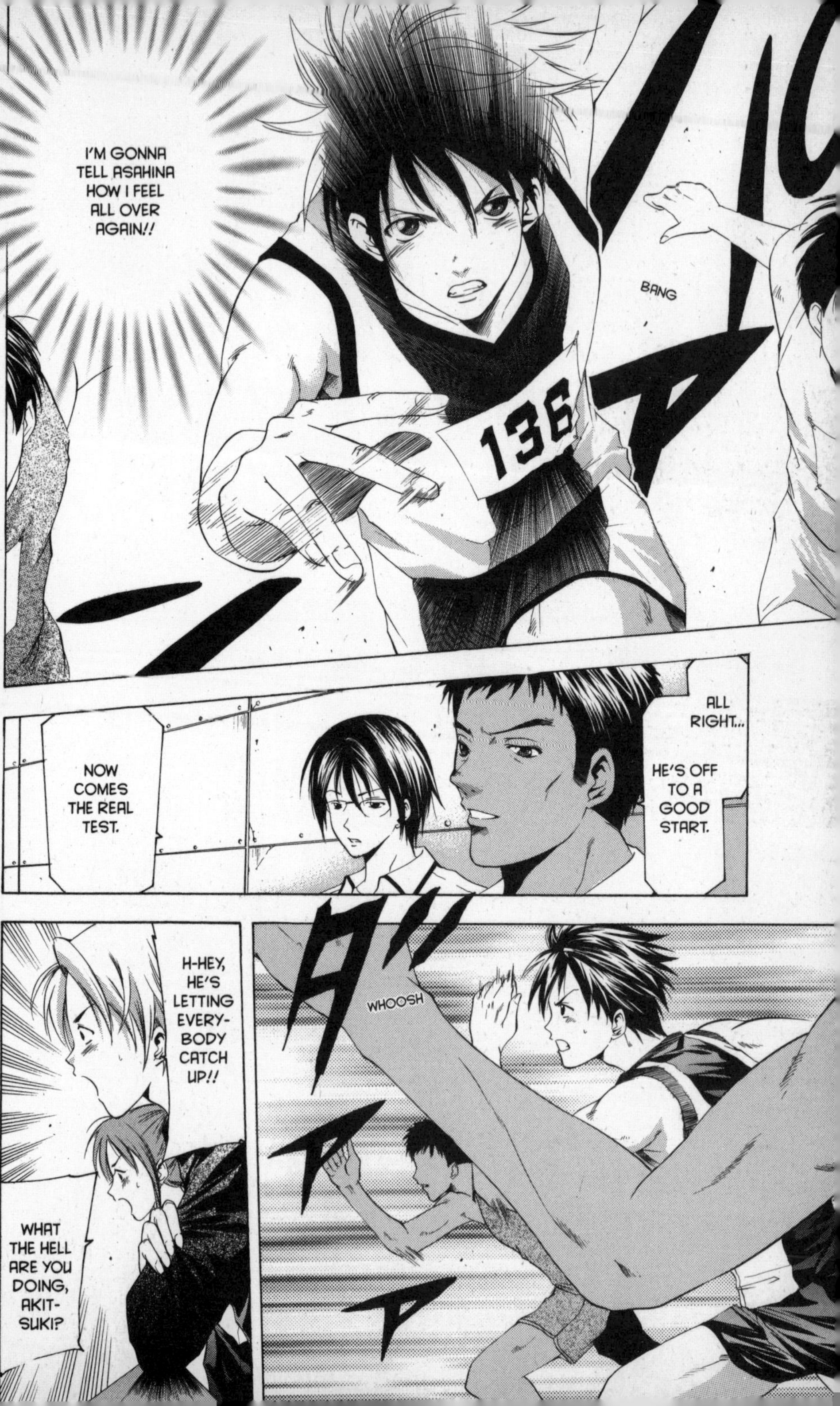
BANG
I'M GONNA TELL ASAHINA HOW I FEEL ALL OVER AGAIN!!
ALL RIGHT...
HE'S OFF TO A GOOD START.
NOW COMES THE REAL TEST.
WHOOSH
H-HEY, HE'S LETTING EVERY-BODY CATCH UP!!
WHAT THE HELL ARE YOU DOING, AKIT-SUKI?

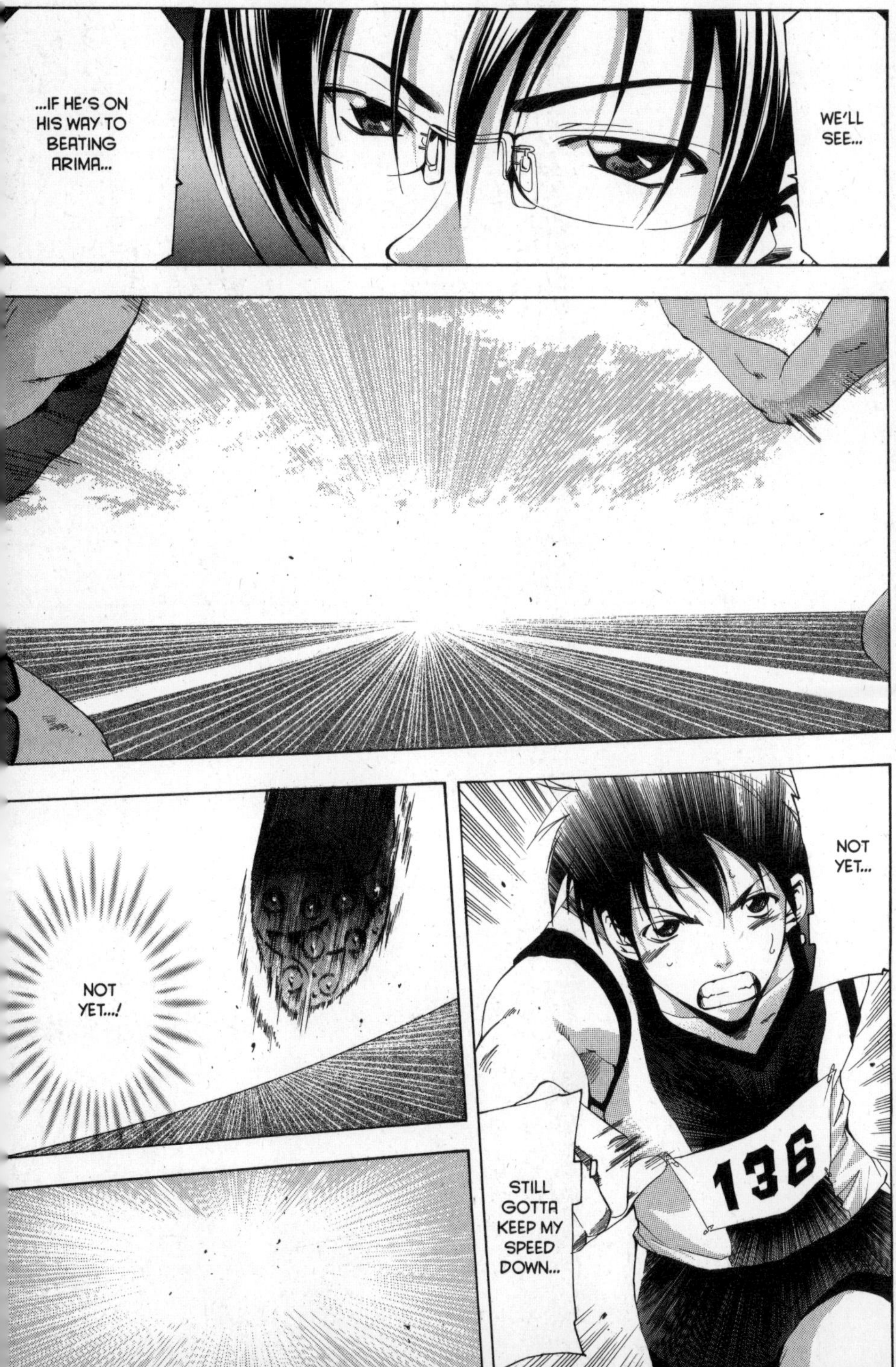
WE'LL SEE...
...IF HE'S ON HIS WAY TO BEATING ARIMA...
NOT YET...
STILL GOTTA KEEP MY SPEED DOWN...
NOT YET...!
136

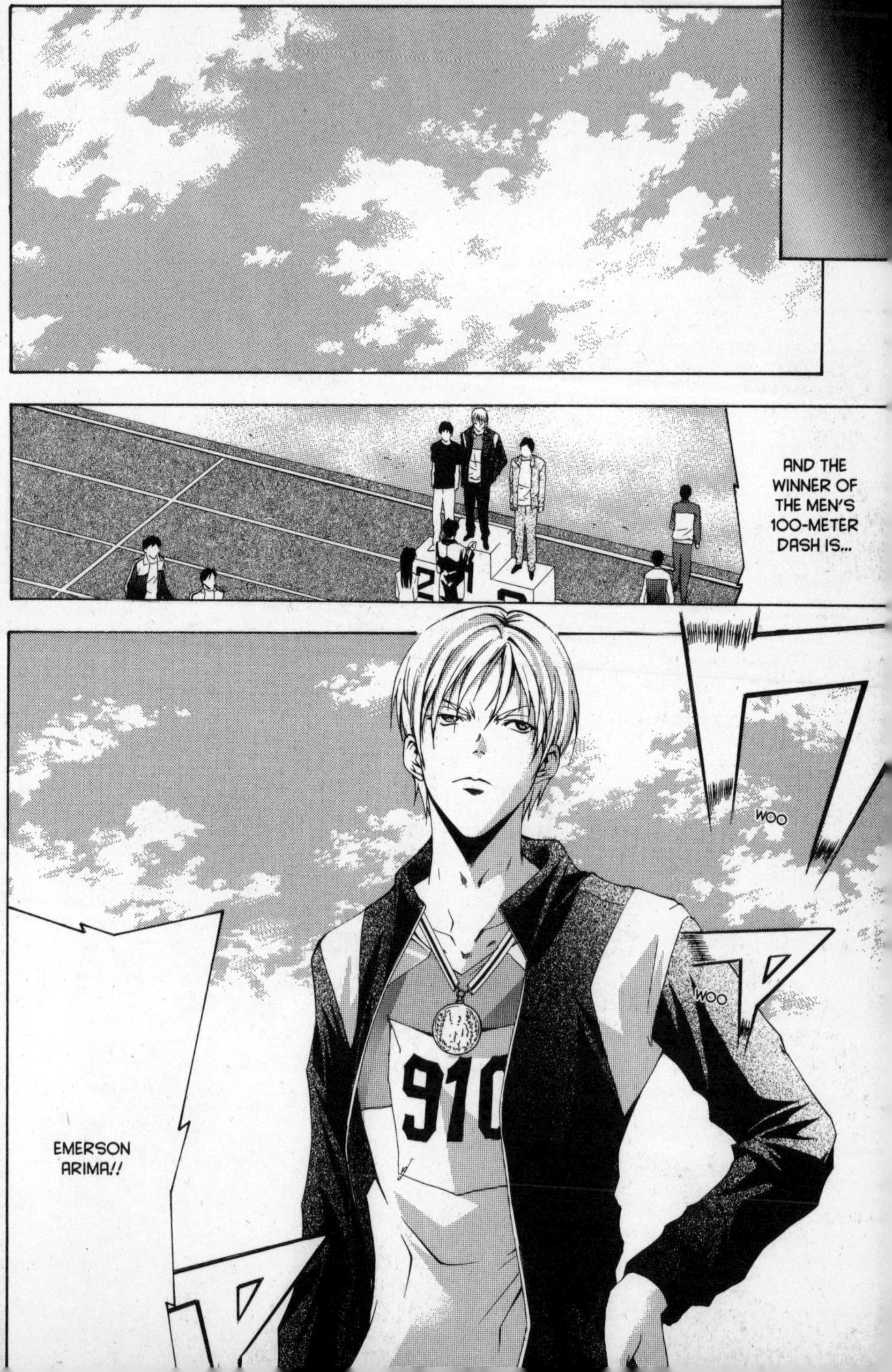
AND THE WINNER OF THE MEN'S 100-METER DASH IS...
WOO
WOO
EMERSON ARIMA!!
910

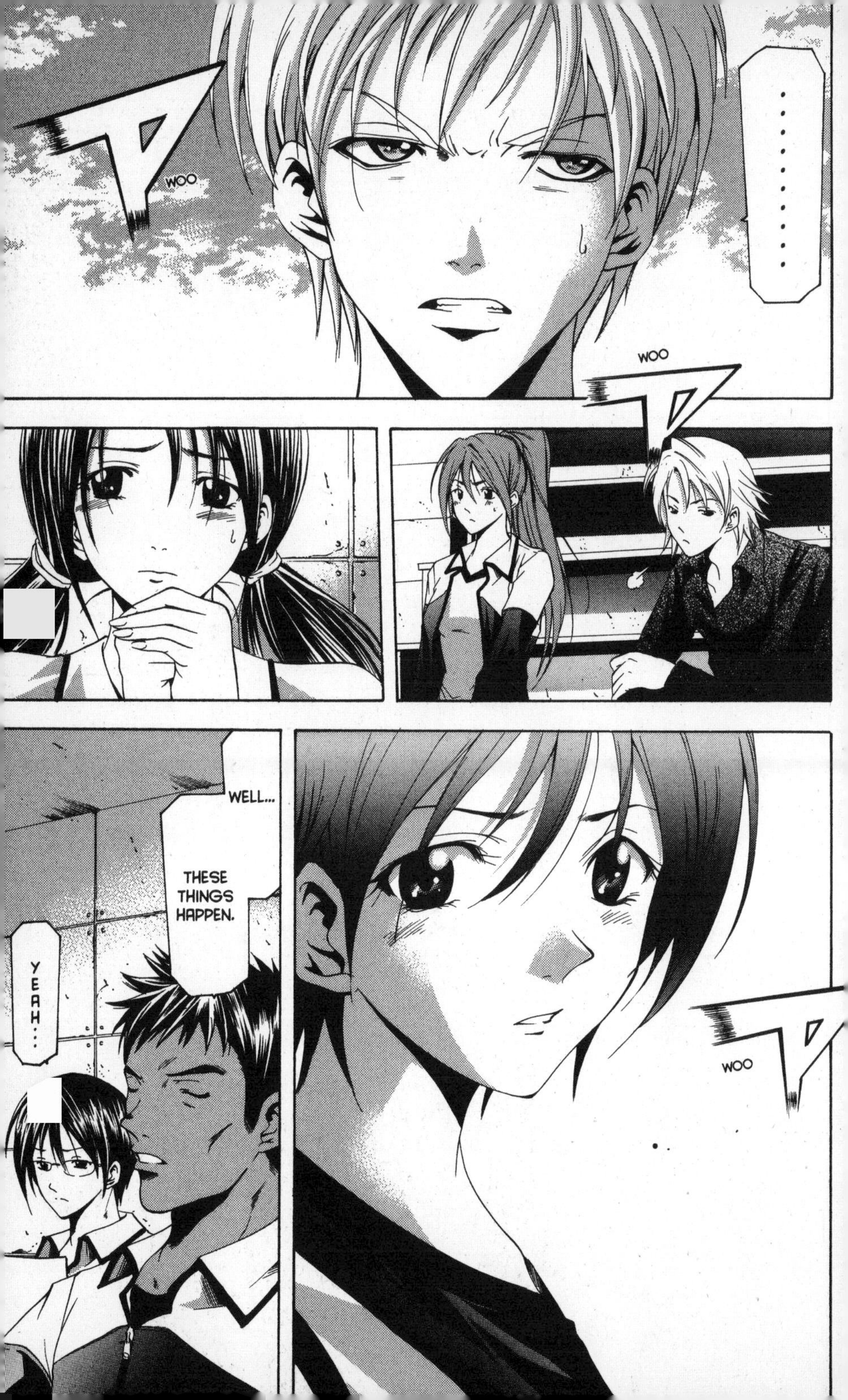
....
WOO
WOO
WOO
..
WELL...
THESE THINGS HAPPEN.
YEAH...

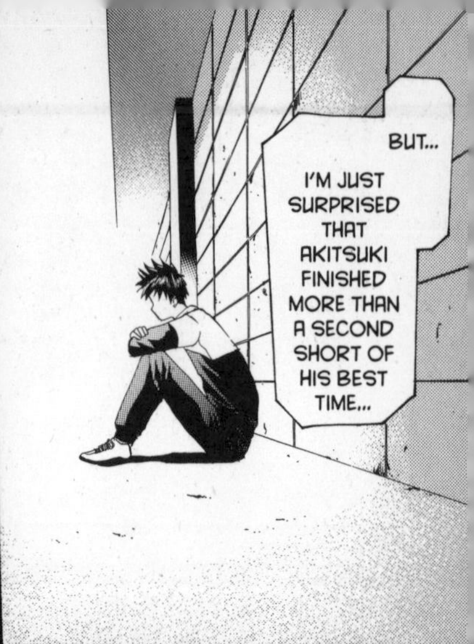
BUT...
I'M JUST SURPRISED THAT AKITSUKI FINISHED MORE THAN A SECOND SHORT OF HIS BEST TIME...

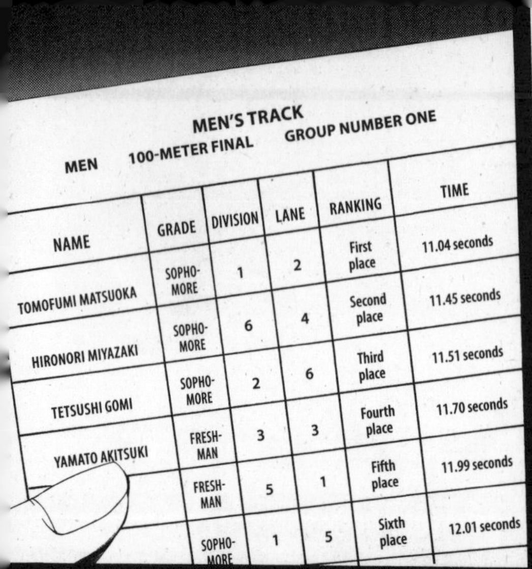

MEN'S TRACK

MEN 100-METER FINAL GROUP NUMBER ONE

NAME	GRADE	DIVISION	LANE	RANKING	TIME
TOMOFUMI MATSUOKA	SOPHOMORE	1	2	First place	11.04 seconds
HIRONORI MIYAZAKI	SOPHOMORE	6	4	Second place	11.45 seconds
TETSUSHI GOMI	SOPHOMORE	2	6	Third place	11.51 seconds
YAMATO AKITSUKI	FRESHMAN	3	3	Fourth place	11.70 seconds
	FRESHMAN	5	1	Fifth place	11.99 seconds
	SOPHOMORE	1	5	Sixth place	12.01 seconds

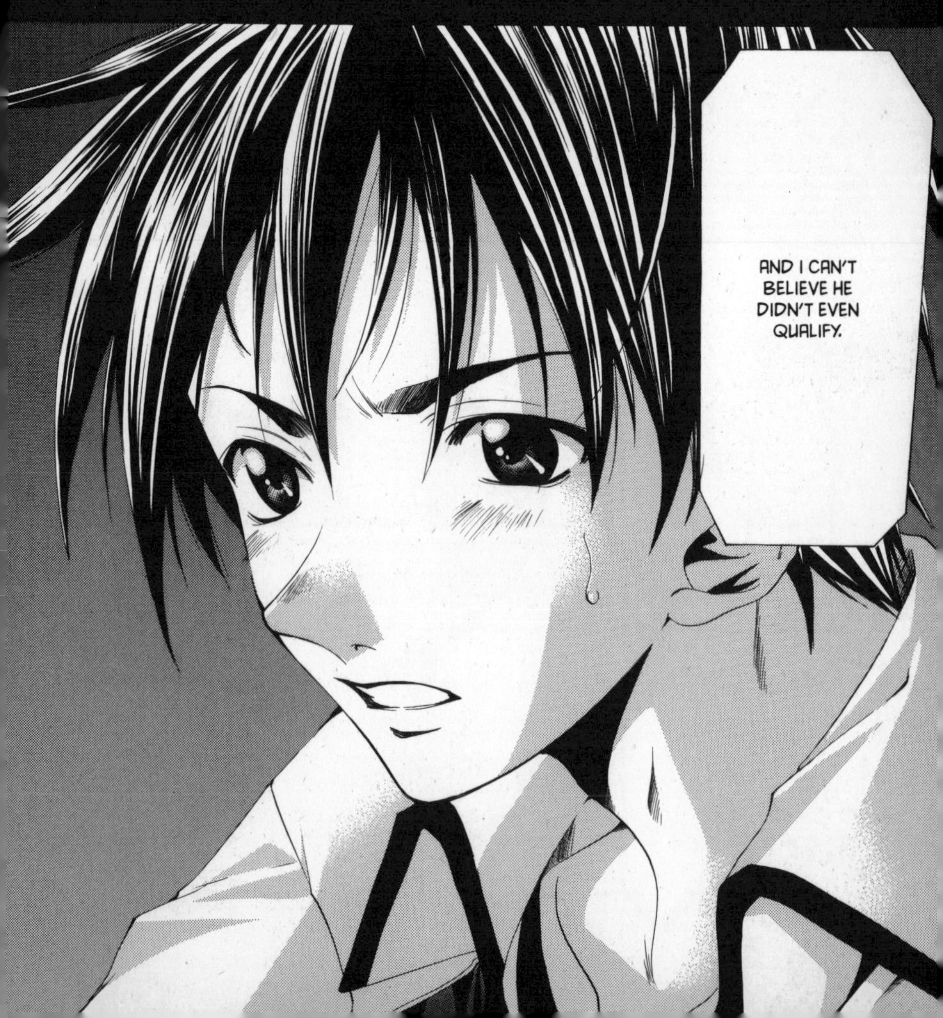
AND I CAN'T BELIEVE HE DIDN'T EVEN QUALIFY.

#66 Miscalculation

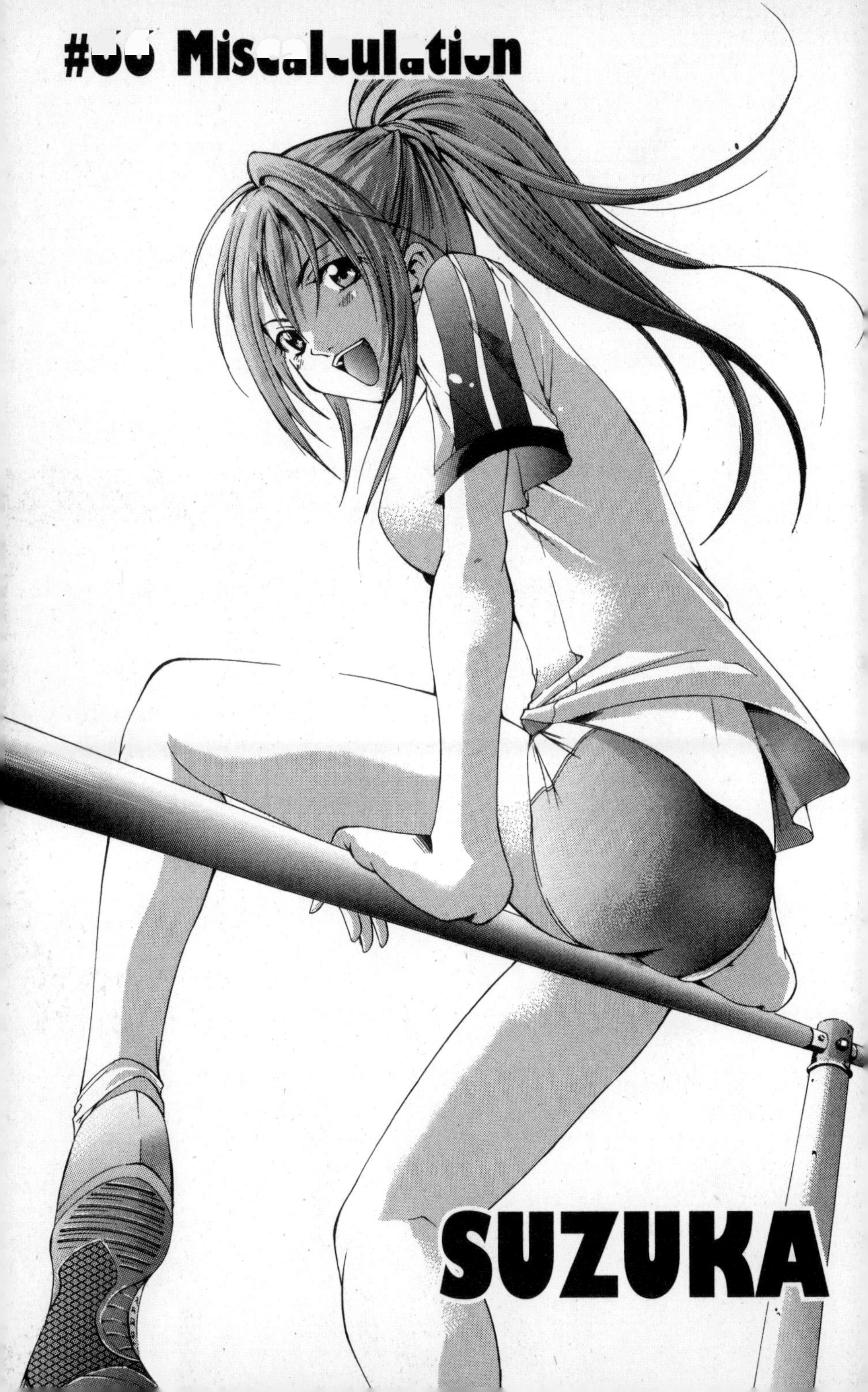
SUZUKA

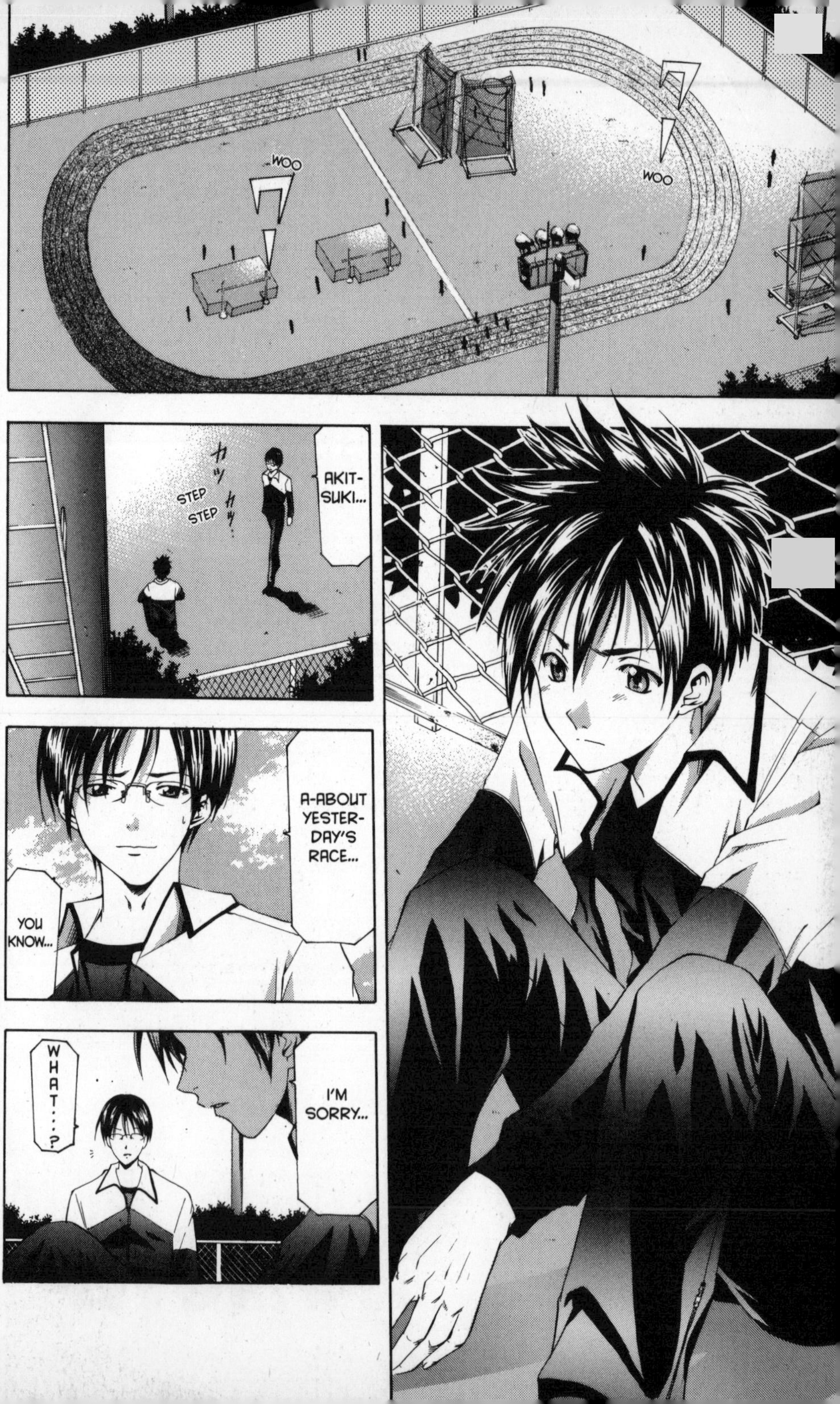
WOO
WOO
AKIT-SUKI...
STEP STEP
カッ カッ
A-ABOUT YESTER-DAY'S RACE...
YOU KNOW...
I'M SORRY...
WHAT...?

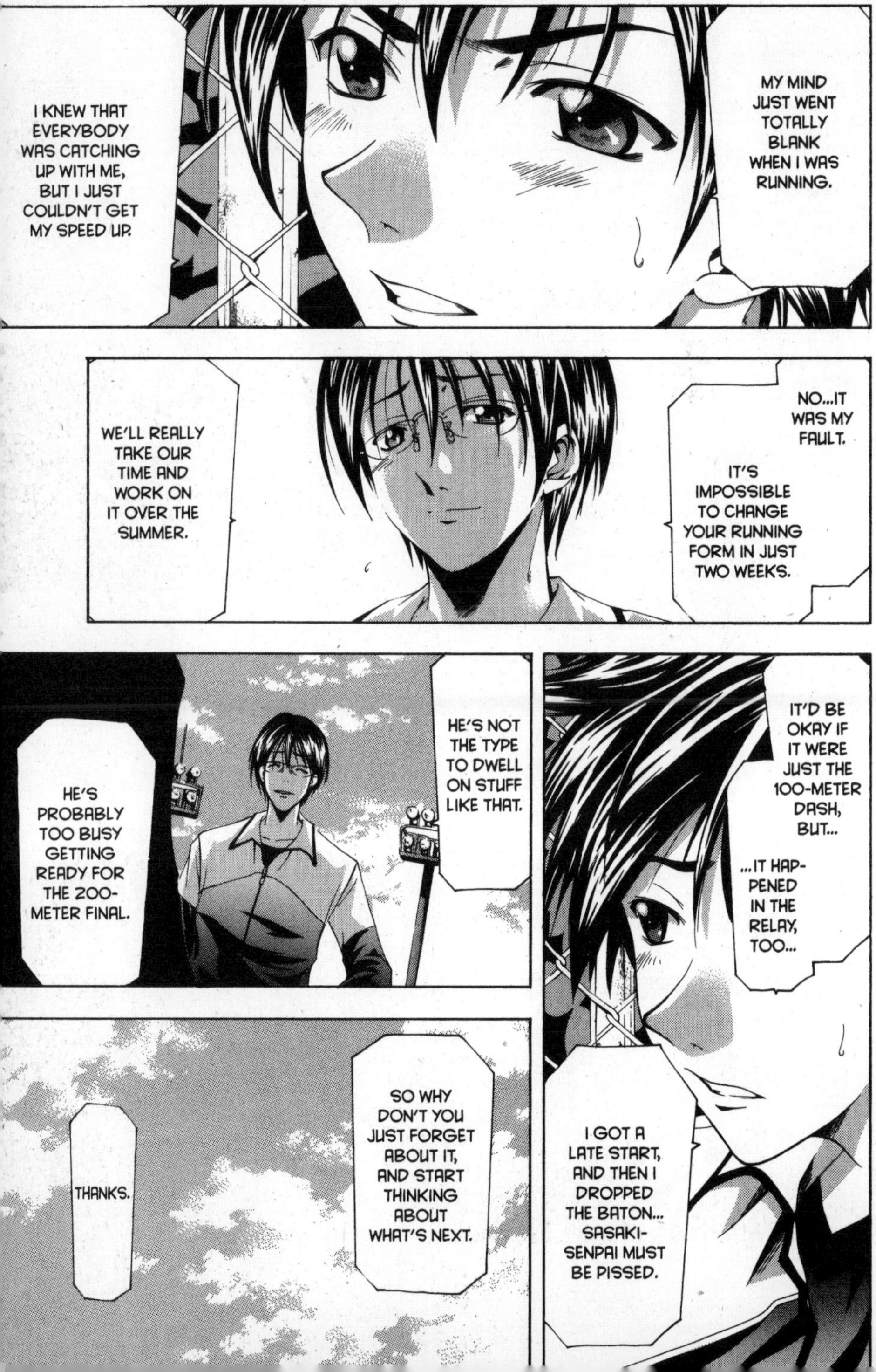
MY MIND JUST WENT TOTALLY BLANK WHEN I WAS RUNNING.
I KNEW THAT EVERYBODY WAS CATCHING UP WITH ME, BUT I JUST COULDN'T GET MY SPEED UP.
NO...IT WAS MY FAULT.
IT'S IMPOSSIBLE TO CHANGE YOUR RUNNING FORM IN JUST TWO WEEKS.
WE'LL REALLY TAKE OUR TIME AND WORK ON IT OVER THE SUMMER.
IT'D BE OKAY IF IT WERE JUST THE 100-METER DASH, BUT...
...IT HAP-PENED IN THE RELAY, TOO...
I GOT A LATE START, AND THEN I DROPPED THE BATON... SASAKI-SENPAI MUST BE PISSED.
HE'S NOT THE TYPE TO DWELL ON STUFF LIKE THAT.
HE'S PROBABLY TOO BUSY GETTING READY FOR THE 200-METER FINAL.
SO WHY DON'T YOU JUST FORGET ABOUT IT, AND START THINKING ABOUT WHAT'S NEXT.
THANKS.

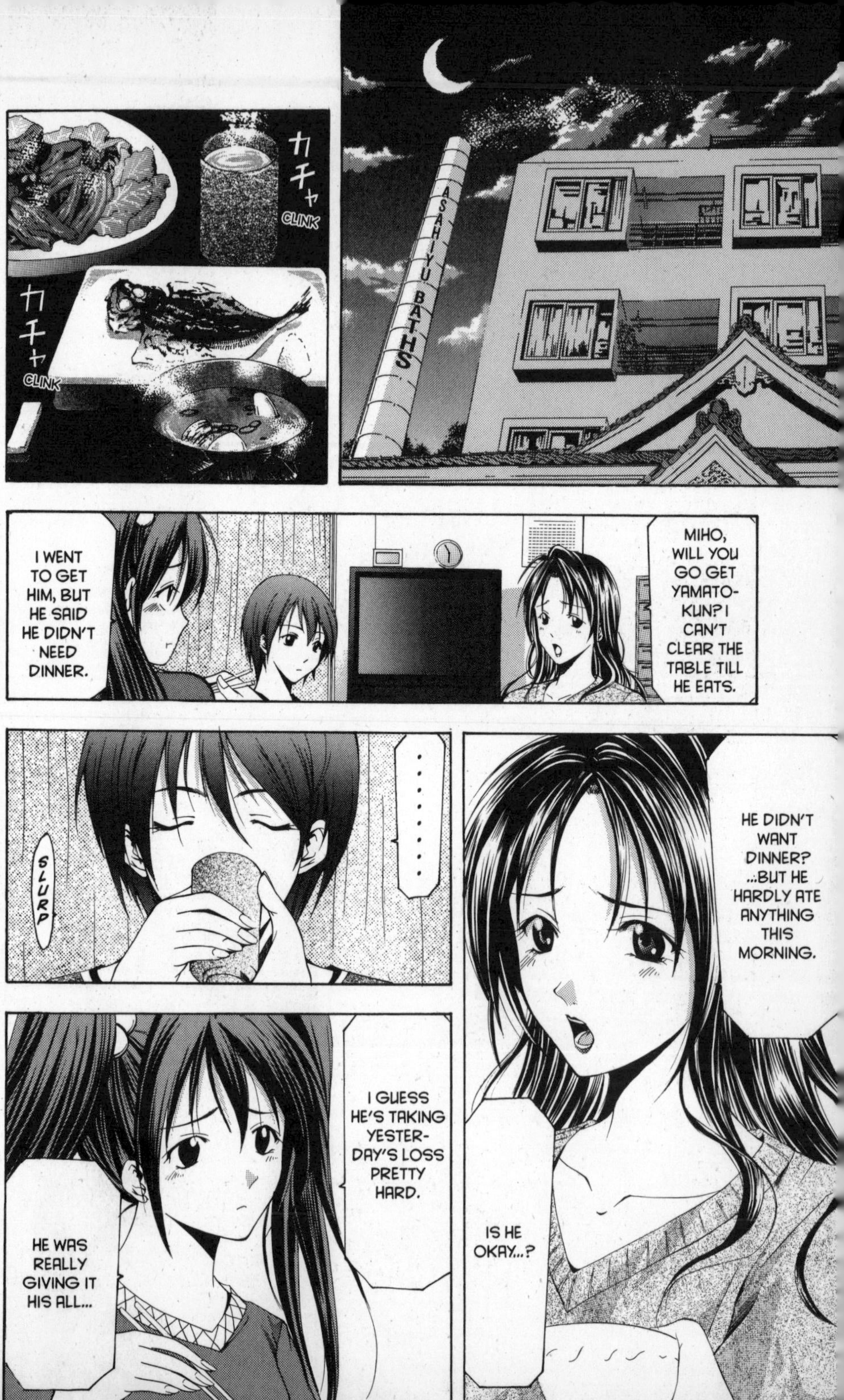

ASAHIYU BATHS
カチャ
CLINK
カチャ
CLINK
MIHO, WILL YOU GO GET YAMATO-KUN? I CAN'T CLEAR THE TABLE TILL HE EATS.
I WENT TO GET HIM, BUT HE SAID HE DIDN'T NEED DINNER.
HE DIDN'T WANT DINNER? ...BUT HE HARDLY ATE ANYTHING THIS MORNING.
IS HE OKAY...?
....
SLURP
I GUESS HE'S TAKING YESTER-DAY'S LOSS PRETTY HARD.
HE WAS REALLY GIVING IT HIS ALL...

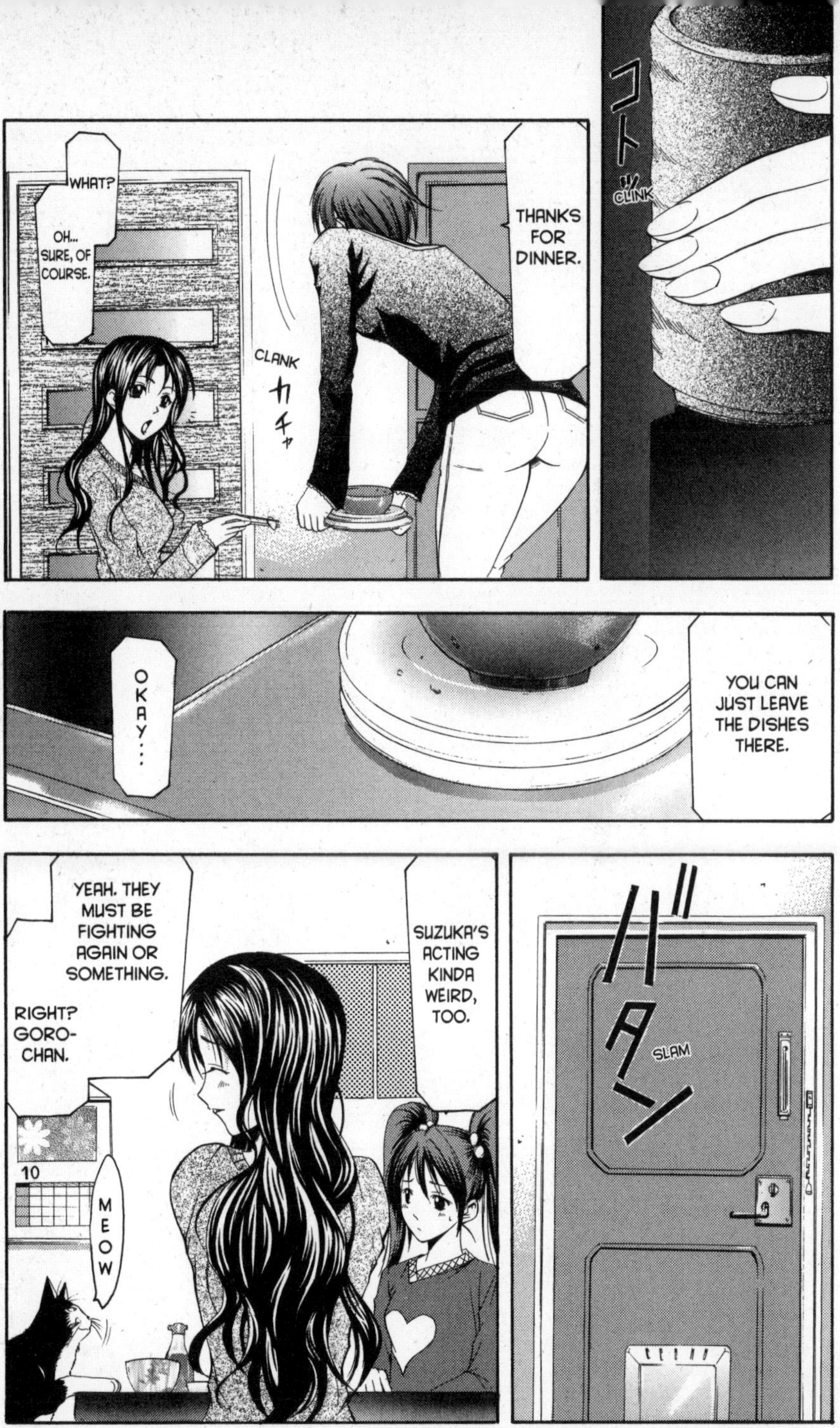
コト
CLINK
THANKS FOR DINNER.
CLANK
カチャ
WHAT?
OH... SURE, OF COURSE.
YOU CAN JUST LEAVE THE DISHES THERE.
OKAY...
バタン
SLAM
SUZUKA'S ACTING KINDA WEIRD, TOO.
YEAH. THEY MUST BE FIGHTING AGAIN OR SOMETHING.
RIGHT? GORO-CHAN.
10
MEOW

YAMATO AKITSUKI

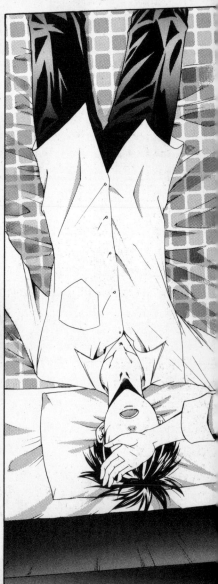

DON'T WORRY ABOUT IT, MAN

IT WAS ONLY YOUR THIRD TOURNAMENT.

SOMETIMES GREAT RUNNERS END UP NOT QUALIFYING, YOU KNOW. IT HAPPENS.

SO, YOUR TIME DROPPED A BIT, IT'S NO BIG DEAL.

THAT'S NOT WHAT I'M BUMMED ABOUT...

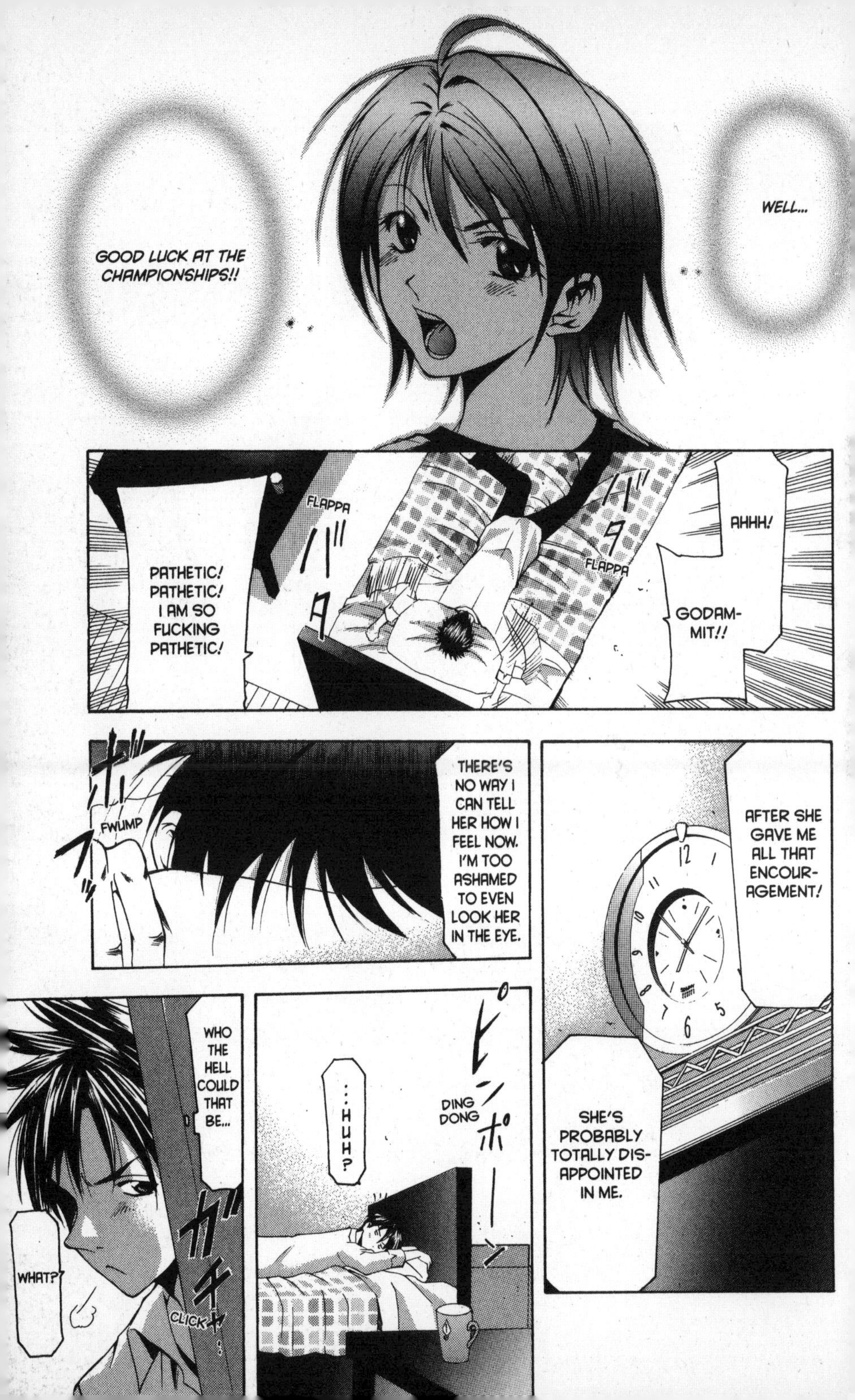
WELL...
GOOD LUCK AT THE CHAMPIONSHIPS!!
AHHH!
GODAM-MIT!!
FLAPPA
FLAPPA
PATHETIC! PATHETIC! I AM SO FUCKING PATHETIC!
AFTER SHE GAVE ME ALL THAT ENCOUR-AGEMENT!
SHE'S PROBABLY TOTALLY DIS-APPOINTED IN ME.
THERE'S NO WAY I CAN TELL HER HOW I FEEL NOW. I'M TOO ASHAMED TO EVEN LOOK HER IN THE EYE.
FWUMP
DING DONG
...HUH?
WHO THE HELL COULD THAT BE...
CLICK
WHAT?

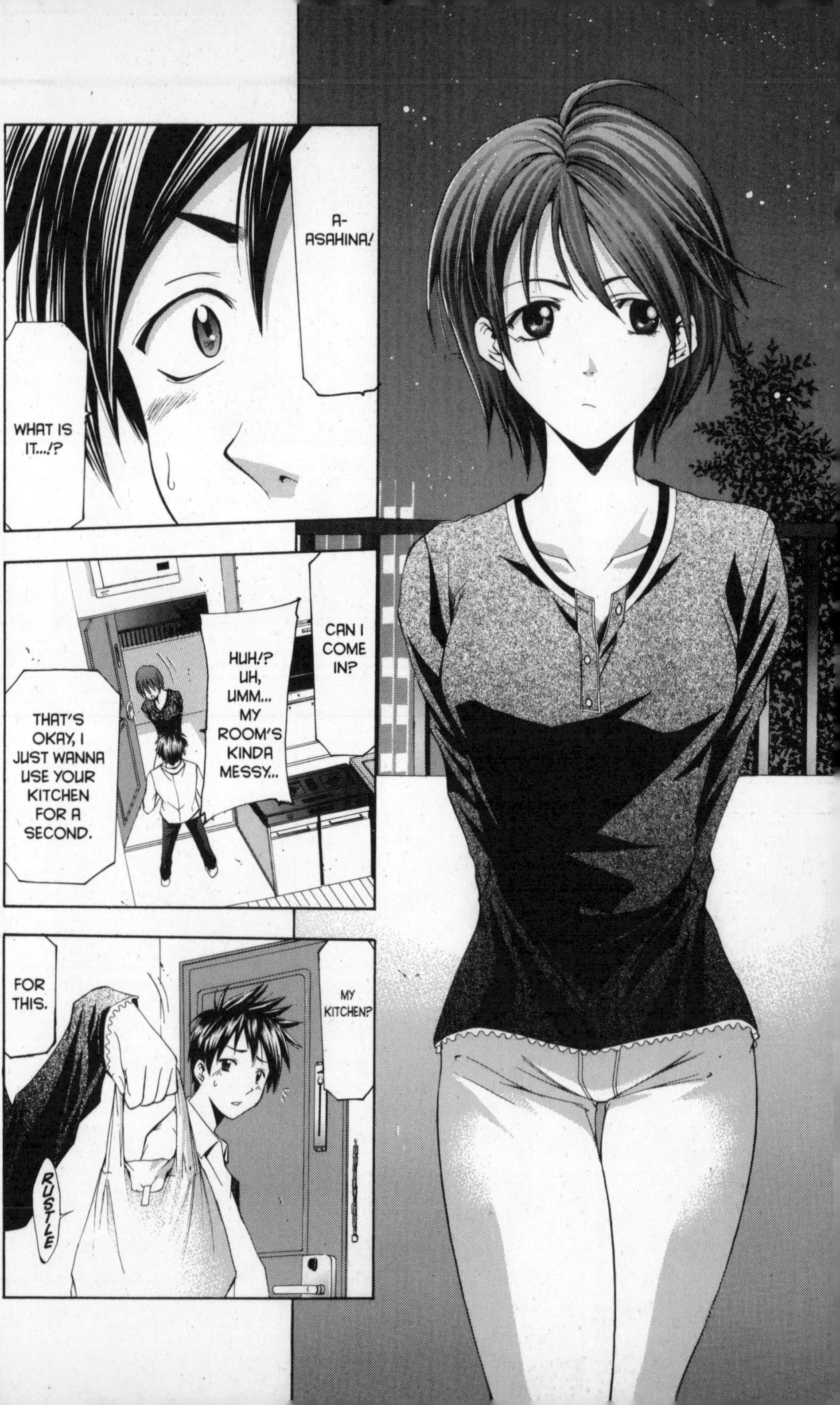
A- ASAHINA!
WHAT IS IT...!?
CAN I COME IN?
HUH!? UH, UMM... MY ROOM'S KINDA MESSY...
THAT'S OKAY, I JUST WANNA USE YOUR KITCHEN FOR A SECOND.
MY KITCHEN?
FOR THIS.
RUSTLE

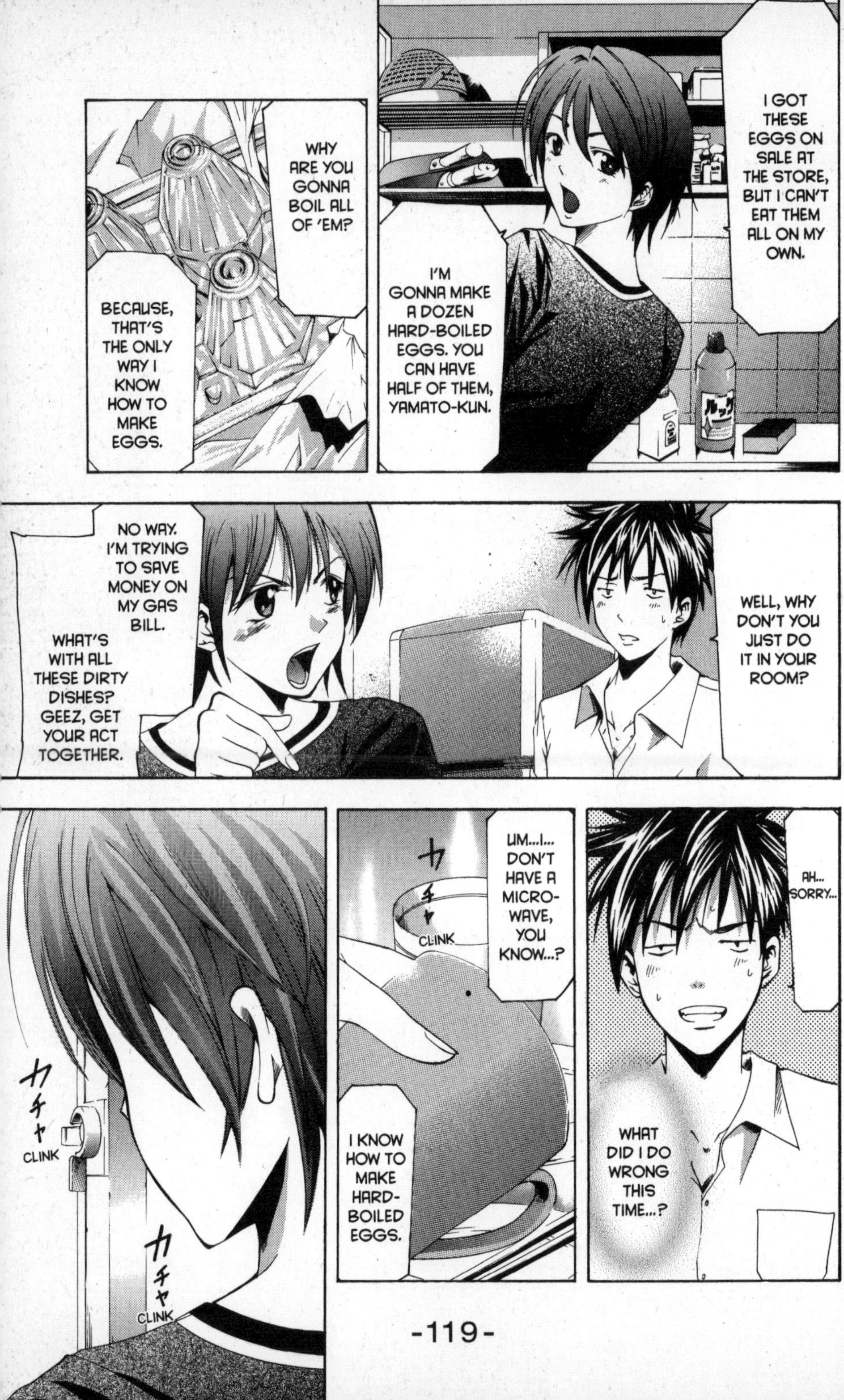
I GOT THESE EGGS ON SALE AT THE STORE, BUT I CAN'T EAT THEM ALL ON MY OWN.
I'M GONNA MAKE A DOZEN HARD-BOILED EGGS. YOU CAN HAVE HALF OF THEM, YAMATO-KUN.
WHY ARE YOU GONNA BOIL ALL OF 'EM?
BECAUSE, THAT'S THE ONLY WAY I KNOW HOW TO MAKE EGGS.
WELL, WHY DON'T YOU JUST DO IT IN YOUR ROOM?
NO WAY. I'M TRYING TO SAVE MONEY ON MY GAS BILL.
WHAT'S WITH ALL THESE DIRTY DISHES? GEEZ, GET YOUR ACT TOGETHER.
AH... SORRY...
WHAT DID I DO WRONG THIS TIME...?
UM...I... DON'T HAVE A MICRO-WAVE, YOU KNOW...?
カチャ
CLINK
I KNOW HOW TO MAKE HARD-BOILED EGGS.
カチャ
CLINK
カチャ
CLINK

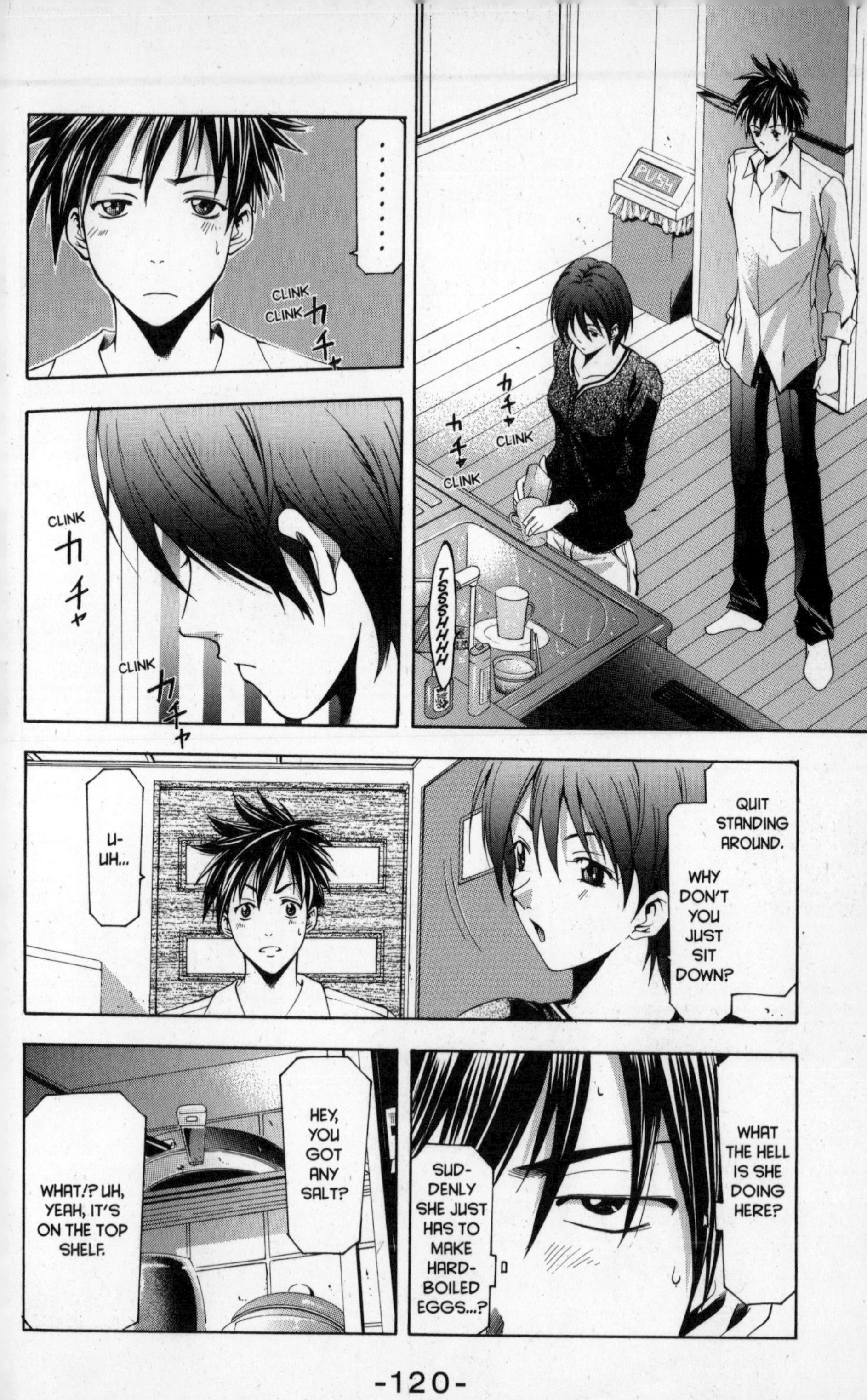
PUSH
カチャ CLINK
カチャ CLINK
TSSSHHHH
......
CLINK CLINK カチャ
CLINK カチャ
CLINK カチャ
QUIT STANDING AROUND.
WHY DON'T YOU JUST SIT DOWN?
U- UH...
WHAT THE HELL IS SHE DOING HERE?
SUD-DENLY SHE JUST HAS TO MAKE HARD-BOILED EGGS...?
HEY, YOU GOT ANY SALT?
WHAT!? UH, YEAH, IT'S ON THE TOP SHELF.

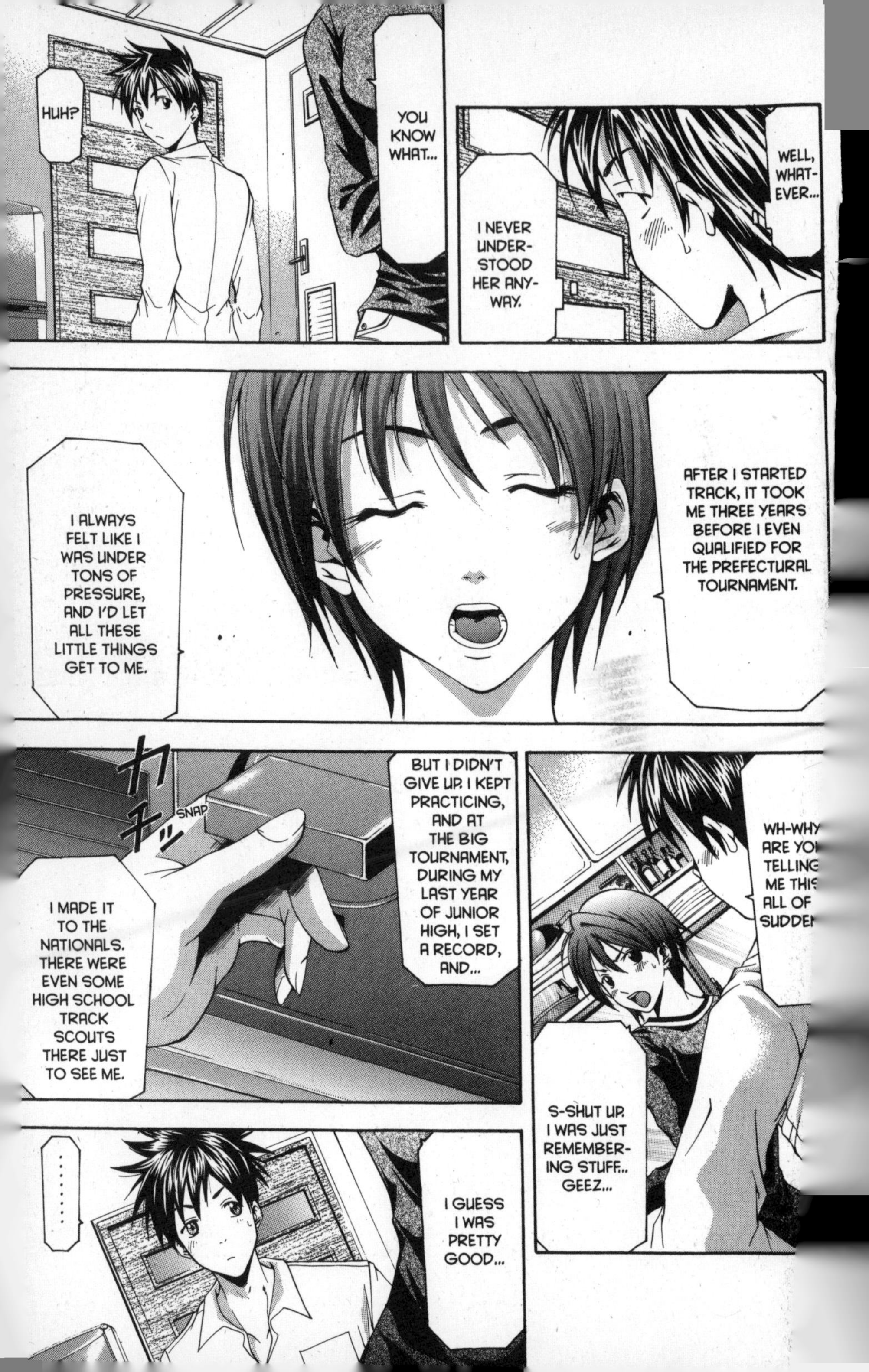
WELL, WHAT-EVER...
I NEVER UNDER-STOOD HER ANY-WAY.
YOU KNOW WHAT...
HUH?
AFTER I STARTED TRACK, IT TOOK ME THREE YEARS BEFORE I EVEN QUALIFIED FOR THE PREFECTURAL TOURNAMENT.
I ALWAYS FELT LIKE I WAS UNDER TONS OF PRESSURE, AND I'D LET ALL THESE LITTLE THINGS GET TO ME.
WH-WHY ARE YO TELLING ME THIS ALL OF SUDDEN
S-SHUT UP. I WAS JUST REMEMBER-ING STUFF... GEEZ...
BUT I DIDN'T GIVE UP. I KEPT PRACTICING, AND AT THE BIG TOURNAMENT, DURING MY LAST YEAR OF JUNIOR HIGH, I SET A RECORD, AND...
カチッ
SNAP
I MADE IT TO THE NATIONALS. THERE WERE EVEN SOME HIGH SCHOOL TRACK SCOUTS THERE JUST TO SEE ME.
I GUESS I WAS PRETTY GOOD...
......

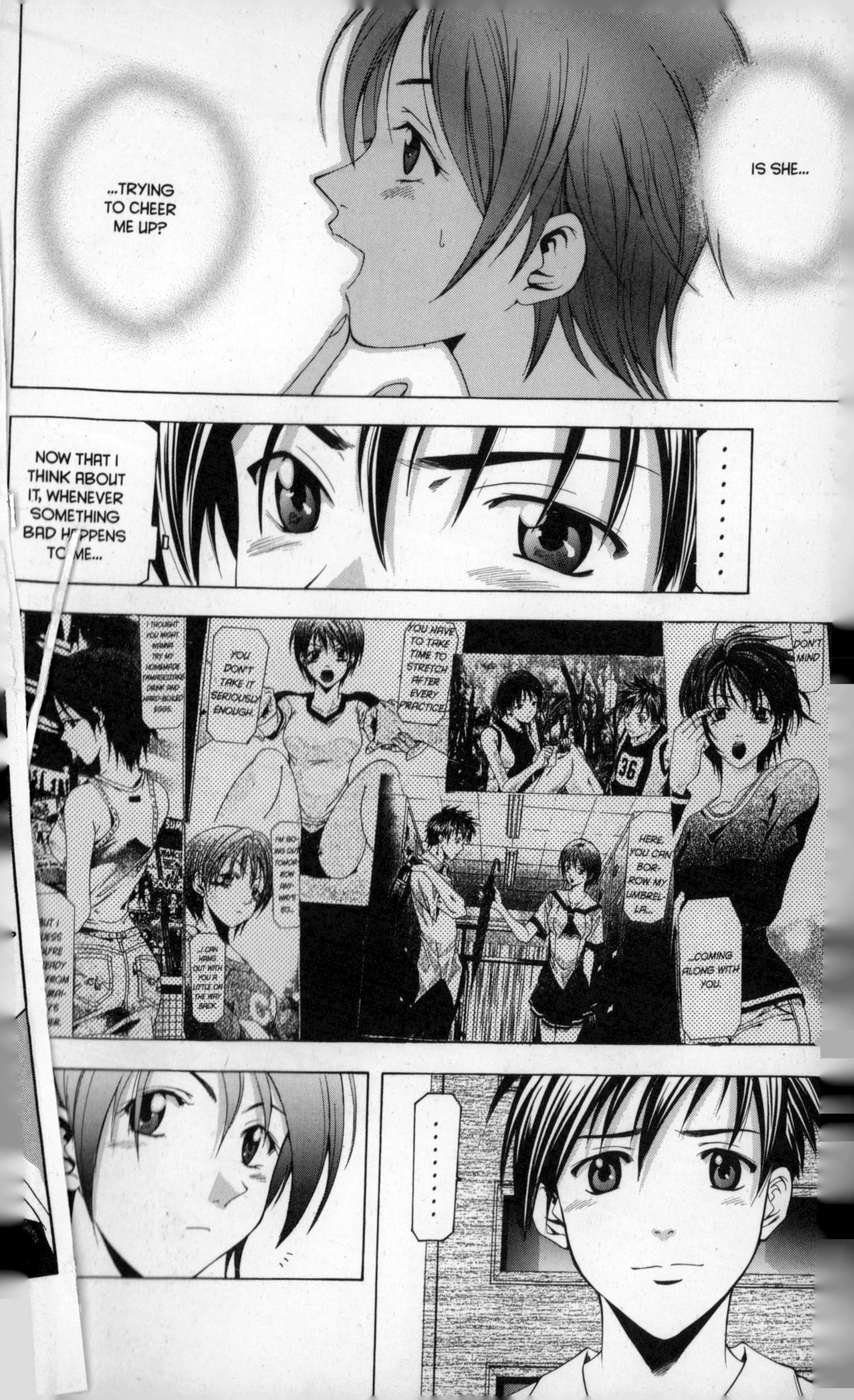
IS SHE...
...TRYING TO CHEER ME UP?
......
NOW THAT I THINK ABOUT IT, WHENEVER SOMETHING BAD HAPPENS TO ME...
...I DON'T MIND
...COMING ALONG WITH YOU.
YOU HAVE TO TAKE TIME TO STRETCH AFTER EVERY PRACTICE.
HERE, YOU CAN BORROW MY UMBRELLA...
YOU DON'T TAKE IT SERIOUSLY ENOUGH.
I'M GOING OUT TOMORROW ANYWAYS SO...
...I CAN HANG OUT WITH YOU A LITTLE ON THE WAY BACK.
I THOUGHT YOU MIGHT WANNA TRY MY HOMEMADE TAMAGOZAKE DRINK AND HARD-BOILED EGGS.
BUT I GUESS YOU'RE READY FROM
......

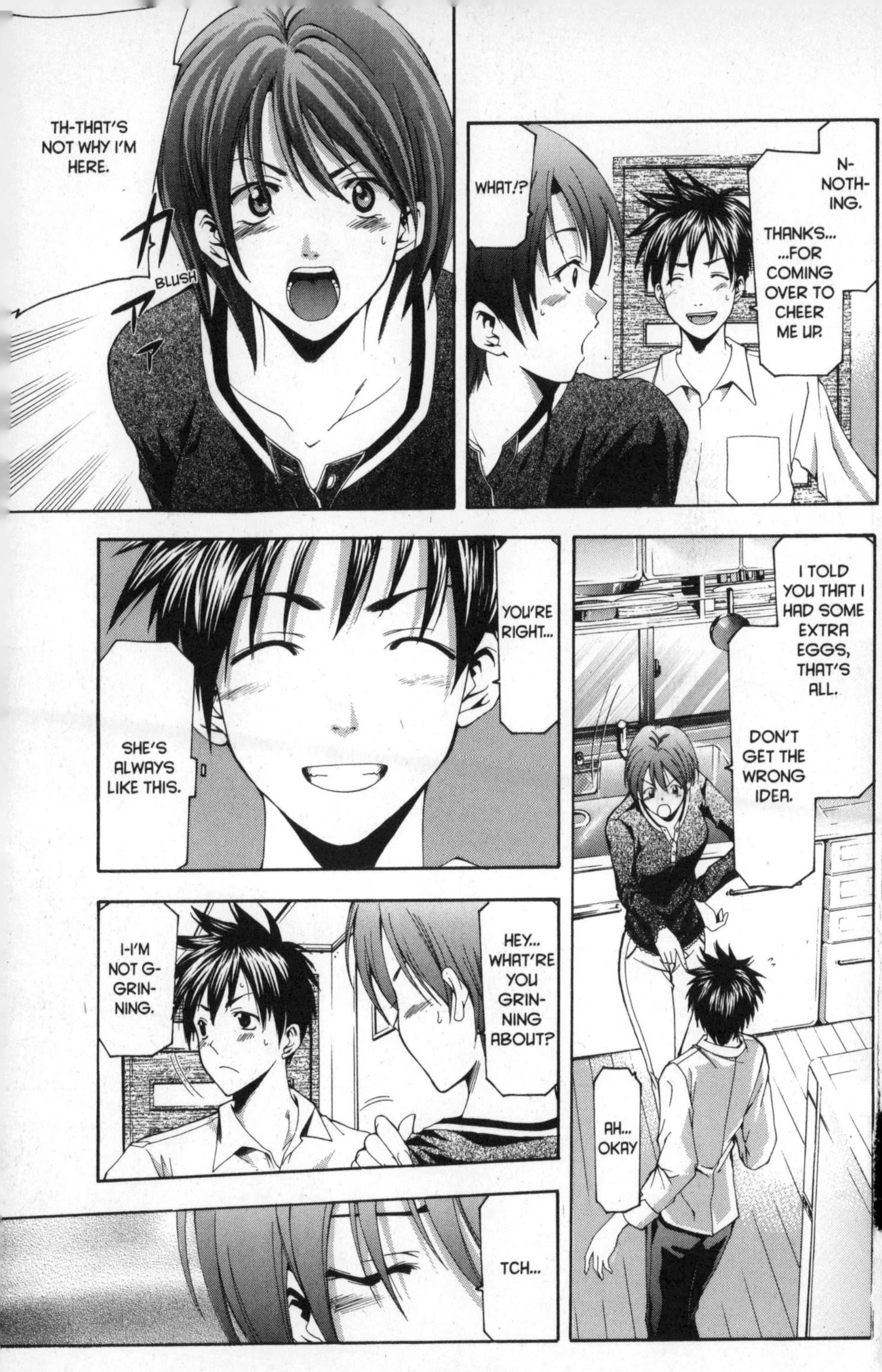
N-NOTHING.
THANKS... ...FOR COMING OVER TO CHEER ME UP.
WHAT!?
TH-THAT'S NOT WHY I'M HERE.
BLUSH
I TOLD YOU THAT I HAD SOME EXTRA EGGS, THAT'S ALL.
DON'T GET THE WRONG IDEA.
AH... OKAY
YOU'RE RIGHT...
SHE'S ALWAYS LIKE THIS.
HEY... WHAT'RE YOU GRINNING ABOUT?
I-I'M NOT G-GRINNING.
TCH...

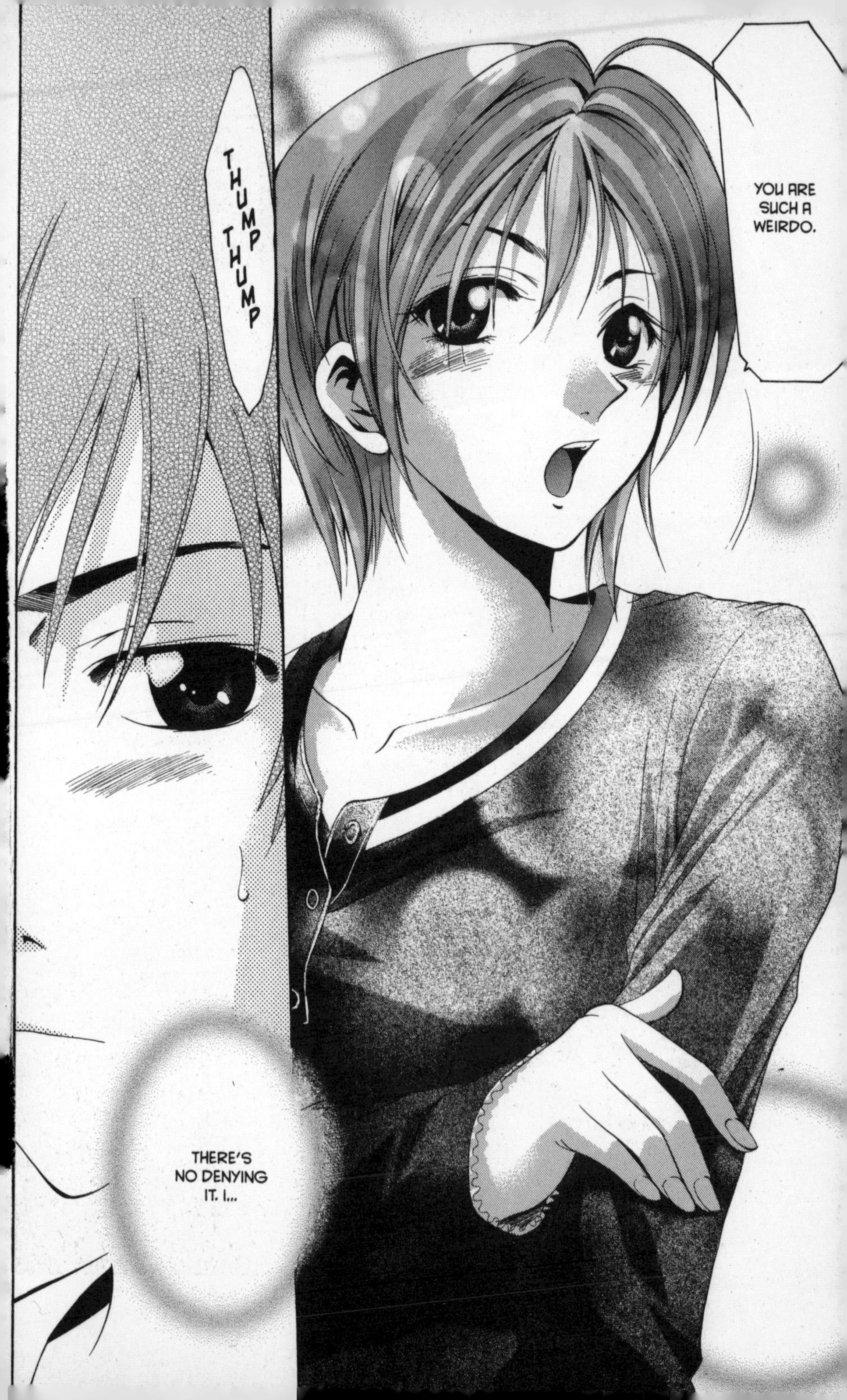
YOU ARE SUCH A WEIRDO.
THUMP THUMP
THERE'S NO DENYING IT. I...

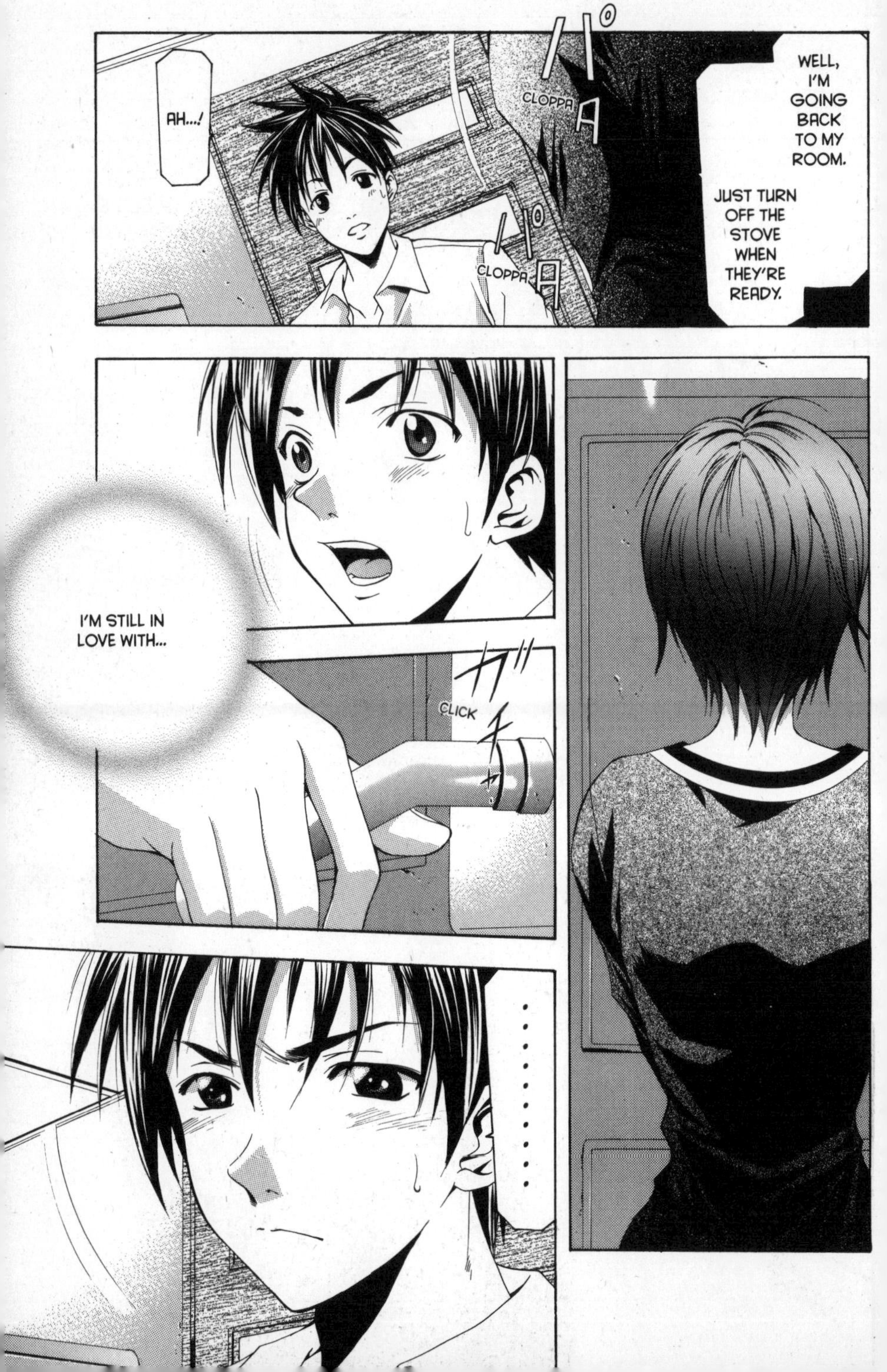
WELL, I'M GOING BACK TO MY ROOM.
JUST TURN OFF THE STOVE WHEN THEY'RE READY.
CLOPPA
CLOPPA
AH...!
I'M STILL IN LOVE WITH...
CLICK
......

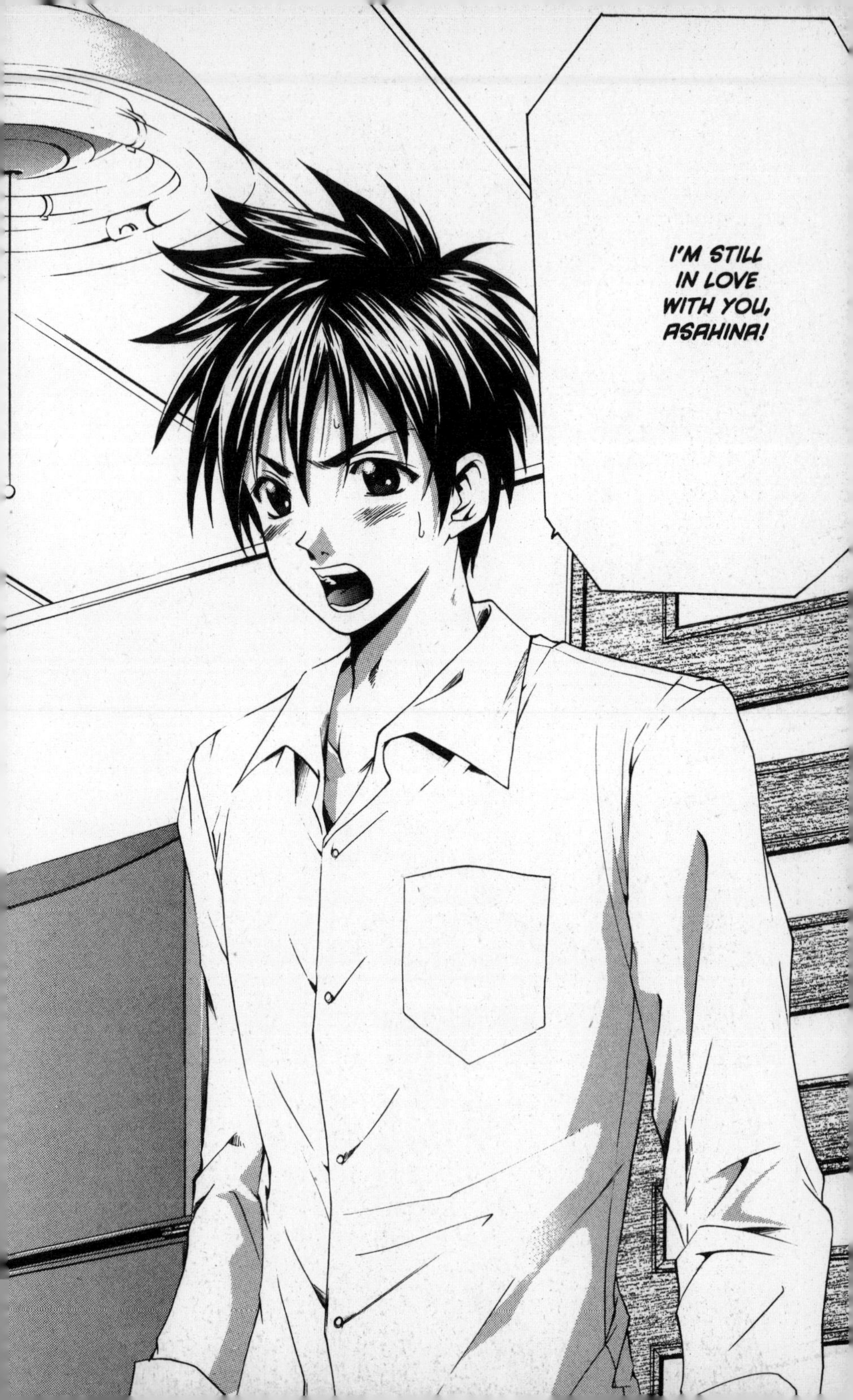
I'M STILL IN LOVE WITH YOU, ASAHINA!

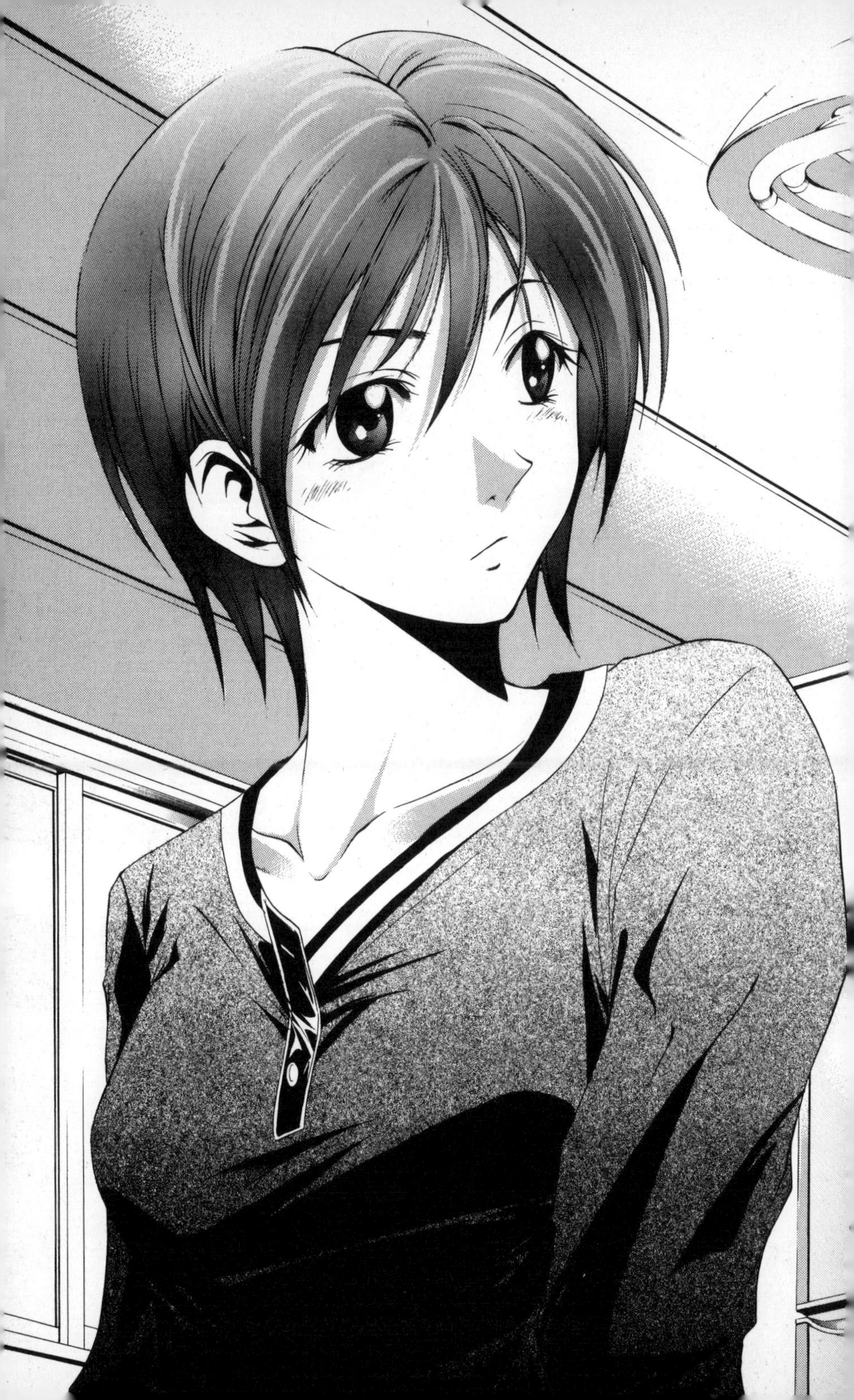

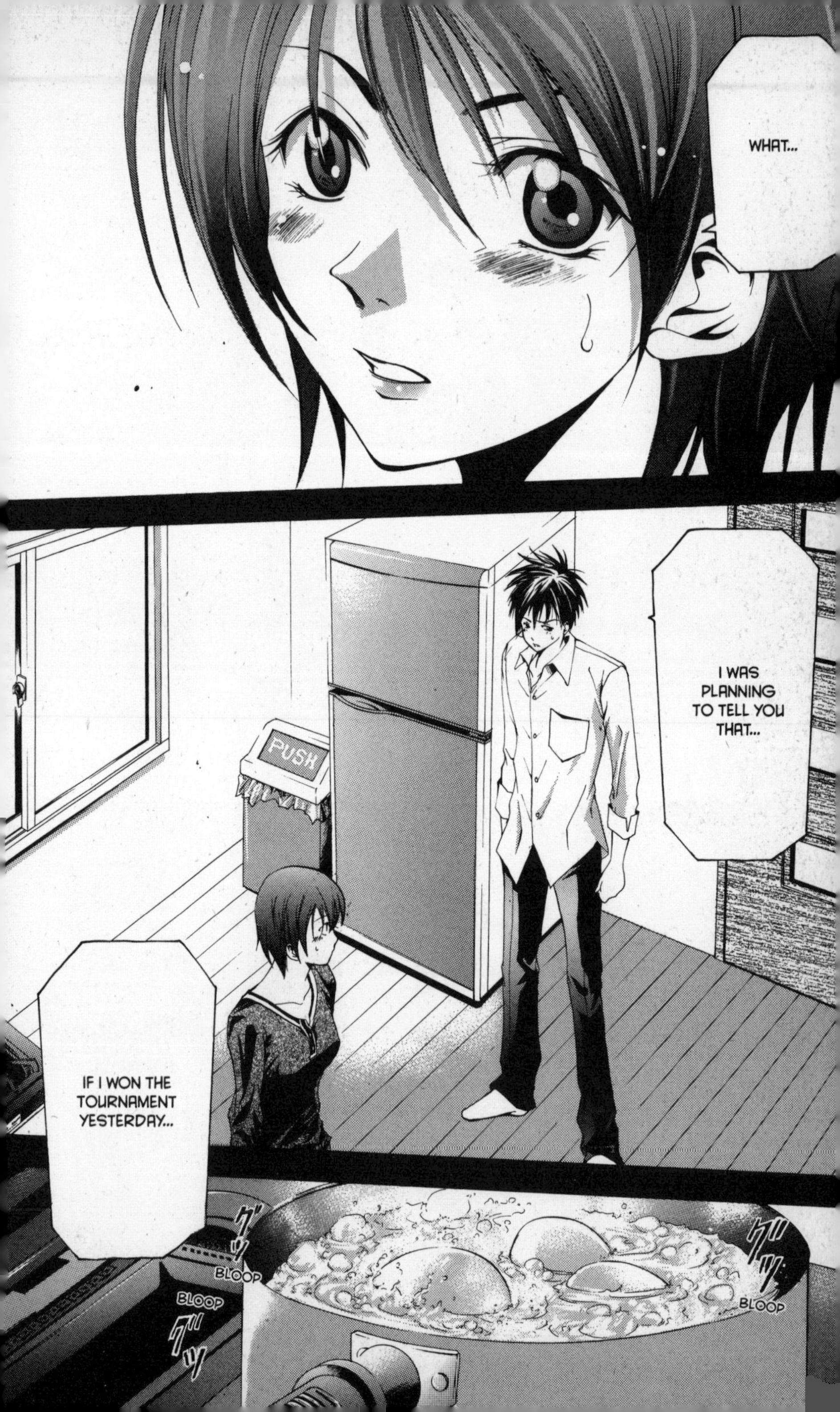
WHAT...
I WAS PLANNING TO TELL YOU THAT...
IF I WON THE TOURNAMENT YESTERDAY...
BLOOP
BLOOP
BLOOP

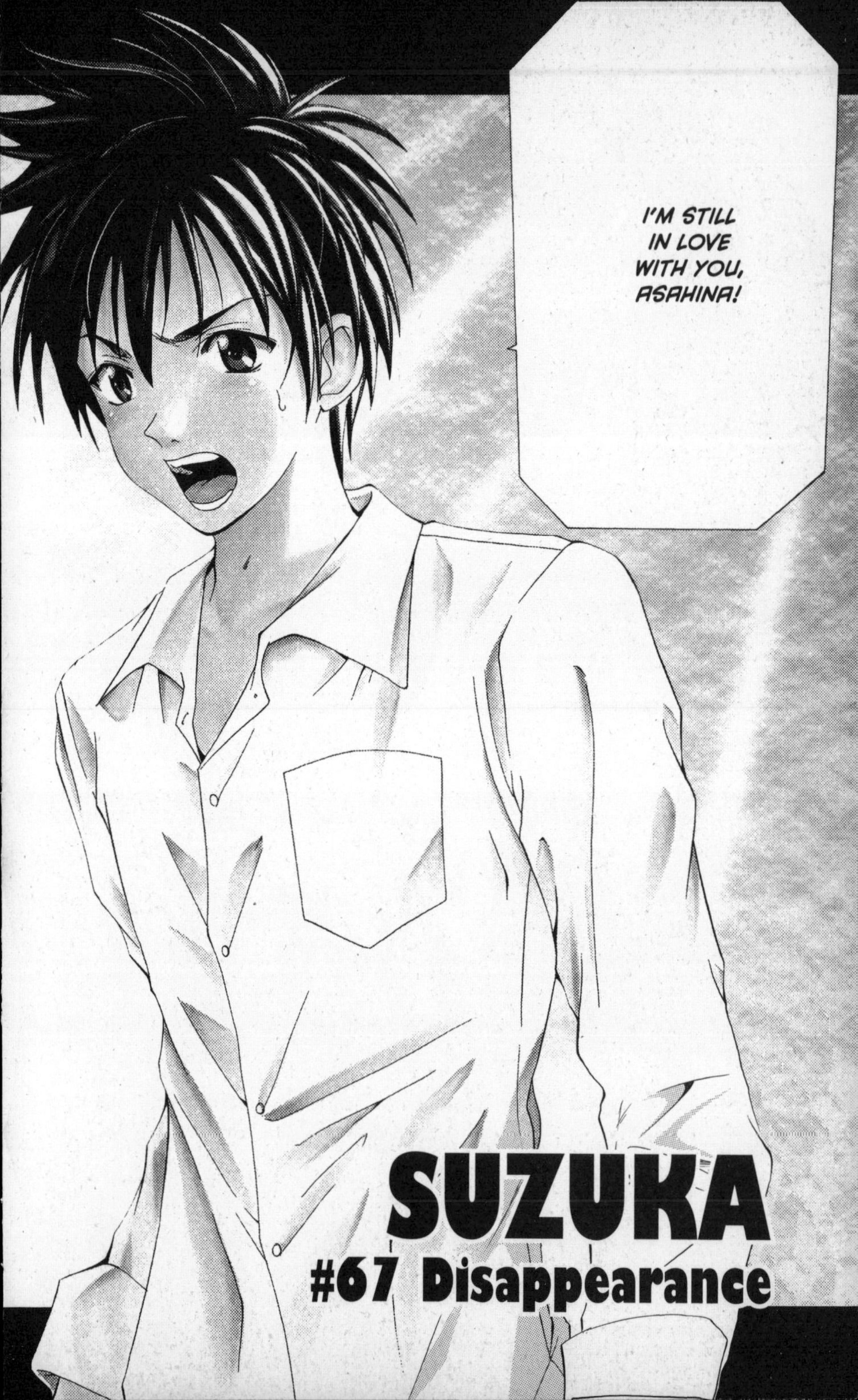
I'M STILL IN LOVE WITH YOU, ASAHINA!
SUZUKA
#67 Disappearance

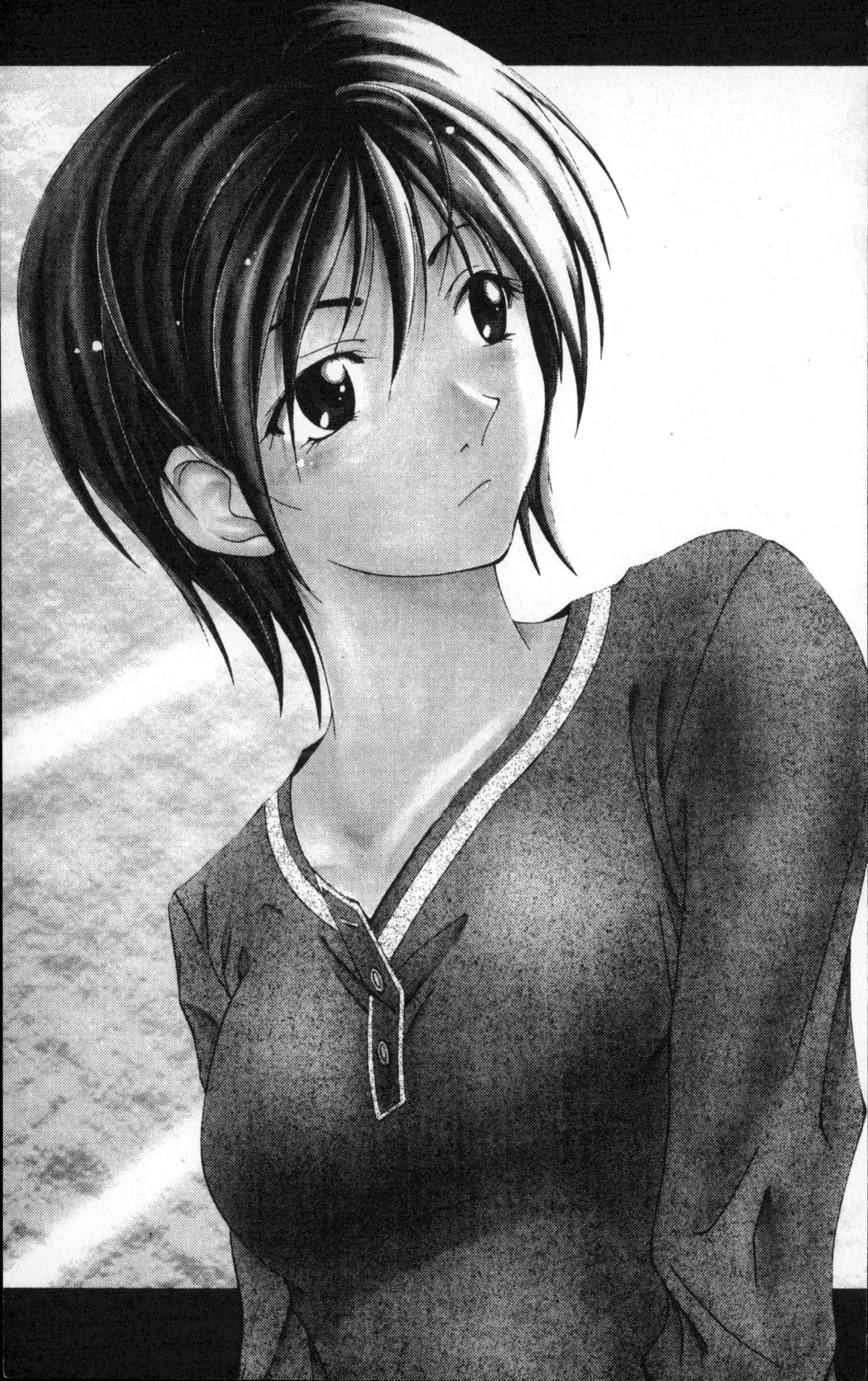

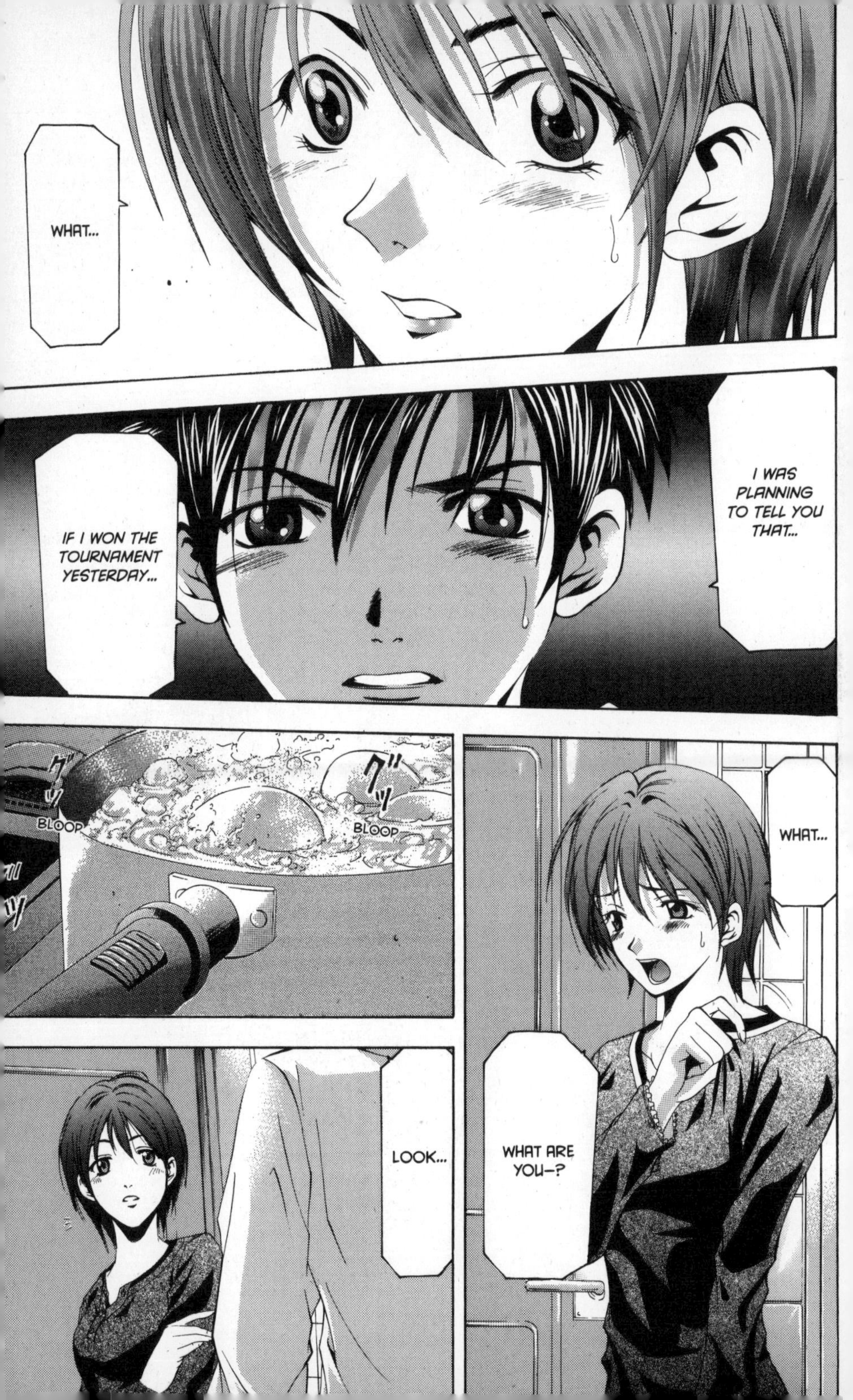

WHAT...
I WAS PLANNING TO TELL YOU THAT...
IF I WON THE TOURNAMENT YESTERDAY...
WHAT...
WHAT ARE YOU-?
グツ
BLOOP
グツ
BLOOP
LOOK...

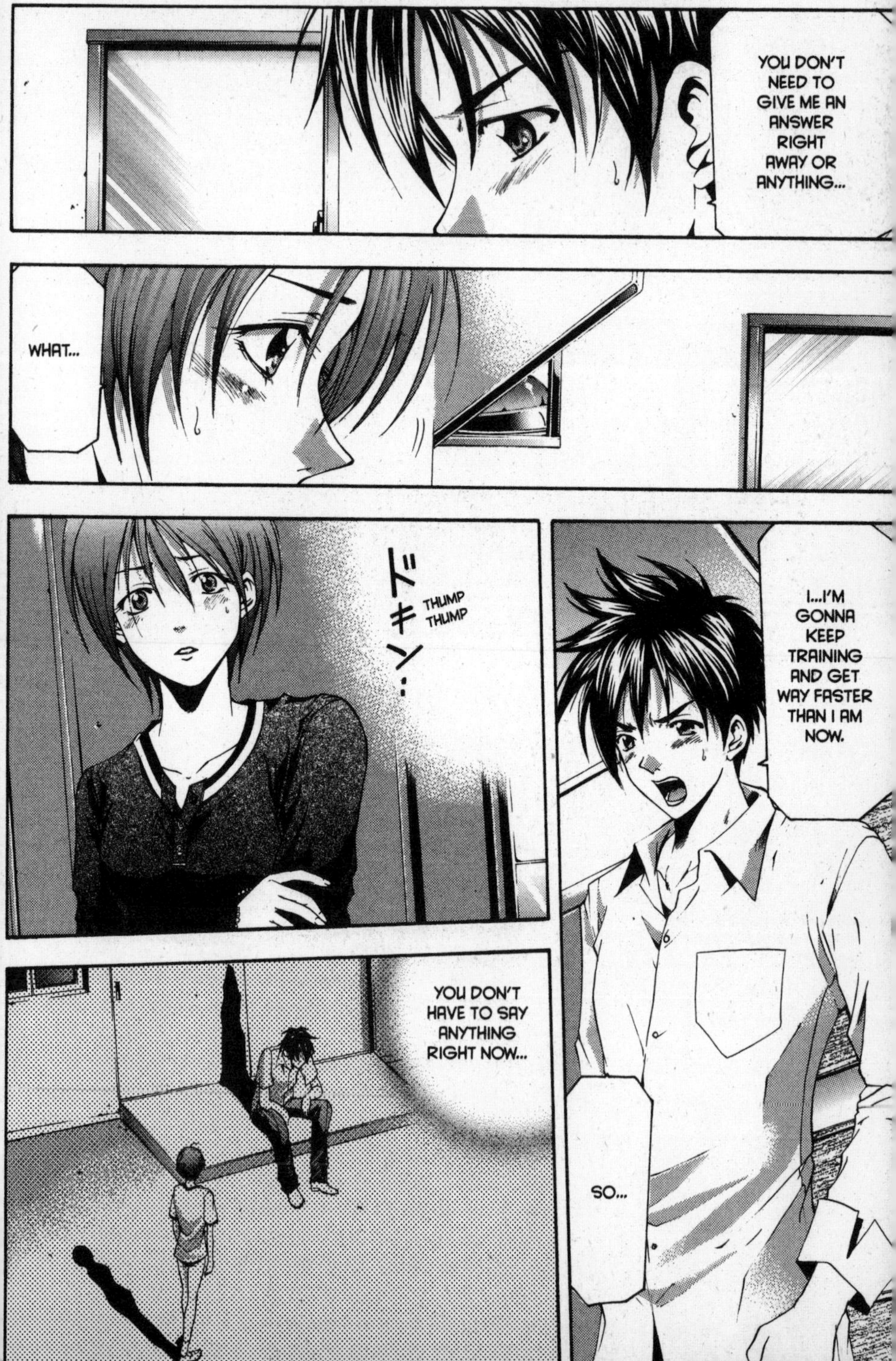
YOU DON'T NEED TO GIVE ME AN ANSWER RIGHT AWAY OR ANYTHING...
WHAT...
I...I'M GONNA KEEP TRAINING AND GET WAY FASTER THAN I AM NOW.
SO...
ドキン
THUMP THUMP
YOU DON'T HAVE TO SAY ANYTHING RIGHT NOW...

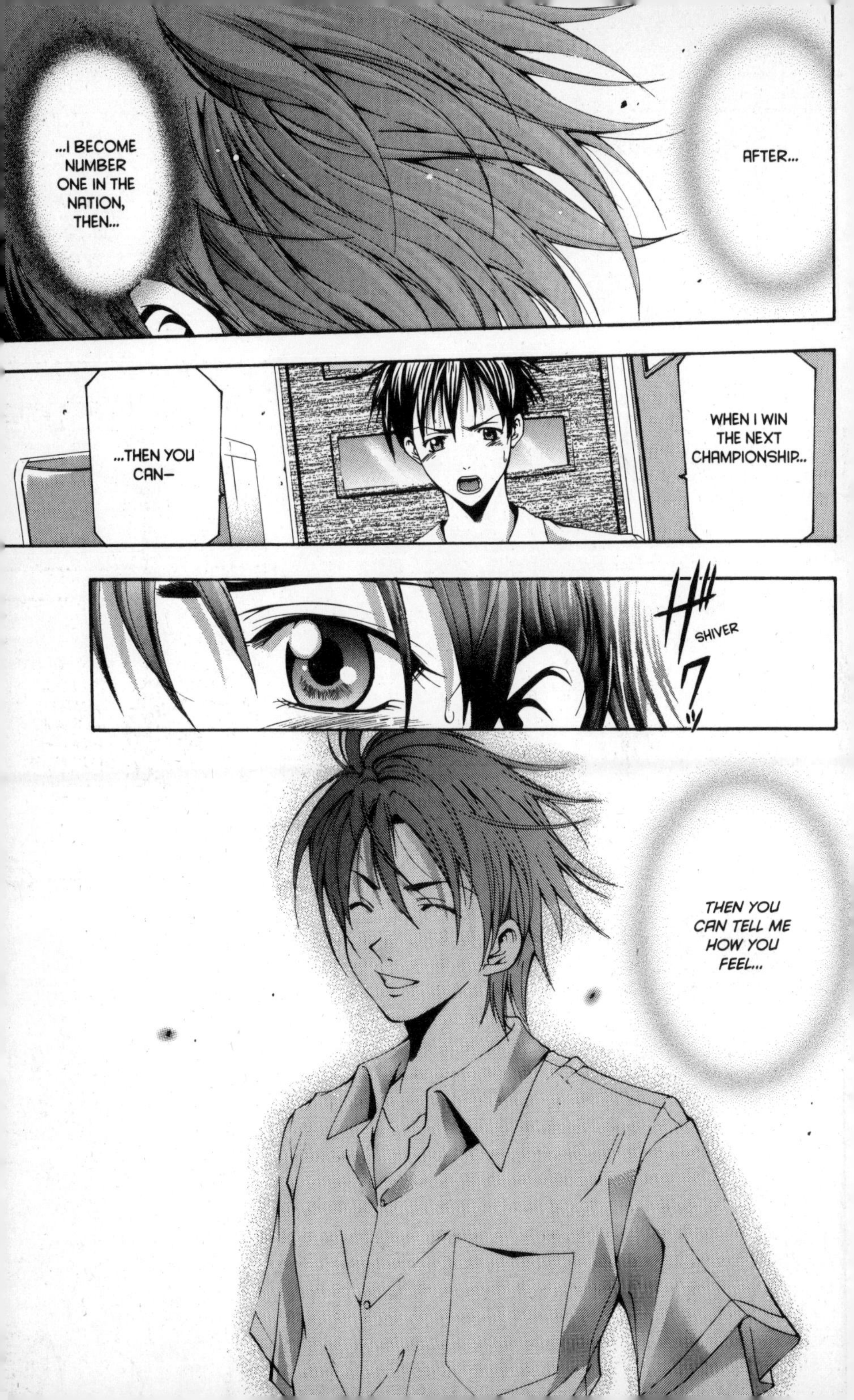
AFTER...
...I BECOME NUMBER ONE IN THE NATION, THEN...
WHEN I WIN THE NEXT CHAMPIONSHIP...
...THEN YOU CAN—
SHIVER
THEN YOU CAN TELL ME HOW YOU FEEL...

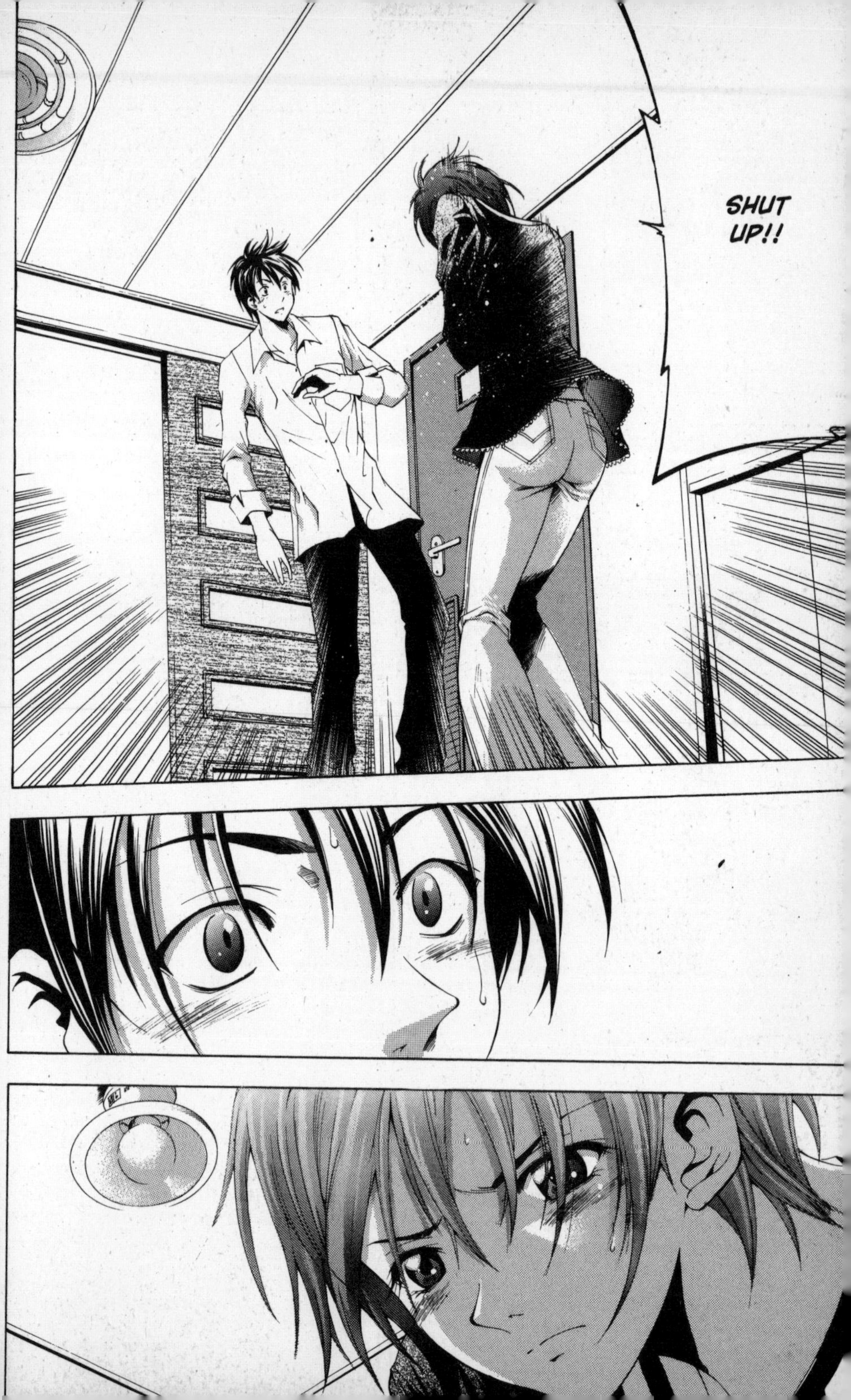
SHUT UP!!

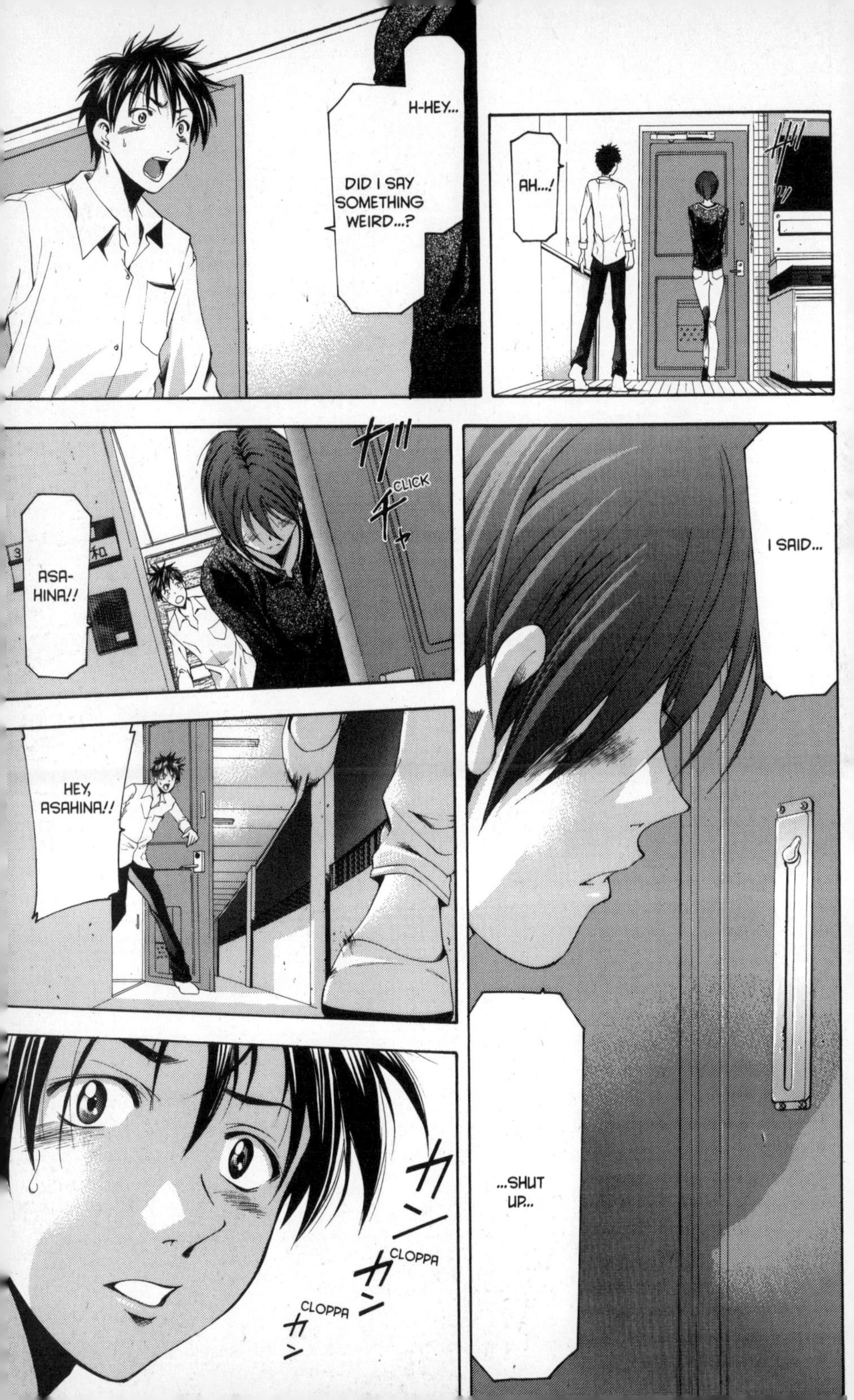
AH...!
H-HEY...
DID I SAY SOMETHING WEIRD...?
I SAID...
...SHUT UP...
ガチャ
CLICK
ASA-HINA!!
HEY, ASAHINA!!
カン
CLOPPA
カン
CLOPPA
カン

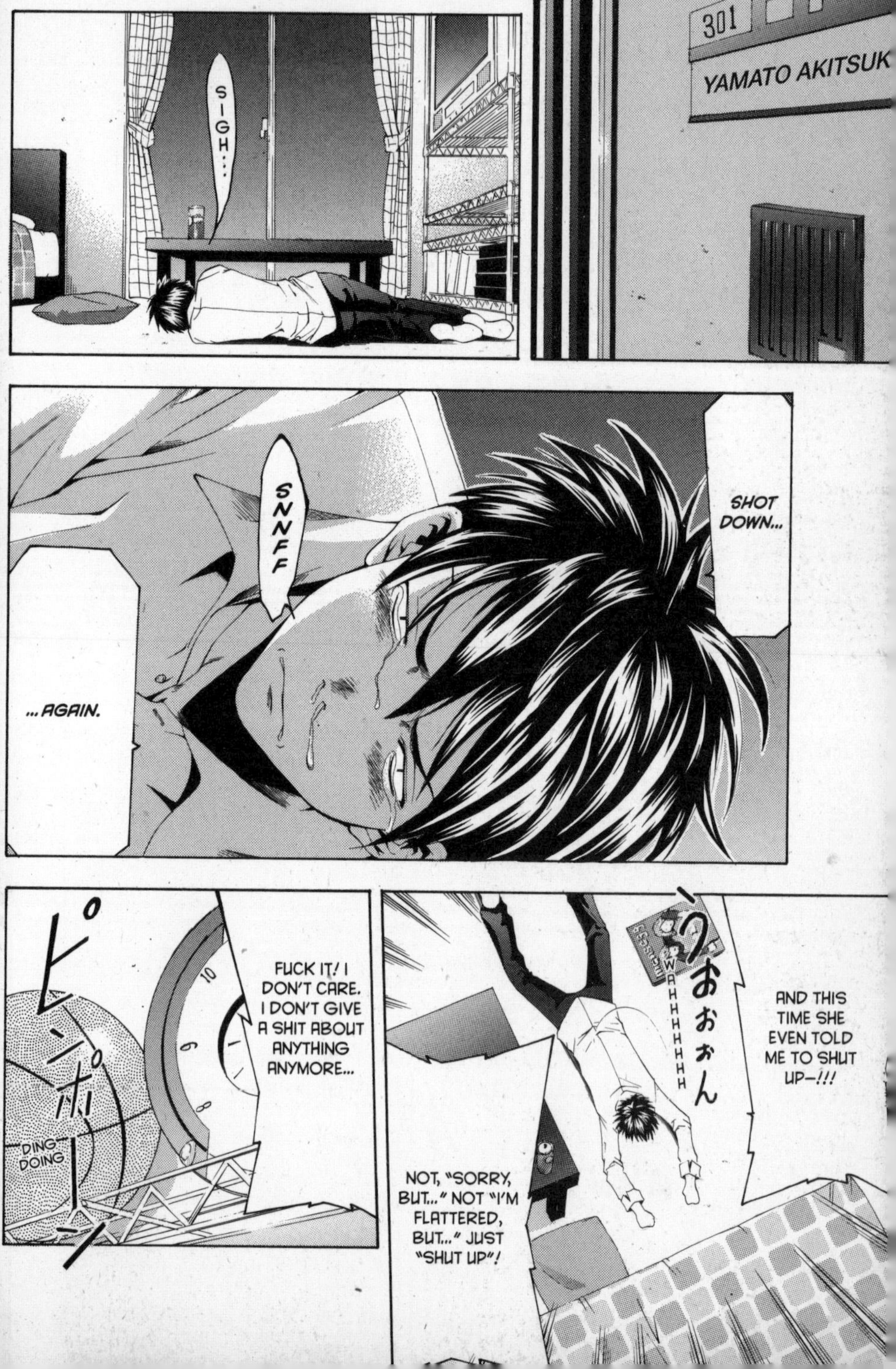
301
YAMATO AKITSUK
SIGH...
SHOT DOWN...
SNNFF
...AGAIN.
うおぉぉん
WAHHHHHHH
AND THIS TIME SHE EVEN TOLD ME TO SHUT UP—!!!
NOT, "SORRY, BUT..." NOT "I'M FLATTERED, BUT..." JUST "SHUT UP"!
FUCK IT! I DON'T CARE. I DON'T GIVE A SHIT ABOUT ANYTHING ANYMORE...
ピンポーン
DING DOING

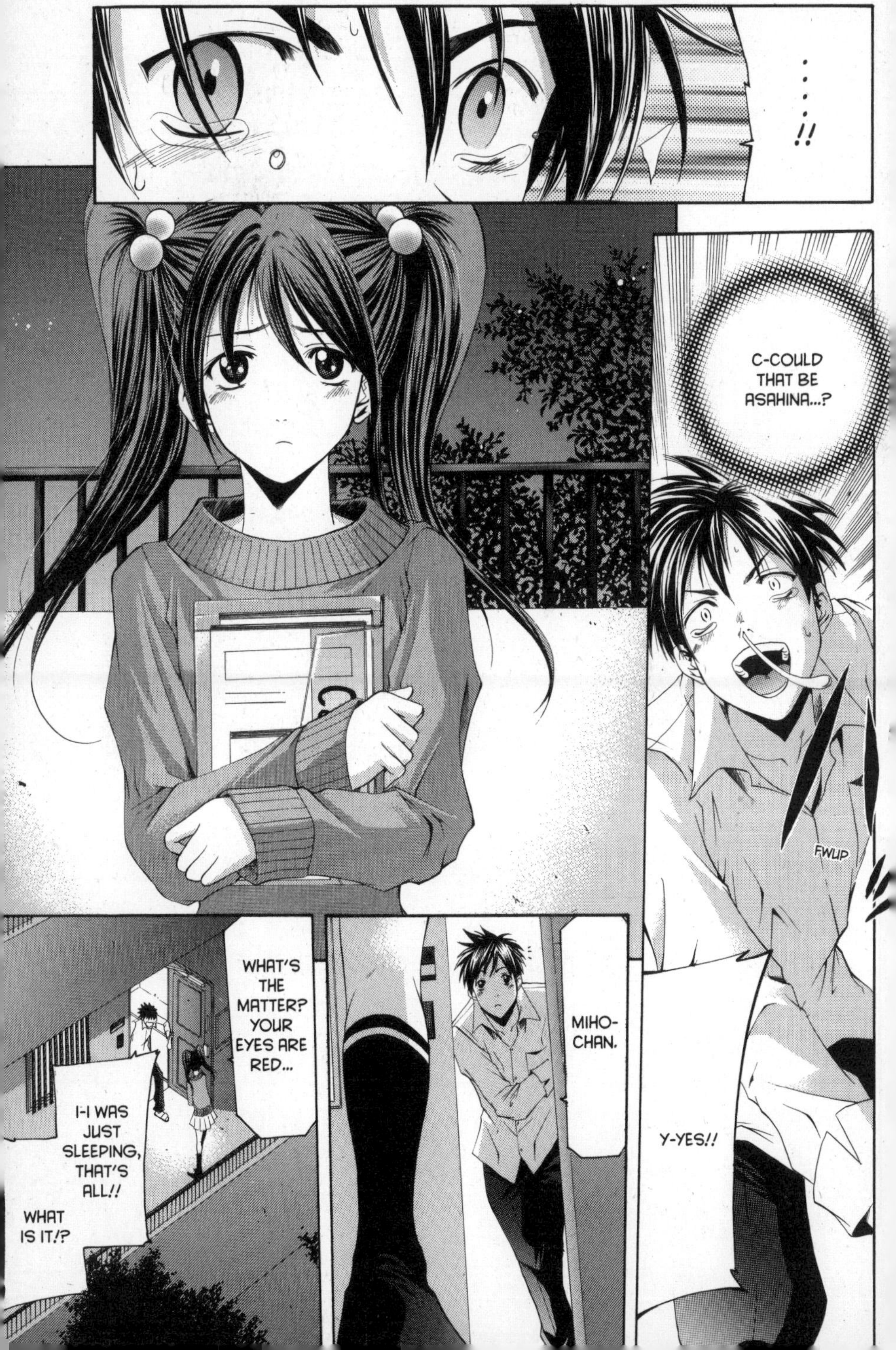
....!!
C-COULD THAT BE ASAHINA...?
FWUP
Y-YES!!
MIHO-CHAN.
WHAT'S THE MATTER? YOUR EYES ARE RED...
I-I WAS JUST SLEEPING, THAT'S ALL!!
WHAT IS IT!?

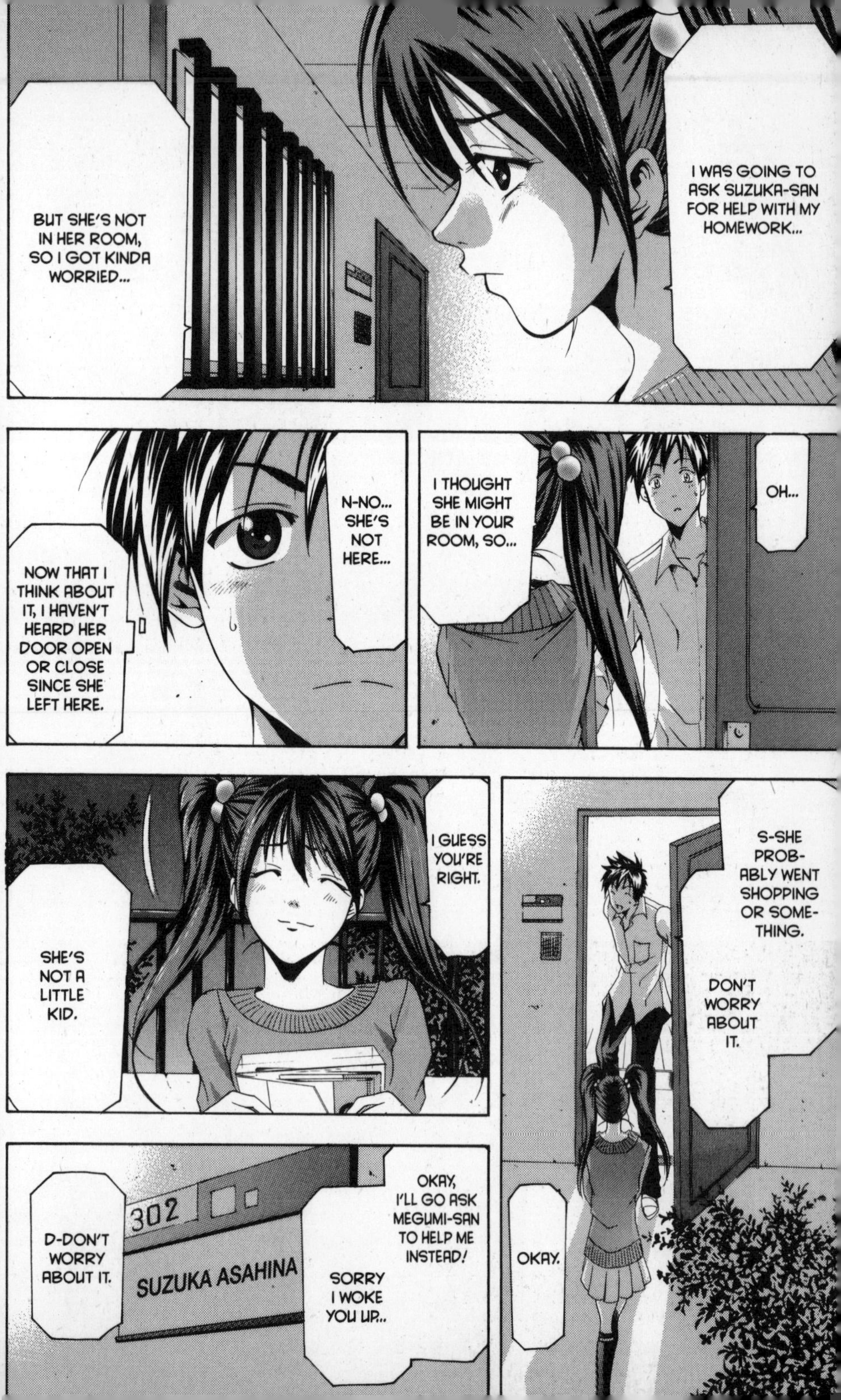
I WAS GOING TO ASK SUZUKA-SAN FOR HELP WITH MY HOMEWORK...
BUT SHE'S NOT IN HER ROOM, SO I GOT KINDA WORRIED...
OH...
I THOUGHT SHE MIGHT BE IN YOUR ROOM, SO...
N-NO... SHE'S NOT HERE...
NOW THAT I THINK ABOUT IT, I HAVEN'T HEARD HER DOOR OPEN OR CLOSE SINCE SHE LEFT HERE.
S-SHE PROBABLY WENT SHOPPING OR SOMETHING.
DON'T WORRY ABOUT IT.
OKAY.
I GUESS YOU'RE RIGHT.
SHE'S NOT A LITTLE KID.
OKAY, I'LL GO ASK MEGUMI-SAN TO HELP ME INSTEAD!
SORRY I WOKE YOU UP...
302
SUZUKA ASAHINA
D-DON'T WORRY ABOUT IT.

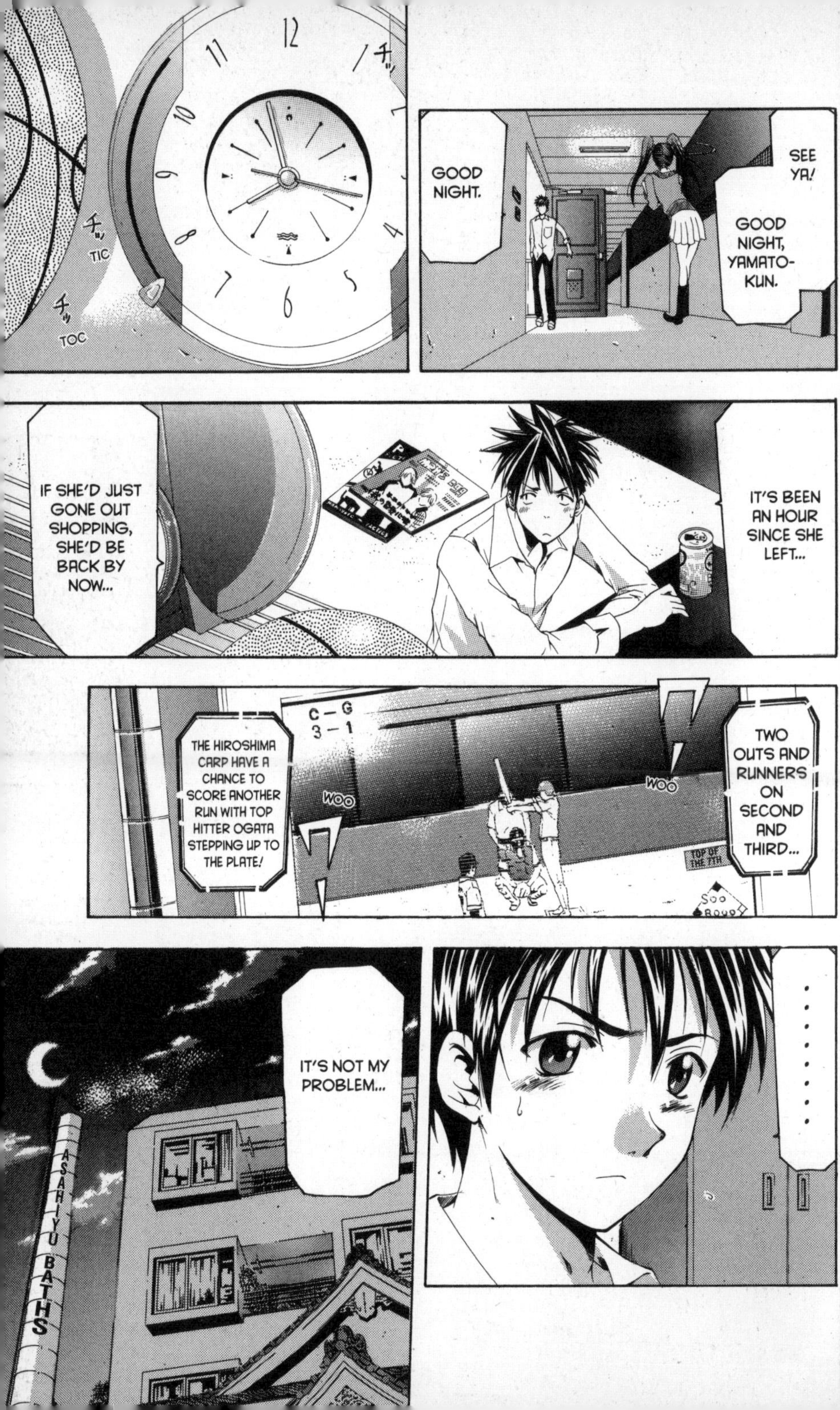
SEE YA!
GOOD NIGHT, YAMATO-KUN.
GOOD NIGHT.
TIC
TOC
IT'S BEEN AN HOUR SINCE SHE LEFT...
IF SHE'D JUST GONE OUT SHOPPING, SHE'D BE BACK BY NOW...
TWO OUTS AND RUNNERS ON SECOND AND THIRD...
WOO
TOP OF THE 7TH
C — G
3 — 1
THE HIROSHIMA CARP HAVE A CHANCE TO SCORE ANOTHER RUN WITH TOP HITTER OGATA STEPPING UP TO THE PLATE!
WOO
....
IT'S NOT MY PROBLEM...
ASAHIYU BATHS

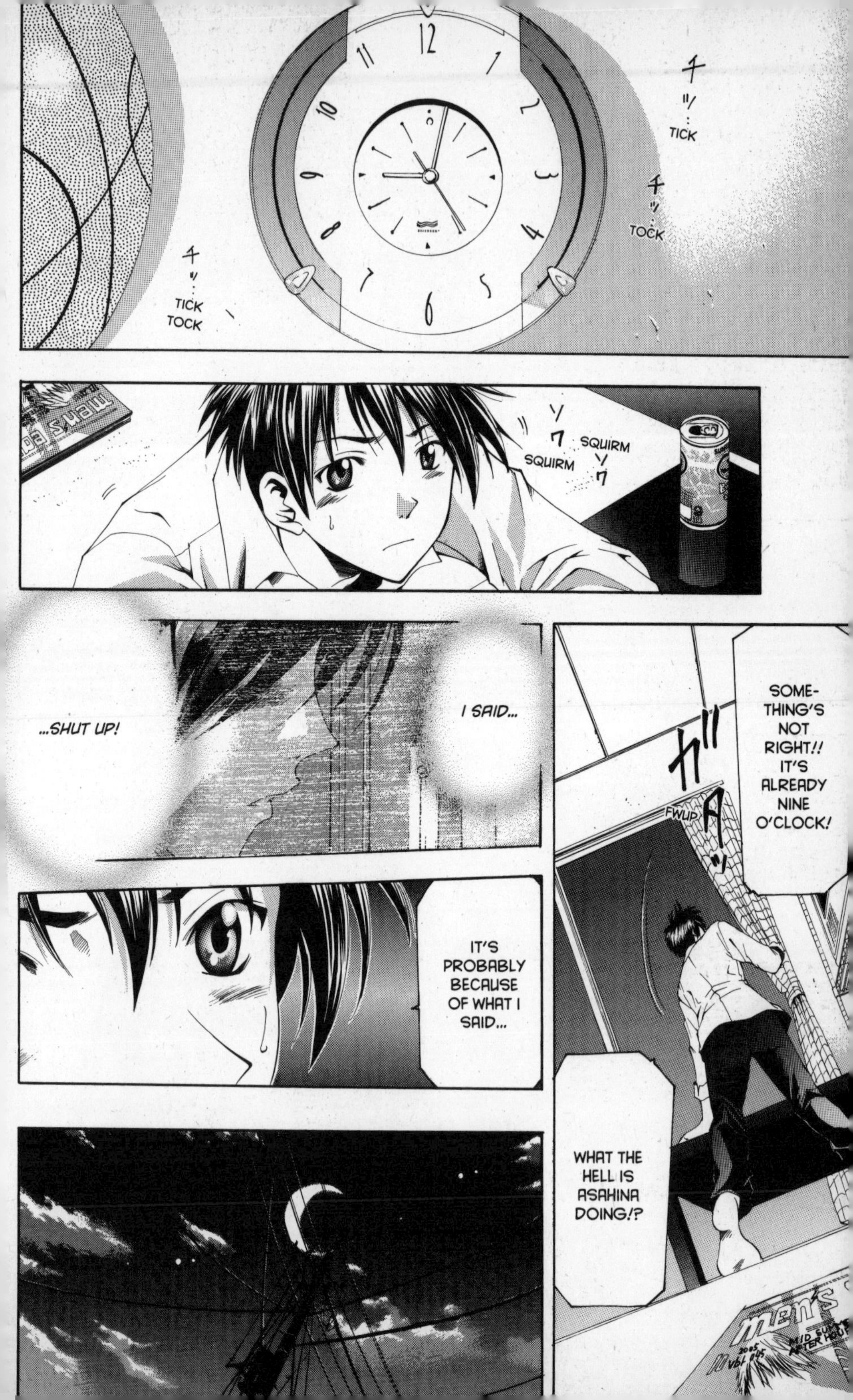

チッ
TICK
チッ
TOCK
チッ
TICK
TOCK
ソワ
SQUIRM
ソワ
SQUIRM
SOME-THING'S NOT RIGHT!! IT'S ALREADY NINE O'CLOCK!
ガバッ
FWUD
WHAT THE HELL IS ASAHINA DOING!?
I SAID...
...SHUT UP!
IT'S PROBABLY BECAUSE OF WHAT I SAID...

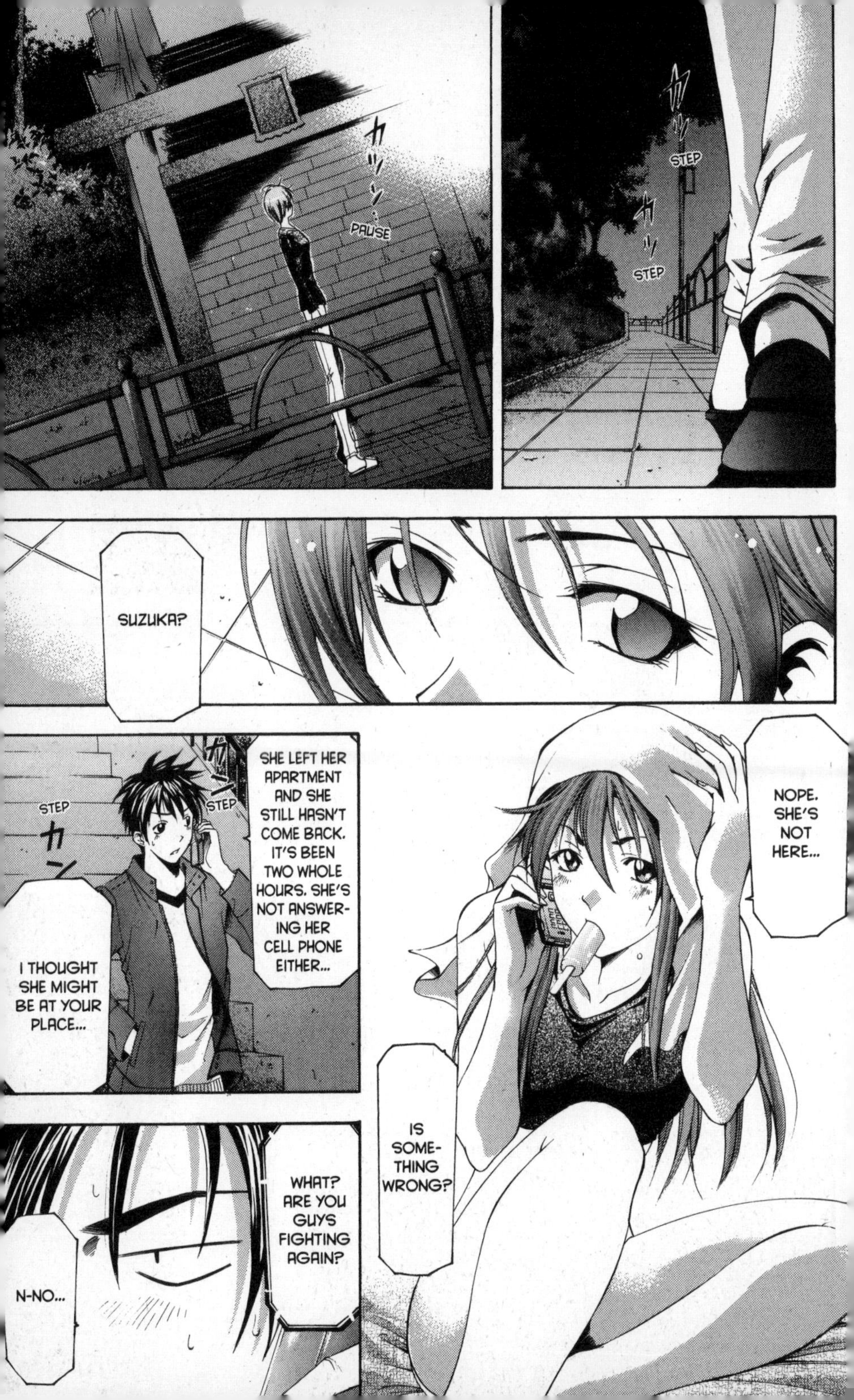
STEP
STEP
PAUSE
SUZUKA?
NOPE. SHE'S NOT HERE...
IS SOME-THING WRONG?
SHE LEFT HER APARTMENT AND SHE STILL HASN'T COME BACK. IT'S BEEN TWO WHOLE HOURS. SHE'S NOT ANSWER-ING HER CELL PHONE EITHER...
STEP
STEP
I THOUGHT SHE MIGHT BE AT YOUR PLACE...
WHAT? ARE YOU GUYS FIGHTING AGAIN?
N-NO...

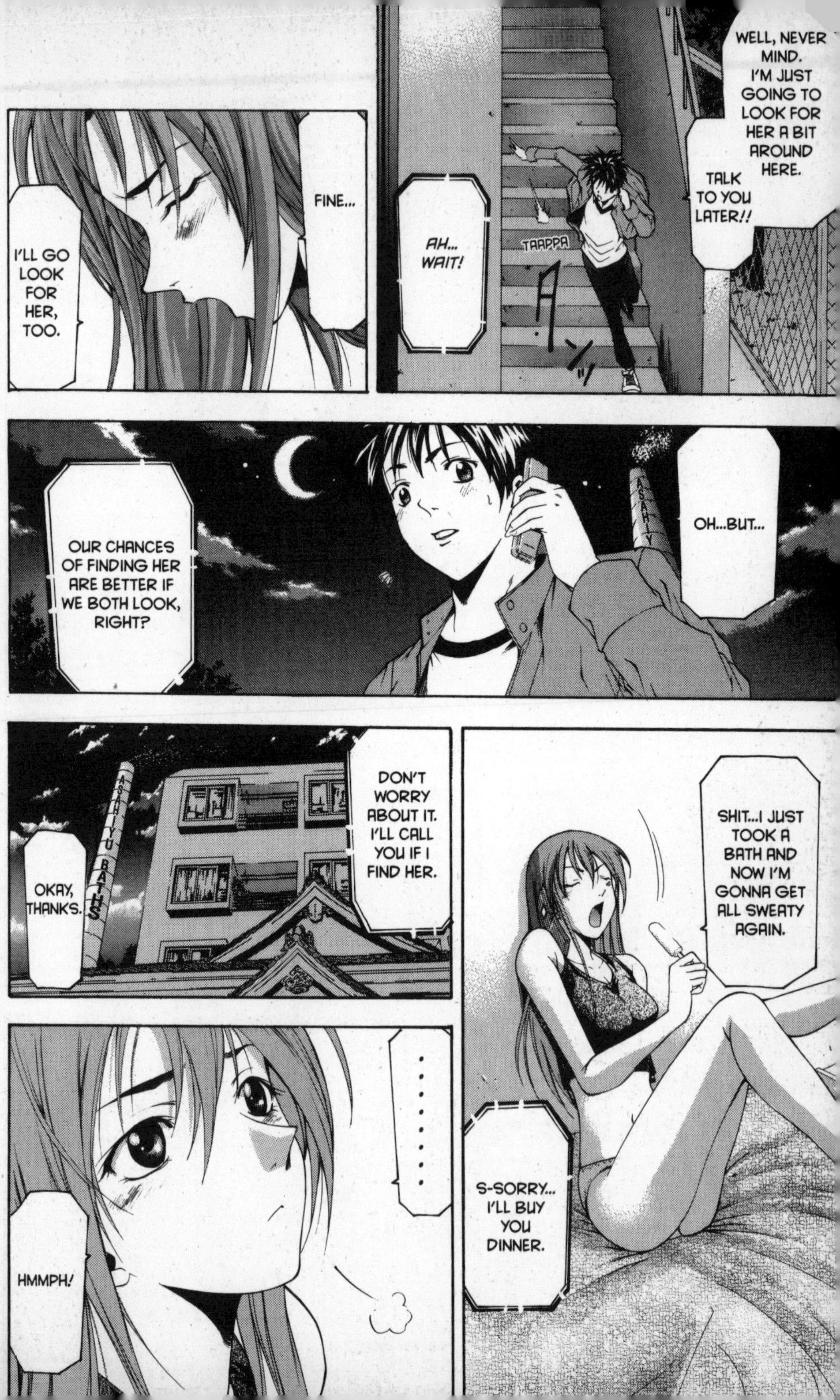
WELL, NEVER MIND. I'M JUST GOING TO LOOK FOR HER A BIT AROUND HERE.
TALK TO YOU LATER!!
TAAPPA
AH... WAIT!
FINE...
I'LL GO LOOK FOR HER, TOO.
OH...BUT...
OUR CHANCES OF FINDING HER ARE BETTER IF WE BOTH LOOK, RIGHT?
DON'T WORRY ABOUT IT. I'LL CALL YOU IF I FIND HER.
ASAHIYU BATHS
OKAY, THANKS.
SHIT...I JUST TOOK A BATH AND NOW I'M GONNA GET ALL SWEATY AGAIN.
S-SORRY... I'LL BUY YOU DINNER.
......
HMMPH!

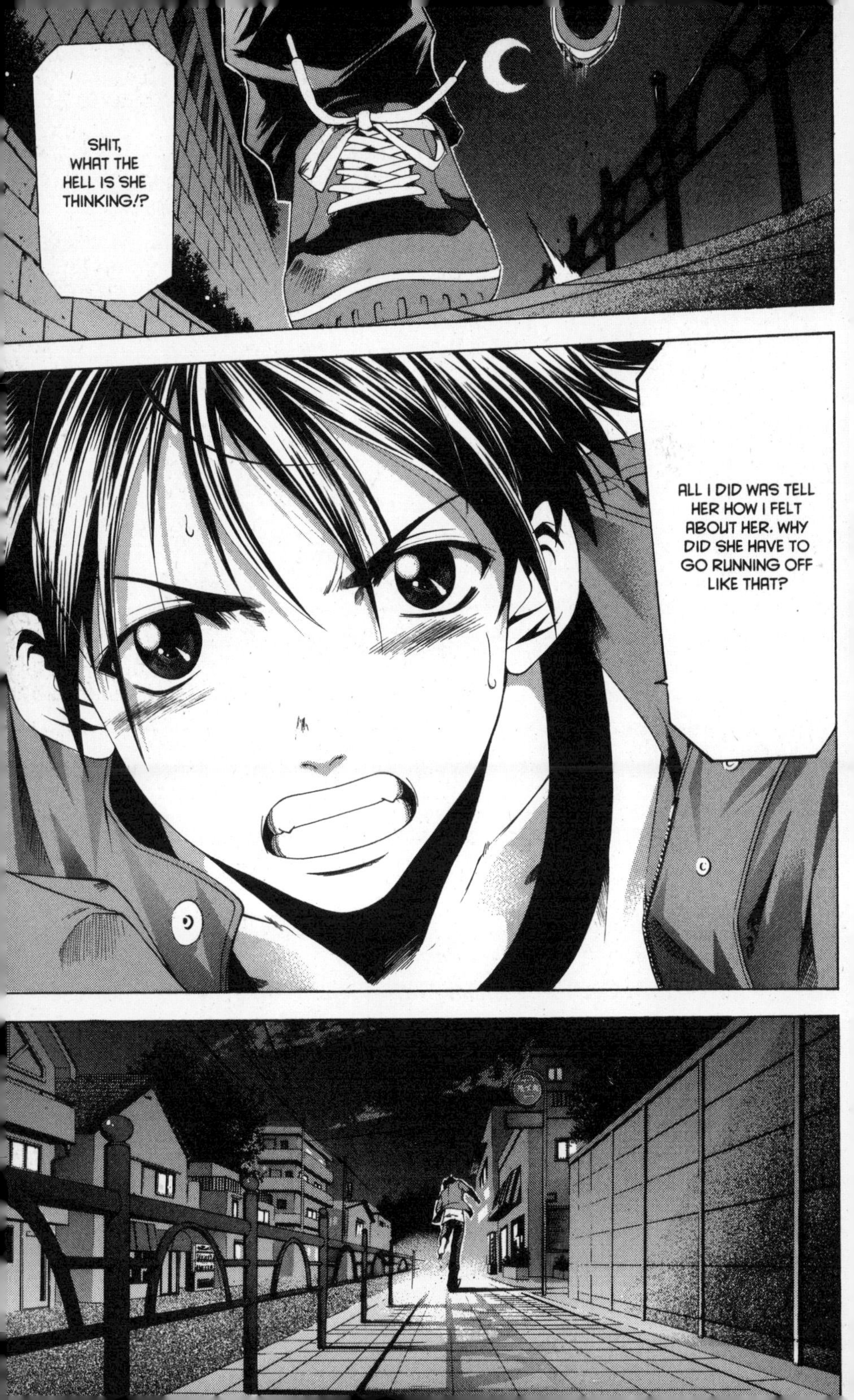
SHIT, WHAT THE HELL IS SHE THINKING!?
ALL I DID WAS TELL HER HOW I FELT ABOUT HER. WHY DID SHE HAVE TO GO RUNNING OFF LIKE THAT?

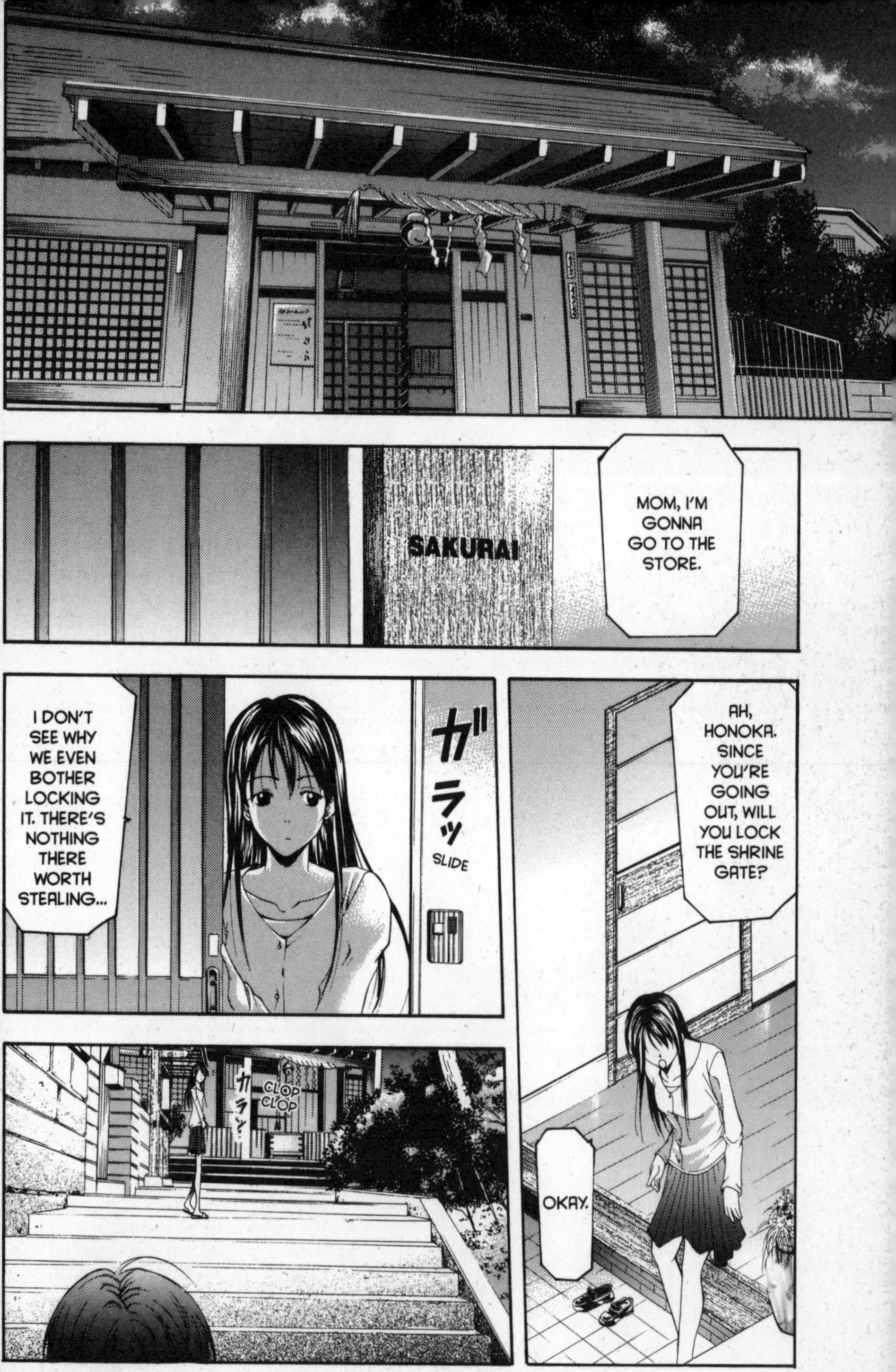
MOM, I'M GONNA GO TO THE STORE.
SAKURAI
AH, HONOKA. SINCE YOU'RE GOING OUT, WILL YOU LOCK THE SHRINE GATE?
OKAY.
ガラッ
SLIDE
I DON'T SEE WHY WE EVEN BOTHER LOCKING IT. THERE'S NOTHING THERE WORTH STEALING...
カラン
CLOP CLOP

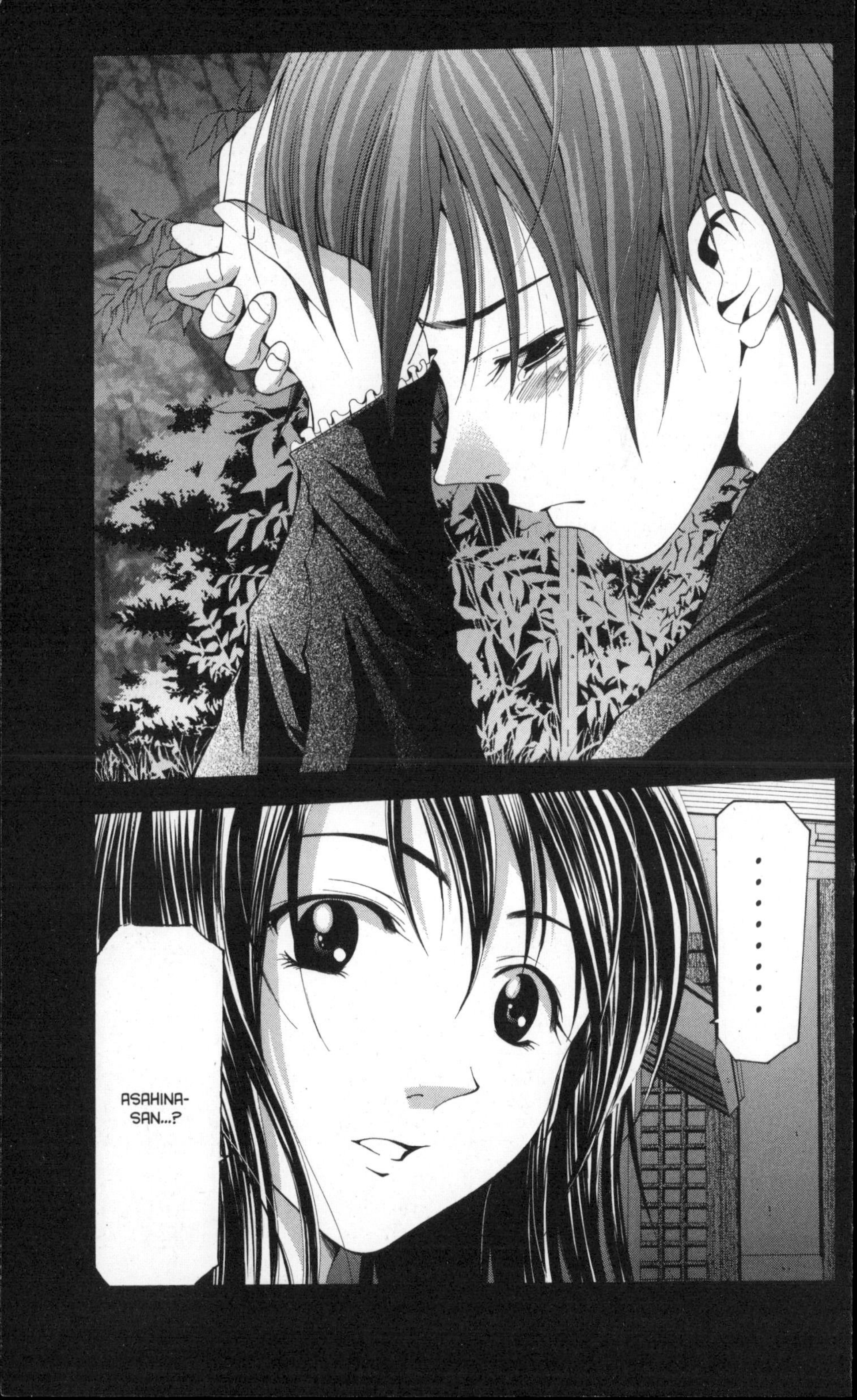
....
ASAHINA-SAN...?

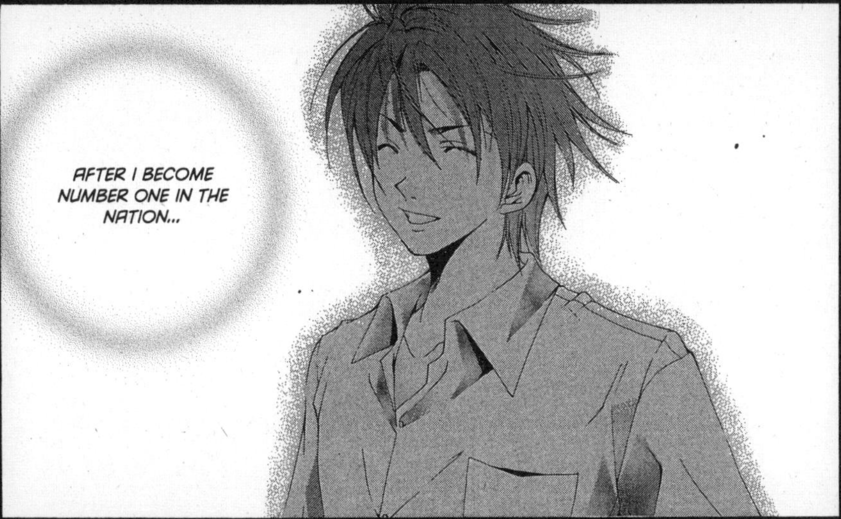
AFTER I BECOME NUMBER ONE IN THE NATION...

SUZUKA

#68 Loss

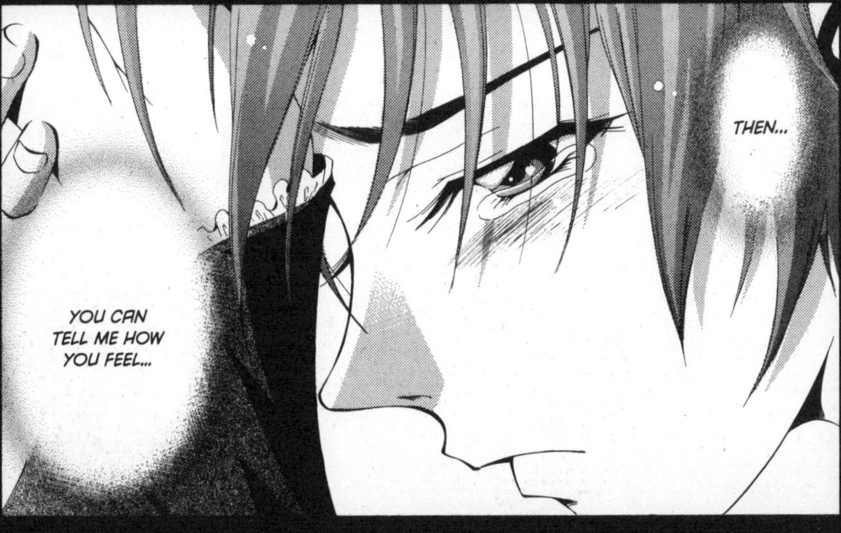
THEN...
YOU CAN TELL ME HOW YOU FEEL...

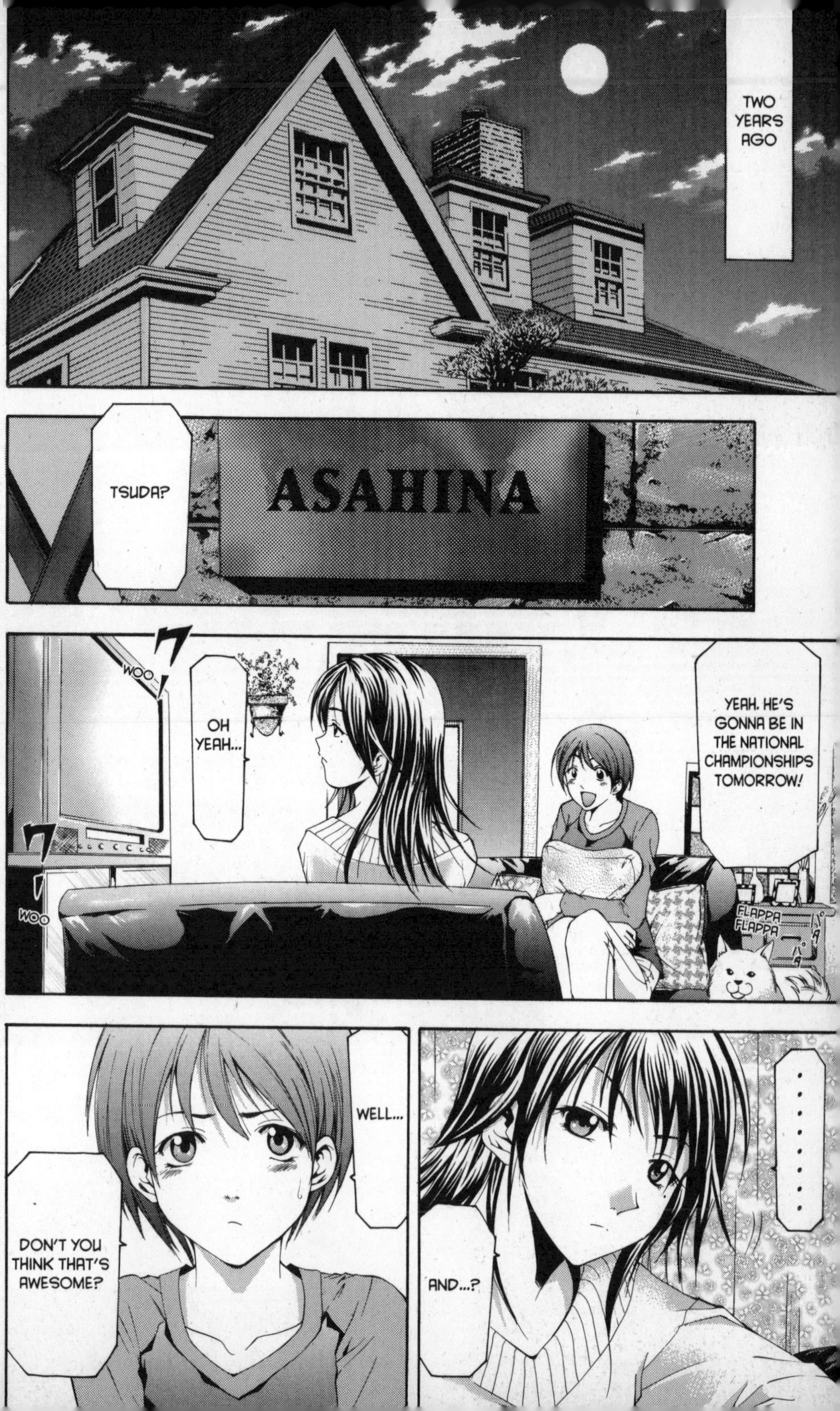
TWO YEARS AGO
ASAHINA
TSUDA?
YEAH. HE'S GONNA BE IN THE NATIONAL CHAMPIONSHIPS TOMORROW!
FLAPPA FLAPPA
OH YEAH...
WOO
WOO
......
AND...?
WELL...
DON'T YOU THINK THAT'S AWESOME?

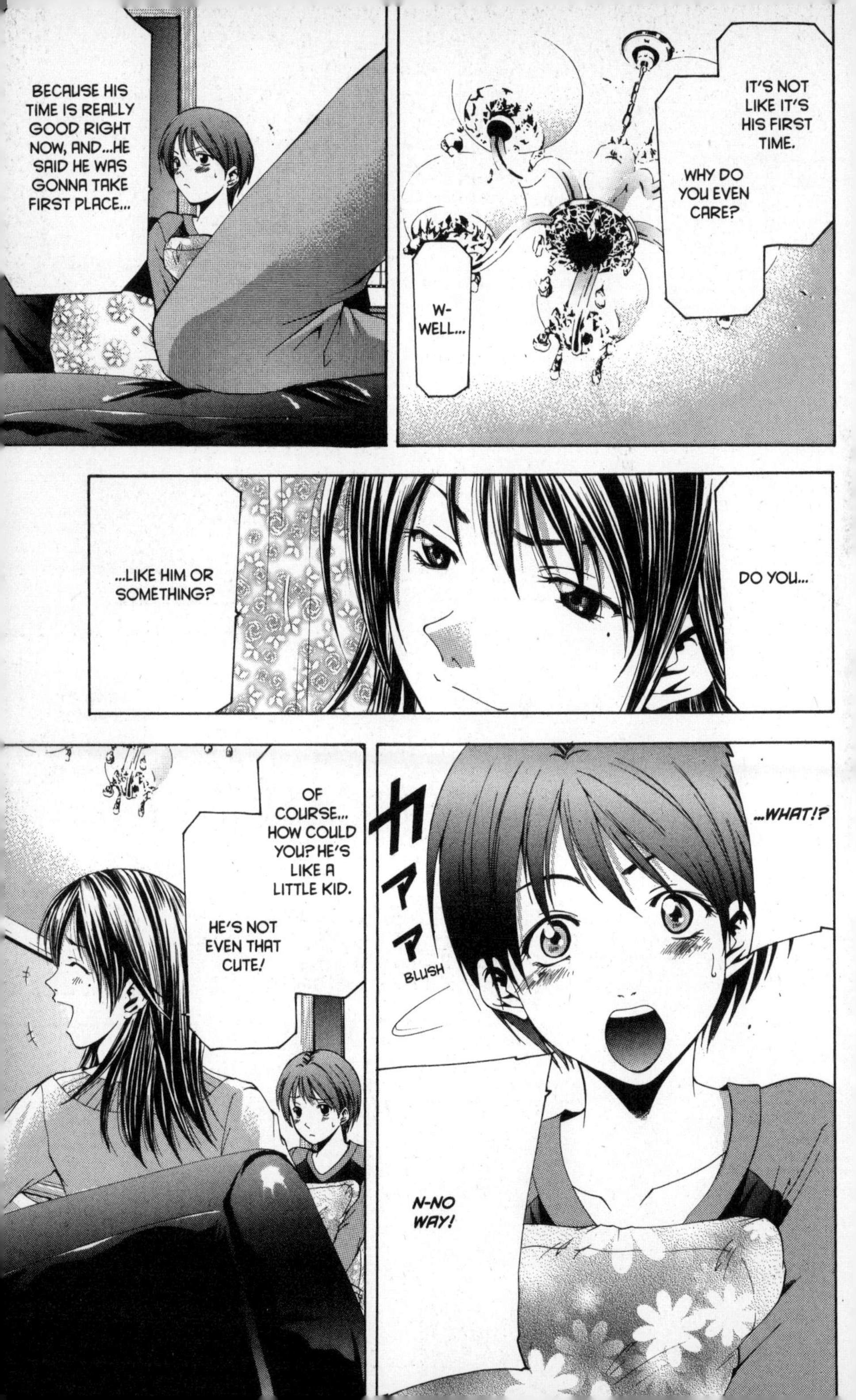
IT'S NOT LIKE IT'S HIS FIRST TIME.
WHY DO YOU EVEN CARE?
W-WELL...
BECAUSE HIS TIME IS REALLY GOOD RIGHT NOW, AND...HE SAID HE WAS GONNA TAKE FIRST PLACE...
DO YOU...
...LIKE HIM OR SOMETHING?
...WHAT!?
カァァ
BLUSH
N-NO WAY!
OF COURSE... HOW COULD YOU? HE'S LIKE A LITTLE KID.
HE'S NOT EVEN THAT CUTE!

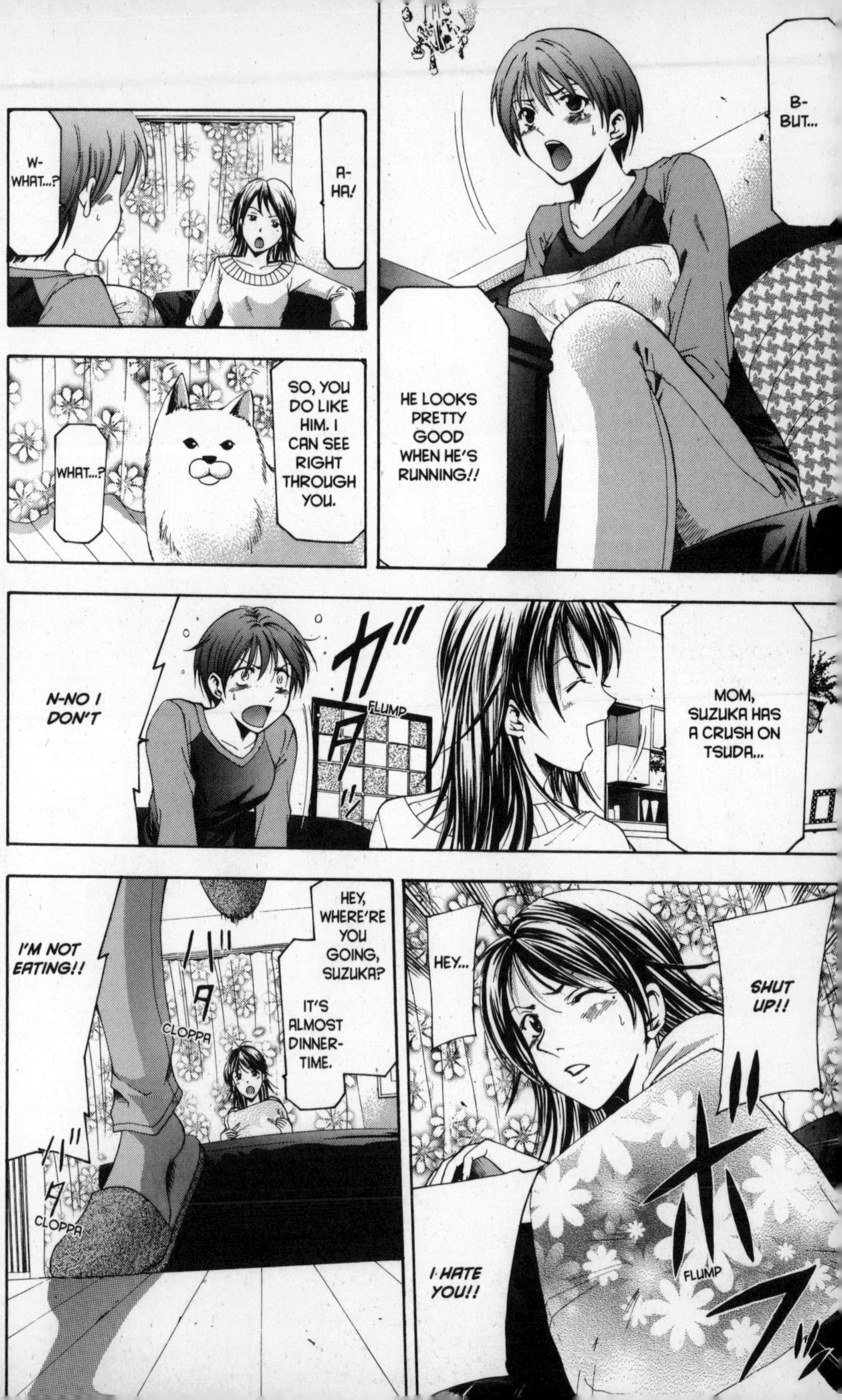
B-BUT...
HE LOOKS PRETTY GOOD WHEN HE'S RUNNING!!
A-HA!
W-WHAT...?
SO, YOU DO LIKE HIM. I CAN SEE RIGHT THROUGH YOU.
WHAT...?
MOM, SUZUKA HAS A CRUSH ON TSUDA...
FLUMP
N-NO I DON'T
SHUT UP!!
HEY...
FLUMP
I HATE YOU!!
HEY, WHERE'RE YOU GOING, SUZUKA?
IT'S ALMOST DINNER-TIME.
I'M NOT EATING!!
CLOPPA
CLOPPA

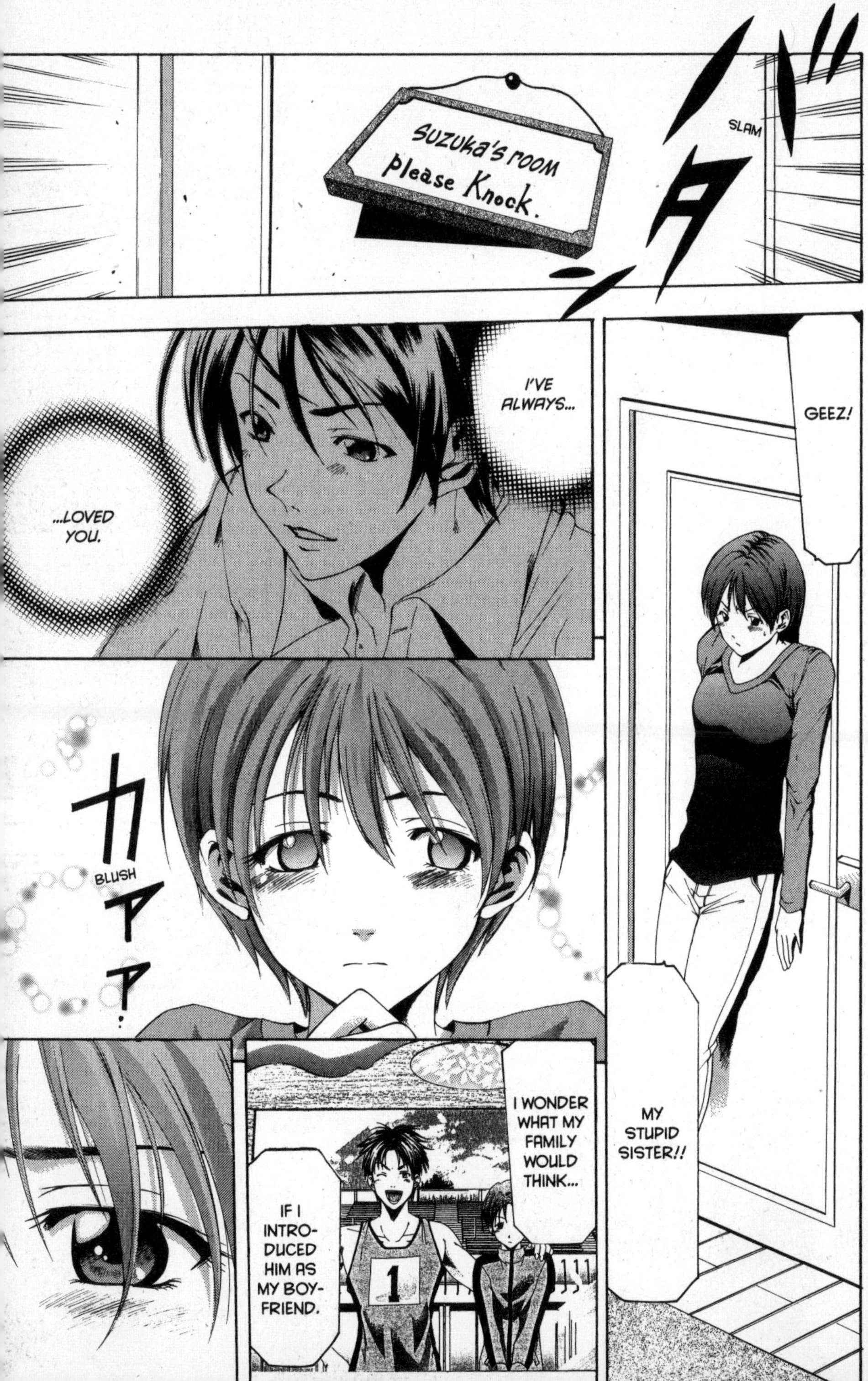
SLAM
SUZUKa's room please Knock.
GEEZ!
MY STUPID SISTER!!
I'VE ALWAYS...
...LOVED YOU.
BLUSH
I WONDER WHAT MY FAMILY WOULD THINK...
IF I INTRO-DUCED HIM AS MY BOY-FRIEND.

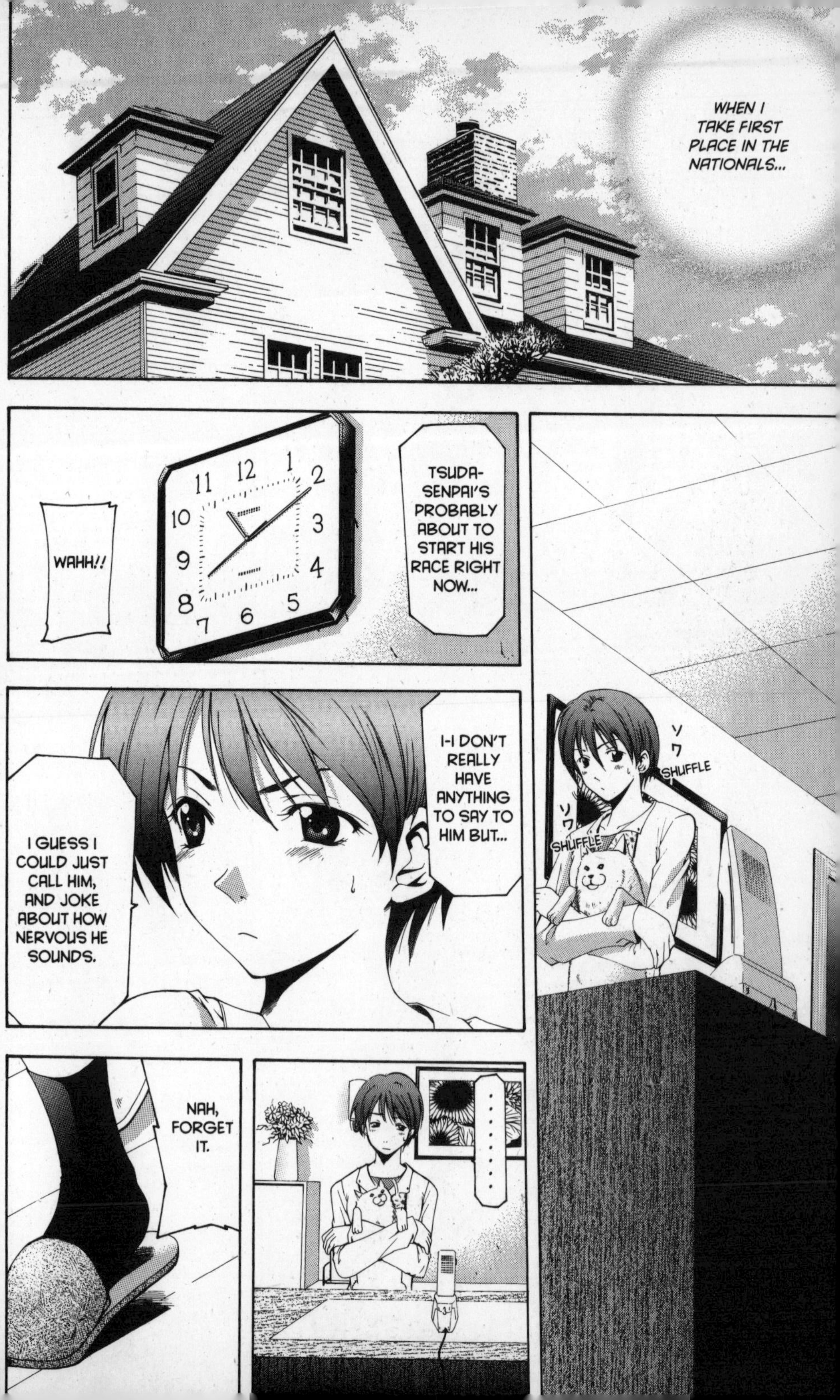
WHEN I TAKE FIRST PLACE IN THE NATIONALS...
ソワ SHUFFLE
ソワ SHUFFLE
TSUDA-SENPAI'S PROBABLY ABOUT TO START HIS RACE RIGHT NOW...
WAHH!!
I-I DON'T REALLY HAVE ANYTHING TO SAY TO HIM BUT...
I GUESS I COULD JUST CALL HIM, AND JOKE ABOUT HOW NERVOUS HE SOUNDS.
......
NAH, FORGET IT.

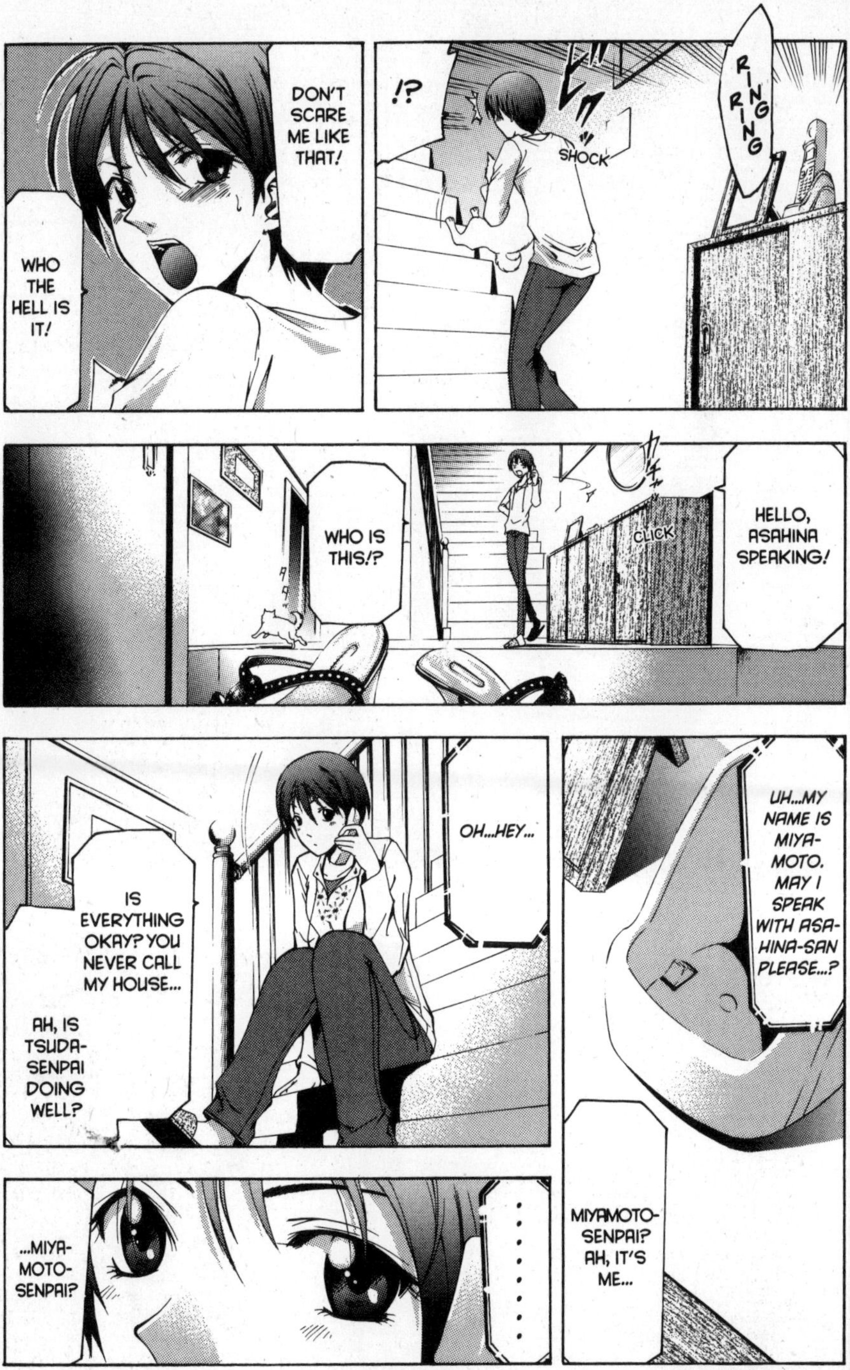
RING RING
SHOCK
!?
DON'T SCARE ME LIKE THAT!
WHO THE HELL IS IT!
HELLO, ASAHINA SPEAKING!
CLICK
WHO IS THIS!?
UH...MY NAME IS MIYA-MOTO. MAY I SPEAK WITH ASA-HINA-SAN PLEASE...?
MIYAMOTO-SENPAI? AH, IT'S ME...
OH...HEY...
IS EVERYTHING OKAY? YOU NEVER CALL MY HOUSE...
AH, IS TSUDA-SENPAI DOING WELL?
......
...MIYA-MOTO-SENPAI?

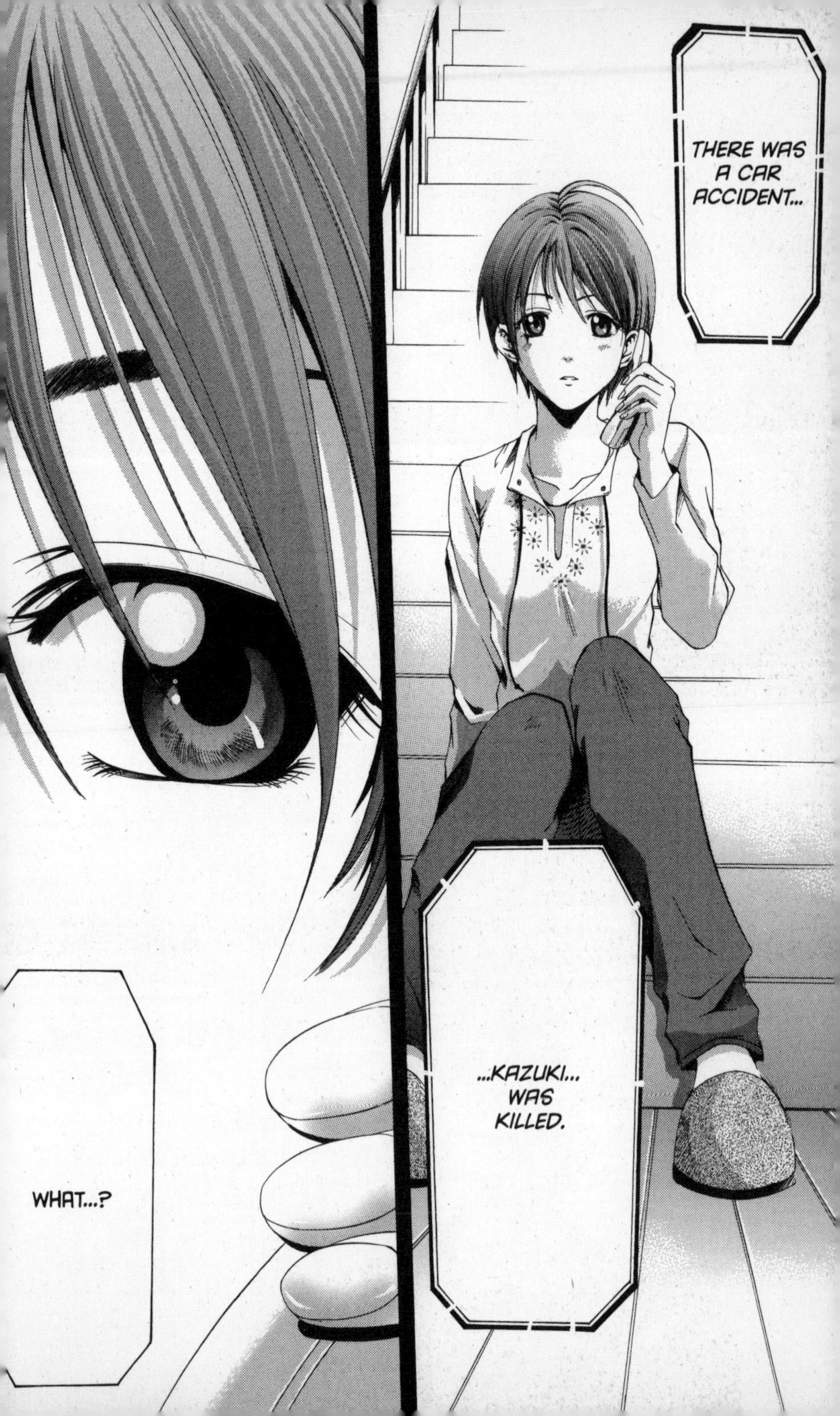
THERE WAS A CAR ACCIDENT...
...KAZUKI... WAS KILLED.
WHAT...?

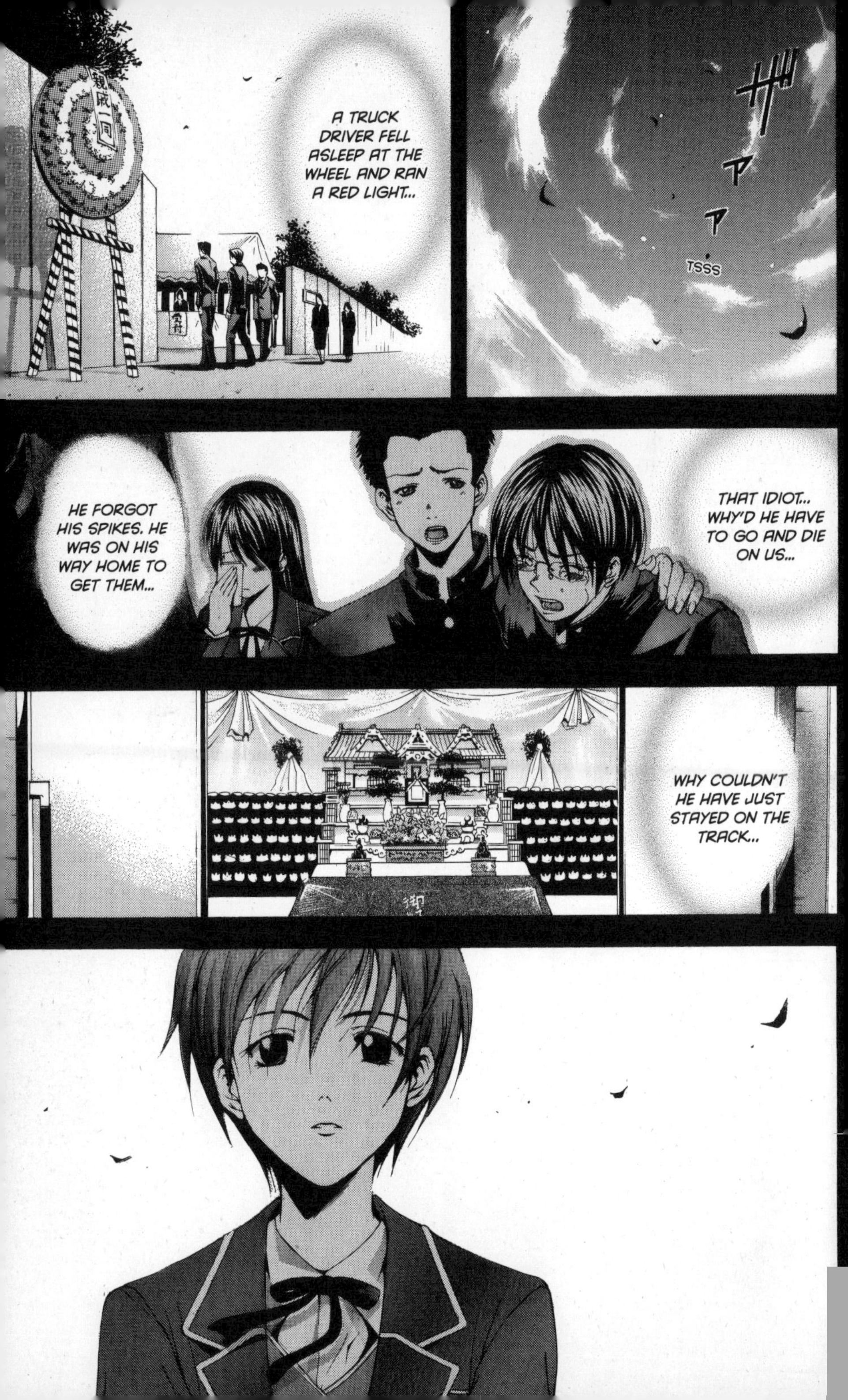
ザァァ
TSSS
A TRUCK DRIVER FELL ASLEEP AT THE WHEEL AND RAN A RED LIGHT...
THAT IDIOT... WHY'D HE HAVE TO GO AND DIE ON US...
HE FORGOT HIS SPIKES. HE WAS ON HIS WAY HOME TO GET THEM...
WHY COULDN'T HE HAVE JUST STAYED ON THE TRACK...

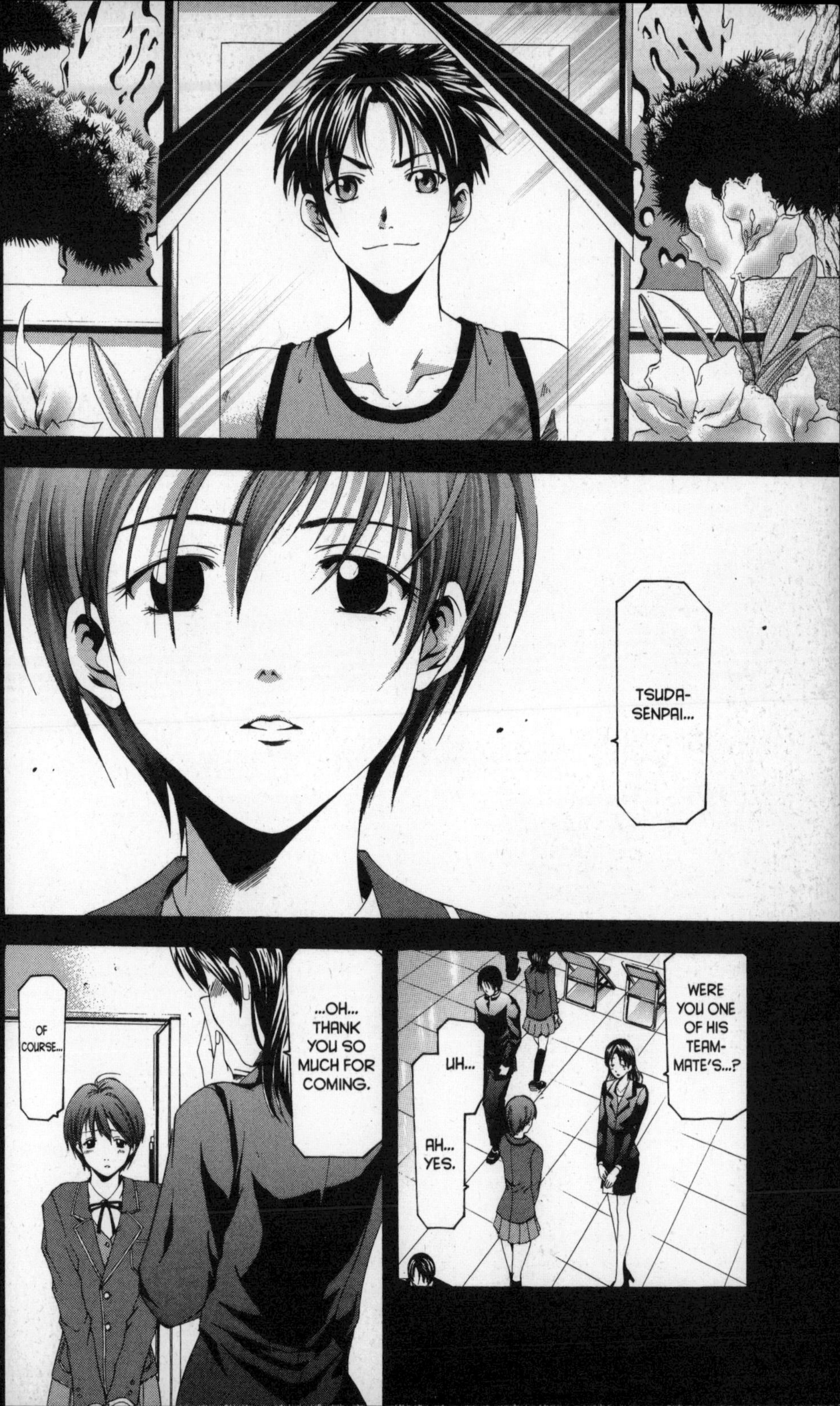
TSUDA-SENPAI...
WERE YOU ONE OF HIS TEAM-MATE'S...?
UH...
AH... YES.
...OH... THANK YOU SO MUCH FOR COMING.
OF COURSE...

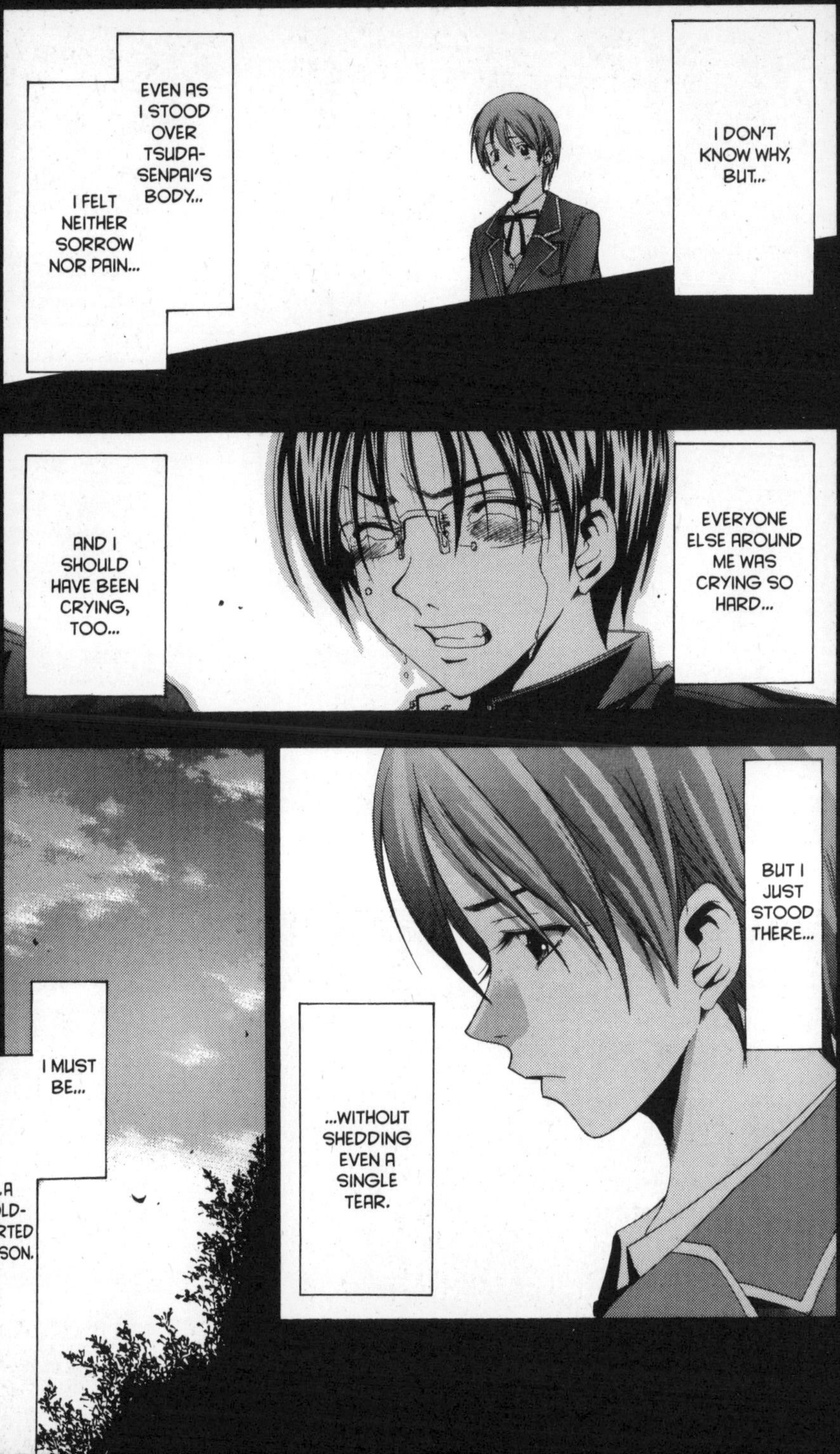
I DON'T KNOW WHY, BUT...
EVEN AS I STOOD OVER TSUDA-SENPAI'S BODY...
I FELT NEITHER SORROW NOR PAIN...
EVERYONE ELSE AROUND ME WAS CRYING SO HARD...
AND I SHOULD HAVE BEEN CRYING, TOO...
BUT I JUST STOOD THERE...
...WITHOUT SHEDDING EVEN A SINGLE TEAR.
I MUST BE...
...A COLD-HEARTED PERSON.

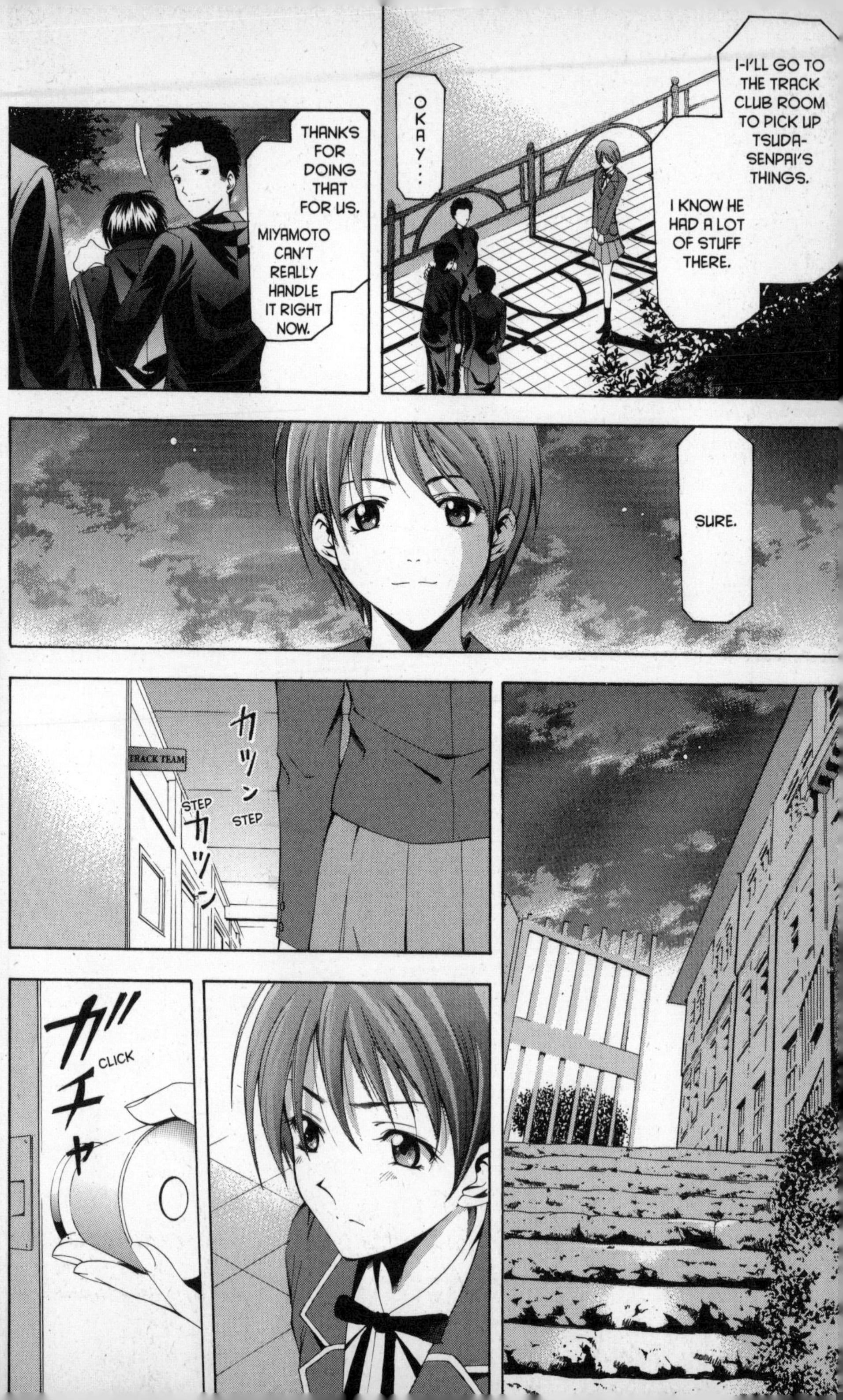
I-I'LL GO TO THE TRACK CLUB ROOM TO PICK UP TSUDA-SENPAI'S THINGS.
I KNOW HE HAD A LOT OF STUFF THERE.
OKAY...
THANKS FOR DOING THAT FOR US.
MIYAMOTO CAN'T REALLY HANDLE IT RIGHT NOW.
SURE.
TRACK TEAM
カツン
STEP
カツン
STEP
ガチャ
CLICK

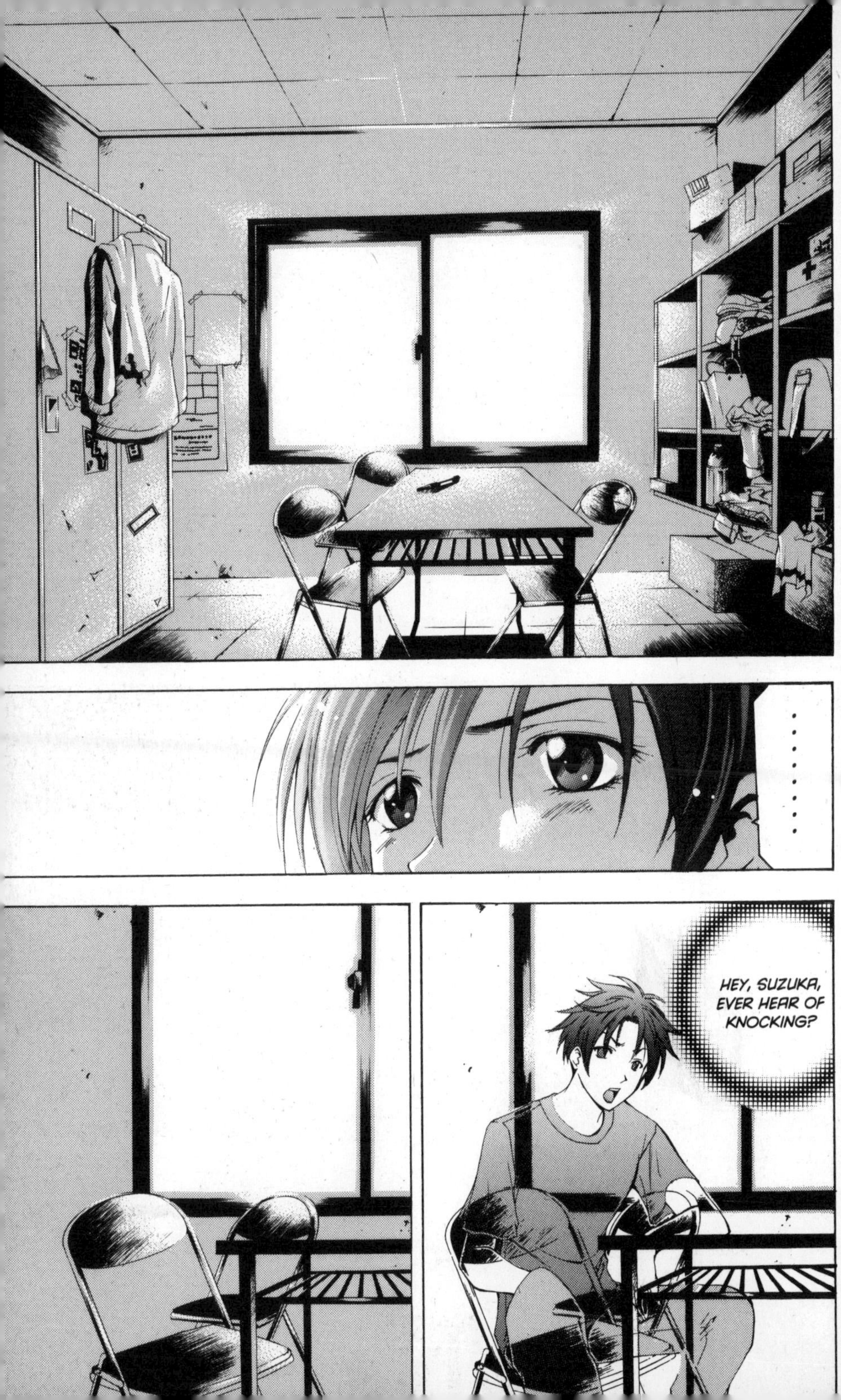

......
HEY, SUZUKA, EVER HEAR OF KNOCKING?

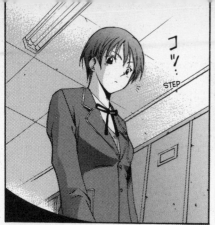

コッ
STEP
コッ…
STEP
Hi-Mckee
Soon to be No.1 in Japan!!
Kazuki Tsuda!!
Suzuka Asahina
AH!! QUIT VANDALIZING THE DESKS!!
TCH... I'M NOT VANDALIZING IT, STUPID... I'M JUST STATING MY GOAL.
Hi Mckee
YEAH, WELL I'M TELLING THE TEACHER.
HEH, WE'LL SEE ABOUT THAT!
I'LL WRITE YOUR NAME, TOO!! NOW YOU'RE AN ACCOMPLICE!!
H-HEY, THAT'S A PERMANENT MARKER!

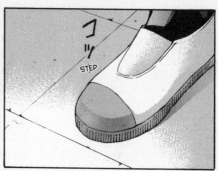

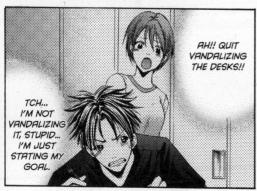

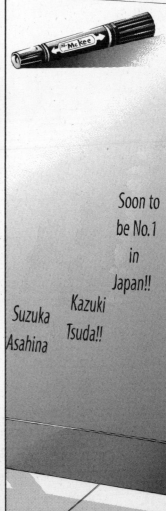

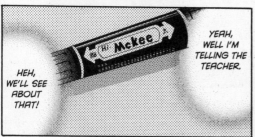

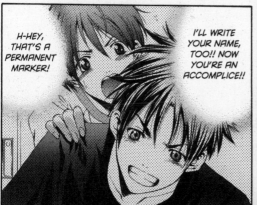

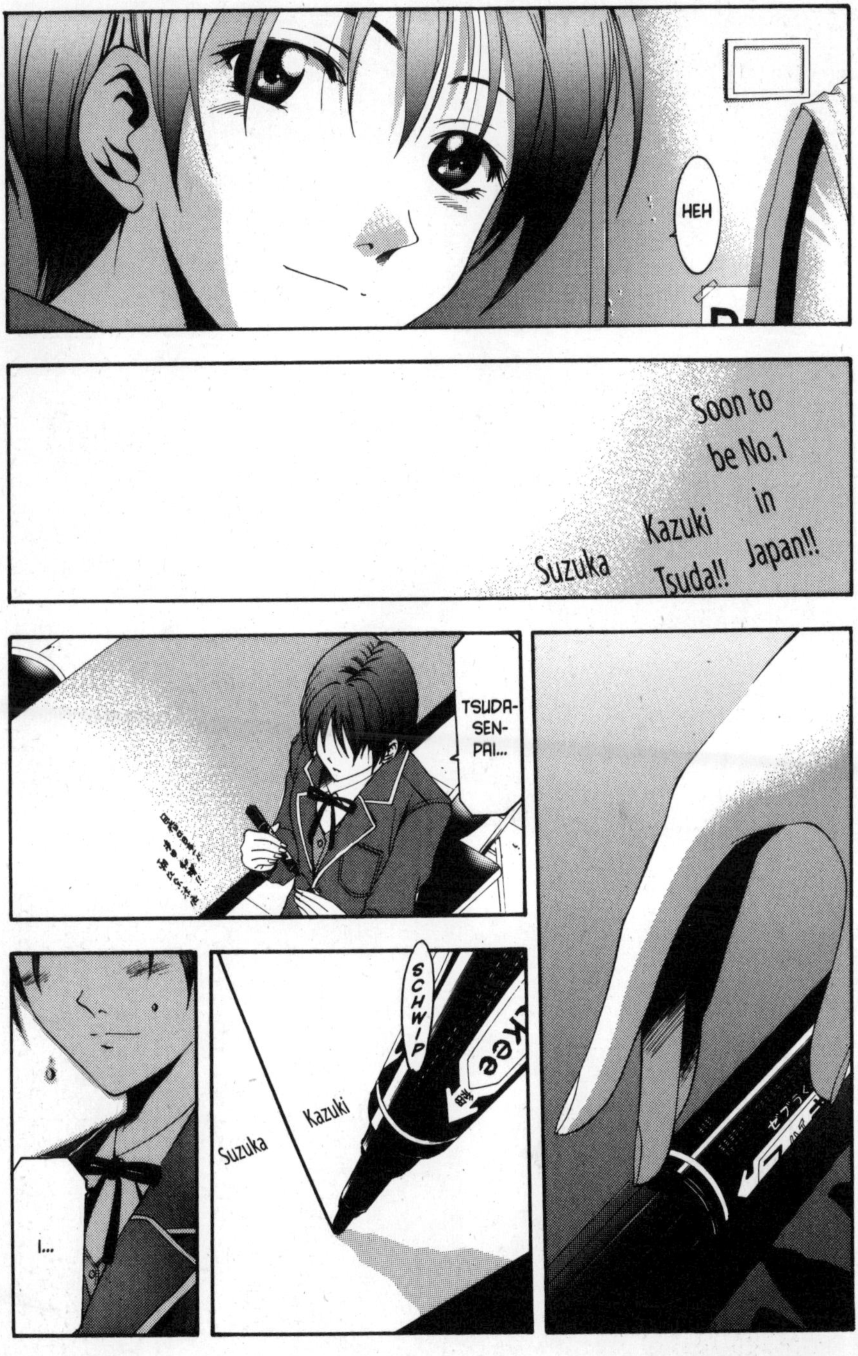
HEH
Soon to be No.1 in Japan!!
Kazuki Tsuda!!
Suzuka
TSUDA-SENPAI...
SCHWIP
Kazuki
Suzuka
I...

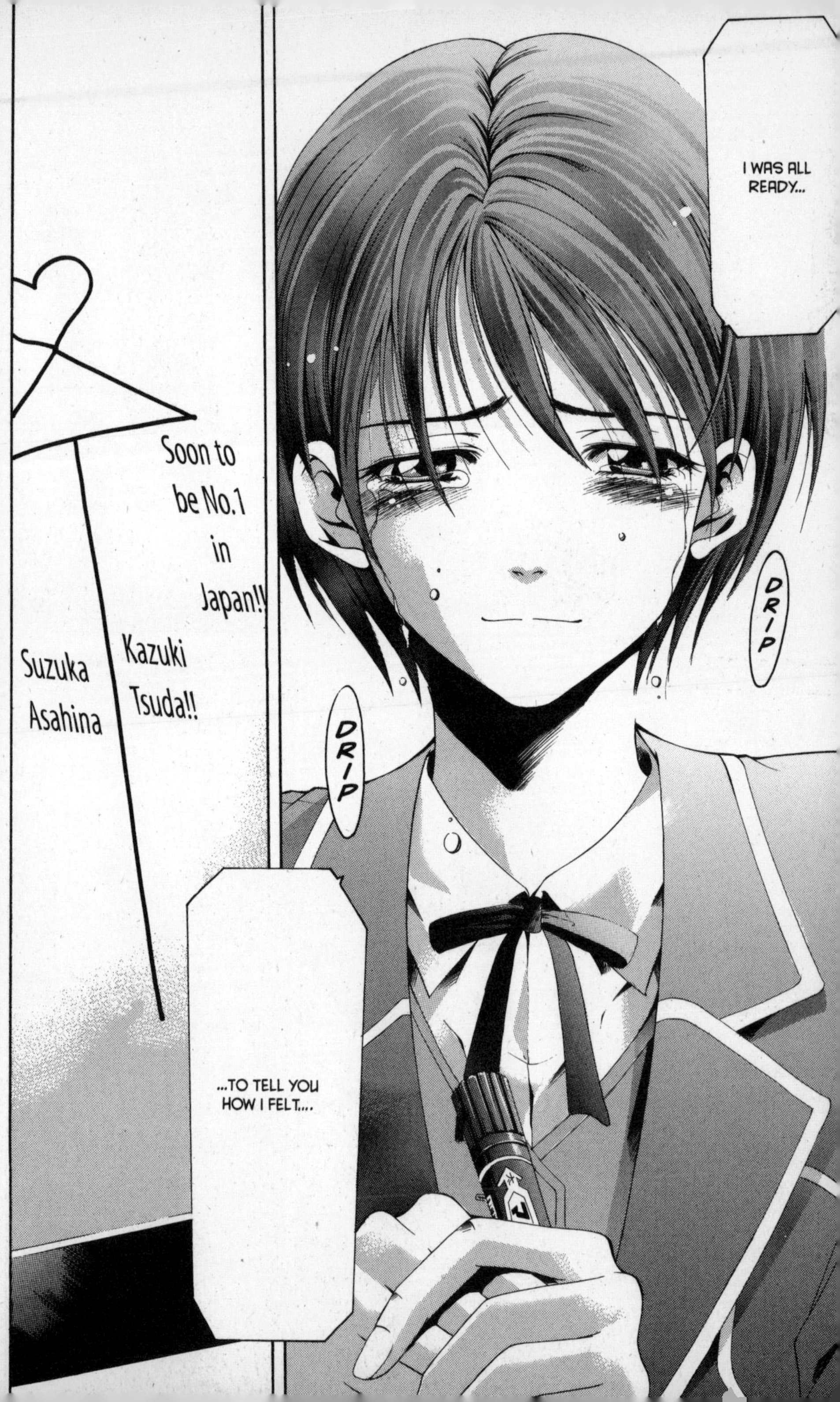
I WAS ALL READY...
DRIP
DRIP
...TO TELL YOU HOW I FELT....
Soon to be No.1 in Japan!!
Kazuki Tsuda!!
Suzuka Asahina

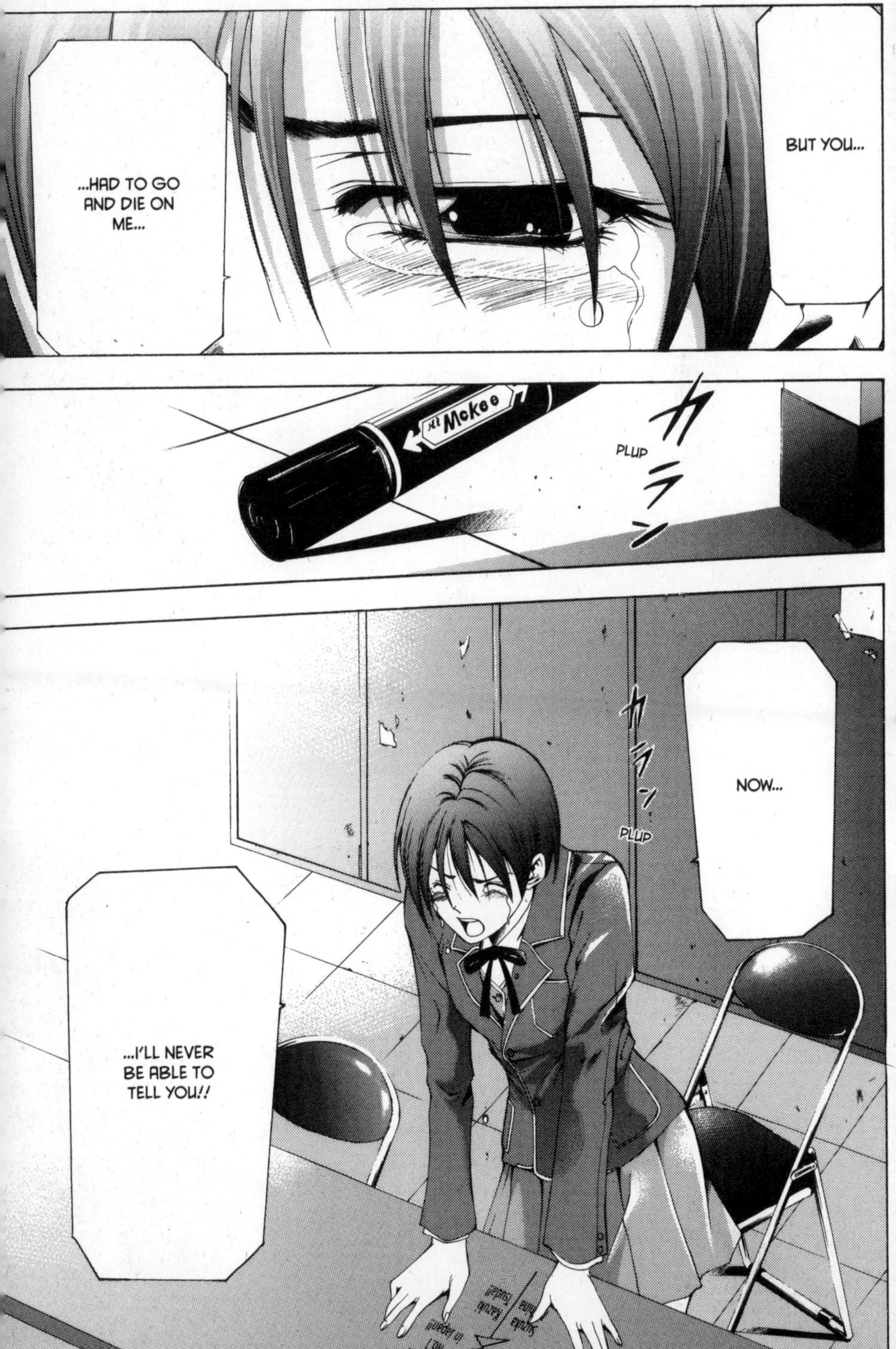
BUT YOU...
...HAD TO GO AND DIE ON ME...
PLUP
Mckee
NOW...
PLUP
...I'LL NEVER BE ABLE TO TELL YOU!!

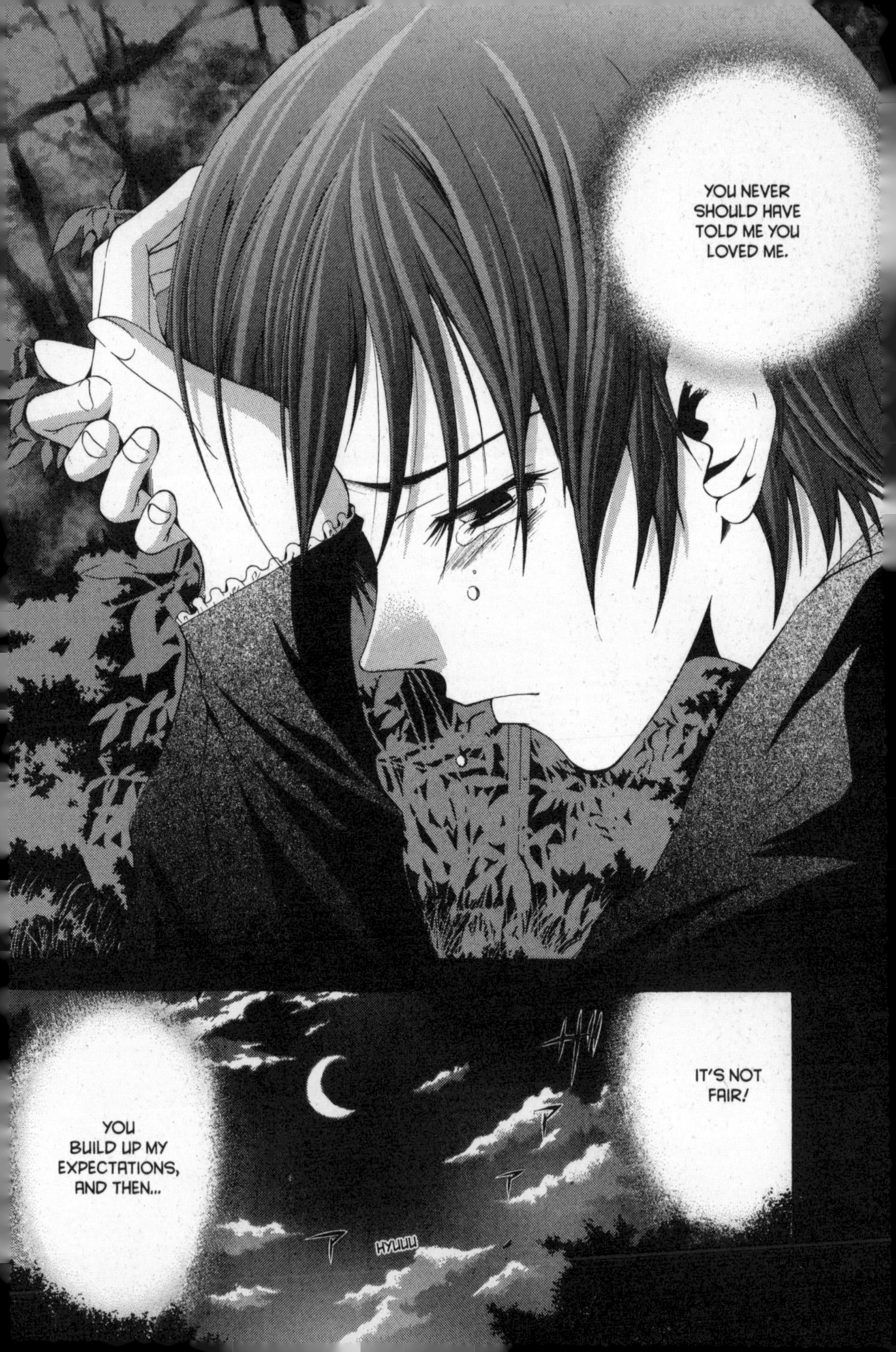
YOU NEVER SHOULD HAVE TOLD ME YOU LOVED ME.
IT'S NOT FAIR!
YOU BUILD UP MY EXPECTATIONS, AND THEN...
HYUUU

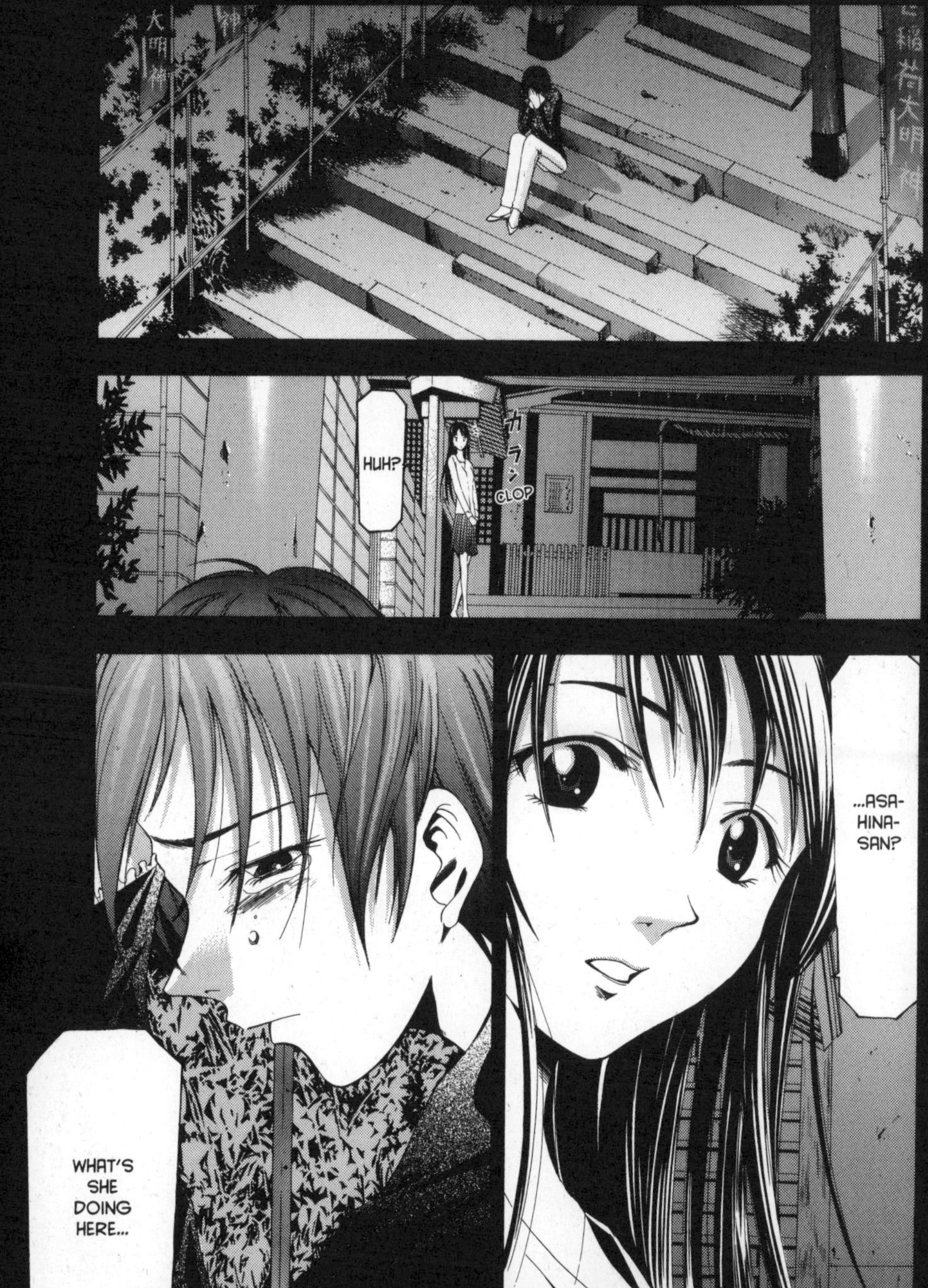
HUH?
カラン
CLOP
...ASA-HINA-SAN?
WHAT'S SHE DOING HERE...

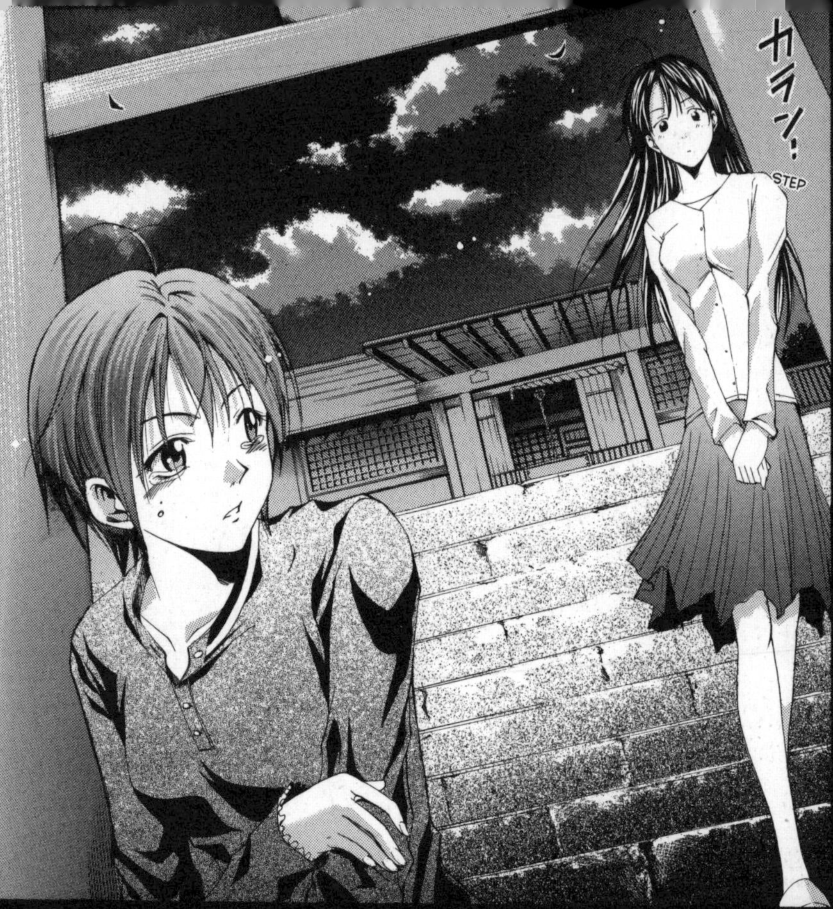
カラン!
STEP

SUZUKA

#69 True Feelings

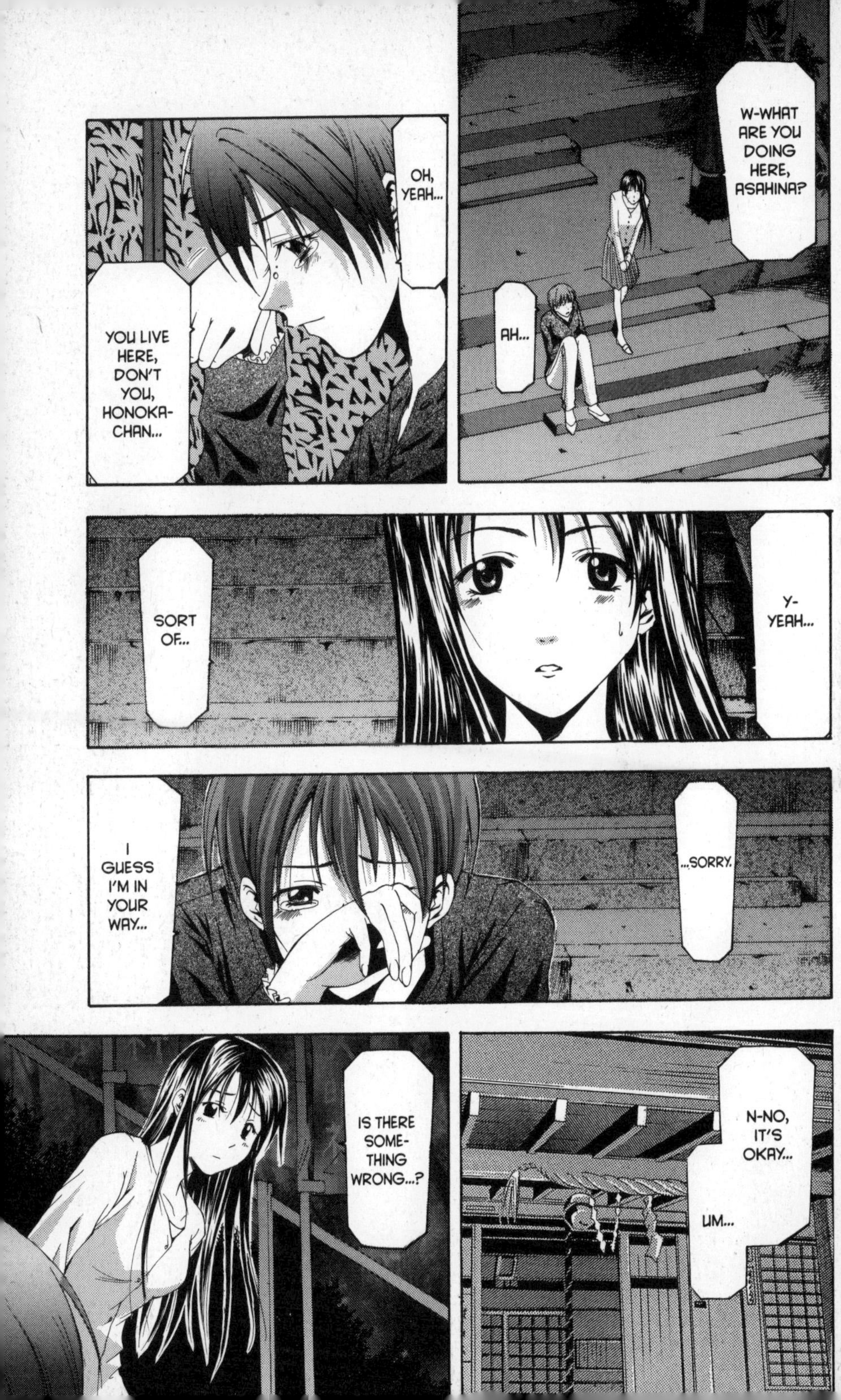
W-WHAT ARE YOU DOING HERE, ASAHINA?
AH...
OH, YEAH...
YOU LIVE HERE, DON'T YOU, HONOKA-CHAN...
Y-YEAH...
SORT OF...
...SORRY.
I GUESS I'M IN YOUR WAY...
N-NO, IT'S OKAY...
UM...
IS THERE SOME-THING WRONG...?

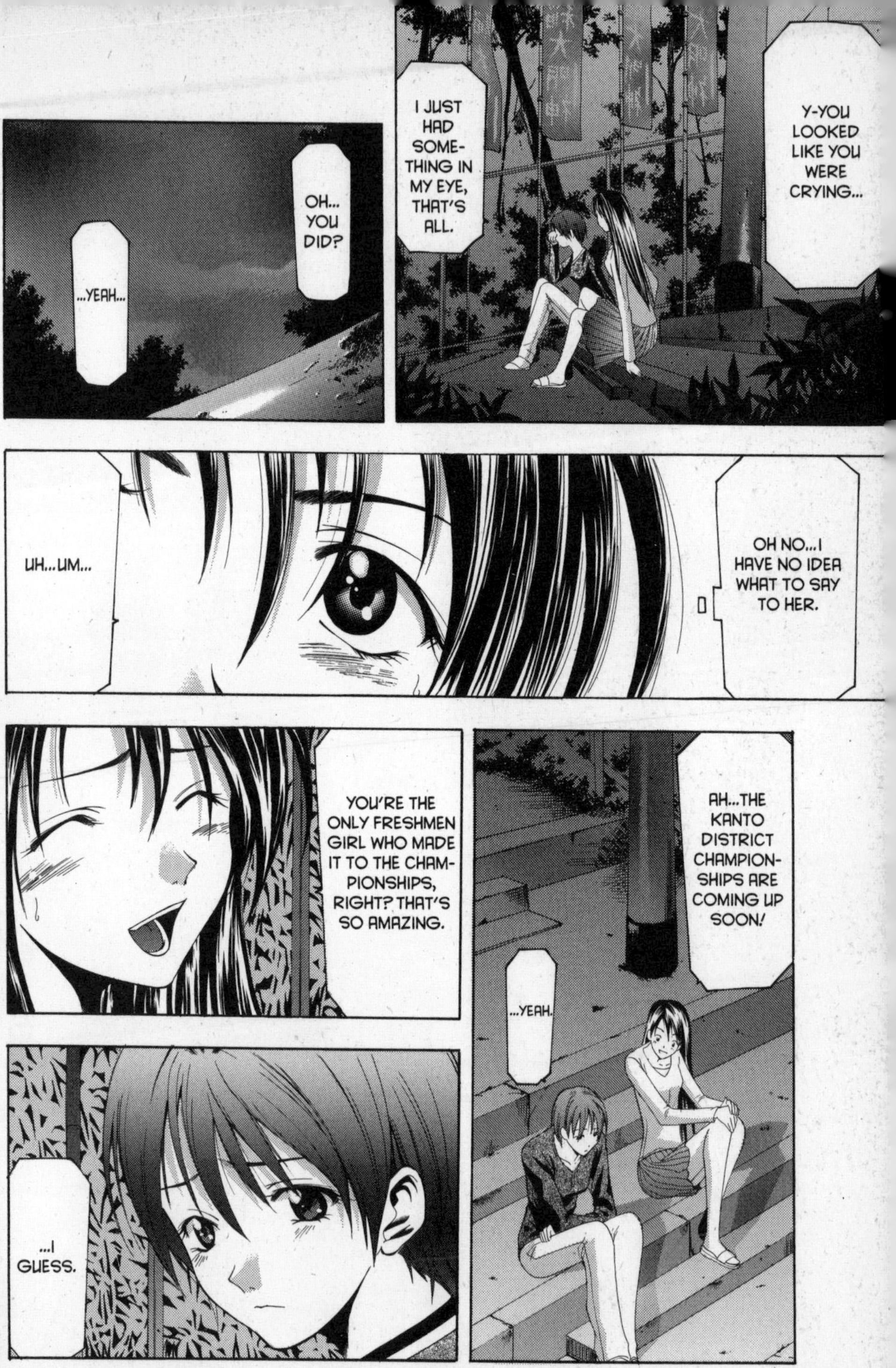
Y-YOU LOOKED LIKE YOU WERE CRYING...
I JUST HAD SOME-THING IN MY EYE, THAT'S ALL.
OH... YOU DID?
...YEAH...
OH NO...I HAVE NO IDEA WHAT TO SAY TO HER.
UH...UM...
AH...THE KANTO DISTRICT CHAMPION-SHIPS ARE COMING UP SOON!
...YEAH.
YOU'RE THE ONLY FRESHMEN GIRL WHO MADE IT TO THE CHAM-PIONSHIPS, RIGHT? THAT'S SO AMAZING.
...I GUESS.

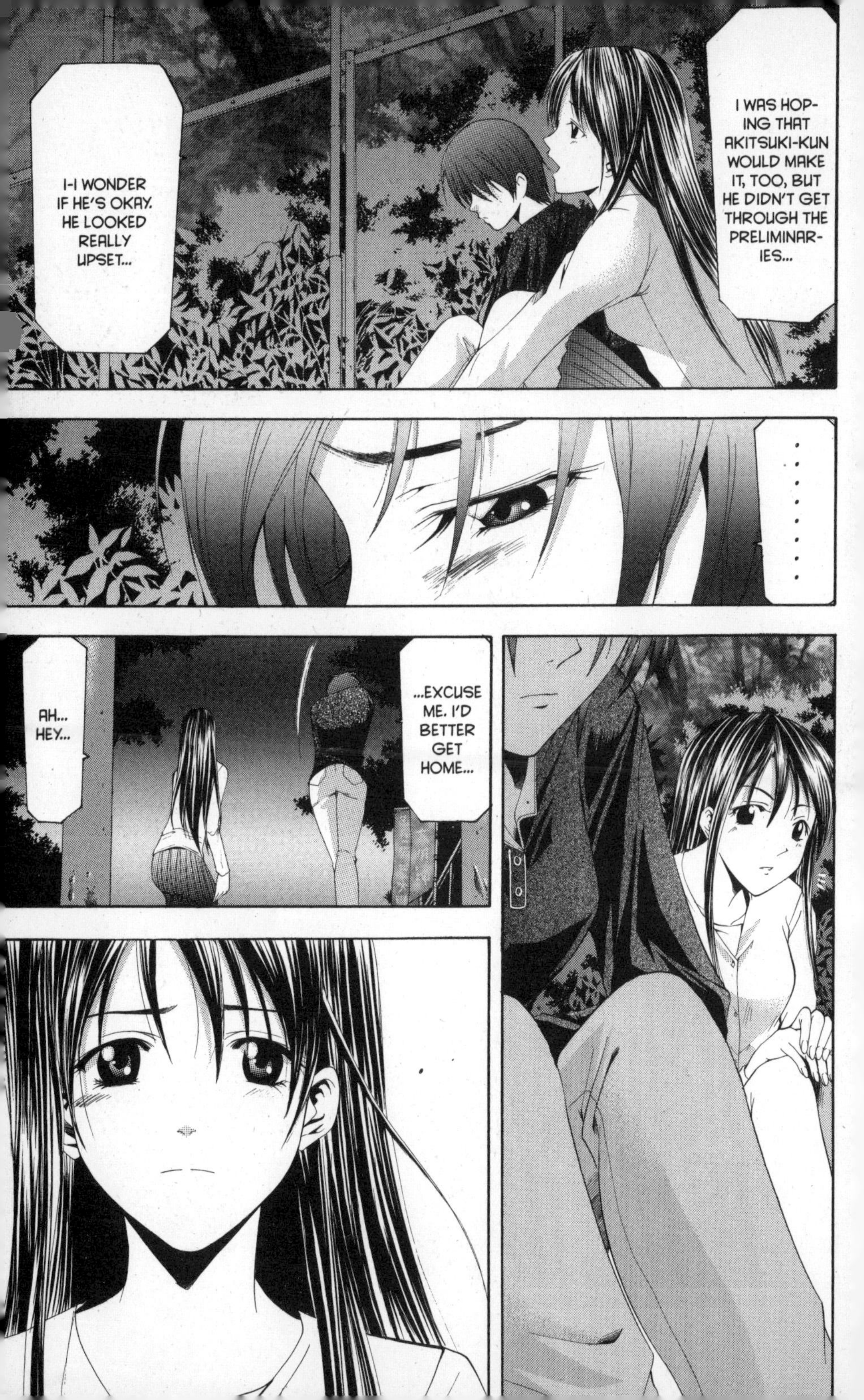
I WAS HOPING THAT AKITSUKI-KUN WOULD MAKE IT, TOO, BUT HE DIDN'T GET THROUGH THE PRELIMINARIES...
I-I WONDER IF HE'S OKAY. HE LOOKED REALLY UPSET...
....
...EXCUSE ME. I'D BETTER GET HOME...
AH... HEY...

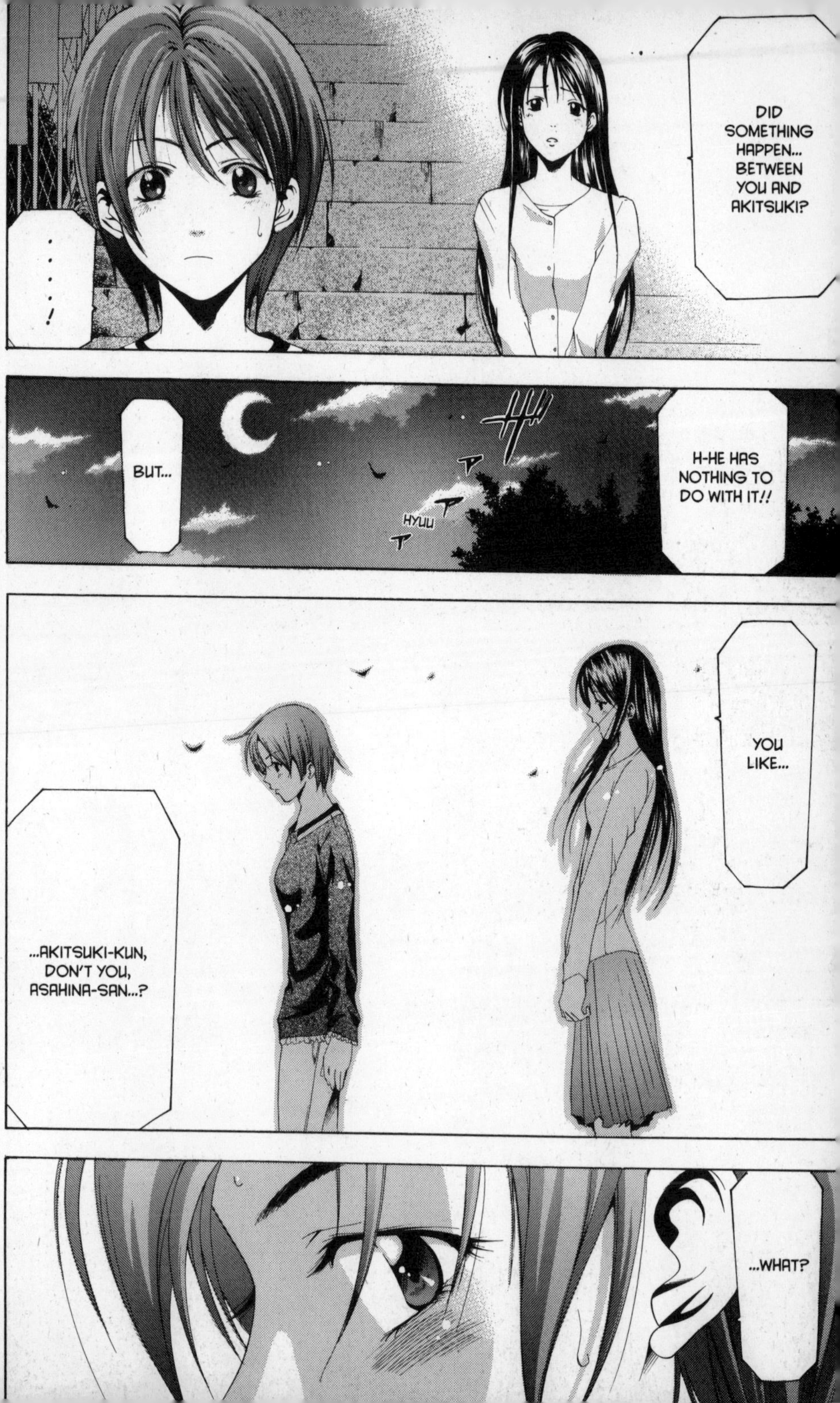
DID SOMETHING HAPPEN... BETWEEN YOU AND AKITSUKI?
......!
H-HE HAS NOTHING TO DO WITH IT!!
HYUU
BUT...
YOU LIKE...
...AKITSUKI-KUN, DON'T YOU, ASAHINA-SAN...?
...WHAT?

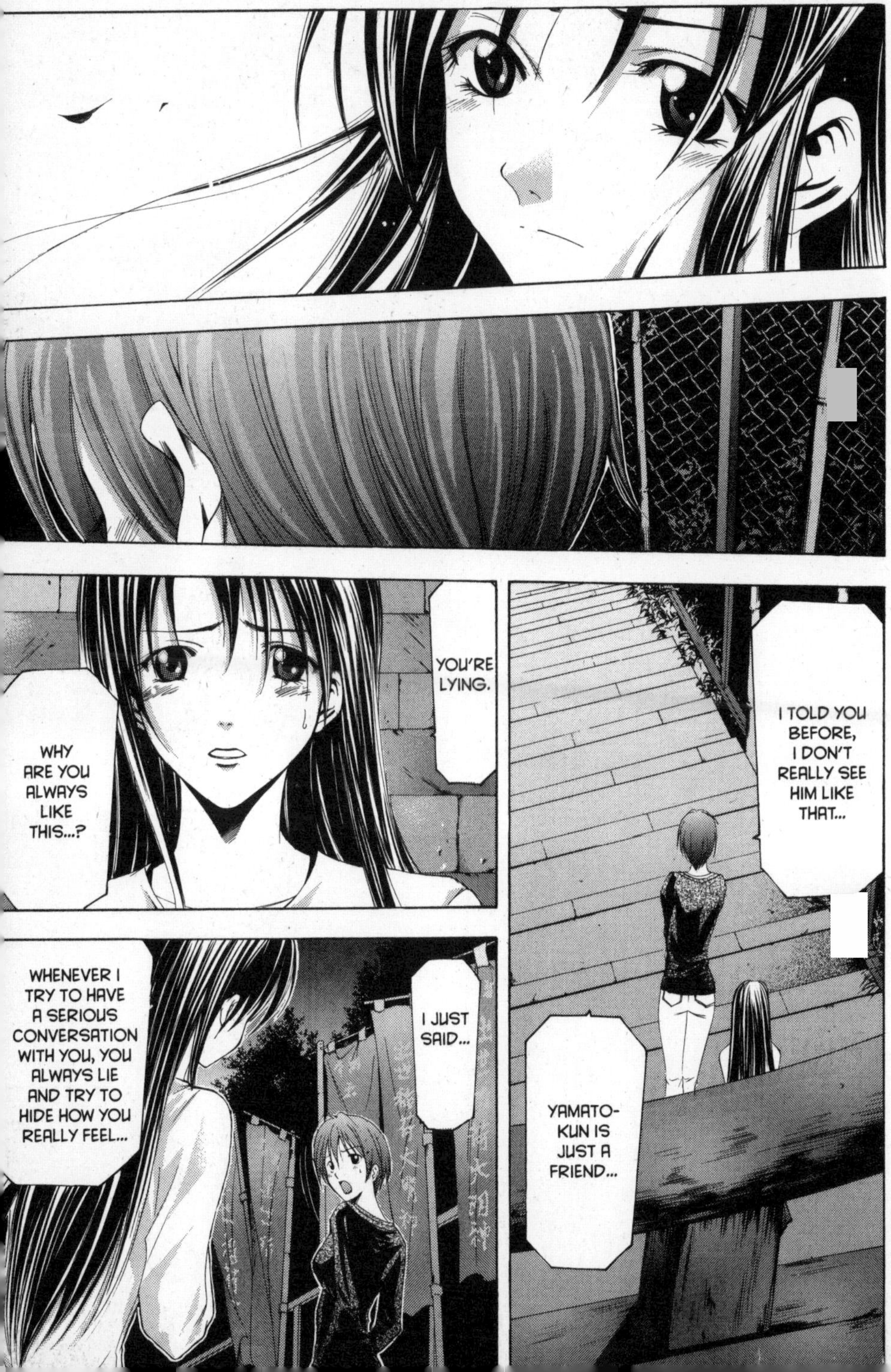
I TOLD YOU BEFORE, I DON'T REALLY SEE HIM LIKE THAT...
YAMATO-KUN IS JUST A FRIEND...
YOU'RE LYING.
WHY ARE YOU ALWAYS LIKE THIS...?
I JUST SAID...
WHENEVER I TRY TO HAVE A SERIOUS CONVERSATION WITH YOU, YOU ALWAYS LIE AND TRY TO HIDE HOW YOU REALLY FEEL...

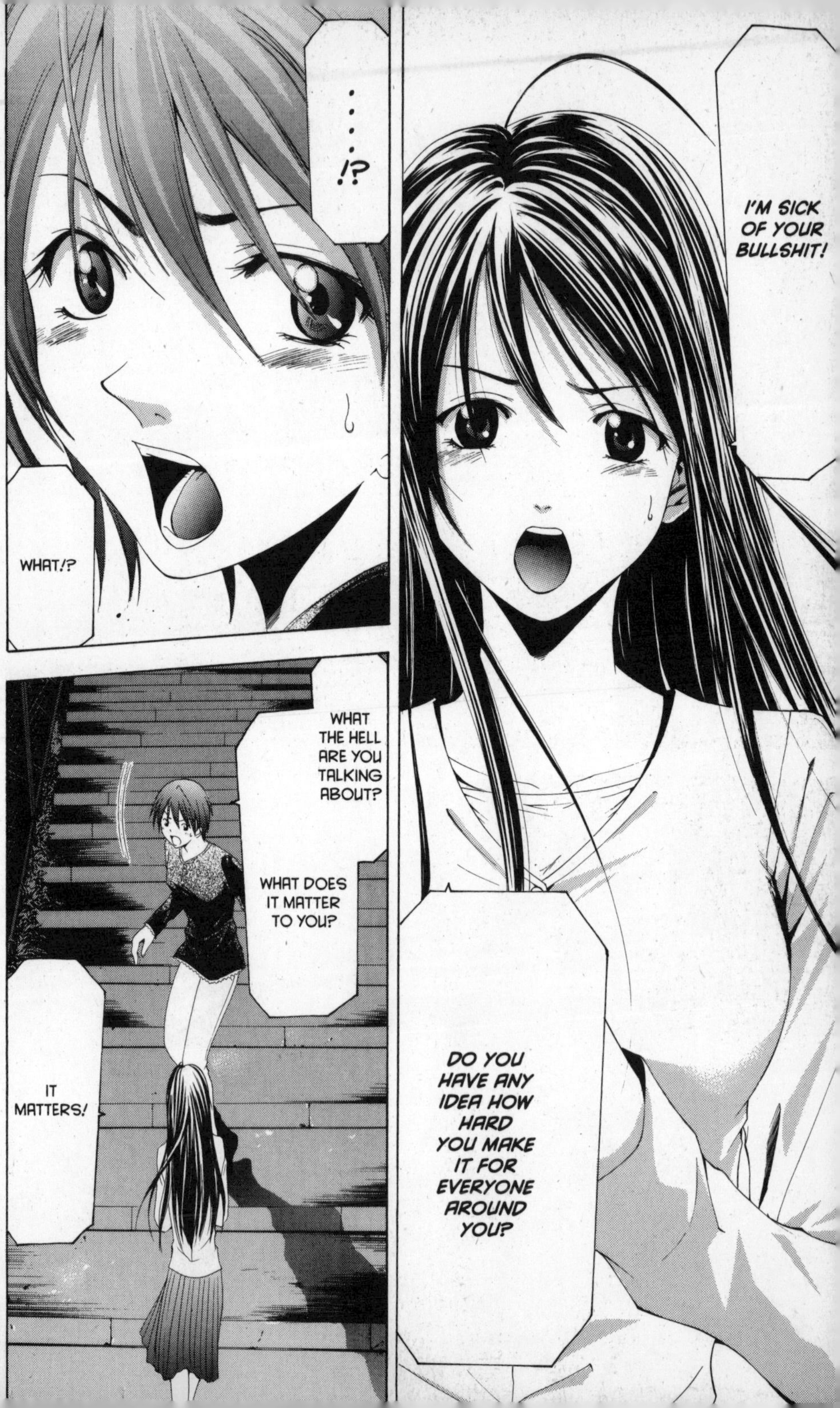
I'M SICK OF YOUR BULLSHIT!
DO YOU HAVE ANY IDEA HOW HARD YOU MAKE IT FOR EVERYONE AROUND YOU?
......!?
WHAT!?
WHAT THE HELL ARE YOU TALKING ABOUT?
WHAT DOES IT MATTER TO YOU?
IT MATTERS!

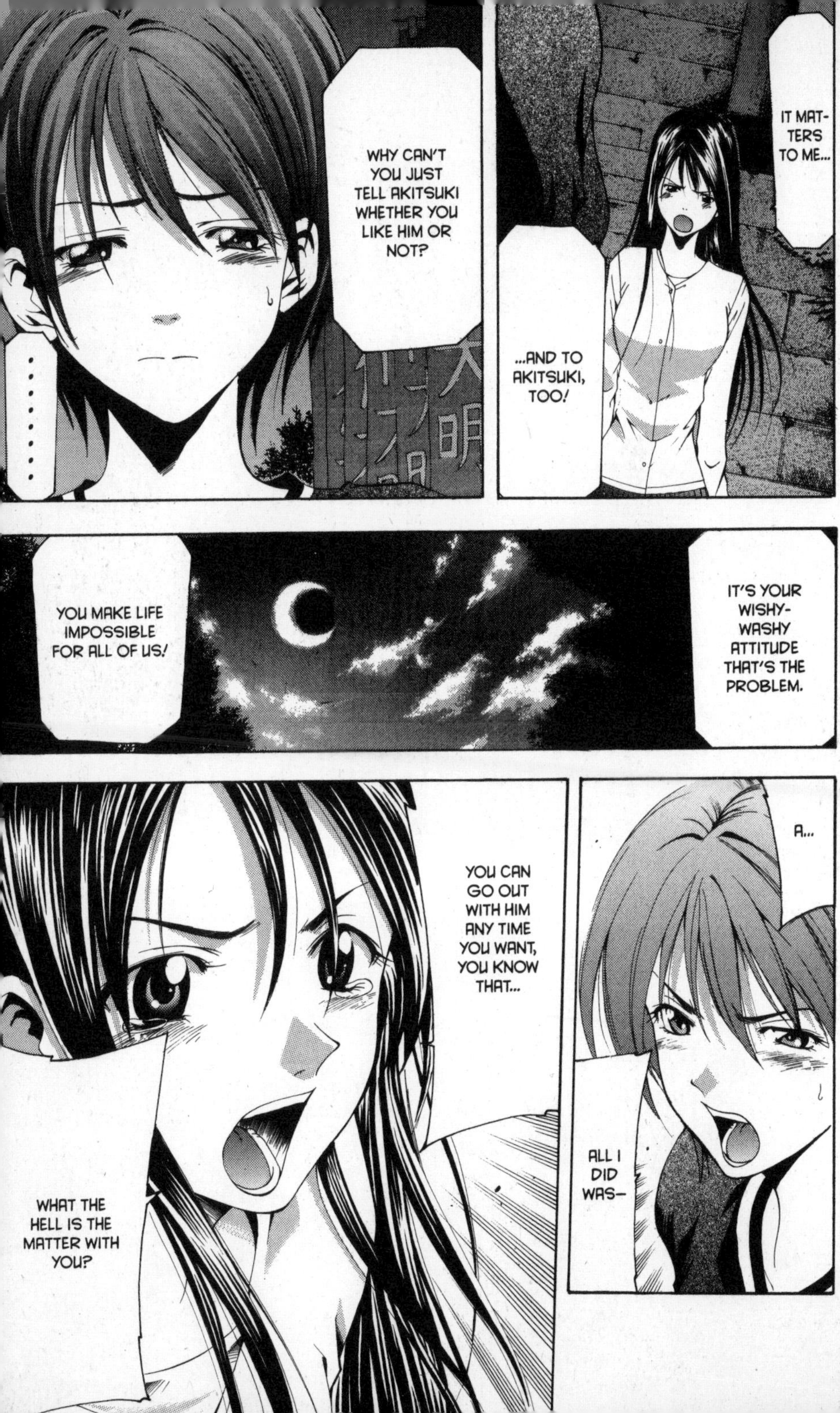
IT MAT-TERS TO ME...
...AND TO AKITSUKI, TOO!
WHY CAN'T YOU JUST TELL AKITSUKI WHETHER YOU LIKE HIM OR NOT?
....
IT'S YOUR WISHY-WASHY ATTITUDE THAT'S THE PROBLEM.
YOU MAKE LIFE IMPOSSIBLE FOR ALL OF US!
A...
ALL I DID WAS—
YOU CAN GO OUT WITH HIM ANY TIME YOU WANT, YOU KNOW THAT...
WHAT THE HELL IS THE MATTER WITH YOU?

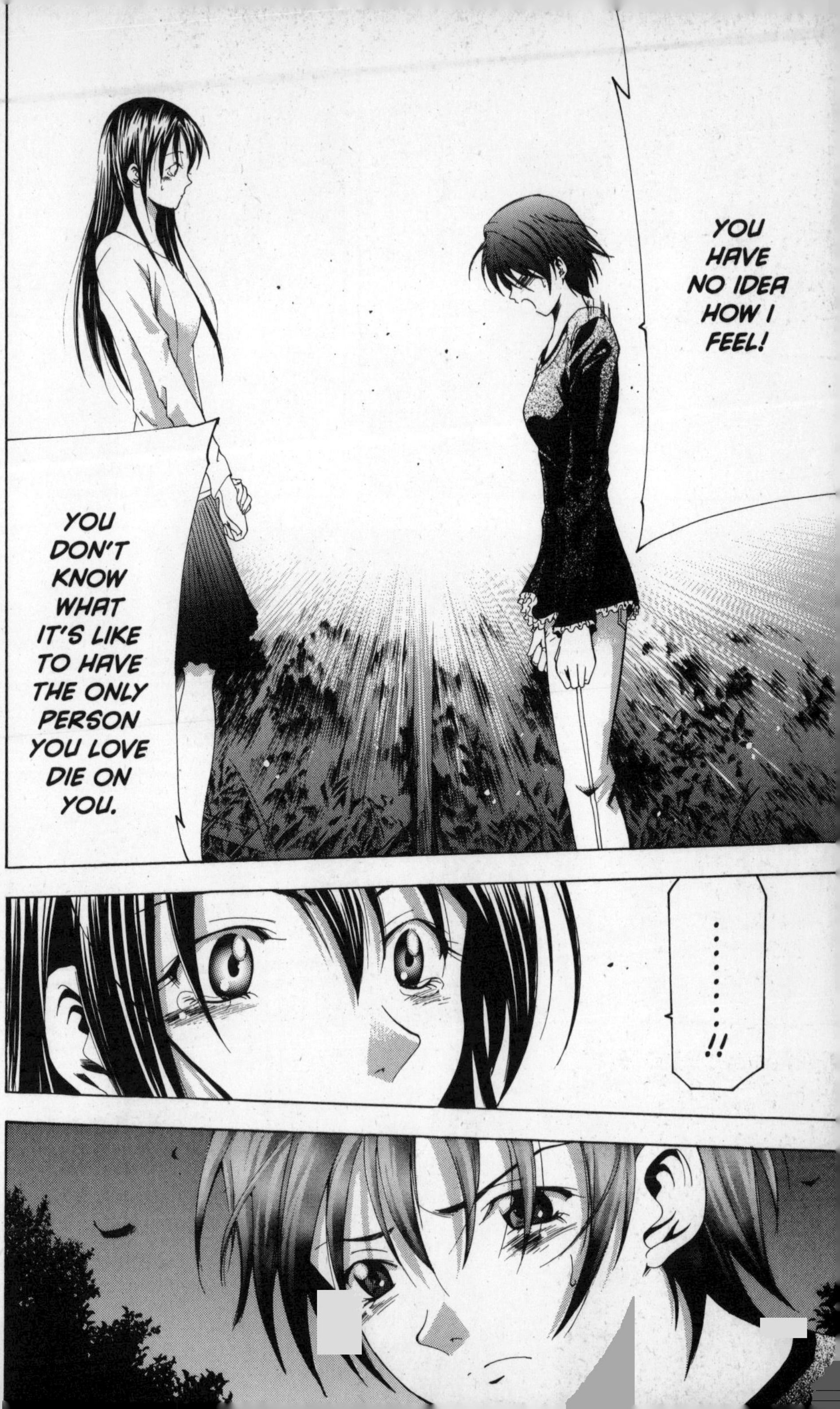
YOU HAVE NO IDEA HOW I FEEL!
YOU DON'T KNOW WHAT IT'S LIKE TO HAVE THE ONLY PERSON YOU LOVE DIE ON YOU.
........!!

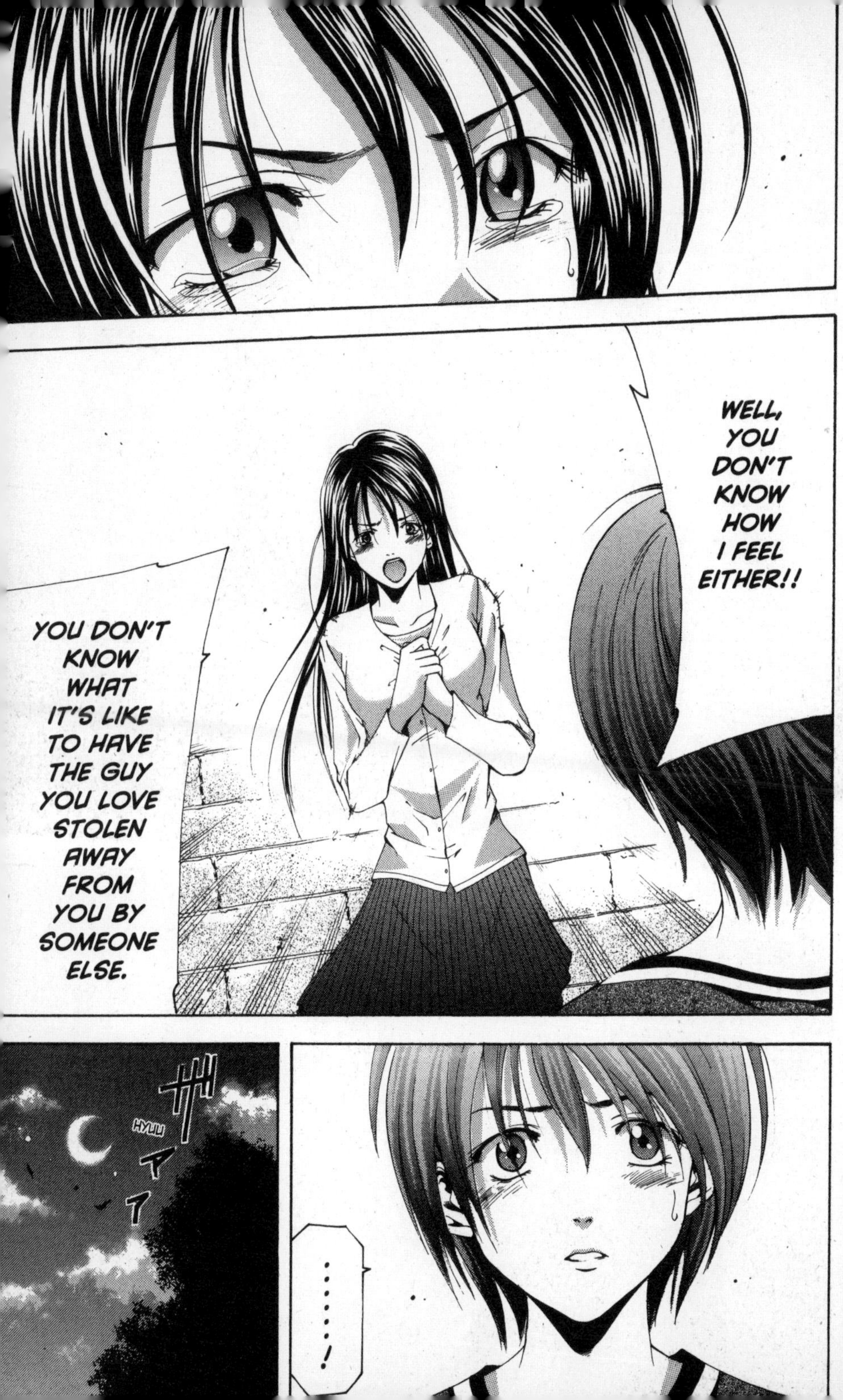
WELL, YOU DON'T KNOW HOW I FEEL EITHER!!
YOU DON'T KNOW WHAT IT'S LIKE TO HAVE THE GUY YOU LOVE STOLEN AWAY FROM YOU BY SOMEONE ELSE.
......!
HYUU

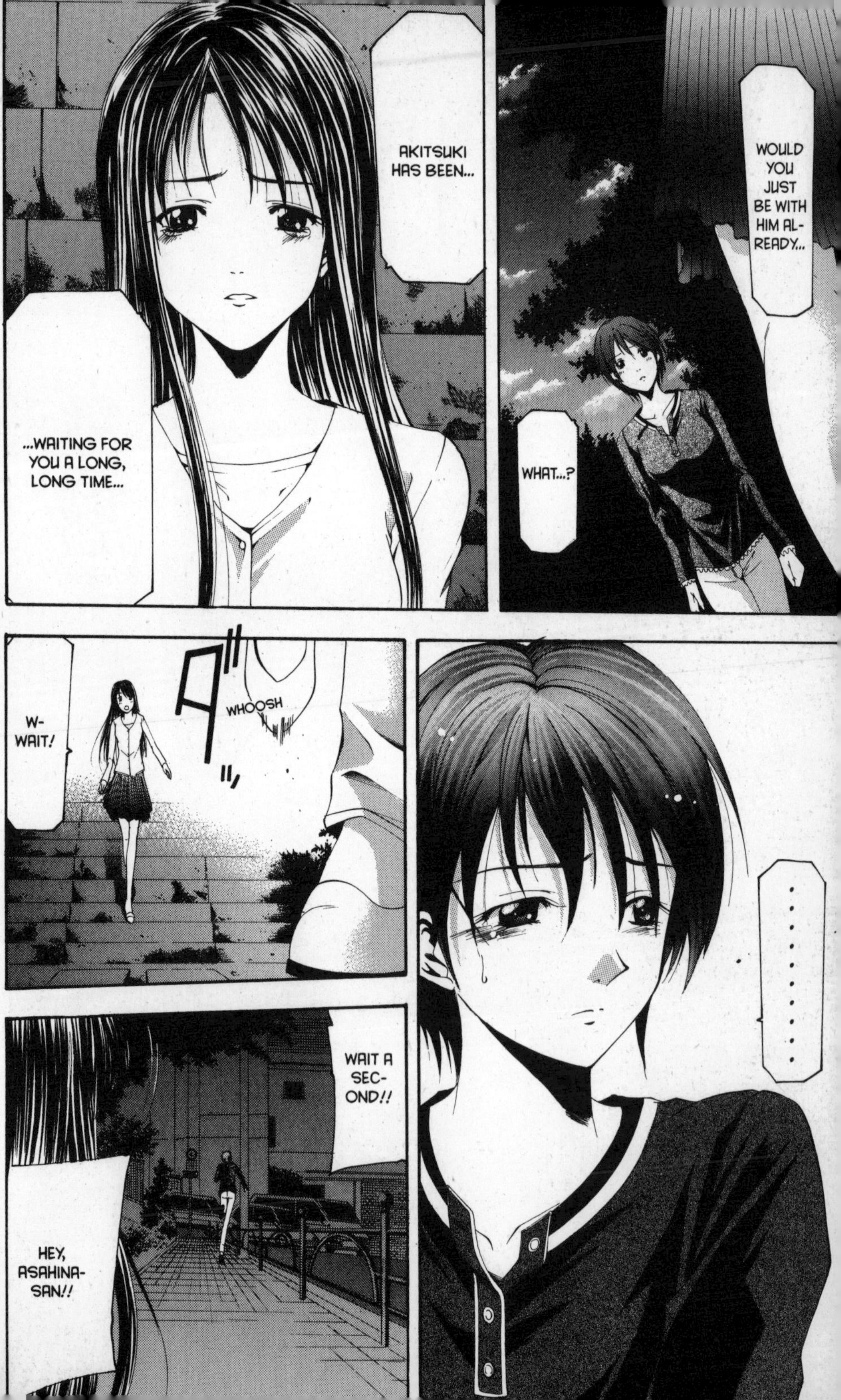
WOULD YOU JUST BE WITH HIM AL-READY...
WHAT...?
AKITSUKI HAS BEEN...
...WAITING FOR YOU A LONG, LONG TIME...
......
W-WAIT!
WHOOSH
WAIT A SEC-OND!!
HEY, ASAHINA-SAN!!

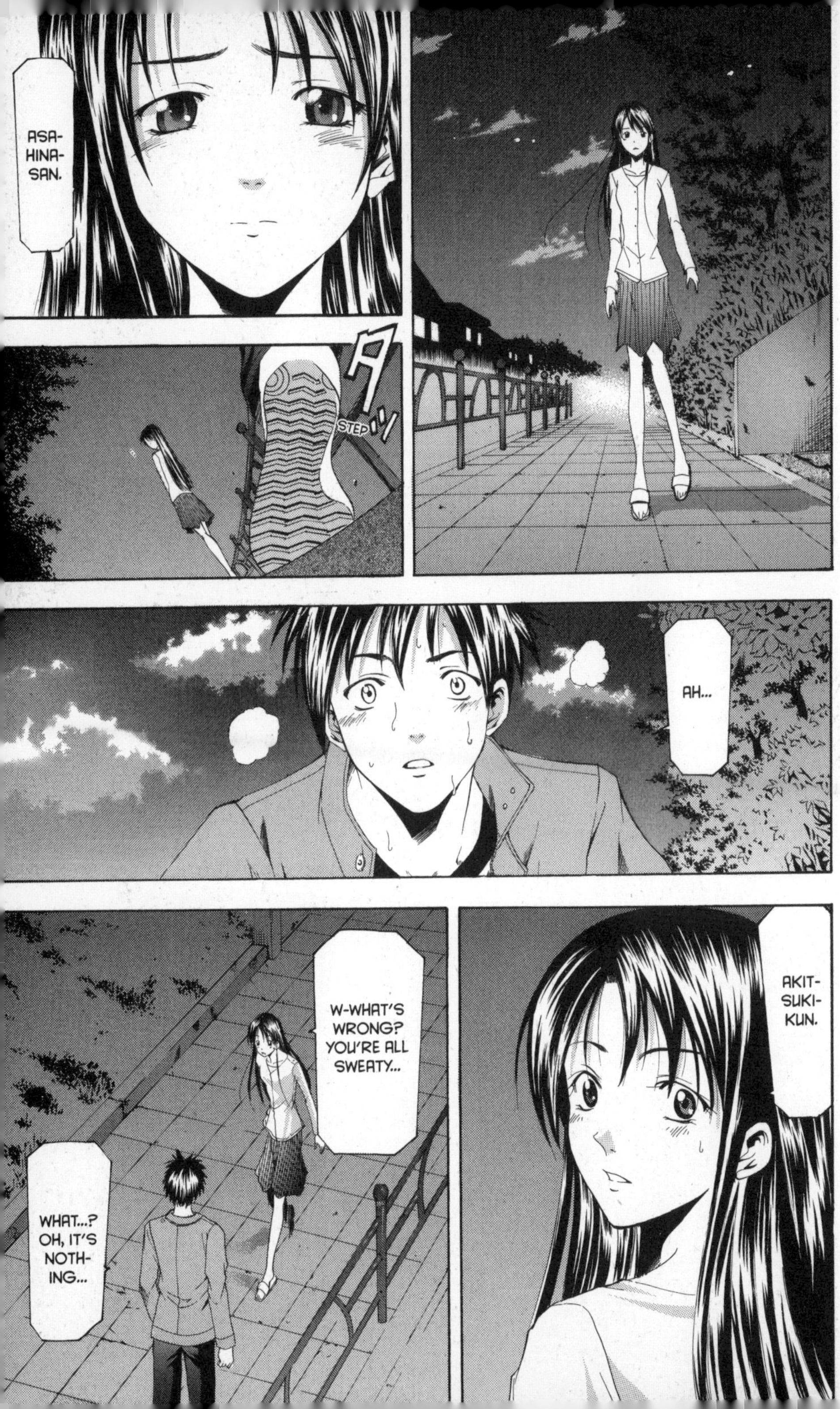
ASA-HINA-SAN.
STEP
AH...
AKIT-SUKI-KUN.
W-WHAT'S WRONG? YOU'RE ALL SWEATY...
WHAT...? OH, IT'S NOTH-ING...

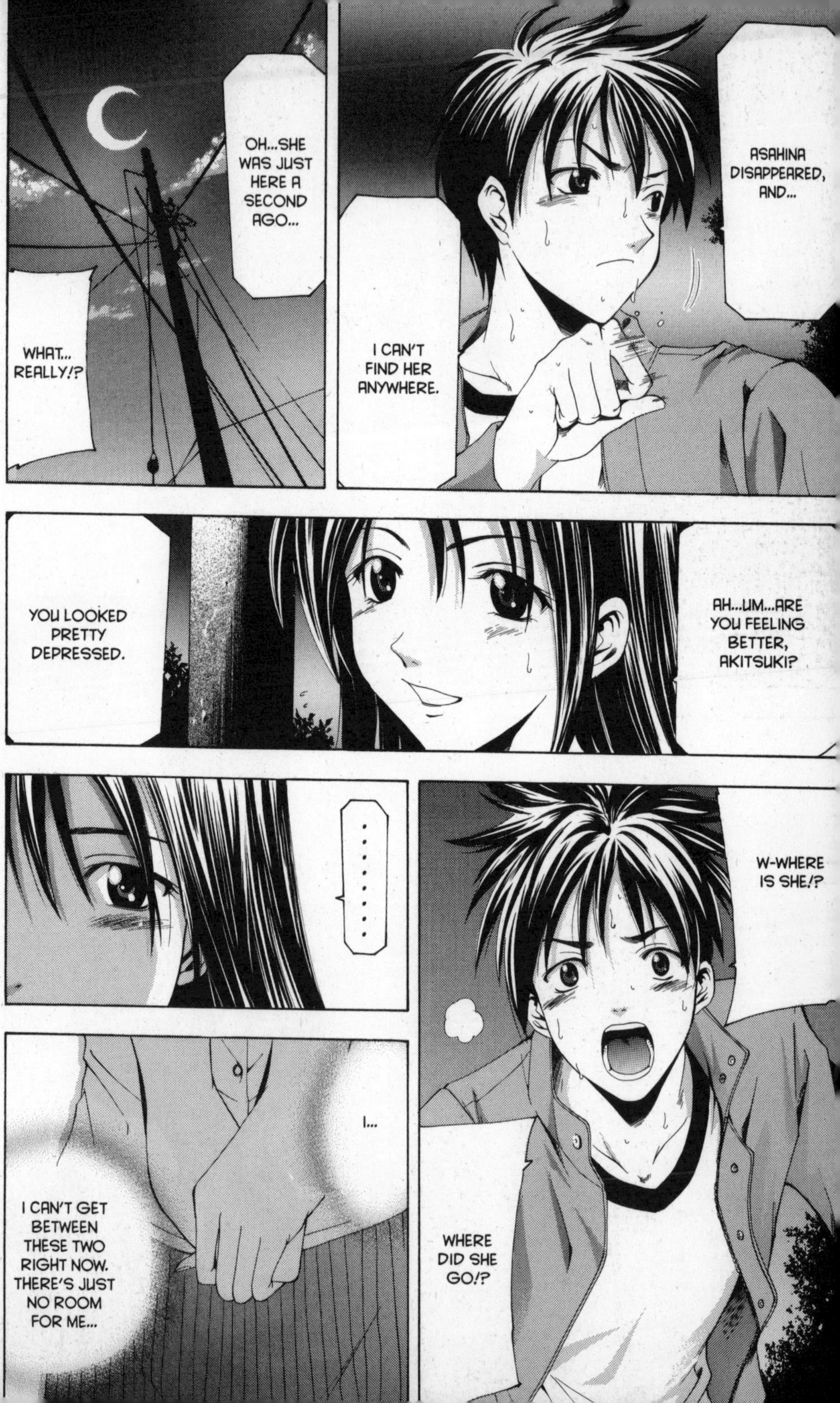
ASAHINA DISAPPEARED, AND...
I CAN'T FIND HER ANYWHERE.
OH...SHE WAS JUST HERE A SECOND AGO...
WHAT... REALLY!?
AH...UM...ARE YOU FEELING BETTER, AKITSUKI?
YOU LOOKED PRETTY DEPRESSED.
W-WHERE IS SHE!?
WHERE DID SHE GO!?
....
I...
I CAN'T GET BETWEEN THESE TWO RIGHT NOW. THERE'S JUST NO ROOM FOR ME...

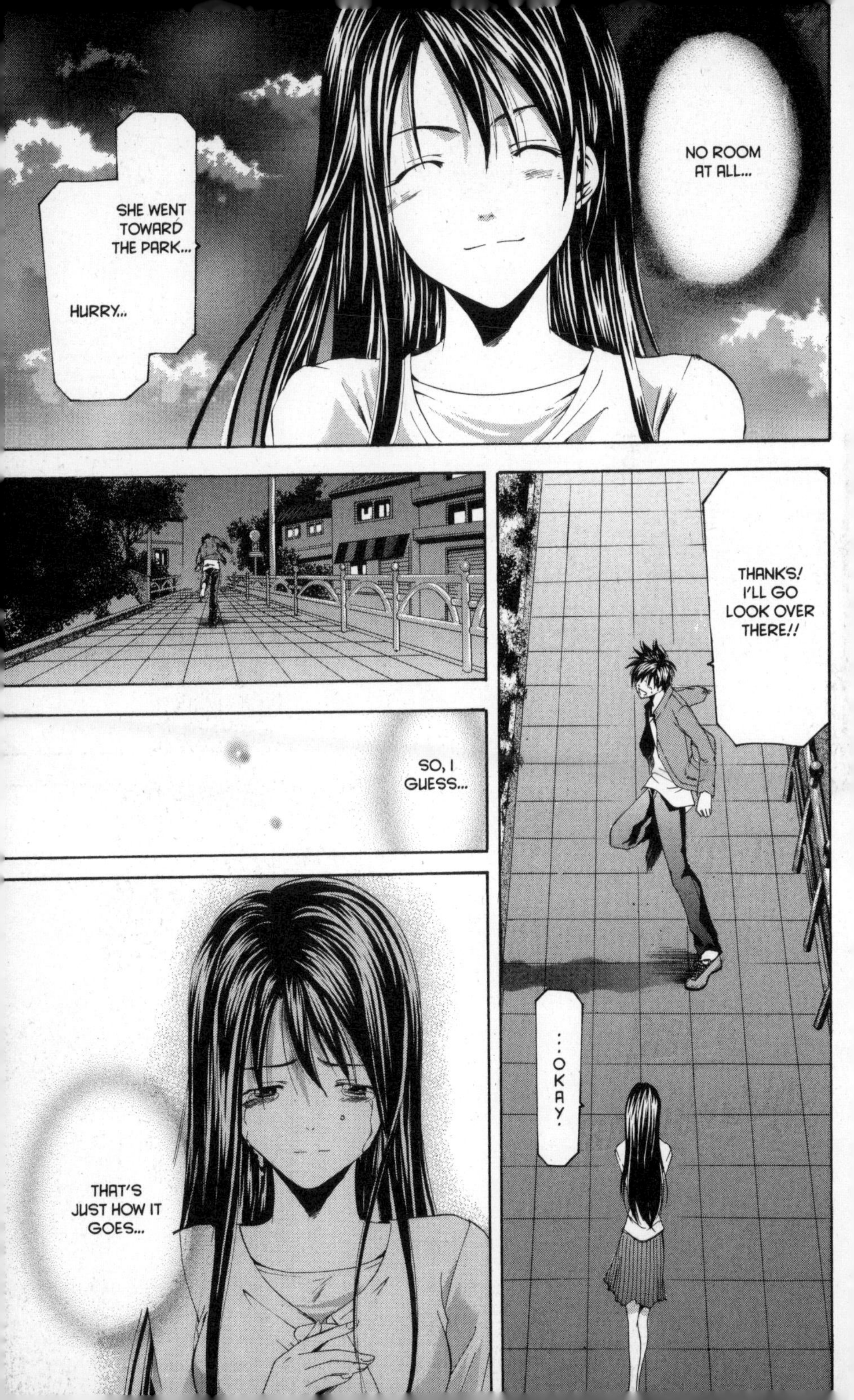
NO ROOM AT ALL...
SHE WENT TOWARD THE PARK...
HURRY...
THANKS! I'LL GO LOOK OVER THERE!!
...OKAY.
SO, I GUESS...
THAT'S JUST HOW IT GOES...

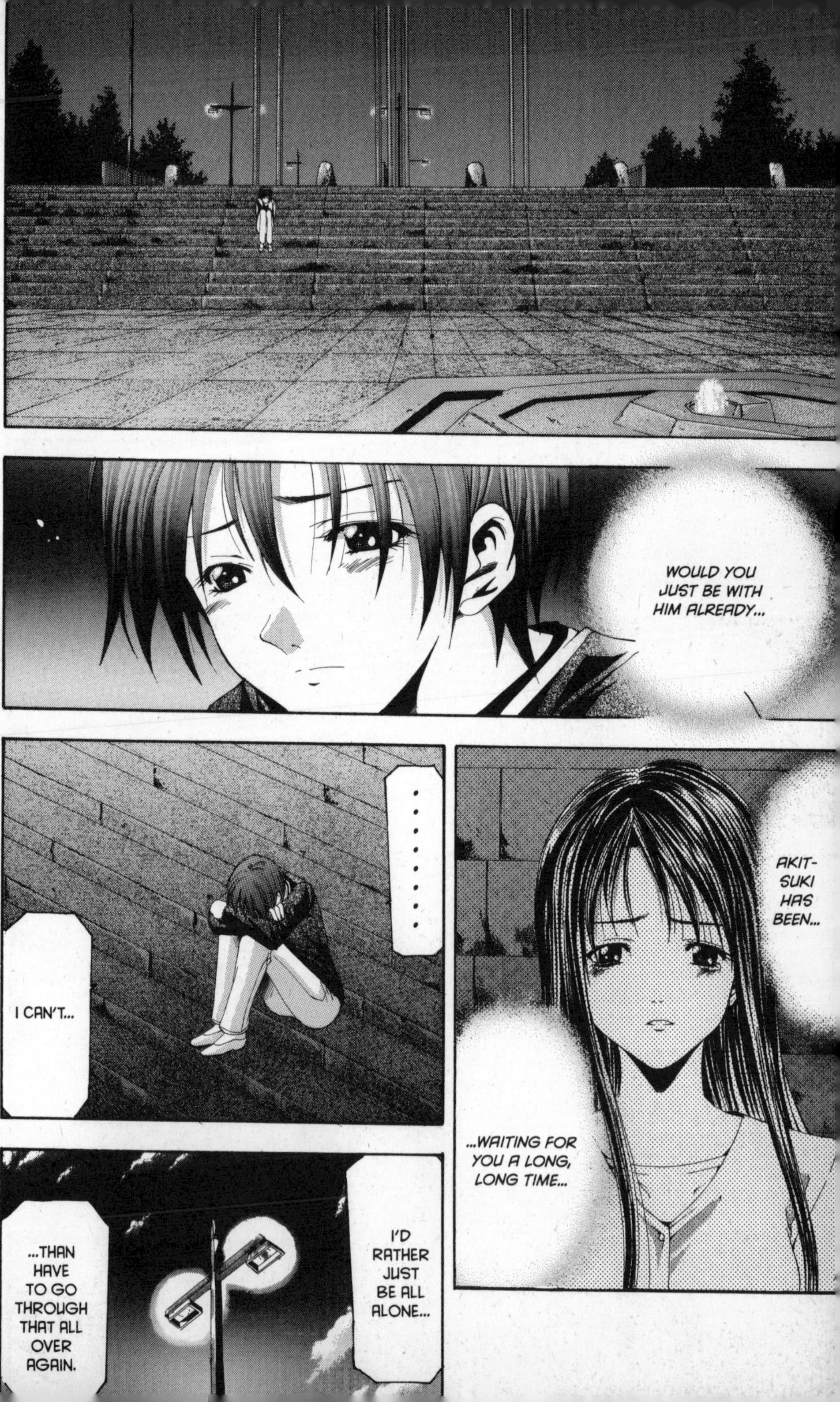
WOULD YOU JUST BE WITH HIM ALREADY...
AKIT-SUKI HAS BEEN...
...WAITING FOR YOU A LONG, LONG TIME...
....
I CAN'T...
I'D RATHER JUST BE ALL ALONE...
...THAN HAVE TO GO THROUGH THAT ALL OVER AGAIN.

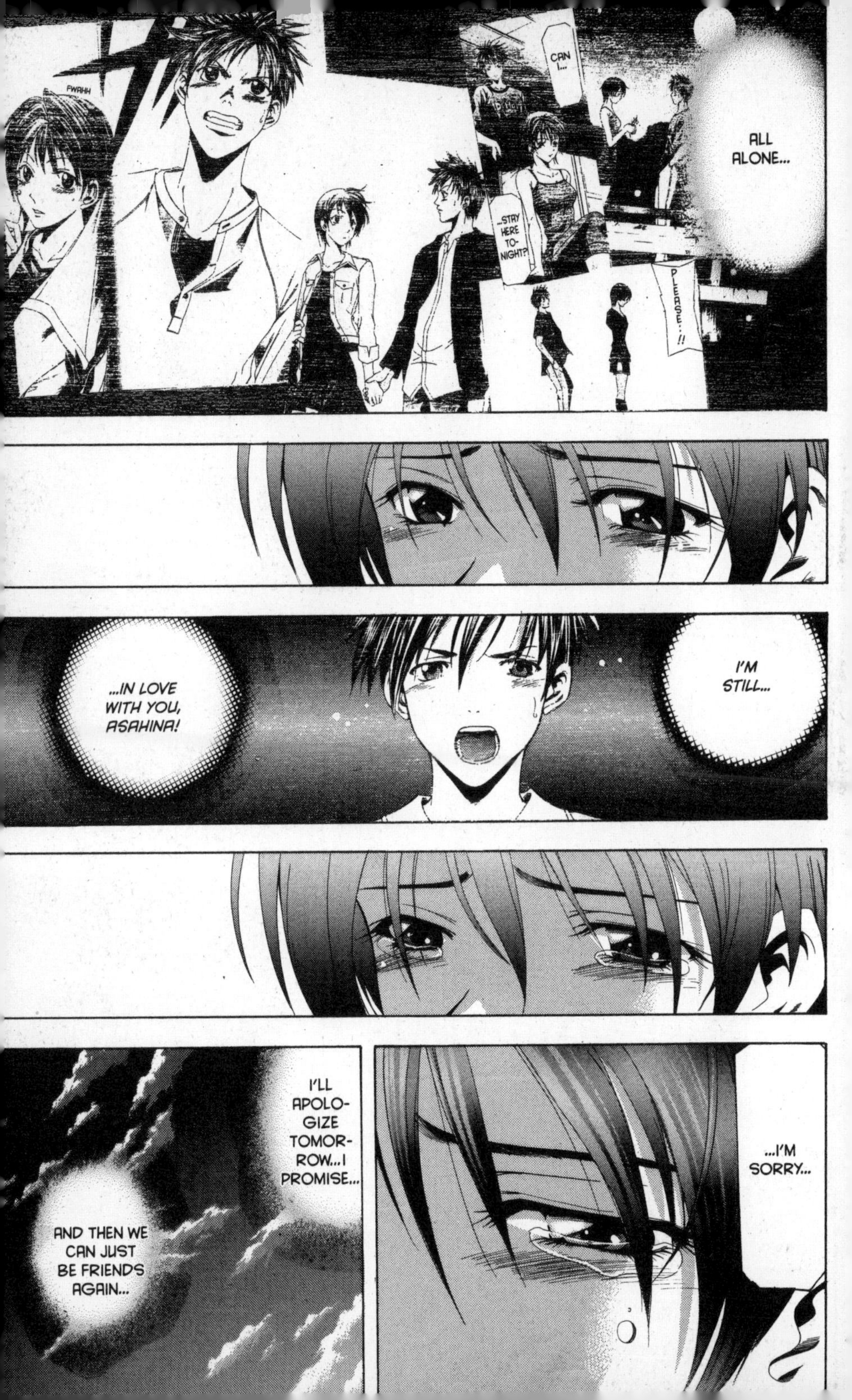
ALL ALONE...
CAN I...
...STAY HERE TO-NIGHT?
PLEASE...!!
FWAHH
I'M STILL...
...IN LOVE WITH YOU, ASAHINA!
...I'M SORRY...
I'LL APOLO-GIZE TOMOR-ROW...I PROMISE...
AND THEN WE CAN JUST BE FRIENDS AGAIN...

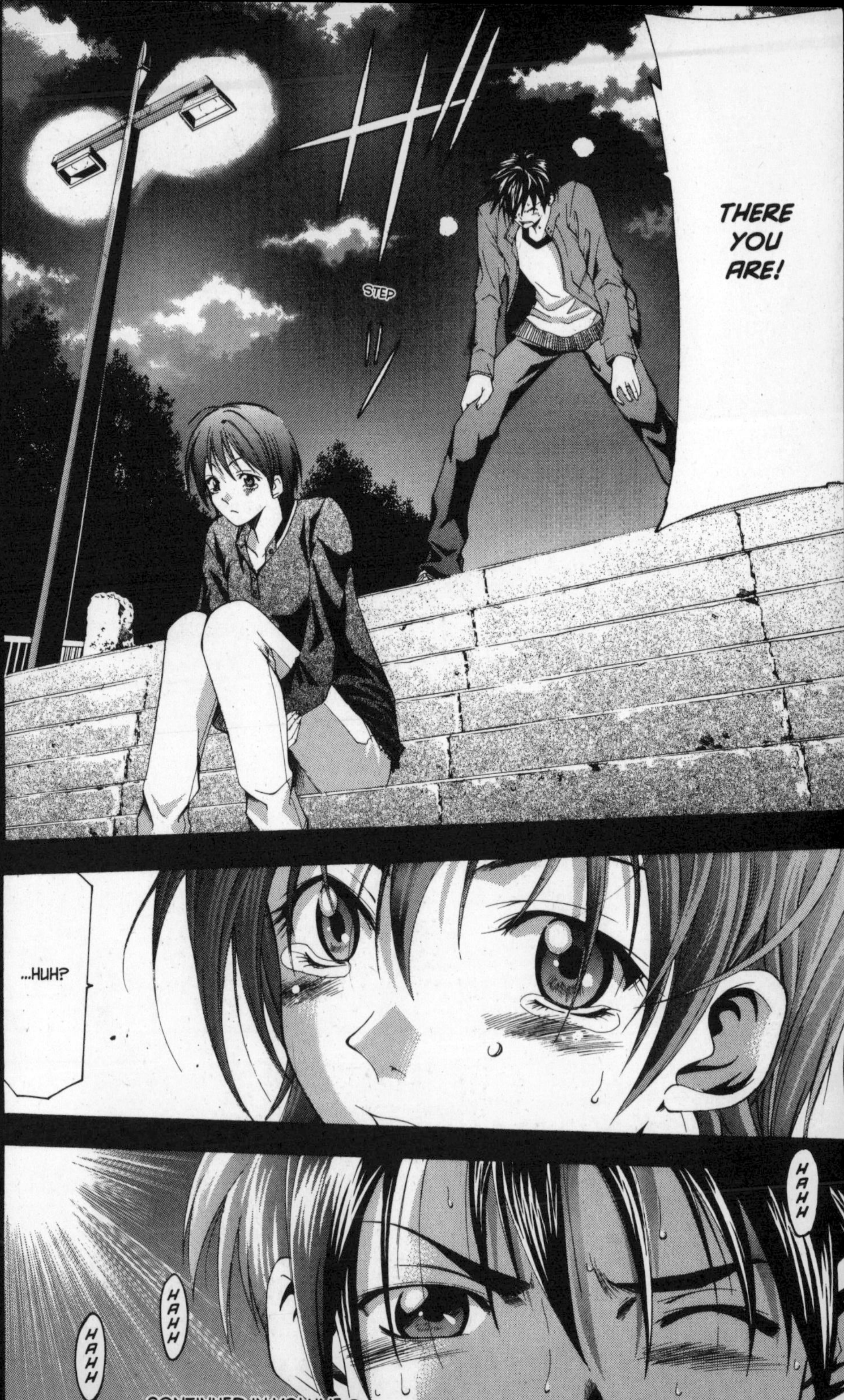
THERE YOU ARE!
STEP
...HUH?
HAHH
HAHH
HAHH

CONTINUED IN VOLUME 9

SPECIAL BONUS MANGA

"PLEASE DON'T DRAG ME OUT IN PUBLIC— PART 2"

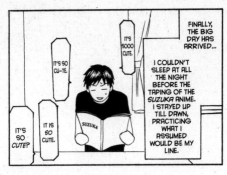

FINALLY, THE BIG DAY HAS ARRIVED...
I COULDN'T SLEEP AT ALL THE NIGHT BEFORE THE TAPING OF THE *SUZUKA* ANIME. I STAYED UP TILL DAWN, PRACTICING WHAT I ASSUMED WOULD BE MY LINE.
IT'S SOOO CUTE.
IT'S SO CU-TE.
SUZUKA
IT IS *SO* CUTE.
IT'S SO *CUTE?*
AND FINALLY IT WAS TIME TO HEAD TO THE STUDIO.
SORRY!!
HARAJUKU STATION
FOR CRYING OUT LOUD, SEO-KUN...
I WAS LATE AS USUAL.
THIS TIME, I BEGGED THE STAFF NOT TO MAKE ME GO ALONE.
HELLO!
I ENDED UP DRAGGING NISHIMOTO-SENSEI, AUTHOR OF THE MANGA *I WON'T DO IT AGAIN*, ALONG WITH ME.
SORRY, THAT DOESN'T LOOK LIKE HIM AT ALL – SEO
I WAS HALF DEAD FROM LACK OF SLEEP AND OVER-ACTIVE NERVES.
PANT
WOBBLE
PANT
WHEN YOU WRITE ABOUT THIS IN *I WON'T DO IT AGAIN*, MAKE ME LOOK COOL, OKAY?
UHHH...I DON'T THINK SO...

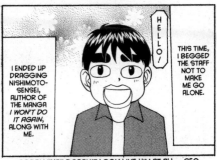

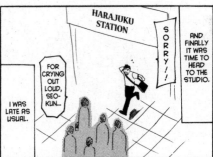

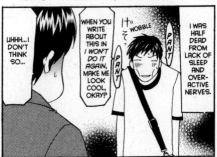

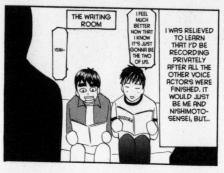

I WAS RELIEVED TO LEARN THAT I'D BE RECORDING PRIVATELY AFTER ALL THE OTHER VOICE ACTORS WERE FINISHED. IT WOULD JUST BE ME AND NISHIMOTO-SENSEI, BUT...
I FEEL MUCH BETTER NOW THAT I KNOW IT'S JUST GONNA BE THE TWO OF US.
THE WAITING ROOM
YEAH-
SUZUKA
ALL RIGHT, IT'S TIME FOR YOU TWO TO COME JOIN EVERY-BODY.
クルッ
FWING
LET'S GO!!
WHAT!?
MITSUYA-SAN SET ME UP.
THERE I STOOD, IN FRONT OF THE MICRO-PHONE AND SUR-ROUNDED BY ALL THOSE PROFES-SIONAL VOICE AC-TORS...
ザワ
CHATTER
HOW DID I GET MY-SELF INTO THIS...?
ザワ
CHATTER
...WISHING I'D NEVER WRITTEN LINES FOR THE CHARAC-TER I WAS SUPPOSED TO BE PLAYING.
AND THE LINE THAT I PRAC-TICED ALL NIGHT, 'IT'S SO CUTE' ...
...TURNED OUT TO BE NISHI-MOTO-SENSEI'S PART.
WHAT!?
ALL RIGHT, SEO-SENSEI'S LINES WILL BE 'WHOA!' AND 'IT'S ALL OVER.' OKAY?

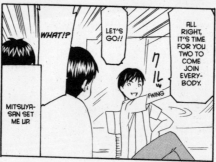

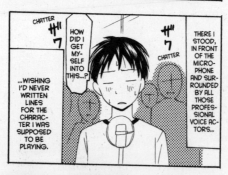

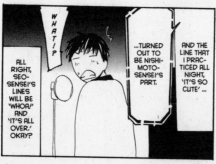

FOR SOME REASON, TWO OF OUR CREW MEMBERS KEPT STANDING RIGHT IN FRONT OF ME, WATCHING WITH HUGE GRINS ON THEIR FACES.

WOULD YOU GUYS JUST LEAVE, PLEASE?

SMIRK SMIRK

UH-UH, NO WAY AM I MISSING THIS.

ME NEI-THER.

I HATE THOSE GUYS.

SOMEHOW I MANAGED TO FINISH RECORDING, AND WAS JUST STARTING TO RELAX.

NOW LET'S HAVE YOU TWO DO SOME BACKGROUND VOCALS FOR US.

CAN YOU JUST AD-LIB SOMETHING?

AD-LIB...?

NOT ONCE IN MY LIFE HAVE I "AD-LIBBED" SOMETHING WITHOUT MEETING DISASTROUS RESULTS...

MITSU-HASHI-SAN, WHO PLAYS SUZUKA, AND THE OTHER ACTORS TRIED TO TALK TO ME AND GET ME TO RELAX, BUT...

YOU MUST BE TIRED, HUH?

SHUDDER

SHUDDER

HEY, ARE YOU LISTENING!?

I TOTALLY IGNORED THEM.

SUZUKA

SUZUKA

I'M REALLY SORRY, GUYS...

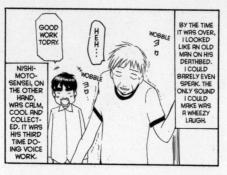

BY THE TIME IT WAS OVER, I LOOKED LIKE AN OLD MAN ON HIS DEATHBED. I COULD BARELY EVEN SPEAK. THE ONLY SOUND I COULD MAKE WAS A WHEEZY LAUGH.
WOBBLE
HEH...
WOBBLE
GOOD WORK TODAY.
NISHIMOTO-SENSEI, ON THE OTHER HAND, WAS CALM, COOL AND COLLECTED. IT WAS HIS THIRD TIME DOING VOICE WORK.
THANK YOU SO MUCH FOR TODAY. I THINK I'LL BE ABLE TO COME UP WITH A GOOD STORY OUT OF ALL THIS.
AH... JUST MAKE ME LOOK COOL, OKAY.
I TOLD YOU THAT'S NOT GONNA HAPPEN.
...GUESS I CAN'T BLAME HIM.
ON THE WAY BACK, WE HAD A MEETING AT A FAMILY RESTAURANT.
THIS IS SO BORING.
SHOCK
WHAT?
THEY TURNED DOWN ALL MY IDEAS.
I COULDN'T HANDLE IT ANYMORE, SO I TURNED TO BOOZE.
ANOTHER BEER, PLEASE. THE BIGGEST SIZE YOU'VE GOT!
SEO-KUN, JUST SO YOU KNOW, WE'RE HAVING A WRAP PARTY AFTER THIS.
SHUDDER

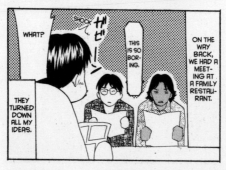

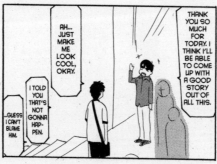

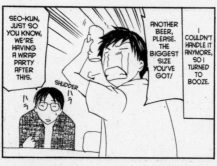

THE WRAP PARTY
GOOD JOB TODAY.
RIGHT IN FRONT OF ME SAT DAISUKE NAKAMURA-SAN, WHO PLAYS YAMATO, AND KANAKO MITSUHASHI-SAN, WHO PLAYS SUZUKA.
...ALONG WITH YUMIKO HOSONO-SAN (HONOKA) AND HATSUMI MIURA-SAN (MEGUMI).
HELLO-
THEY'RE ALSO MEMBERS OF THE BAND COACH WHO SING THE *SUZUKA* OPENING THEME SONG.
THEY ARE BOTH ABSOLUTELY GORGEOUS.
WAH...
SHINE
THEY'RE LIKE ANGELS...
I WAS SO NERVOUS I COULD HARDLY EVEN TALK...
THE NEXT THING I KNEW...
THE HIROSHIMA CARP ARE THE BEST TEAM IN BASEBALL, AM I RIGHT, FUKUTOMI-SAN!?
SUZUKA DIRECTOR, HIROSHI FUKUTOMI-SAN
YEP, THE HIROSHIMA CARP CAN'T BE BEAT!
... I WAS STUCK DRINKING WITH THE OTHER GUYS.

THE END

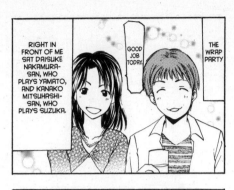

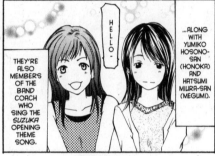

COMING SOON IN THE BONUS MANGA SECTION IT'S... *"YOU SCARED OF HEIGHTS? HOW THE HELL SHOULD I KNOW?"*

WHEREIN KOUJI SEO TAKES ON PARAGLIDING IN AN ATTEMPT TO GET BACK AT HIS COWORKERS!!

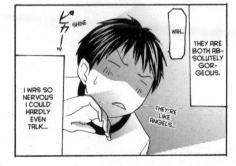

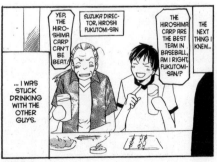

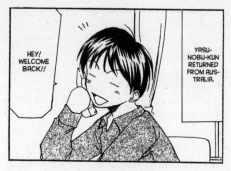

SUPER SPECIAL BONUS MANGA

"WELCOME HOME! YASUNOBU-KUN"

YASU-NOBU-KUN RETURNED FROM AUS-TRALIA.
HEY! WELCOME BACK!!
HOW WAS AUSTRA-LIA?
WAS IT EXPEN-SIVE THERE?
UH... WILL YOU RECORD THE SOCCER GAME FOR ME? THE JAPAN MATCH.
HUH...?
I'M AT MY GIRLFRIEND'S HOUSE, SO I CAN'T REALLY TALK. BYE.
CLICK...
BEEP
BEEP
WELCOME BACK...

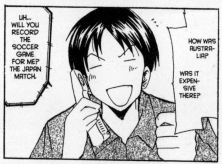

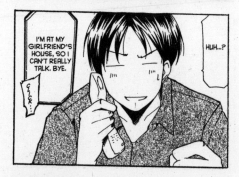

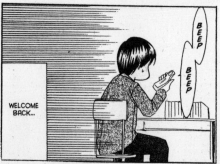

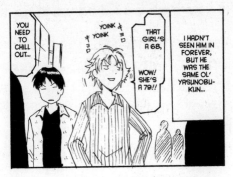

I HADN'T SEEN HIM IN FOREVER, BUT HE WAS THE SAME OL' YASUNOBU-KUN...
THAT GIRL'S A 68,
WOW! SHE'S A 79!!
YOINK キョロ
YOINK キョロ
YOU NEED TO CHILL OUT...
YOU KEEP RATING ALL THESE GIRLS...SO WHAT ABOUT THE CUTEST GIRL YOU'VE EVER SEEN...HOW HIGH DID SHE SCORE?
LET'S SEE... ABOUT 85 MAYBE...
OH YEAH? SO...WHAT CELEB-RITY WOULD SCORE 100?
WHAT? I NEVER GIVE ANYBODY 100.
IF I FOUND PERFEC-TION, I'D HAVE NOTHING LEFT TO LIVE FOR. THE GAME WOULD BE OVER.
HEH フフン
WHAT DO YOU HAVE TO LIVE FOR NOW...?
LEAVE IT TO YASUNOBU-KUN TO SAY SOMETHING TOTALLY IDIOTIC AND ACT AS IF IT'S THE COOLEST THING IN THE WORLD.

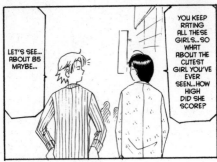

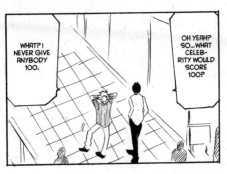

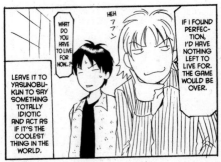

Translation Notes

Japanese is a tricky language for most Westerners, and translation is often more an art than a science. For your edification and reading pleasure, here are notes on some of the places where we could have gone in a different direction or where a Japanese cultural reference is used.

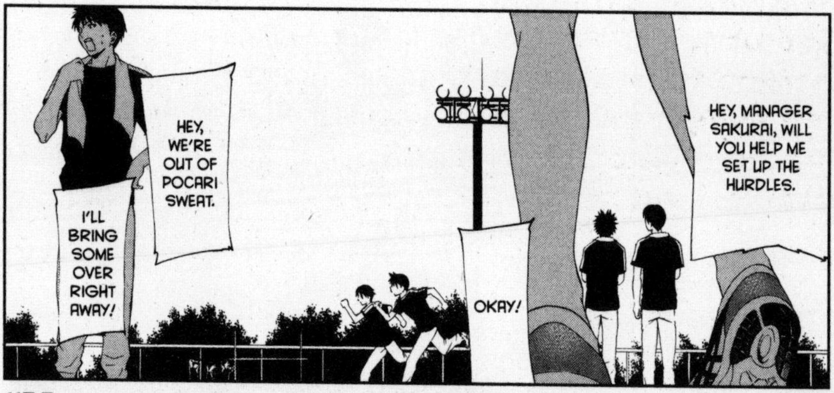
HEY, MANAGER SAKURAI, WILL YOU HELP ME SET UP THE HURDLES.
OKAY!
HEY, WE'RE OUT OF POCARI SWEAT.
I'LL BRING SOME OVER RIGHT AWAY!

"Mmmmm Sweat," page 39

Pocari Sweat is a popular Japanese sports drink.

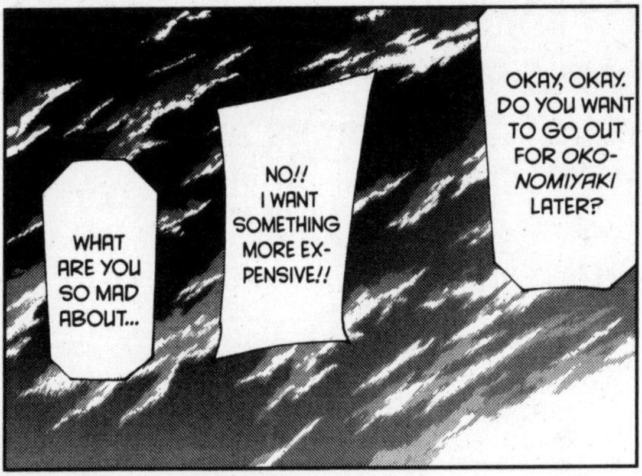
OKAY, OKAY. DO YOU WANT TO GO OUT FOR *OKO-NOMIYAKI* LATER?
NO!! I WANT SOMETHING MORE EX-PENSIVE!!
WHAT ARE YOU SO MAD ABOUT...

***Okonomiyaki*, page 73**

Okonomiyaki is often referred to as a Japanese pancake. It's a concoction made of batter and a mixture of meat, vegetables, egg, and sometimes noodles. At most *okonomiyaki* restaurants your table will have a built in grill, and you can cook your own *okonomiyaki* right at the table.

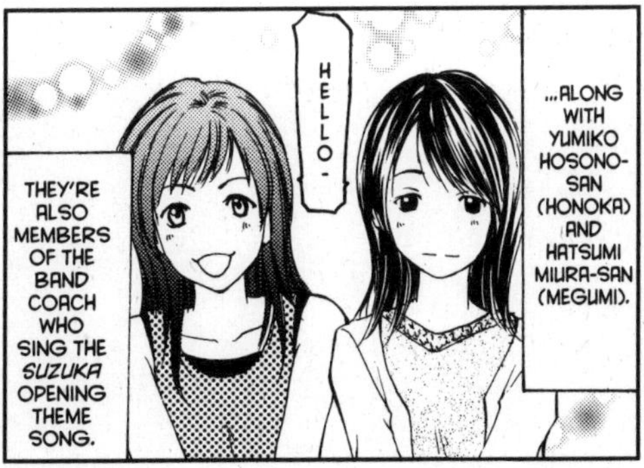
THEY'RE ALSO MEMBERS OF THE BAND COACH WHO SING THE *SUZUKA* OPENING THEME SONG.
HELLO-
...ALONG WITH YUMIKO HOSONO-SAN (HONOKA) AND HATSUMI MIURA-SAN (MEGUMI).

Coach, page 189

Coach is a band made up of Yumiko Hosono, Hatsumi Miura, Ai Hayashi, Satomi Akesaka, and Michie Kitaura.

Preview of Volume 9

We're pleased to present you a preview from *Suzuka* volume 9. Please check our website (www.delreymanga.com) to see when this volume will be available in English. For now you'll have to make do with Japanese!

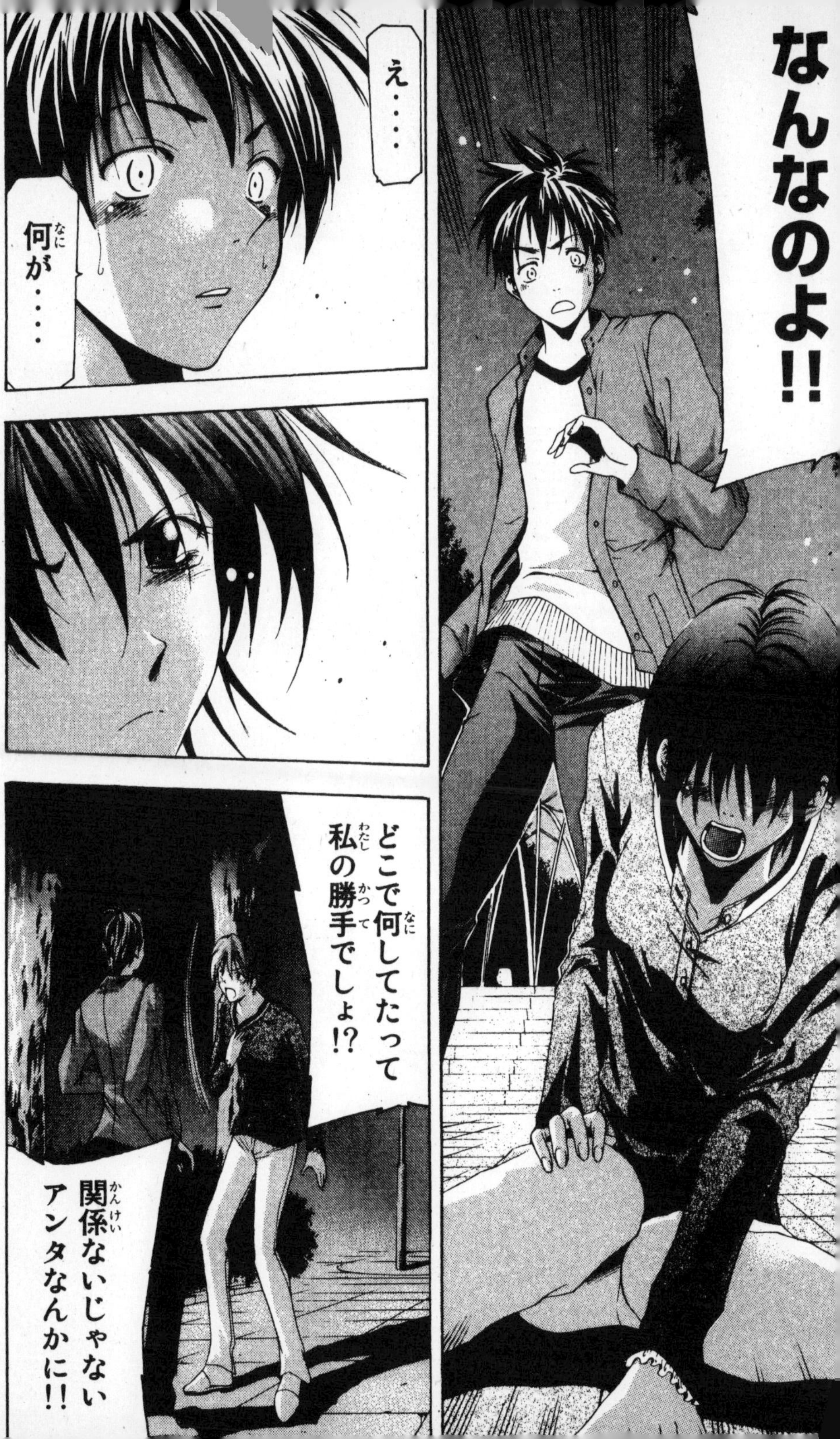
なんなのよ!!
え・・・・
何が・・・・
どこで何してたって
私の勝手でしょ!?
関係ないじゃない
アンタなんかに!!

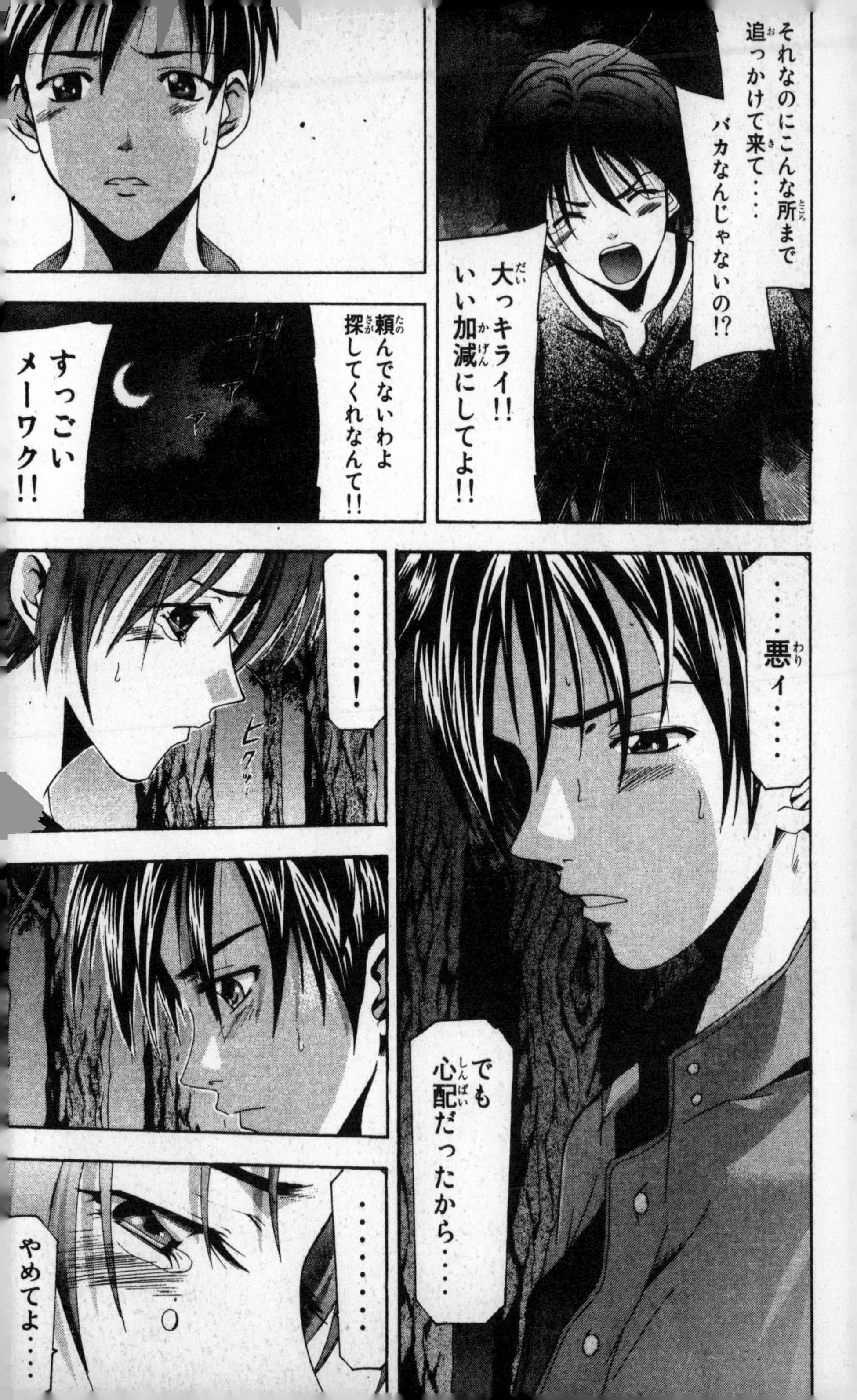
それなのにこんな所まで追っかけて来て‥‥
バカなんじゃないの!?
大っキライ!!
いい加減にしてよ!!
頼んでないわよ探してくれなんて!!
すっごいメーワク!!
‥‥悪イ‥‥
でも心配だったから‥‥
‥‥‥‥!
ヒクッ
‥‥‥‥
やめてよ‥‥

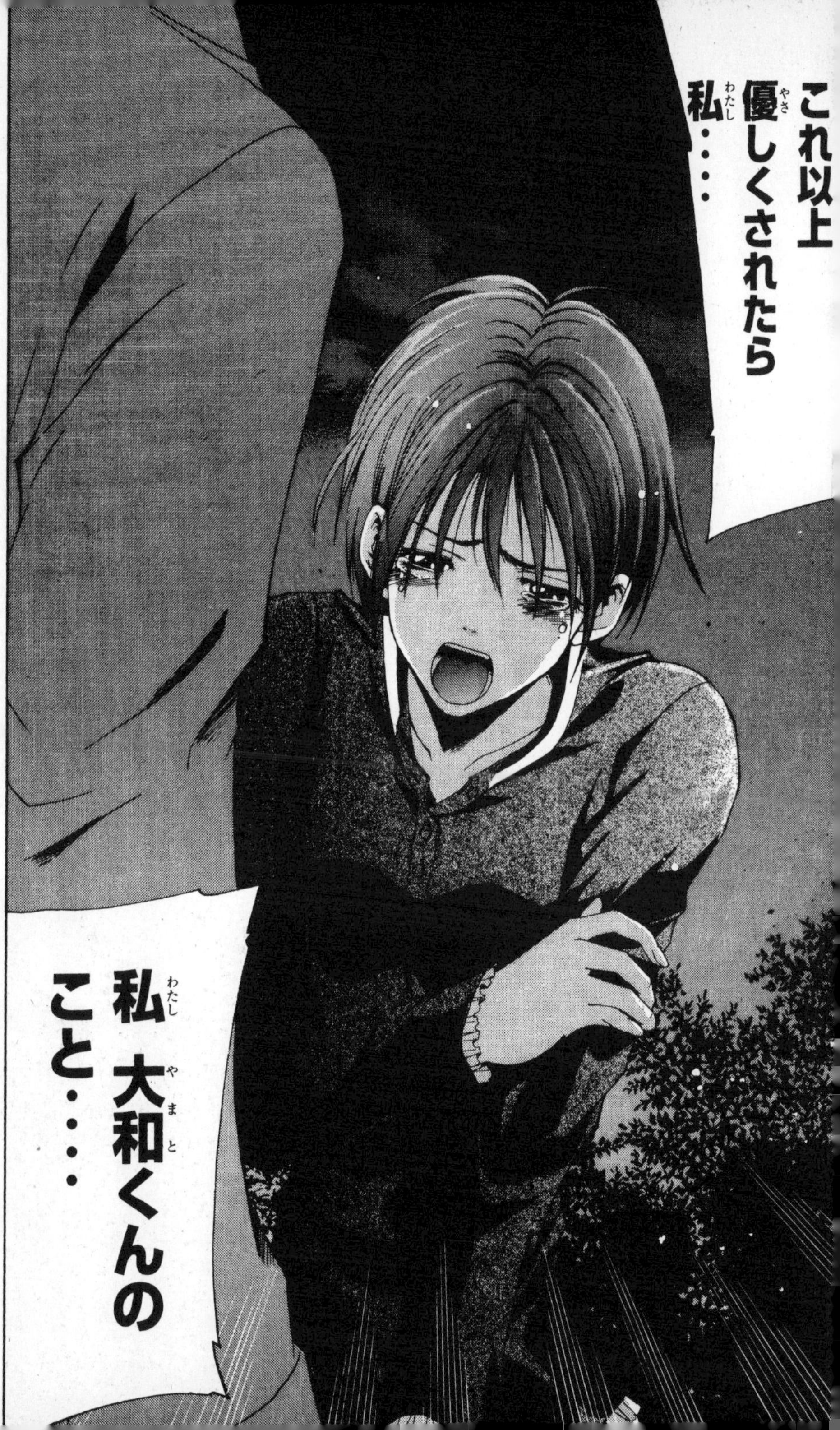
これ以上
優しくされたら
私・・・
私 大和くんの
こと・・・

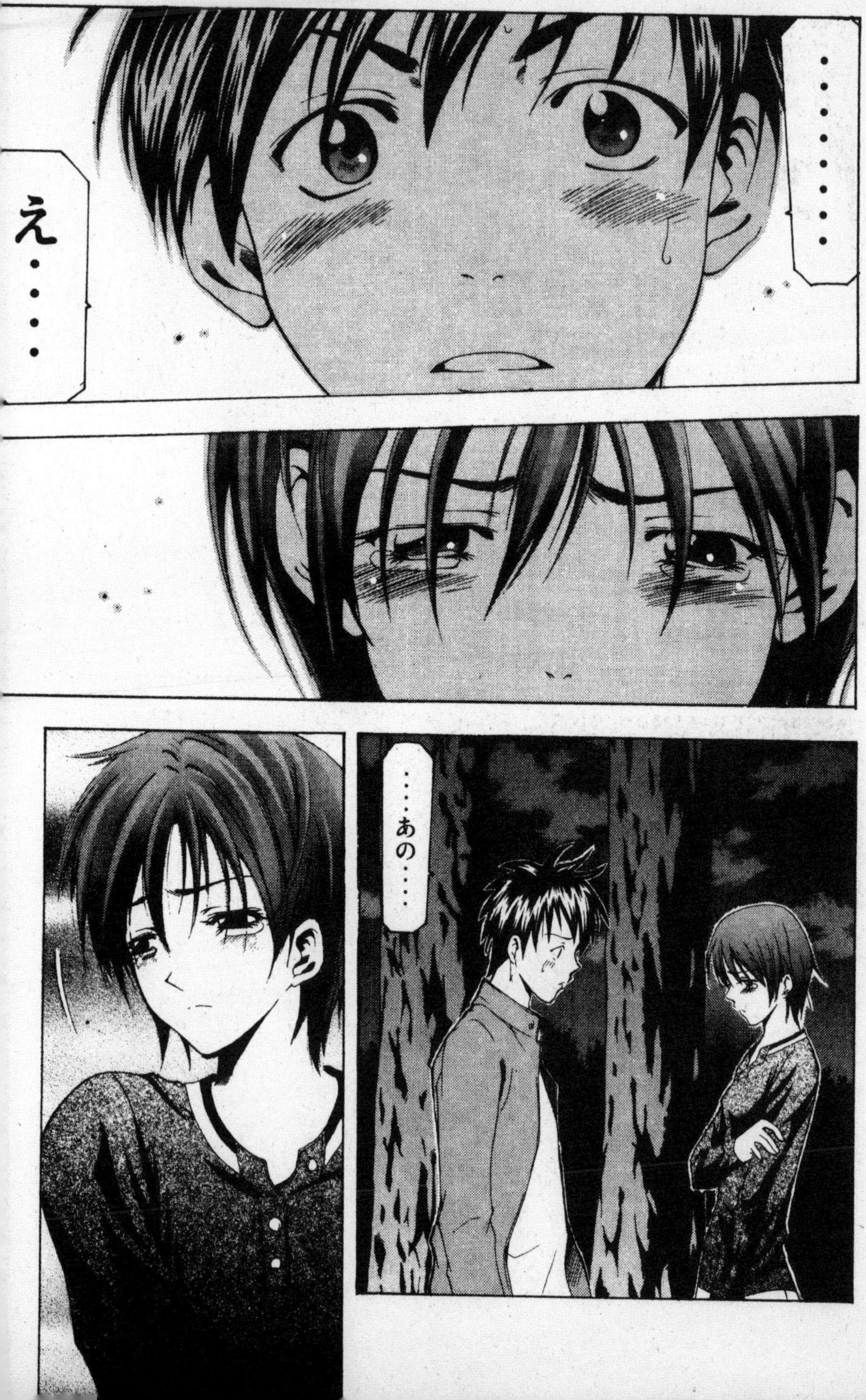
・・・・・・・・
え・・・・
・・・・あの・・・・

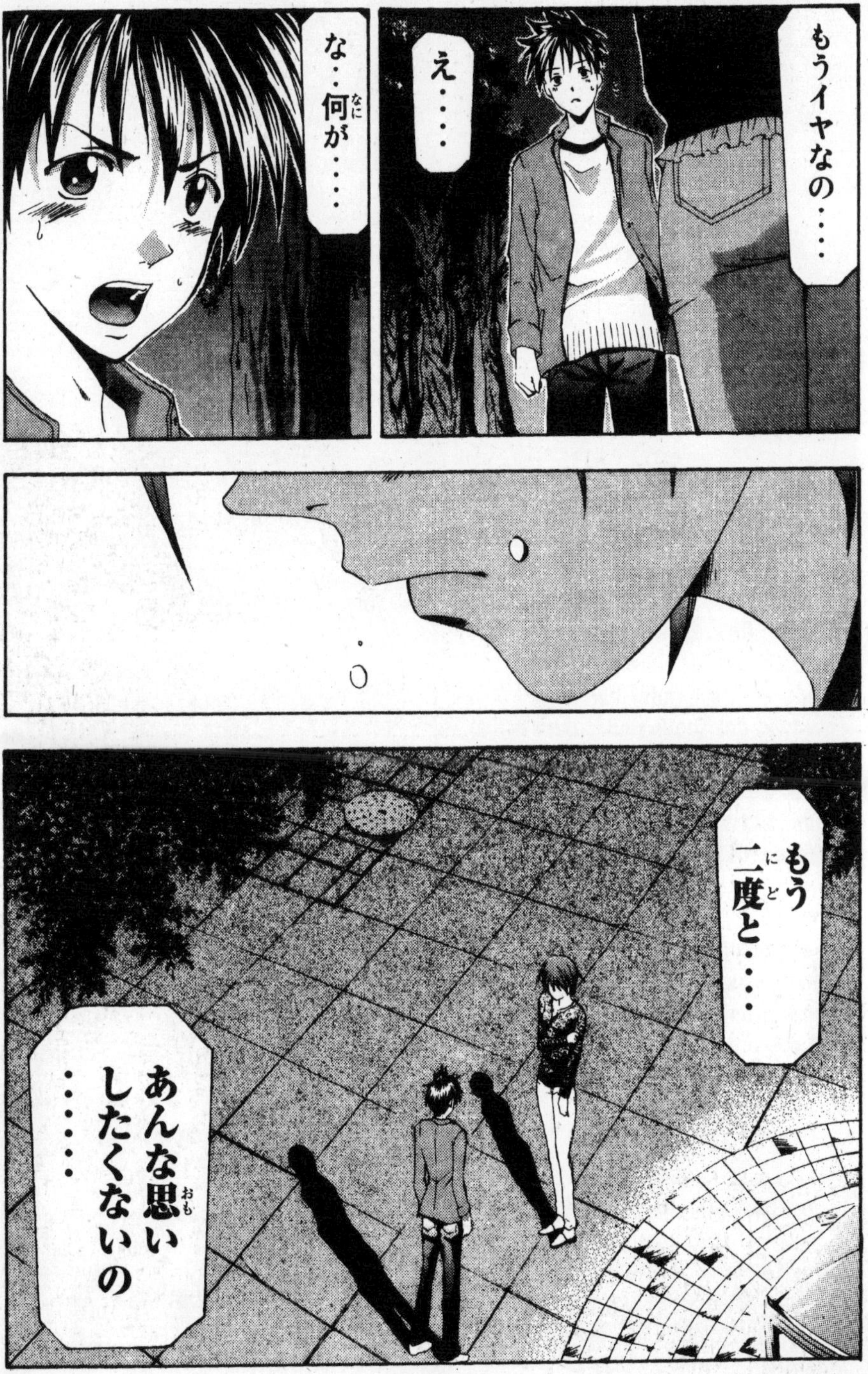
もうイヤなの・・・・
え・・・・
な・・何が・・・・
もう二度と・・・・
あんな思いしたくないの・・・・・

HIROYUKI TAMAKOSHI

JUST ONE OF THE GIRLS

A whole new Gacha Gacha story line begins! Akira Hatsushiba is just your typical, average high school kid . . . until a glitch in a Gacha Gacha video game changes his life forever. Now, every time Akira sneezes, his entire body undergoes a gender-bending switcheroo! That's right, Akira is always just an *achoo* away from getting in touch with his feminine side. But it's not all bad. Akira has had a crush on Yurika Sakuraba ever since he first laid eyes on her. He's always been too shy, but now that he can change into a girl, Akira finally has a chance to get close to Yurika. Being a girl certainly has its advantages!

Special extras in each volume! Read them all!

VISIT WWW.DELREYMANGA.COM TO:
• Read sample pages
• View release date calendars for upcoming volumes
• Sign up for Del Rey's free manga e-newsletter
• Find out the latest about new Del Rey Manga series

RATING M AGES 18+

 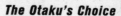 DEL REY MANGA

The Otaku's Choice

Gacha Gacha: The Next Revolution © 2004 Hiroyuki Tamakoshi / KODANSHA LTD. All rights reserved.

The Yagyu Ninja Scrolls

REVENGE OF THE HORI CLAN

ORIGINAL STORY BY FŪTARO YAMADA
MANGA BY MASAKI SEGAWA

VOW OF VENGEANCE!

Seventeenth-century Japan: A rebellion in the Aizu territory has been brutally crushed, leaving twenty-one brave warriors dead and most of the nuns of the local convent slaughtered. Now the surviving nuns have sworn to seek revenge.

• From the creators of *Basilisk*

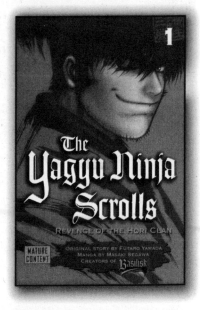

Special extras in each volume! Read them all!

VISIT WWW.DELREYMANGA.COM TO:
• Read sample pages
• View release date calendars for upcoming volumes
• Sign up for Del Rey's free manga e-newsletter
• Find out the latest about new Del Rey Manga series

RATING   M AGES 18+

DEL REY MANGA デルレイ

The Otaku's Choice.™

The Yagyu Ninja Scrolls: Revenge of the Hori Clan © 2005 Fūtaro Yamada and Masaki Segawa / KODANSHA LTD. All rights reserved.

TOMARE!

[STOP!]

You are going the wrong way!

Manga is a completely different
type of reading experience.

To start at the *beginning,* go to the *end*!

That's right! Authentic manga is read the traditional Japanese
way—from right to left, exactly the *opposite* of how American
books are read. It's easy to follow: Just go to the other end of
the book, and read each page—and each panel—from right side
to left side, starting at the top right. Now you're experiencing
manga as it was meant to be.